# Sustainability Accounting and Accountability

The management and balancing of social, environmental and economic sustainability is one of the most complex and urgent challenges facing both private and public sector organizations today, with these challenges of sustainability posing many risks to, and many opportunities for, advancing the aims and performance of organizations. Accounting and accountability processes and practices provide key tools to help organizations to more effectively identify and manage the risks and opportunities of sustainability.

Popular features from the first edition are retained, while recent developments in theory and practice are accounted for. New substantive chapters on water resource accounting, carbon accounting and decision making have been introduced and the book continues to benefit from a host of expert contributors from around the world, including Jesse Dillard, Rob Gray and Craig Deegan.

This comprehensive and authoritative textbook will continue to be a key resource for students of accounting and sustainability, as well as being a vital tool for researchers.

**Jan Bebbington** is Professor of Accounting and Sustainable Development in the School of Management at the University of St Andrews, UK.

**Jeffrey Unerman** is Professor of Accounting and Corporate Accountability and Head of the School of Management at Royal Holloway University of London, UK.

**Brendan O'Dwyer** is Professor of Accounting and Dean of Research at the University of Amsterdam Business School in the Netherlands.

This book is a useful contribution as an update to the traditional world of 'ESG' and 'triple bottom line' which has been on the agenda for some years.

Paul Druckman, *Chief Executive Officer, The International Integrated Reporting Council*

In a still emerging field, *Sustainability Accounting and Accountability* gives a comprehensive overview of the state of play and puts the developments to date in a rich context. In addition to theoretical reflections the authors address practical challenges as a basis for future discussions. Sincerely recommended to those who will meet sustainability during their professional career, which includes accounting and MBA students, and to those who want to get an overview of the topic.

Wim Bartels, *Global Head Sustainability Reporting & Assurance at KPMG, The Netherlands*

A key theme in the field of sustainability accounting and accountability, and one that runs explicitly through this book, is that critique is energising, life giving. A commitment to sustainability demands critical analysis and action; not a search for praise and a longing for congratulatory niceties. So, let's be clear, this book does not provide you with a 'check-list' of approved sustainability accounting practices. It certainly does not reassure you that contemporary sustainability accounting and associated systems of accountability are 'sustainable'. But, in the process, the book gives you something fundamentally more important. It challenges and encourages you to think differently. It makes you realise that when accounting for sustainability gets comfortable, it cannot be sustainable. Likewise, an accounting profession that fails to create and maintain space for radical rethinking in terms of sustainability accounting and associated systems of accountability, will soon find that its own social relevance and value is placed in serious question.

Chris Humphrey, *Professor of Accounting, University of Manchester, UK*

# Sustainability Accounting and Accountability

## Second edition

**Edited by
Jan Bebbington, Jeffrey Unerman
and Brendan O'Dwyer**

LONDON AND NEW YORK

First published 2007
Second Edition 2014
by Routledge
2 Park Square, Milton Park, Abingdon, Oxon OX14 4RN

and by Routledge
711 Third Avenue, New York, NY 10017

*Routledge is an imprint of the Taylor & Francis Group, an informa business*

*British Library Cataloguing in Publication Data*
A catalogue record for this book is available from the British Library

*Library of Congress Cataloging-in-Publication Data*
Sustainability accounting and accountability/edited by Jan Bebbington,
Jeffrey Unerman and Brendan O'Dwyer. – Second Edition.
pages cm
Includes bibliographical references and index.
ISBN 978-0-415-69557-2 (hardback) – ISBN 978-0-415-69558-9
(paperback) – ISBN 978-1-315-84841-9 (ebook) 1. Sustainable
development reporting. 2. Social accounting. I. Bebbington, Jan.
II. Unerman, Jeffrey. III. O'Dwyer, Brendan.
HD60.3.S87 2014
657–dc23
2013041326

ISBN: 978-0-415-69557-2 (hbk)
ISBN: 978-0-415-69558-9 (pbk)
ISBN: 978-1-315-84841-9 (ebk)

Typeset in Times New Roman
by Cenveo Publisher Services

Printed and bound in Great Britain by
TJ International Ltd, Padstow, Cornwall

From Brendan to Kim, Tim and Seán
and in memory of Michael and Frances.

From Jan to Jason.

From Jeffrey to Franco, Alan, Hazel and Martin.

# Contents

# Figures

# Tables

# Notes on contributors

**Amanda Ball's** research focuses on the public sector and its role in the broader pursuit of sustainable development. Amanda is currently Professor of Accounting at the Newcastle University Business School having previously held a chair at the University of Canterbury in Christchurch, NZ.

**Jan Bebbington** holds a Chair in Accounting and Sustainable Development in the School of Management at the University of St Andrews and is also the Director of the St Andrews Sustainability Institute, formed in 2006 to coordinate interdisciplinary research in sustainable development. Her research interests focus around the themes of organizational responses to the global climate change agenda as well as how governance regimes for sustainable development might be developed at organizational, regional and country level. Professor Bebbington was also Vice-Chair (Scotland) of the UK's Sustainable Development Commission from 2006–11 and brings substantial policy experience to her academic work.

**Jeff Birchall**, PhD, lectures on climate change science, mitigation and adaptation in the School of Urban and Regional Planning, Ryerson University, and previously in the College of Business and Economics, University of Canterbury, where he was the recipient of the prestigious Royal Society of New Zealand Marsden Scholarship.

**Roel Boomsma** is an Assistant Professor of Accounting at the Amsterdam Business School, University of Amsterdam. His current research interests lie in the field of non-governmental organization (NGO) accounting and accountability. Roel completed his PhD in 2013 in which he investigated over an extended time period the construction of accountability in the relationship between NGOs and a governmental funder. He also examined the operationalization of proposed accountability solutions on a practical level within a group of development NGOs. Roel has taught a number of courses at bachelor and masters level, including courses in Qualitative Research Methods and Sustainability, Accountability and Ethics.

**Nola Buhr**, PhD, CA, is a Professor of Accounting in the Edwards School of Business at the University of Saskatchewan in Saskatoon, SK. Her research, both contemporaneous and historical in nature, focuses on accounting and reporting practices in the absence of standards. She has published widely in the areas of accountability and environmental and sustainability reporting and sits on seven editorial boards. Nola also has an interest in government accounting and governance in the public sector. From 2003–9 she spent six years as a member of the Public Sector Accounting Board (PSAB) of Canada, serving as the Chair of PSAB for the last two of those years. Nola is currently a member of the Departmental Audit Committees for two federal government departments: Canadian Heritage, and Aboriginal Affairs and Northern Development Canada.

**David Collison** is Professor of Accounting and Society in the School of Business at the University of Dundee. After training as an accountant in the National Health Service and with Thomson McLintock (a forerunner of KPMG) he qualified as an accountant (with Association of Chartered Certified Accountants [ACCA]) in 1980, and worked in West Africa and the UK before entering academia. He joined the University of Dundee in 1989 and has undertaken a range of research projects in the broad area of social and environmental accounting. These interests led to his serving on a number of professional bodies' committees in the sustainability area. He is a member of ACCA's Global Forum on Sustainability, and of the Sustainability Advisory Group of the Institute of Chartered Accountants of Scotland (ICAS) which he represented for many years on the Sustainability Group of the European Federation of Accountants (FEE). In addition to an interest in accounting and accountability issues in relation to sustainability, he is also particularly interested in varieties of capitalism. In this area his recent work has investigated the systemically poor performance of Anglo-American countries across a range of social indicators and the significance of Anglo-American accounting, finance and corporate governance traditions as explanatory factors.

**Stuart Cooper** is Professor of Accounting at the University of Bristol. His research interests are in the areas of social and environmental accounting and accountability. Recently this has tended to focus on accounting and measurement issues relating to climate change in both the private and public sectors.

**Andrea B. Coulson** is a Senior Lecturer in Accounting at the University of Strathclyde and Chair of the Association of Chartered Certified Accountants (ACCA)'s Global Sustainability Forum. Her research and teaching interests include environmental and social accounting and accountability and accounting for risk. She has over 15 years' experience working with the financial sector on environmental risk management projects and accounting for climate adaptation strategies. Over the years she has developed an international network of public and private sector collaborators engaged in accounting for sustainability, risk mitigation and management. Andrea has conducted research commissioned by the ACCA/IIRC (International Integrated Reporting Council), Economic and Social Research Council (ESRC), F&C Asset Management plc, the Ministry of Malaysia, the Scottish Executive, Social Sciences and Humanities Research Council (SSHRC), United Nations Conference on Trade and Development (UNCTAD), UNEP FI (United Nations Environment Programme Finance Initiative) and UniCredit Group. As consultant to UNCTAD on environmental accounting Andrea has developed and delivered workshops in Africa, Asia, Central Europe and South America. This role helps add a practical, international perspective to both her research and teaching in accounting for sustainability and risk.

**Craig Deegan**, B Com (UNSW), M Com (Hons) (UNSW), PhD (UQLD) is Professor of Accounting in the School of Accounting at Royal Melbourne Institute of Technology (RMIT) University, Melbourne, VIC. His main research interests are in the area of social and environmental accountability, financial accounting, and financial accounting theory, and he has published in numerous leading international accounting journals, including *Accounting Organizations and Society*, *Accounting, Auditing and Accountability Journal*, *Journal of Business Ethics*, *Critical Perspectives on Accounting*, *Accounting and Business Research*, *British Accounting Review*, *International Journal of Accounting*, and *Accounting and Finance*. He consults widely with government, industry and corporations on various social, environmental and financial accountability issues and is the author of a number of leading textbooks, including *Australian Financial Accounting* (McGraw Hill, Sydney, NSW, 2012) and *Financial Accounting Theory* (McGraw Hill, Sydney, NSW, 2013).

**Colin Dey** is a Senior Lecturer in Accounting at the University of Stirling. His research explores accountability issues with a particular focus on social accounting and reporting. He has worked with the fair-trade organization Traidcraft plc to develop new forms of social accounting and bookkeeping, and undertaken research on behalf of Prince Charles's Accounting for Sustainability charity.

**Jesse Dillard** holds appointments as Adjunct Professor at Victoria University, Welllington, NZ; Investigador Vinculat a la Universitat, Universitat Autonoma de Barcelona; and Emeritus Professor at Portland State University, Portland, OR. He is an Associate Editor of *Critical Perspectives on Accounting* and *Accounting Forum*, and Consulting Editor for *Contemporary Accounting Research*, as well as serving on several editorial boards. Jesse has published widely in the accounting and business literature. His current interests relate to the ethical and public interest applications of administrative and information technology particularly as they affect social and environmental accountability.

**John Ferguson** is currently a Reader in Accounting at the University of Strathclyde. He has published in the areas of accountability, governance and the accounting profession. John is currently Joint Editor of *Social and Environmental Accountability Journal*.

**Michael Fraser** is the Director of Technical Services for the New Zealand Institute of Chartered Accountants (NZICA). Prior to joining NZICA Michael completed an FRST (Foundation for Research Science and Technology) funded PhD and received a Highly Commended Emerald Outstanding Doctoral Research Award. Michael has gone on to research and publish in the areas of *sustainability accounting* and *organizational change*. Michael is a Chartered Accountant and was previously a Senior Lecturer at Victoria University of Wellington, NZ.

**Jane Gibbon** is a Senior Lecturer in Accounting at Newcastle University Business School. Her research focus is the practice of social accounting using action research approaches. She has advised and worked with third sector organizations in fair trade, leisure services, social housing and health to develop better understandings of their social outcomes.

**Rob Gray** is Professor of Social and Environmental Accounting in the School of Management at the University of St Andrews. He is a qualified Chartered and Chartered Certified Accountant and is the author/co-author of over 300 articles, chapters, monographs and books – mainly on social and environmental accounting, sustainability, social responsibility and education. He founded CSEAR (Centre for Social and Environmental Accounting Research) in 1991 and for 21 years was its Director. He serves on the editorial boards of 15 learned journals and has worked with a wide range of international and local commercial and non-commercial organizations including from time to time collaborations with the United Nations. In 2001 he was elected British Accounting Association Distinguished Academic Fellow and in 2004 became one of the 14 founding members of the British Accounting Association Hall of Fame. He was awarded an MBE in the Queen's 2009 Birthday Honours List and was elected to the Academy of Social Science in 2012.

**Suzana Grubnic** is a Senior Lecturer in Management Accounting at Loughborough University. Her research interests include sustainability accounting and accountability, and organizational change, particularly as related to public services. Current work-in-progress draws upon the Prince of Wales Accounting for Sustainability Project as well as a study funded by the Chartered Institute of Management Accountants (CIMA). Suzana has published in various accounting and public administration journals such as *Accounting, Auditing & Accountability Journal, Financial Accountability & Management Journal* and *Journal of Public Administration Research and Theory*.

**Colin Higgins** is a Senior Lecturer in the Deakin Graduate School of Business at Deakin University in Melbourne, VIC. His research explores the processes and outcomes of institutionalization, especially in relation to sustainability reporting and corporate social responsibility.

**Carlos Larrinaga** is Professor of Accounting at the University of Burgos, Spain, and a Research Fellow of the University of Trento. His interests focus on the role of business in sustainable development, particularly the disclosure of their social and environmental impacts. His research has been published in journals such as *Accounting, Organizations and Society, Accounting, Auditing and Accountability Journal, Critical Perspectives on Accounting, Environmental Management* and *European Accounting Review*.

**Linda Lewis** is a Senior Lecturer in Accounting within the Management School at the University of Sheffield. Her current teaching and research interests lie in corporate social responsibility, social and environmental reporting, accounting for sustainability, regulatory and institutional frameworks for sustainability and the relationship between management accounting for sustainability and externally reported information. A number of research projects have also been funded by the Engineering and Physical Sciences Research Council (EPSRC) working within the water industry developing and applying whole-life costing, incorporating sustainability criteria, in order to optimize asset management decisions and to study the efficacy of stakeholder engagement practices in the implementation of technologies for sustainable water management.

**Markus J. Milne** is Professor of Accounting in the School of Business and Economics at the University of Canterbury, Christchurch, NZ. He has published more than 80 papers and book chapters, and his work is widely cited in the field. In 2009, he and his co-authors received the Mary Parker Follet award for best paper, in volume 22 of the *Accounting, Auditing and Accountability Journal*. Markus currently serves as Associate Editor of the *British Accounting Review*, and as Accounting Section Editor for the *Journal of Business Ethics*, and advises on a further ten international editorial boards. He has acted as a guest co-editor for special issues of the *Accounting, Auditing and Accountability Journal*, of which the 2012 issue on climate change and greenhouse gas accounting (with Suzana Grubnic) received the outstanding special issue award from Emerald Publishing. Markus has served as a member of the Economics and the Human and Behavioural Sciences Panel for the Royal Society of New Zealand's Marsden Fund. In 2002 and 2009, he was co-recipient of two Marsden research awards, one to critically investigate the sustainability discourse of New Zealand Business, and one to critically investigate the phenomenon of carbon neutrality in New Zealand organizations.

**Brendan O'Dwyer** is Professor of Accounting and Dean of Research at the University of Amsterdam Business School in the Netherlands. His research investigates themes surrounding sustainability reporting and assurance, NGO accounting and accountability and the regulation of the accounting profession. His work has been published in leading accounting journals including *Accounting, Organizations and Society, Accounting and Business Research, Accounting, Auditing and Accountability Journal*, and *Contemporary Accounting Research*. Brendan is an Associate Editor of *Accounting, Auditing and Accountability Journal* and a member of the editorial boards of *Accounting, Organizations and Society, Auditing; A Journal of Practice and Theory* and *Contemporary Accounting Research*. He is a Fellow of the Irish Institute of Chartered Accountants.

**Niamh O'Sullivan** is a post-doctoral Researcher and Lecturer at the University of Amsterdam Business School. Her research primarily focuses on the social accountability and institutional processes associated with sustainable finance, in particular those related to the Equator Principles. She previously worked as a project manager with the United Nations Environment Programme Finance Initiative (UNEP FI).

**David Owen** is an Emeritus Professor at the International Centre for Corporate Social Responsibility, Nottingham University Business School. He is also an Honorary Fellow of the Centre for Social and Environmental Accounting Research (CSEAR), University of St Andrews).

**Leonardo Rinaldi** is Lecturer in Accounting in the School of Management and member of the Centre for Research into Sustainability (CRIS) at Royal Holloway University of London. His research revolves around several interdisciplinary strands with particular emphasis on the extent to which sustainability accounting and accountability practices have been used as a governing means to create, spread and maintain power and the centrality of dialogue to widespread accountability initiatives. His academic work has been published in top-ranking international accounting outlets – including *Accounting, Organizations and Society* – and in reports credited with informing global policy documents for professional accountancy bodies.

**Shona Russell** is a Lecturer in Knowledge and Practice in the School of Management at the University of St Andrews. Shona's research interests concern governance and accountability in the context of human–environmental relations, particularly concerning fresh water and climate change. She has a proven track record of collaborative and interdisciplinary research in Scotland and New Zealand with public, private and community organizations.

**Lorna Stevenson** is a Reader in Accounting at the University of St Andrews. She is a qualified Chartered Accountant and has worked in different Scottish universities since 1993. The social, environmental and economic consequences of accounting, and the implications of these for both wider forms of accountancy and accountants' and managers' education, are research interests. Lorna's research is informed by her professional and education experiences.

**Ian Thomson** is a Professor of Accountancy at Heriot-Watt University, Edinburgh. His research has included interdisciplinary studies on implementation of cleaner technology, establishing industrial ecologies, effective stakeholder engagement, risk governance in water and salmon farming, sustainable development indicators, government policymaking and external accounting. He has been called as an expert witness to the Scottish Parliament's Finance and Infrastructure and Capital Investment Committees, Special Policy Advisor to the Scottish Parliament's Transport, Infrastructure and Climate Change Committee and member of the expert stakeholder panel for the Sustainable Development Commission (Scotland). His current projects include shadow accounting, carbon accountability and sustainable outcome measurement. In 2012 he was elected Convener of the governing council of the Centre for Social and Environmental Accounting Research (CSEAR).

**Carol Tilt** is a Professor of Accounting and former Dean at Flinders Business School in Adelaide, SA. She has published over 50 refereed articles and conference papers, and numerous other papers in the area of corporate social and environmental reporting. She is on the editorial board of a number of journals, including *Accounting, Auditing and Accountability Journal*; she is a member of the Accounting and Finance Association of Australia and New Zealand (AFAANZ) and of the Centre for Social and Environmental Accounting Research (CSEAR) in Scotland. Professor Tilt teaches accounting theory and research methods. In December 2013 she took up the position of Dean of the Australian Institute of Business (AIB), Adelaide, SA.

**Jeffrey Unerman** is Professor of Accounting and Corporate Accountability and Head of the School of Management at Royal Holloway University of London. He researches the role of accounting and accountability practices in helping organizations become more sustainable, recognizing the interdependencies between economic, social and environmental sustainability. He is co-editor of *Accounting for Sustainability: Practical Insights* (Earthscan, London, 2010) and co-author of *Financial Accounting Theory – European Edition* (McGraw Hill, Sydney, NSW 2011). He holds a PhD in social and environmental accounting from the University of Sheffield, is a member of the Institute of Chartered Accountants in England and Wales (ICAEW) and the Association of Chartered Certified Accountants (ACCA), and is an honorary member of CPA (Certified Practising Accountants) Australia.

# Acknowledgements

We are very grateful to the editorial team at Routledge for their help and encouragement in the writing and compilation of this book. In particular we would like to thank Sinead Waldron, Terry Clague and the copyeditor Pat Baxter.

We are also deeply indebted to the authors of all the chapters in this book for the timely and high quality completion of their chapters.

We also thank the reviewers of this book, including Professor Sumit Lodhia and Mr James Hazelton.

# Part I

# Setting the context for sustainability accounting and accountability

# 1 Introduction to sustainability accounting and accountability

*Jan Bebbington, Jeffrey Unerman and Brendan O'Dwyer*

In what kind of world do you want current and future people to live? Do you want them to live in a world characterized by social justice? Or would you be happy for them to live in a world riven by social conflict, where 'justice' is only available to a few members of society? Do you want them to live in a world where nature provides what is needed to sustain life? Or would you be satisfied for them to live in a world where the ecosphere had been damaged to the extent that life is lived at the margins of existence, where weather patterns have become so unsettled that storms regularly kill many people, the supply of food and water is erratic, and many species of plants, animals and insects have become extinct? Do you want them to live in an economically prosperous world where all needs are met? Or would you be satisfied for them to live in a world where the economy had failed and they were therefore unable to enjoy a prosperous life where wellbeing was enhanced?

Some of these scenarios might be considered unrealistically extreme by many, and in practice future generations are likely to experience a society, ecosphere and economy between these positions. In other words, like many scenarios which are presented to us in stark black and white terms, these scenarios may be false dichotomies. But the fact that future social, ecological and economic scenarios are often portrayed in a headline-grabbing manner characterized by stark images of doom and gloom should not prevent us from acknowledging that current human activities will have a future impact on the shape of society, the ecosphere and the economy. Some may argue that one or more of these future impacts will be beneficial, while others may argue the reverse. Some may argue that the negative impacts will not be as detrimental as suggested by the scenarios of social collapse, an ecosphere unable to sustain life, and/or an economy in long-term deep recession. It seems incontrovertible, however, that the negative consequences of our current way of life presently do (and hence are likely to in the future) cause a situation where possibilities for social justice, ecological integrity and economic stability are compromised.

For example, a scientific consensus exists that human activity is a contributory factor to the global warming that is causing social, environmental and economic damage (with future damage likely to accelerate). Some commentators point out that (for a variety of complex reasons) the 'doom-laden' scenarios set out in the opening paragraph of this chapter are a current reality for many people in the world – for example, those living in poverty across the globe.

There are reasons why poverty and ecological degradation exist that relate to particular times and places, but there are also systemic reasons behind these phenomena. Many people argue that social injustice and damage to the ecosphere are a result of the dominant (and rarely questioned) objective of organizing economies so as to maximize economic growth.

At the same time, commentators observe (and several arguments supporting this linkage are discussed in this and other chapters in this book) that economic growth (characterized by energy and material intensive production, and exploitative social relations) is socially and environmentally unsustainable.

It is these issues of sustainability that form the focus of this book. One way to look at these issues is in terms of the long-term need to ensure that economic activity is socially and environmentally sustainable. In the short term it might be possible to have economic growth while damaging society and the environment; however, in the long term this is impossible. For example, organizations need stable social and ecological conditions in which to operate (although some businesses might generate profits from addressing the outcomes of social conflicts, such as businesses offering security services). Therefore, if business as a whole operates in a manner that causes damage to society and undermines a stable context in which to operate then such activities are neither economically nor socially sustainable. In the longer term, if organizational activities cause a level of damage to the ecosphere such that it cannot sustain human life on the scale we currently enjoy, then this is clearly unsustainable against all social, economic and ecological standards. Thus, if the quest for economic growth causes significant damage to society and the environment, such economic growth is not economically, socially or environmentally sustainable in the longer term.

These may seem like obvious points. But what might be less immediately obvious is how these points relate to issues of accounting and accountability. Accounting is a powerful tool (or range of tools) which has conventionally been used to seek to optimize the economic performance of organizations. A range of management accounting techniques has helped managers plan and control their activities so that they (for commercial organizations) maximize their profits and (for those providing public services) maximize the benefits of funding available to them. A range of financial accounting techniques has helped communicate aspects of the economic performance of organizations to a range of stakeholders (primarily owners in the case of larger for-profit entities) who are not involved in the day-to-day running of the organization. As such, these financial accounting techniques have provided the mechanisms through which managers have been able to discharge duties of accountability to shareholders or stockholders (owners) who are not involved in the day-to-day running of the business.

Just as conventional management and financial accounting have provided tools in the management, planning, control and accountability of the economic aspects of an organization, broader techniques of sustainability accounting and accountability have the potential to be tools in the management, planning, control and accountability of organizations for their social and environmental impacts (or, in other words, for the social and environmental in addition to the more conventional economic impacts of organizations).

In practice, attempts to account for social, environmental and economic impacts have become much more common among many organizations in the past few years. At the same time, the concept of sustainable development has become a central organizing theme within contemporary society, which in many ways is an astonishing achievement for an idea that is usually thought to have arrived on the public policy scene in 1987 with the publication of the *Brundtland Report*. Sustainable development concerns tend to focus on how to organize and manage human activities in such a way that they meet physical and psychological needs without compromising the ecological, social or economic base that enables these needs to be met. The role of private and public sector organizations in this process is significant in most countries around the globe, and especially so in the industrialized West: the epicentre of the choices and actions which disproportionately drive environmental change.

In public statements on their sustainable development policies and practices, many organizations claim that they recognize their social and environmental, in addition to their economic, responsibilities, and are seeking to manage and account for these activities in an appropriate manner. Some of their critics, however, argue that many organizations are simply using sustainability accounting techniques as a public relations tool to win (or maintain) the approval of those stakeholders whose continued support is crucial for the perceived legitimacy of their activities. In this latter case (and especially if they relate to profit-seeking organizations), the social and environmental reporting practices adopted might be perceived as addressing the interests of the most powerful stakeholders in any particular organization, while leaving marginalized the interests and needs of less powerful stakeholders.

Whichever is the case (and the truth is likely to lie somewhere between these two positions), the use of sustainability accounting and accountability techniques has increased in recent years. An understanding of the basis of these techniques and the ability to critically evaluate them is important because of the central role of accounting in the management and accountability of organizations. As a result, forms of accounting and reporting will affect our ability, at a societal level, to pursue sustainable development. Furthermore, the sustainable development agenda is likely to impact on how accounts are created and the ends to which they are used. This book attempts to sketch the terrain on which these interrelationships are and will be played out. It sets out to provide an explanation of the key issues involved in sustainability accounting and accountability, and thereby to provide a basis from which readers will be equipped to help both develop and critique these practices. To contribute towards realizing these aims, each chapter in this book has been written by leading thinkers in the topic area considered.

As the purpose of this book is to provide an introduction as to how the study of accounting might contribute to a transition to sustainable development (or, possibly, moving away from unsustainability), it is first necessary to explain what is meant by sustainable development and the current state of thinking around sustainable development. The next section of this introductory chapter, Framing the Field, will introduce this explanation of sustainable development and link this to accounting-related activities. The final section, How to Use this Book, will then provide a guide as to how this book might be used to support a course of study in this topic area.

## Framing the field of accounting and accountability for sustainable development

While many readers may be familiar with the *Brundtland Report* definition of sustainable development (as 'development that meets the needs of the present without compromising the ability of future generations to meet their own needs' [UNWCED, 1987, p. 8]), the field of sustainable development studies has proliferated since this report was published. A more formal and extended introduction to current framings of social, environmental and economic sustainability is therefore necessary to provide a context for the topics explored in this book. In order to introduce this sustainable development context, the most influential thinking in the area of the environment, social justice and economic development will be outlined. While this outline does not draw explicitly on accounting sources (and we are not seeking to make readers knowledgeable in the diverse areas that surround sustainable development thinking), a familiarity with these concerns is necessary in order to situate accounting work that relates to sustainable development.

Concern about the extent to which the natural world is being destroyed by human activity and the implications of this destruction (both in terms of the way this might undermine future human development as well as in terms of the intrinsic undesirability of destruction of nature) remains high. Two ways of framing this debate have emerged in recent years, namely: *planetary boundaries identification* and *ecosystem services framing*.

### Planetary boundaries identification

Planetary boundaries research has involved consortiums of scientists from different backgrounds working together to define the state of earth systems that underpin human flourishing. A primary purpose of this area of research is to provide society and political leaders (along with policymakers) with evidence about how extensively elements of the natural environment have been affected or changed by human activities and which of these aspects are in need of urgent action. The most influential work in this area is that of Rockström and colleagues, who suggest that biodiversity[1] loss, the nitrogen cycle[2] and climate change are beyond planetary boundaries, while a number of other areas are approaching those limits (see http://www.stockholmresilience.org/planetary-boundaries for more detail on this initiative). This implies that collective action (including action for organizations, guided and shaped by accounting and reporting activities) is required to address these issues.

### Ecosystem services framing

At the same time as the planetary boundaries framing emerged, a long-standing United Nations programme of work was coming to fruition around thinking of ecology in terms of ecosystem services. This is a framing that seeks to link environmental quality to the ability of humans (and other species) to flourish and sees nature as providing services to enable this flourishing. The usefulness of the ecosystem services framing is that it allows us to think about how to sustain this flow of services and links human flourishing directly to the state of the ecology (see the Economics of Ecosystems and Biodiversity project at http://www. teebweb.org/ (accessed 10 October 2013) which explains this framing in more detail). While this framing is especially relevant for organizations in the productive sectors (such as beverages; fishing; food; fibre;[3] and forestry, where the reliance of well-functioning ecosystems is obvious) it is also valuable for other industries (for example, the tourism industry would be an example of a sector that requires stable ecological conditions).

### The Millennium Development Goals

Alongside this ecological focus, work with a focus on human development has continued. There are two significant contemporary developments in this area. The first of these relates to the Millennium Development Goals (see also the http://www.un.org/millenniumgoals/ [accessed 10 October 2013]) process, while the second links the work of Rockström et al. (2009) with the idea of minimum conditions for flourishing that are explicit in the work that is deemed necessary for the achievement of (and moving beyond) the Millennium Development Goals.[4]

The Millennium Development Goals encompass eight areas that affect the lives of people on the planet and these goals were signed up to by all United Nations member countries with the intention of these being achieved by 2015 (an outline of the goals and a progress

*Table 1.1* Millennium Development Goals progress

| Goal (with sample sub targets) | Progress commentary |
|---|---|
| Eradicate extreme poverty and hunger (measured in terms of the proportion of people living on less than $1 a day) | Poverty rates have been halved between 1990 and 2015 meaning 700 million fewer people living in extreme poverty<br>As many as 1.2 million people still live in extreme poverty<br>The economic crisis undermines progress on this goal |
| Achieve universal primary education (ensure boys and girls will complete a full course of primary education) | On current trends will not be achieved<br>By 2011, 57 million children were out of school (compared to 102 million in 2000), half of whom live in sub-Saharan Africa<br>There remains a lack of literacy skills (with girls making up 61% of this group) |
| Promote gender equality and empower women (on a variety of participation metrics) | Gains have been made in all areas but progress towards equality is not yet achieved<br>Workforce participation by women has increased but not in all job roles<br>In 2013 the average share of women members in parliaments worldwide was 20% |
| Reduce child mortality (reduce the under-five mortality rate by two-thirds) | Since 1990 child mortality has dropped by 41% equating to a drop in child deaths of 14,000 each day<br>6.9 million children under five died in 2011 from preventable diseases<br>Death rates in sub-Saharan Africa are 16 times the average of those for developed regions |
| Improve maternal health (reduce maternal mortality ratio by three-quarters) | Maternal mortality has declined by nearly 50% since 1990 but the target is not yet achieved<br>Eastern Asia, Northern Africa and Southern Asia have met the target<br>Only 50% of pregnant women in developing regions receive recommended antenatal care visits |
| Combat HIV/AIDS, malaria and other diseases (reverse HIV/AIDS spread; halt and reverse the incidence of other diseases) | Incidence of HIV is declining in most regions and access to antiretroviral therapy for those affected has increased rapidly (but still falls short of 100%)<br>In the ten years since 2000, 1.1 million deaths from malaria were averted<br>Treatment for tuberculosis saved some 20 million lives between 1995 and 2011 |
| Ensure environmental sustainability | Greenhouse gas emissions are rising; environmental stocks are depleting; and risk of extinction is increasing<br>More than 2.1 billion people have gained access to improved drinking water sources since 1990 |
| Develop a global partnership for development | Of least developed country exports, 83% enter developed countries duty free<br>Debt servicing of developing countries consumes 3% of their export revenues (down from 12% in 2000) |

commentary are contained in Table 1.1). The Millennium Development Goals mechanism has resulted in significant progress in poverty alleviation, although there is still much that needs to be achieved. However, the links from this global equality debate to organizational actions are less direct than those for environmental sustainability. Despite this, how organizations operate does affect poverty outcomes, especially in terms of both employment practices and supply-chain connections. This is especially the case for organizations that are operating in countries which face poverty challenges (with these most often being firms in the extractive industries or in primary production, such as palm oil producers).

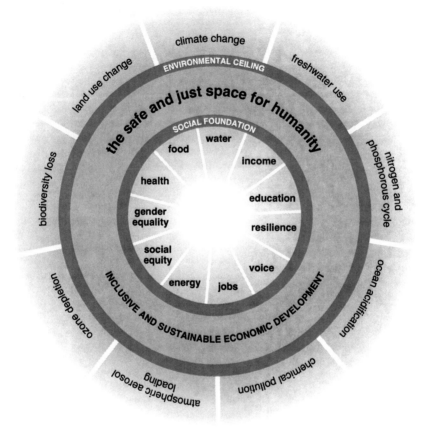

*Figure 1.1* A safe and just operating space for humanity.

Source: Raworth (2012, p. 4*)

* See http://www.oxfam.org/en/grow/policy/safe-and-just-space-humanity (accessed 10 October 2013) for more information on this initiative.

The Millennium Development Goals ethos also underpins another framing device that we introduce here, as the goals act as one expression of a social foundation – that is, the minimum social outcomes that we might find morally acceptable. Indeed, Figure 1.1 depicts how Raworth (2012) links the Rockström et al. (2009) work with the ideals of the Millennium Development Goals to identify a 'donut' (or life-saving ring if you like) where a safe and just space for human activities might be found. This framing is proving influential and builds on the ideas of ecosystem services by introducing a fairness dimension.

### Rethinking economics

The final element in this quick tour of the 'triple bottom line' of sustainable development is consideration of where the debate about the nature of our economic systems has developed. As you might imagine given the global financial crisis (dating from 2008), this has been an area of contention because while economic growth often impairs the natural environment and reduces social equality, economic contraction can also have a devastating effect on individuals, communities and countries.

The debates in this area have mostly focused on the way countries measure progress and how a narrow focus on *gross domestic product* (GDP) means that sustainable development outcomes are not pursued (see Stiglitz et al., 2009, for the best example of this work). Likewise, the extent to which unreformed economic growth is likely to drive ecological damage and hence the need to move to prosperity without growth (Jackson, 2009) has also been widely discussed. Both issues have salience for organizations in terms of how they might measure performance (and especially how most social and environmental externalities are not accounted for in financial and management accounting and reporting) as well as the concern that pursuing profits will override desires to be socially and environmentally responsible. This is a theme that comes through the chapters of this book and which Barter and Bebbington (2009) explore in terms of the relative efficiencies required if growth is allowed within the system.

Taken together, the above elements of sustainable development frame any discipline's engagement with the concept – even if specific aspects of these concerns do not fully inform all aspects of accounting directly. In addition, these broader trends raise questions as to whether sustainable development is even possible and it is here that some observations from Raworth (2012) are insightful (see Tables 1.2 and 1.3 respectively). What these tables suggest is that the goals of environmental security and poverty alleviation are not inherently incompatible. Likewise, Table 1.3 in particular shines light on the actions of the 'rich' (into which category we writers of this text fall, and within which you as readers are likely to also be included) and how responsibility for changes might rest more firmly with those of us with greater wealth. This raises important personal questions for us all and in many ways goes to the heart of how we think about development, how it might be conceptualized and what our role might be in any transition towards sustainability.

## Accounting themes

As may be seen from the preceding section, Framing the Field, the array of issues and concerns that are addressed under the guise of sustainable development is complex and covers a wide array of topics. These themes (of ecological security, social justice and economic resilience) are relevant for the discipline of accounting in both conceptual and practical terms. Indeed, this book was originally written in an attempt to provide a bridge between the concerns of sustainable development and accounting. Likewise, in practice, accountants

*Table 1.2* Ending poverty need not destroy the planet

'The first imperative of sustainable development is poverty eradication, and achieving that need not be a source of stress on planetary boundaries. Data available for some critical dimensions of deprivation indicate that bringing every person alive today above the social foundation could be achieved with strikingly little additional demand on resources:

*Food:* Providing the additional calories needed by the 13% of the world's population facing hunger (850m people) would require just 1% of the current global food supply.

*Energy:* Bringing electricity to the 19% of the world's population (1.3bn people) who currently lack it could be achieved with less than a 1% increase in global $CO_2$ emissions.

*Income:* Ending income poverty for the 21% of the global population who live on less than $1.25 a day (1.4bn people) would require just 0.2% of global income.'

Source: Raworth (2012, p.19).

*Table 1.3* The impact of the wealthy is disproportionate

'The biggest source of planetary boundary stress today is the excessive consumption levels of roughly the wealthiest 10% of people in the world, and the production patterns of the companies producing the goods and services that they buy:

*Carbon emissions:* Just 11% of the global population generate around 50% of global carbon emissions, while 50% of people create only 11%.

*Incomes:* The richest 10% of people in the world hold 57% of global income. The poorest 20% of people hold just 2%.

*Purchasing power and electric power:* High-income countries – home to 16% of the world's population – account for 64% of the world's spending on consumer products and use 57% of the world's electricity.

*Nitrogen:* Humanity is using nitrogen at four times the globally sustainable rate. The European Union – home to just 7% of the world's population – uses up 33% of the globally sustainable nitrogen budget simply to grow and import animal feed, while many Europeans eat far more meat and dairy products than is suitable for a healthy diet.'

Source: Raworth (2012, p.19).

have not been ignoring issues of sustainable development and increasingly some of the practical efforts to address social and environmental impacts of development (in terms of accounting, managing and reporting the outcomes of these efforts) have been framed as sustainable development work. Indeed (and since the publication of the first edition of this book) a number of new initiatives have developed in this space.[5]

For example, the Prince's Accounting for Sustainability Project (one of the Prince of Wales's charities) has garnered a considerable level of support from private and public sector organizations (including many large and influential professional accounting bodies) from countries across the globe in developing practices that seek to embed considerations of sustainable development into organizational decision making. A research project commissioned by the Accounting for Sustainability Project (Hopwood et al., 2010) involved a number of accounting academics undertaking case studies that examined different aspects of how eight organizations had developed and used a variety of accounting techniques to help embed understandings of the risks and opportunities arising from their sustainability impacts into decisions taken at all levels (strategic, tactical and operational), and how this led to more effective decisions.

Another example is the rapid development of integrated reporting, which seeks to report a concise integrated picture of an organization's social, environmental, economic and governance performance and impacts. This is intended to be different from the practices of sustainability reporting, for example those guided by the Global Reporting Initiative's (GRI) G3, G3.1 and G4 reporting guidelines. Where GRI compliant sustainability reports might present in a single document an analysis of the organization's environmental impacts separately from its social impacts and both of these separately from its economic impacts, a combined report is intended to communicate the integrated impact of key actions across and between social, environmental and economic spheres. In South Africa, a form of integrated reporting governed by local South African regulations[6] has been compulsory (on a comply or explain non-compliance basis) since 2010 for all corporations whose shares are listed on the Johannesburg Stock Exchange. Internationally, the International Integrated Reporting Council (IIRC) has been developing a set of unified reporting guidelines with the support of many large and influential organizations (including multinational corporations, public sector bodies, large accounting firms, professional accounting bodies and other accounting regulatory bodies) and, at the time of this book going to press, had over 100 organizations piloting a variety of approaches to combined reporting as part of its development of integrated reporting guidelines.

Although integrated reporting proposals and practices have been developing rapidly, and are likely to continue changing shape after this book has been published, in 2013 it was becoming clear that the IIRC approach to integrated reporting was developing in a subtly different direction from South African integrated reporting. While South African integrated reporting appeared to be aimed at providing for the combined information needs of a range of stakeholders, IIRC integrated reporting was moving towards a focus on the unified social, environmental, economic and governance information needs of providers of capital rather than of a broader range of stakeholders. While some thought this a regrettable direction as they considered it a missed opportunity to develop a framework that would address broader sustainability impacts of the reporting organization, others argued that it was a more pragmatic approach to ensure that some integrated sustainability information would be reported by companies in situations where a reporting guideline addressing the sustainable development information needs of a broader array of stakeholders risked simply being ignored or dismissed by many powerful corporations.

In addition to these specific initiatives, the field of social and environmental accounting research[7] has continued to evolve with topic areas emerging since the last edition of the book. Some of these topic areas are covered in the current edition as there is sufficient high quality research output that has been produced to be able to provide a summary of the work (for example, in the case of climate change and water – Chapters 12 and 13 respectively). Two other areas that are emerging as we go to press and that point towards future sustainable development related accounting work are biodiversity (with a special issue being produced by *Accounting, Auditing and Accountability Journal* in 2013) and human rights (which is starting to garner a lively research community; see particularly a special issue of *Critical Perspectives on Accounting* 2011).

As these fields emerge they will inform any consideration of accounting for sustainable development. Indeed, we hope it can be seen that the concerns introduced in the earlier section on framing accounting and accountability for sustainable development link to the roles that organizations, management activities, accounting and reporting play in these various areas. Some aspects of the sustainable development agenda are more appropriately the responsibility of governments (together or collectively). For example, poverty alleviation is not directly the responsibility of organizations. Likewise, governments are the appropriate body to set governance regimes that will ensure that sustainable development outcomes might be attained, while the manner in which organizations interact with these regimes (and in some cases exceed expectations in these areas) will affect the outcomes. This makes any pursuit of sustainability/unsustainability complex; and while accounting is not the sole way in which any transitions might be made, it is a part of the process by which many academic disciplines might come together to address substantive issues of our time.

## How to use this book

This book is intended to be of use to a variety of readers. In addition to providing a broadly based view of current issues in sustainability accounting and accountability to anyone with an interest in the subject, it should also provide a good starting point for anyone wanting to conduct research in this area by enabling them to identify relevant prior studies in the specific area they wish to research, and to locate this area within the broader context of sustainability accounting and accountability research. It is also intended to support the growing number of courses in this area, both where such courses are stand-alone sustainability accounting and accountability courses, and where material on sustainability accounting and accountability is incorporated as part of broader accounting courses.

The book is divided into five parts, each of which focuses on cognate areas of investigation. Part I provides a context to the issues examined in the rest of the book and, in addition to this introduction, contains two chapters – the first maps the terrain of sustainability accounting and accountability, while the second explores some issues related to sustainability accounting and accountability in the education process. Part II then provides perspectives on some of the practices that have developed in seeking to account for and finance aspects of sustainable development – covering some of the histories, rationales and future prospects for sustainability reporting; independent assurance of sustainability reports; stakeholder dialogue and engagement; developing silent and shadow accounts; environmental and social assessment in sustainable finance; and sustainability accounting and organizational change. Part III of the book moves on to explore accounting for sustainable development in other organizational settings – specifically non-governmental organizations (NGOs) and the public services. Part IV focuses on accounting in relation to the specific biophysical concerns of carbon emissions and water resource use. Finally, Part V provides some overarching conceptual interpretations in the form of chapters examining: philosophical underpinnings of sustainability and organizational accountability; organizational legitimacy as a motive for sustainability reporting; and insights into sustainability reporting from institutional theory. A concluding chapter, Chapter 17, ties together all of the major insights from the book.

There is increasing recognition in many universities globally that as ever more organizations across the private, public and third sectors adopt and develop sustainability accounting and accountability practices, the study of accounting solely focusing on its financial or economic aspects without the social and environmental sustainability dimensions does not adequately equip students with the accounting knowledge and understanding they will

*Table 1.4* An outline of a potential module using this book

| Week | Topic | Chapters from this book |
|---|---|---|
| 1 | Introduction and understanding the context for sustainability accounting and accountability | 1, 2 and 3 |
| 2 | Development and credibility of sustainability reporting | 4 and 5 |
| 3 | Role of stakeholders in internal and external sustainability, accountability and reporting | 6 and 7 |
| 4 | Environmental and social assessment in sustainable finance | 8 |
| 5 | Sustainability accounting and organizational change | 9 |
| 6 | Sustainability accounting and accountability in the public sector and in NGOs | 10 and 11 |
| 7 | Perspectives on carbon accounting and accounting for water resource use | 12 and 13 |
| 8 | Philosophical underpinnings of sustainability and organizational accountability | 14 |
| 9 | Motives underlying sustainability reporting | 15 and 16 |
| 10 | Holistic review of the current and potential roles of accounting in sustainable development | 17 |

require once they have graduated. Therefore a growing number of more broadly based financial and management accounting courses are now incorporating elements of sustainability accounting and accountability, and chapters from this book can be used, either individually or in combination, to support the teaching and learning of these elements.

There is also a growing number of universities that are developing whole courses in sustainability accounting and accountability – at both undergraduate and postgraduate levels. This book provides the ideal text for such courses, as the chapters can be combined to support the typical ten to 12 week single term (or semester) course. One example of how this could be achieved for a ten-week course is as presented in Table 1.4.

We hope that readers will find the material presented in this book both useful and informative. As it has been written to inform a variety of readers about the current and potential role of accounting in the crucially important area of sustainable development, we hope that it also helps contribute towards both practical and theoretical developments in accounting and accountability practices, such that accounting can contribute towards more sustainable, or less unsustainable, business, public sector and third sector operations.

Any comments that readers may have on the structure and content of this book are most welcome.

## Notes

1  Biodiversity is a term used to describe the degree of variety of living organisms observed in any location. It is also used to describe the total number (which is a highly uncertain figure) of different living organisms there are on the planet. High levels of biodiversity are thought to be good (overall, but not necessarily in every place of the planet) as they allow for more robust ecological systems to exist.

2  The most obvious way concerns about changes in the nitrogen cycle evidence themselves in accounting studies is through a consideration of the production of fertilizers (which cause particular disruption to this area) as well as a consideration of how food-producing organizations are affecting this natural cycle. This is an example of an environmental pressure that might not be obviously linked to accounting or organizational concerns but where hidden connections exist.

3  Such as in the building and clothing industries.

4  Indeed, there is a process currently in play within the United Nations that is looking at whether or not the Millennium Development Goals will be replaced by Sustainable Development Goals (when the Millennium Development Goals process is due to close after 2015).

5  As you will see when you read various chapters, these initiatives infuse various topic areas.

6  The 2009 King Report on Governance for South Africa, commonly referred to simply as King III.

7  This is a large and diverse research community with a global scale and reach. Many members of that community also belong to the Centre for Social and Environmental Accounting Research (http://www.st-andrews.ac.uk/csear/), which produces a journal dedicated to this area (http://www.tandfonline.com/toc/reaj20/current#.Ujgjij88DTo) as well as hosting resources for study of these issues (including educational resources – https://sites.google.com/site/cseareducation/). (all accessed 10 October 2013).

## References

Barter, N. and Bebbington, J. (2009), Factor 4/10/20/130: A briefing note, *Social and Environmental Accountability Journal*, 29(1): 23–26.

Hopwood, A., Unerman, J. and Fries, J. (2010), *Accounting for Sustainability: Practical Insights*, Earthscan: Abingdon.

International Integrated Reporting Council (IIRC) (2013), available at http://www.theiirc.org/, accessed 10 October 2013.

Jackson, T. (2009), *Prosperity without Growth: Economics for a Finite Planet*. Earthscan: London.

Raworth, K. (2012), *A Safe and Just Space for Humanity*. Oxfam: Oxford.

Rockstrom, J., Steffen, W., Noone, K., Persson, A., Chapin, F. S., Lambin, E. F., Foley, J. A. (2009), A safe operating space for humanity, *Nature*, 461(7263): 472–5.

Stiglitz, J., Sen, A. and Fitoussi, J. (2009), *Report by the Commission on the Measurement of Economic and Social Progress*.

Unerman, J., Bebbington, J. and O'Dwyer, B. (2007), *Sustainability Accounting and Accountability*, Routledge: Abingdon.

United Nations (2013), *The Millennium Development Goals Report 2013*. United Nations: New York.

United Nations World Council for Environment and Development (1987), *Report of the World Commission on Environment and Development: Our Common Future*. Oxford University Press: Oxford.

# 2　Mapping the terrain of sustainability and accounting for sustainability

*Ian Thomson*

## Introduction

Sustainable accounting research should contribute towards sustainable transformation and reducing societies' negative sustainability impact on our planet. Accounting-sustainability research should produce and communicate knowledge that points the way to a sustainable future. Accounting-sustainability research should critically: confront the unsustainable way the world is; create new accounting knowledge, processes and practices; and problematize, disrupt and engage constructively with transformation processes. The 'so-what' question for accounting-sustainability research articles should be: how does this article help with the resolution of the urgent and wicked problems faced by society?

This chapter reports on a review of all the research articles published in the period 2008–12 in the 21 accounting journals euphemistically referred to as the 'top' accountancy journals.[1] This review examined over 3,200 articles to identify their coverage of topics and issues associated with the political and scientific sustainability programmatic discourses. A series of maps was constructed to represent the accounting-sustainability research terrain in a period where there has been growing political and scientific consensus on the scale of the unsustainability problems confronting humanity. In total, 235 research articles (7 per cent of the total published) were identified as covering issues related to the contested arenas associated with unsustainability and contributing to the research led discourses of the problematic interface between accounting and sustainability. It is important to place this chapter's analysis in the wider accounting research terrain. While 235 articles could be considered a positive contribution to accounting-sustainability discourses, there still remains a number of serious limitations and omissions in the research literature. The majority of accounting research articles do not address or question the actions of corporations or financial markets that contribute to the planet's ecological and social unsustainability, with billions living in unacceptable levels of poverty, hunger, oppression, ill-health, species loss, ecological damage and resource depletion (see also Gray, 2010).

The maps presented in this chapter are stylized representations of the accounting-sustainability research terrain ordered intuitively according to a spatial arrangement based on key sustainability policy and scientific arenas (Georgakopoulos and Thomson, 2008). These maps are intended to help contextualize, simplify and make sense of the interaction between the programmatic discourses of accounting and sustainability. Mapping contemporary accounting-sustainability research creates a visual representation of a complex and dynamic field that complements the actual reading of these texts. The mapping of concepts, attributes and things creates opportunities for visualizing relationships among concepts, stimulating idea generation, organizing ideas, communicating complex ideas and evaluating contributions (actual and potential) to the mapped field (see Benking, 2001; Buzan and Buzan, 2003; Laszlo, 1994). As will be discussed in the Personal Observations section of this chapter, the mapped fields identify areas of weakness and omissions as well as the need for an active and energetic discourse on the future research agenda for accounting sustainably. These maps are intended to shape the wider discourse on the current and future trajectory of accounting-sustainability research and complement other reviews or critiques of this research field (e.g. Bebbington and Larrinaga-Gonzalez, 2012; Gray, 2010; Gray *et al.*, 2009; Lehman, 2002; Parker, 2011; Spence *et al.*, 2010).

The maps are a personal representation of selected accounting-sustainability research articles. I would like to repeat the warning from Thomson (2007) that these maps are intended to represent the field, but there is a danger that these maps may capture, omit and/or constrain knowledge of the field. These maps are intended as learning devices to aid knowledge development, help determine the shared understanding of the accounting-sustainability community and drive transformation.

The maps in this chapter differ from those in Thomson (2007), which mapped the research publications considered influential in the establishment of accounting-sustainability as a legitimate research terrain. This chapter looks at the intersections of research published in the 'top' accountancy journals and the contested arenas and problems that sustainability science and practitioners are engaged in resolving. I argue that it is these contested arenas and wicked problems that accounting-sustainability researchers should use to shape their future research programmes and engagement activities. The use of contested arenas to map accounting research highlights the conflicts and problems accounting researchers are choosing, as well as those areas where more research effort is needed in the field of sustainability accounting and accountability research. The chapter will conclude with some suggestions on constructing an effective sustainability accounting research agenda and research questions.

## Designing the maps

### Constructing a conceptual map of sustainability's contested arenas

This chapter draws on a number of different sources to construct a conceptual map of the conflict areas associated with sustainability. These sources include critiques of accounting-sustainability research (e.g. Gray, 2010; Gray *et al.*, 2009; Lehman, 2002; Spence *et al.*, 2010); strategies and policies intended to implement sustainable transformations along a sustainability trajectory (e.g. Frame *et al.*, 2010; Scottish Executive, 2005; SDC, 2011); review of sustainability science literature (Bebbington and Larrinaga-Gonzalez, 2012; Frame and O'Connor, 2011; Oels, 2005); and critique of research methods, in particular when constructing research questions (Parker, 2011; Sandberg and Alvesson, 2011).

There were many problems with dividing accounting research publications into *sustainability* and *non-sustainability*, particularly given the holistic and multifaceted nature of sustainability. All accounting research could be construed to be concerned with sustainability impacts. Unfortunately these impacts are very rarely considered. The overwhelming mass of accounting research publications, particularly from 'top' North American journals, is underpinned by unsustainable methodological stances. The publications in many of these journals implicitly, and often explicitly, promote and perpetuate ways of governing society that are unjust, oppressive, and ecologically and socially destructive. This is observed by the predominance of glorifying shareholder wealth maximization at the expense of consumers, workers, local communities, animals, flora and fauna, habitats and the intrinsic beauty of nature.

A choice was made to define accounting-sustainability research as research that problematized or offered solutions to unsustainable social and ecological processes, practices and ways of thinking. Unsustainability was determined with reference to contested arenas where unsustainable forces rub against or confront sustainable forces. This is conceptually similar to the method used in Thomson (2007) where papers were included if they dealt with key attributes of sustainability, i.e. eco-efficiency, eco-justice and eco-effectiveness, social and ethical issues that challenged unsustainable systems of governance, control and markets. However, in Thomson (2007) these concepts emerged from the review of these articles, whereas in this chapter the conceptual mapping structure was undertaken prior to the review of the accounting literature.

This conceptual map attempts to identify the sustainability conflicts that accounting research could engage with. It was constructed through an iterative process. First, individual maps were constructed from an analysis of a number of documents relating to sustainability strategy documents (e.g. Scottish Executive, 2005; SDC, 2011); report of sustainable development practices (Frame *et al.*, 2010); and selected articles (Bebbington and Larrinaga-Gonzalez, 2012; Frame and O'Connor, 2011; Gray, 2010; Lehman, 2002; Oels, 2005; Parker, 2011). From these individual maps common themes, structures and issues could be observed, and so these maps were revised, overlayed and distilled (eventually) into a single map of sustainability contested arenas (see Figure 2.1) that had some plausible connection to accounting research. Just for the record, that last sentence appears to imply a rather orderly process which bears little resemblance to the flipchart strewn shambles that was my kitchen during this exercise. This map consists of 110 conflict arenas arranged into 15 themes. Unfortunately it was not possible to adequately represent the complex interconnectedness of these arenas; however, it is hoped that Figure 2.1 does begin to convey the scope of the problems with which sustainable development needs to be engaged.

### *What constitutes accounting research?*

Establishing the parameters for what constitutes accounting research was a problematic process, and after much pondering, I decided to take the easy way out and made a pragmatic decision to use the ABS (2010) journal ranking categories to identify 'accounting journals' and then use a subset of those journals classified as '3' or '4'. This decision was not taken lightly as I have, like many fellow academics, major problems with this crude attempt to *calculate* the 'quality' of research, not least in that it results in a lazy and an arithmetic judgment of research that allows evaluation without the 'trouble' of actually reading the research. However, it has to be accepted that journal rankings play a powerful role in legitimating accounting research across the whole research community. ABS (2010) is used as a proxy of generally accepted accounting research publications and is considered a reasonable empirical site to identify the penetration of sustainability into accounting research. The exclusion of journals allocated scores of less than '3' is a major limitation of this chapter as is the omission of new journals not yet considered by ABS (2010), in particular the *Social and Environmental Accountability Journal* and *Sustainability Accounting, Management and Policy Journal*. These new journals are publishing interesting and insightful research related to accounting sustainability and management and their output should be considered in any future studies of this type.

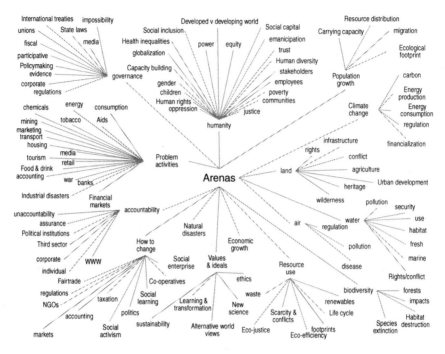

*Figure 2.1* Mapping sustainability in accounting research publications 2008–12.

Another important limitation is that this map relies exclusively on academic journal articles on accounting. It is restricted to one communication channel and that a channel which is not always appropriate to researchers involved in engagement action programmes or interdisciplinary research. There are a number of difficulties in translating these activities into peer-reviewed accounting journal articles. It is also the case that alternative media and communication channels are more relevant to those driving change in policymaking and organizational processes and practices. Research monographs, books, press articles, policy consultations, policy engagements, speaking at political, NGO (non-governmental organizations) and/or business conferences, contributing to NGO shadow accounts, and direct action are all channels for researchers to use to engage with a wider group of people rather than only other academics. These discourses/publications are at present 'off-radar' from this chapter.

The content pages and abstracts of each journal issue in the publication window January 2008–December 2012 were used to classify each of the 3,200 articles using the conceptual map of contested arenas (Figure 2.1). This task was not as onerous as it seems as it was relatively easy to identify that most articles were unrelated to sustainability and there were even whole journals that had published nothing on sustainability in the last five years! Where it was not possible to classify an article based on the abstract, then the actual paper was read. Often an article was classified with multiple contested arenas (on average each article was associated with four arenas). Each article map was used to build up a topology (Benking, 2001) that represented the frequency with which accounting research articles could be linked to arenas. In total 235 articles (7 per cent) were deemed to have links with sustainability's contested arenas; however, these articles were not evenly distributed across the 21 selected journals.

Figures 2.2a and 2.2b illustrate the uneven distribution of accounting-sustainability research articles across journals. It is noticeable that there is a concentration of publications in a small number of journals: *Accounting, Auditing and Accountability Journal*; *Critical Perspectives on Accounting*; *Accounting Forum*; *Accounting Organisations and Society*. With the exception of *Accounting Organisations and Society* there was an almost total absence of accounting-sustainability research in the 'elite' international journals. This absence was 'contradicted' by the publication of three articles in the May 2012 *Accounting Review*, which was so unusual that it merited a special mention by the editor.

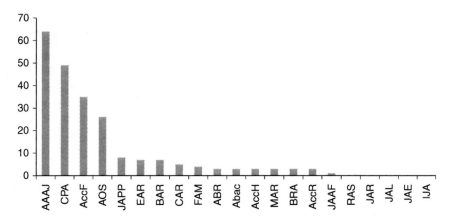

*Figure 2.2a* Sustainability-related publications by journal 2008–12.

Key to journal abbreviations:
*AAAJ – Accounting, Auditing and Accountability Journal; CPA – Critical Perspectives on Accounting; AccF – Accounting Forum; AOS – Accounting Organisations and Society; EAR – European Accounting Review; BAR – British Accounting Review; JAPP – Journal of Accounting and Public Policy; CAR – Contemporary Accounting Research; FAM – Financial Accountability and Management; ABR – Accounting Business Research; Abac – Abacus; AccH – Accounting Horizons; JAAF – Journal of Accounting Auditing and Finance; RAS – Review of Accounting Studies; MAR – Management Accounting Research; JAR – Journal of Accounting Research; JAL – Journal of Accounting Literature; JAE – Journal of Accounting and Economics; IJA – International Journal of Accounting; BRA – Behavioural Research in Accounting; AccR – Accounting Review*

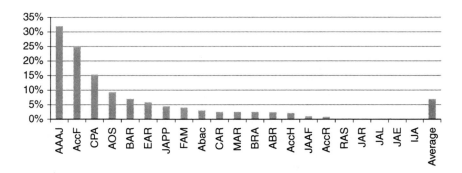

*Figure 2.2b* Sustainability articles as percentage of total articles published 2008–12.

Naturally, an approach that considers non-shareholder maximizing behavior is likely to generate a range of strong reactions among different accounting scholars, but I view that as a healthy prospect. This approach also appears to be consistent with the spirit of recent American Accounting Association efforts to promote innovative accounting research. With the preceding background and disclosures in mind, it is now up to you, the readers, and the market more generally to decide to what extent this 'forum on corporate social responsibility (CSR) research in accounting' contributes to future accounting scholarship

(Evans, 2012, p. 722)

The relative absence of accounting-sustainability articles in these 'elite-mainstream' journals does beg the question as to how 'quality' is determined by ABS (2010). It would appear that relevance of journal articles to the problems that threaten the very existence of our planet is not a factor in 'quality evaluation'. It does not seem unreasonable that relevance to contemporary world problems should be 'at least' one criterion for journal ranking, something that ABS and others seem to be blindly ignoring. The image of 'elite' academics sitting at their computers fiddling with share-price movements and absurd, ill-thought-out variables while the planet burns, Arctic ice sheet melts and half the world's population starves is both absurd and worrying on so many levels.

## *Constructing the terrain of accounting-sustainability research*

The concept map represents the scope of possible accounting-related sustainability conflicts, but it does not illustrate the volume or intensity of accounting research publications associated with these contested arenas. Therefore a partial topology of accounting-sustainability research was constructed (Benking, 2001; Laszlo, 1994), which maps the scope and activity levels of the conflicts associated with accounting research in the publication window 2008–12. The terrain maps (Figures 2.3–2.7) were constructed from the analysis of each individual article and the vertical height was built up based on the frequency of coverage. Simply, the more articles associated with the topic the higher that part of the terrain. Iterating this process for each article led to the construction of the wider accounting-sustainability research terrain. It proved too complex to present and interpret the whole of the conceptual map of all 110 contested arenas, so five sub-maps were produced. Figure 2.3 relates to the 13 level 1 conflict arena themes, whereas Figures 2.4–2.7 represent selections of the 110 level 2 contested arenas. Figure 2.3 provides a thematic overview of the accounting-sustainability field whereas Figures 2.4–2.7 collectively provide a more detailed representation of the accounting-sustainability research published during 2008–12.

*Table 2.1* Values to assist interpreting Figures 2.3–2.7 (excluding 2.6)

| Figure | | Frequency |
| --- | --- | --- |
| 2.3 | Humanity | 123 |
| 2.4 | Financialization | 13 |
| 2.5 | Stakeholders | 14 |
| 2.7 | Political institutions | 16 |

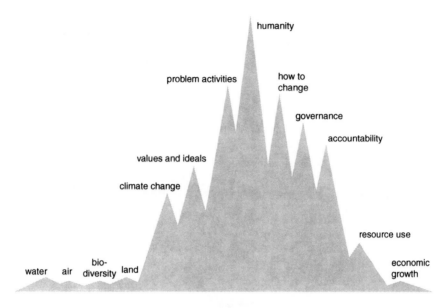

*Figure 2.3* Level 1 themes: accounting-sustainability terrain.

Figures 2.4–2.7 use a constant scale with the vertical height of the triangle representing their frequency of coverage, with empty triangles with dotted borders denoting an absence of coverage. These figures are designed to produce a qualitative impression of the field, by juxtapositioning different elements rather than providing a quantitative analysis. However, to help with making sense of the maps Table 2.1 provides some indicative values to the frequencies of coverage. Note for presentational purposes a different scale is used in Figure 2.3 to take account of the fact that it is representing the aggregate coverage of each of the 13 level 1 conflict arenas.

In the spirit of conceptual mapping and a dialogical approach to learning (Thomson and Bebbington, 2004), I will provide my interpretations of the figures used in this paper *after* the presentation of the topology maps, rather than providing a detailed critique of each individual image.

## Personal observations

In the period 2008–12 the sustainability contested arenas have been covered by an encouraging volume and scope of accounting publications as illustrated by Figure 2.3. There has been no observable reduction in the volume of publications in this field since Thomson (2007) although there appears to be an increase in the frequency of publications related to human conflicts, problematizing activities, how to change, alternative values and ideals, systems of governance and accountability issues. Perhaps surprisingly environmental themes such as land, air, water, biodiversity, population growth and resource use were not covered in so much depth. There does appear to be a concentration on the social attributes of sustainability despite the dominance of the contemporary sustainability policy discourse on climate change. Climate change has emerged quite suddenly into the research terrain, but not as much as might have been anticipated.

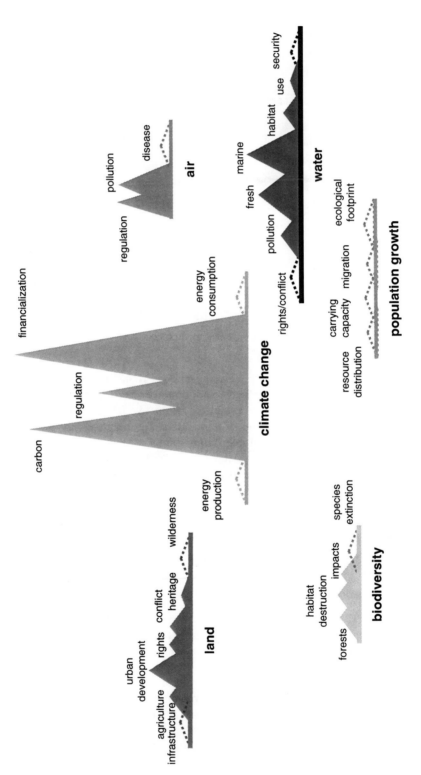

*Figure 2.4* Level 2 accounting-sustainability terrain (1).

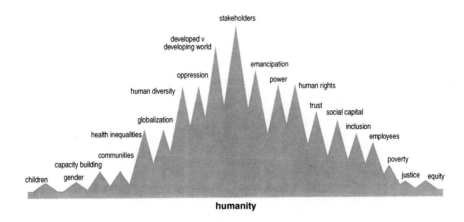

*Figure 2.5* Level 2 accounting-sustainability terrain (2).

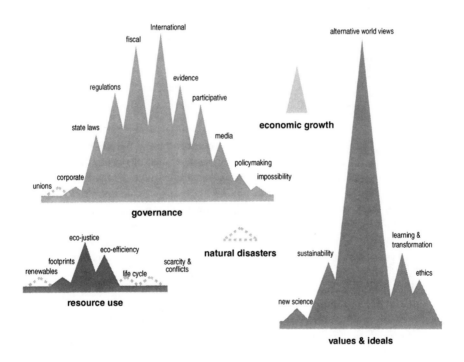

*Figure 2.6* Level 2 accounting-sustainability terrain (3).

Since 2007 a number of 'new' topics can now be seen to be part of the accounting-sustainability terrain, e.g. carbon accounting, conflict, emancipation, accounting for NGOs, political institutions, resource use and biodiversity, Although publication frequencies are relatively few in number, it does suggest a limited co-evolution with the sustainability science literature and the contested arenas of unsustainability. However, many of the observations from Thomson (2007) still remain valid. These include a numeric domination of

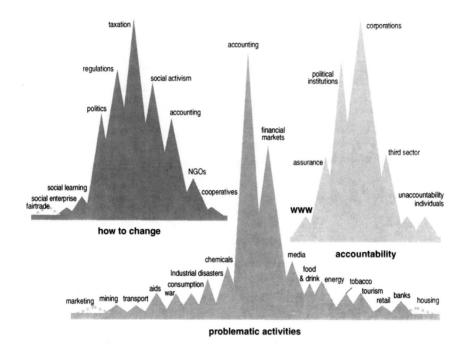

*Figure 2.7* Level 2 accounting-sustainability terrain (4).

content analysis of social and environmental reports, substantial numbers of papers without an explicit theoretical framework that rely on the business case or generic faith in the market to solve problems. There is an empirical focus on profit-oriented organizations traded on some stock exchange in developed Anglo-Saxon, English-speaking countries. Far too many papers still limit their contributions to describing practice within a managerialist framework with limited engagement using prior theoretically informed research.

On a more positive note it would appear that many more unsustainable accounting practices and processes have now been extensively problematized. Accounting was identified in Figure 2.7 as the most frequent problematic activity, as were issues of poor accountability. Many more important conflicts have begun to be incorporated into publications particularly in relation to humanity (see Figure 2.5) and the social dimension of sustainability. Figure 2.4 illustrates a number of contested arenas that has formed part of the wider sustainability discourse that is now forming part of the accounting-sustainability terrain. Interestingly there are special issues scheduled in *Social and Environment Accountability* journal on water and indigenous peoples; and in *Accounting, Auditing and Accountability* on biodiversity. Arguably, Figure 2.4 maps a number of critical public policy discourses related to sustainability and is likely to contain a rich potential source of research questions and empirical sites. The accounting literature is wide ranging in terms of those issues it regards as problematic (Figures 2.3–2.7), which also includes a fundamental questioning of our underlying values and vision of an acceptable and desirable future (see Figure 2.6).

On a negative note, the scope and volume of published research does not appear to stop researchers from trawling over the same ground, as evidenced by the problematic activities in Figure 2.7 and some of the suggestions in how to change (see also Figures 2.4 (Climate Change), 2.5, 2.6 (Governance), 2.7 (How to change)). It is apparent that many recent research articles appear to be ignorant of the fact that there is already a rich accounting-sustainability literature. There is evidence that at its core the accounting-sustainability research literature is co-evolving with changes in sustainability conflicts, policies and practice; but there is an absence of a strong sustainability dynamic in the research literature. The continued popularity of content analysis of annual financial reports is surprising and many of the 'solutions' lack a theoretical understanding of sustainability concepts, sustainability science or sustainability transformational praxis. Many of the proposed solutions contained in recent publications have already been found wanting in prior academic publications (see taxation in Figure 2.7, financialization in Figure 2.4, fiscal measures in Figure 2.6). The volume of publications that are re-problematizing those issues already accepted as problematic is troubling and wasteful, as is the lack of transformative accounting-sustainability solutions. A considerable volume of articles stop at problematizing corporations' accounting-sustainability practices without considering why this was the case or how things could be transformed.

The terrain maps do reveal a number of contradictions in the accounting-sustainability terrain. There are clusters of papers that propose the accountingization of sustainability, along the lines of pristine capitalism (Gray, 2010), as the solution to the world's problems. In their ontologies there are not enough markets, not enough accounting, not enough powers or incentives for the rational shareholders to sort out this mess.

There are clusters of papers that take the exact opposite stance. There are too many markets, too much accounting, too many powers for shareholders and this has caused and is now accelerating the social, economic and ecological crisis. Their ontological positions question the ability of accounting, however constituted, to do anything other than perpetuate current unsustainable activities and ways of behaving. There is a cluster of papers that sits somewhere in-between. They normally dismiss most of the pristine capitalism arguments; however, they exhibit a belief, normally based on qualitative empirical research, that some form of reconstructed accounting processes and practices could contribute somehow to a sustainable transformation.

There is a problem with the cohesion, focus and persistence of research into accounting sustainability and accountability. My personal stance is that the urgency and immediacy of the threats posed by unsustainability require all concerned with sustainable transformation to focus on how and whether accounting can contribute to governing these threats. If accounting in whatever form can contribute to sustainable transformation then we should be identifying and developing processes and practices, expertise that can be hybridized or integrated into existing or new sustainable governance processes, practices and expertise; or exploring how accounting should be constituted if it is to effectively and authentically engage with sustainable transformation. Much of the published research in accounting sustainability, and accounting in general, does not discuss how the provision of new accounting information or novel accounting processes, practices and expertise would bring about a shift towards more sustainable behaviour.

To sum up this section I would argue that despite some promising developments in the accounting-sustainability literature, there is still a feeling of the same old stuff reappearing in journals and I fear that this is likely to continue. This is a problem shared by other social science disciplines. In their insightful analysis of the management research literature Sandberg and Alvesson (2011) identify a number of reasons for the conservative nature of 'elite' management research. One observation pertinent to this chapter is the dominance of 'gap-spotting' in the formulation of 'acceptable' research questions. The research question acts as a foundational framework for any subsequent research and if the process for setting research questions is problematic then any research output is also likely to be problematic.

Sandberg and Alvesson (2011) suggest that the majority of management researchers construct their research questions not from 'real-world' problems or the risks and hazards confronting people or our planet, but rather from perceived gaps in their academic literature. They also outline clear, if perverse, structural incentives and mechanisms that drive researchers into this mode of formulating research questions. Gap spotting is an easy, uncontroversial and safe way of identifying what to research. The accumulation of knowledge over time through peer verification and legitimation lies at the core of historic approaches to science. Gap spotting has been a successful strategy for many researchers, one actively encouraged by research institutions and many 'top' journals. Gap spotting under certain conditions can also produce high-quality valuable knowledge, but in 2014 it is inappropriate for accounting-sustainability research, although it may at least force researchers to be aware that there is an existing accounting-sustainability research literature.

Gap spotting reinforces the status quo and works within the existing parameters of a research field. It assumes that all of the problems with which a discipline is concerned have already been identified and processes are under way to address them. Gap spotting does not open up new research problems or resolve long-running controversies; nor does it integrate different opinions or interface with different disciplines. Gap spotting accepts the received wisdom and does not challenge axiomatic assumptions or disrupt belief structures. Gap spotting also perpetuates any error, myopia and ignorance contained within a discipline; I would refer you to the discussion in the Personal Observations section on the lack of substantive coverage of sustainable conflicts in all but one of the journals ranked 'four' on the ABS journal list. Gap spotting in the accounting academic literature is a very poor strategy for setting research questions for effective accounting-sustainability research concerned with sustainable transformations. The mapping process undertaken for this chapter (and Thomson, 2007) would suggest that large parts of the accounting research community privilege gap spotting strategies and the prevalence of gap spotting partially explains the publication topologies mapped in this chapter.

However, there was evidence of researchers adopting a different approach to setting their research questions or challenging the questions accounting-sustainability researchers were asking (see also Bebbington and Larrinaga-Gonzalez, 2012; Gray, 2010; Gray *et al.*, 2009; Parker, 2011). A small group of papers could be seen to disrupt the status quo and change the conceptual terrain of accounting-sustainability research in alignment with emerging sustainable science and pressing social and ecological hazards.

Sandberg and Alvesson (2011) propose a problematizing or disruptive strategy to setting research questions in order to facilitate the development of interesting and influential theories and knowledge. Problematization explores the extent to which it is possible to think differently, instead of accepting what is already known, and to consider how to use this new thinking and/or knowledge to transform our existential reality along a more sustainable path. The radical nature of sustainable transformations (Bebbington and Larrinaga-Gonzalez, 2012; Gray, 2010; Parker, 2011) requires our research questions to be more radical and ambitious. As a community, we need to be challenging assumptions, engaging in actions and thinking that seeks to resist unsustainable practices, participating effectively in sustainability conflicts and focusing on solving problems. Fortunately for sustainability-accounting researchers, as illustrated in this chapter's conceptual map, there are many sites of conflict requiring accounting research participation. It is also the case that a wider debate needs to be initiated on the vision of accounting sustainability and accountability. Establishing a vision of what is possible rather than evaluating current practice is a critical stage in any transformation process (Freire, 1970; Stevenson, 2009). This vision should not be regarded as a normative prescription of what must be, but rather part of an ongoing discourse, a discourse that has been surprisingly limited in the accounting-sustainability research community (Adams and Whelan, 2009; Gray, 2010; Lehman, 2002).

### *Establishing a vision for sustainable accounting and accounting-sustainability research*

Gray (2002, 2010) raised a number of challenges to future research and the development of accounting-sustainability practices. Using his wide-ranging criticisms of contemporary accounting-sustainability research and practice as a starting point, it was possible to construct a set of attributes associated with effective accounting-sustainability that would counter his critique. In order to invigorate this debate I would like to offer the following vision for accounting sustainability and accountability.

Sustainable accounts should contribute to the sustainable narratives within and about an entity as part of sustainable dialogues in the context of governing transformation towards sustainable societies in a sustainable world. Sustainable accounting entities should incorporate all organizations and collectives that either inhibit or promote sustainable transformation, and not be restricted to destructive, profit-oriented corporations. All entities should be accountable for the unsustainable consequences of their actions and intentions and prepare sustainable accounts in the public's and planets' interest. The intention of producing these accounts should be to educate others as to how the entity is (or is not) contributing towards sustainable transformation. These accounts should be mandatory, plausible, understandable, truthful and reliable, and form part of a series of dialogic engagements with relevant stakeholders, political institutions and regulatory bodies. The content of these accounts should not focus on ecological housekeeping arrangements or successes but should make visible the interrelationships and future consequences of that entity's actions and intentions on social, ecological and economic sustainability. These accounts should be an appropriate blend of scientific, economic, financial, statistic, ethical and aesthetic narratives that reflect the urgency for action given our unsustainable state. The sustainability and accountability of any entity should be accounted for in series of reflexive engagements involving different participants representing a plurality of interests, powers, epistemological and ontological perspectives.

### Final comment

There is an urgency in constructing a new accounting-sustainability research agenda with research questions aligned with the unfolding sustainability science discourse.[2] Sustainability science has certain characteristics that are relevant to building on the successes of the accounting-sustainability research programme. Sustainability science is problem driven and is prioritized by the risks posed and the urgency of a solution, as should be accounting-sustainability research. Sustainability science seeks to produce knowledge that can help reduce negative sustainability impacts and contribute to any sustainable transformations, as should accounting-sustainability research. Sustainability science is concerned with developing an interdisciplinary, post-normal understanding of the inherently complex, reflexive relationships between nature and society, as should accounting-sustainability research.

Sustainability science is underpinned by notions of participatory and democratic involvement with a normative bias and seeks to participate in policy and practice discussions, as should accounting-sustainability research. Sustainability science often takes the form of social learning, as should accounting-sustainability research. There are considerable merits in developing problematizing sustainability accounting research along the same trajectory as sustainability science.

I would argue that there is a need to use sustainability theories/concepts to first directly disrupt accounting processes, practices and expertise; and second, as the foundation for exploring new forms of sustainability accounting and accountability. With a few exceptions, accounting-sustainability researchers have used established social theories from other disciplines to disrupt accounting and then tried to infer from their analysis the implications for sustainable transformations. There are merits in reformulating accounting research from a sustainability science perspective and in using different approaches to imagine and develop transformative accounting for a sustainable world.

## Notes

1  Reluctantly, I have used the ABS ranking list as a generally accepted way of classifying journals. Personally I have problems with this ranking and do not wish to endorse this as a way of judging research quality.
2  For a more in-depth discussion of sustainability science and accounting, see Bebbington and Larrinaga-Gonzalez (2012).

## References

Adams, C.A. and Whelan, G. (2009), Conceptualising future change in corporate sustainability reporting, *Accounting Auditing and Accountability Journal* 21(1): 118–43.
Association of Business Schools (ABS) (2010), *ABS Academic Journal Quality Guide v4*, available at http://www.associationofbusinessschools.org, accessed November 2012.
Bebbington, J. and Larrinaga-Gonzalez, C. (2012), Accounting for sustainable development: (re)constructing the agenda, paper presented at the Centre for Social and Environmental Accounting Research Conference, St Andrews, Scotland, September.
Benking, H. (2001), Setting the common frame of reason, *Knowledge Management, Auditing and Mapping Journal* 1(5), available at http://benking.de/Global-Change/spatial-spacial.html, accessed November 2012.
Buzan, T. and Buzan, B. (2003), *The Mind Map Book: Radiant Thinking – Major Evolution in Human Thought*, BBC Books, London.
Evans, J. (2012), Introduction, *The Accounting Review* 87(3): 721–2.
Frame, B. and O'Connor, M. (2011), Integrating valuation and deliberation: the purposes of sustainability assessment, *Environment Science and Policy* 14(1): 1–10.
Frame, B., Gordon, R. and Mortimer, C. (2010), *Hatched: The Capacity for Sustainable Development*, Landcare Research, Auckland.
Freire, P. (1970), *The Pedagogy of the Oppressed*, Seabury, New York.
Georgakopoulos, G. and Thomson, I. (2008), Social reporting, engagements, controversies and conflict in an arena context, *Accounting Auditing & Accountability Journal* 21(8): 1116–43.
Gray, R. (2010), Is accounting for sustainability actually accounting for sustainability ... and how would we know? An exploration of narratives of organisations and the planet, *Accounting, Organizations and Society* 35(1): 47–62.
Gray, R., Dillard, J. and Spence, C. (2009), Social accounting research as if the world matters: postalgia and a new absurdism, *Public Management Review* 11(5): 545–73.

Gray, R.H. (2002), The social accounting project and accounting organizations and society privileging engagement, imaginings, new accountings and pragmatism over critique? *Accounting, Organizations and Society* 27: 687–708.

Laszlo, S. (1994), *Changing Vision: Human Cognitive Maps – Past, Present and Future*, Adamantine Press, London.

Lehman, G. (2001), Reclaiming the public sphere: problems and prospects for corporate social and environmental accounting, *Critical Perspectives on Accounting* 12(6): 713–33.

Lehman, G. (2002), Global accountability and sustainability: research prospects, *Accounting Forum* 26(3/4): 219–32.

Oels, A. (2005), Rendering climate change governable: from biopower to advance liberal government? *Journal of Environmental Policy and Planning* 7(3): 185–207.

Parker, L. (2011), Building bridges to the future: mapping the territory for developing social and environmental accountability, *Social Environmental Accountability Journal* 31(1): 7–24.

Sandberg, J. and Alvesson, M. (2011), Ways of constructing research questions: Gap-spotting or problematization?, *Organisation* 18(1): 23–44.

Scottish Executive (2005), *Choosing Our Future: Scotland's Sustainable Development Strategy*, Scottish Office, Edinburgh.

Spence, C., Husillos, J. and Correa-Ruiz, C. (2010), Cargo cult science and the death of politics: a critical review of social and environmental accounting research, *Critical Perspectives on Accounting* 21(1): 76–89.

Stevenson, T. (2009), Enacting the vision for sustainable development, *Future* 41: 246–52.

Sustainable Development Commission (SDC) (2011), *Prosperity without Growth: The Transition to a Sustainable Economy*, SDC, London.

Thomson, I. (2007), Accounting and sustainability: mapping the terrain, in J. Bebbington, B. O'Dwyer and J. Unerman (eds) *Sustainable Accounting and Accountability*, Routledge, London.

Thomson, I. and Bebbington, J. (2004), It doesn't matter what you teach? *Critical Perspectives on Accounting* 15(4/5): 609–28.

# 3  Sustainability accounting and education

*David Collison, John Ferguson and Lorna Stevenson[1]*

[E]ducation is the most vital of all resources ... education, which fails to clarify our central convictions is mere training or indulgence. For it is our central convictions that are in disorder, and, as long as the present anti-metaphysical temper persists, the disorder will grow worse. Education, far from ranking as man's greatest resource, will then be an agent of destruction.

(Schumacher, 1973, pp. 64, 83)

## Introduction

In its *Call for Action* (2010, p. 4) the Association for the Advancement of Sustainability in Higher Education (AASHE) stated 'What is needed is a curriculum that prepares learners for living sustainably, both professionally and personally, and that explicitly helps the learner deeply understand the iterations, inter-connections, and the consequences of actions and decisions'. This chapter seeks to explore the accounting education curriculum in the context of this call for action.

The term 'sustainability accounting' is often taken to equate to the range of topics normally included within social and environmental accounting (SEA).[2] To some extent, the terms will be used interchangeably[3] in this chapter, though we acknowledge that much of what constitutes SEA stops seriously short of engaging with the notion of sustainability. Within the SEA canon we could include technical eco-efficiency issues including environmental management accounting, implications for and critiques of conventional accounting and reporting, and critiques and prescriptions of innovative forms of reporting: 'sustainability accounting' draws on all these areas but, ideally, also explicitly recognizes the limitations of the biosphere and its profound implications for peaceful human coexistence. Such implications are graphically highlighted by Meadows *et al.* (2005, p. 234):

> Once the population and economy have overshot physical limits of the Earth there are only two ways back: involuntary collapse caused by escalating shortages and crises, or controlled reduction of the ecological footprint by deliberate social choice.

Our chapter takes the position that these potential scenarios be considered in the context of the following statement, also by Meadows *et al.* (2005, p. 234):

> Technology and markets typically serve the most powerful segments of society. If the primary goal is growth, they produce growth as long as they can. If the primary goals were equity and sustainability they could also serve those goals.

In this chapter we therefore address: the socializing effects of education itself; the values implicit in accounting and business education and whether the changes – which we believe to be necessary – can be achieved through more learning or are impossible without 'unlearning' (see Ghoshal, 2005; Schumacher, 1973); the development of SEA education in universities; as well as professional perspectives and developments. Outside the study of accounting and its related disciplines, sustainability education initiatives have led to eponymous multidisciplinary degrees, and UK government rhetoric purports to be embedding sustainability in the curriculum at all levels. Indeed the time of writing coincides with the last stage of the United Nations Decade of Education for Sustainable Development (2005–14). While these developments go beyond the scope of this essay, they are acknowledged as part of the wider context, to which the first section, The Socializing Effects of Education, is readily applicable.

The need for wider societal acceptance of the requirement for fundamental changes in values and aspirations, and the reflexive relationship of this acceptance with political will and leadership, as attenuated by the hegemonic power of vested interests, bestride all discussions of this issue. The education of those, in particular, who will exercise leadership and offer expertise in matters of economic and business decisions is no trivial matter in this wider context, and is often referred to in international calls for action.

Before considering sustainability accounting education[4] *per se*, it seems necessary first to consider the nature of education itself. The truly awesome challenges presented by expanding an already unsustainable, ecological footprint in our fragile world require a fundamental shift in societal values; in Einstein's words: 'No problem can be solved from the same consciousness that created it. We have to learn to see the world anew' (Sterling, 2001, p. 12). This need prompts us to consider central aspects of the nature and role of education.

## The socializing effects of education

Functionalist perspectives on education that view the education system as being a meritocracy which serves as the 'engine of democracy' have been repeatedly challenged in the sociology literature since the early 1960s (Apple, 1995, p. 9). In particular, a range of perspectives emerged which recognized the significance of conflict and ideology in education (Karabel and Halsey, 1977). While there are serious disagreements within this literature in terms of how education contributes to existing power asymmetries, prominent figures within this field, such as Althusser, Apple, Bernstein, Bourdieu, Gramsci, and Illich, all acknowledge the importance of examining the role of education in reproducing and sustaining relations of power (Karabel and Halsey, 1977, p. 4; see also Apple, 1995).

One aspect of the education process, the curriculum (or more precisely, the selection and organization of knowledge) has received considerable attention in terms of the role it plays in the 'creation and recreation of ideological hegemony' (Apple, 1995, p. 17).[5] As Apple and Christian-Smith (1991) point out, it is naive to consider the curriculum to be a 'neutral' collection of knowledge. On the contrary, what is considered to be 'legitimate' or 'official' knowledge is the result of complex power relations which 'signal more profound political, economic and cultural relations and histories' (Apple and Christian-Smith, 1991, p. 3). In describing what he calls the 'selective tradition', and which could equally describe the selective processes in education curricula, Raymond Williams (1989, p. 58) states:

> From a whole possible area of past and present, in a particular culture, certain meanings and practices are selected for emphasis and certain other meanings and practices are

neglected or excluded. Yet within a particular hegemony, and as one of its decisive processes, this selection is presented and usually successfully passed off as 'the tradition', 'the significant past'. What has then to be said about any tradition is that it is in this sense an aspect of contemporary social and cultural organization, in the interest of the dominance of a specific class.

Therefore, the knowledge and culture of powerful groups is defined and passed on as not only the most 'legitimate', but as common sense (Apple, 1995).

In the case of the accounting curriculum, the official curriculum is developed, both directly and indirectly, through complex power relations between a range of constituents including: professional accounting bodies (through the development of accounting standards and accreditation requirements for university programmes); corporate law (which sets the way in which companies must report – and in whose interests they should be run (for an exploration, see Collison *et al.*, 2011)); lobbyists (who play a significant role in influencing company law and accounting standards); and universities, lecturers and students. In addition, each of these constituents will be 'structured by the class, gender, sexual and race inequalities' that organize society (Apple, 2004, p. 189).

While the structuring effects of class, gender, sex and race may not be formally included on the 'overt' curriculum, the norms and values which they embody will underpin it to the extent that they will still inform students' sense of what is right and wrong. This is referred to by Illich as the 'hidden curriculum' (see also Apple, 1995; Bebbington and Thomson, 2001). In business and accounting education, the knowledge and values produced and distributed to students tend to implicitly privilege a particular group of people – corporate shareholders (this argument will be further developed in the following subsection, Values Implicit in Accounting Education). Furthermore, this privileging is taken as common sense, as natural. According to Bebbington and Thomson (2001), it is the prevalence of these hidden assumptions which explain why 'bolt-on' courses on corporate social responsibility (CSR)[6] or business ethics[7] ultimately fail – because they do not sufficiently challenge the underlying common-sense assumptions that help maintain and reproduce current social arrangements.

This can be further explained by reference to one aspect of the hegemonic process. In order to maintain its own legitimacy, the dominant ideology must integrate many interests, 'even opposing groups under its banner' (Apple, 1995, p. 27). One way of integrating oppositional cultures (in the context of the curriculum) is to pay them lip service; to allow them to be mentioned, or, in the case of CSR, to be included as an addition or an option, but never to integrate them to the extent that they modify the core values which the curriculum embodies.[8] Thus it is important to realize that, while the selection of knowledge is never a neutral activity, it is neither, nor need it be, a *complete* 'mirror reflection of ruling class ideas' (Luke, 1988, p. 24; see also McIntosh, 2002).

### Values implicit in accounting education

The relationship between accounting and the values implicit in neoclassical economic theory have long been acknowledged in the accounting literature (Cooper, 1980; Cooper and Sherer, 1984; Tinker, 1980). For example, Tinker (1980, p. 149) points out that neoclassical economic theory has 'probably contributed more than any other [theory] to the practice of accounting'. Drawing primarily on a positivist philosophy, both neoclassical economics, and (hence) much accounting theory, both make claims to be 'value-neutral', liberated from any particular political view of the world. However, such claims conceal the 'value-impregnated' underpinnings of this perspective, which can be considered ideological in the sense that it is 'imbued with certain beliefs' which help maintain relations of domination (Frankfurter and McGoun, 1999, p. 161; see also Thompson, 1990).

In particular, neoclassical economics assumes individuals are free to act in their own (economic) self-interest and that, by doing so, economic growth ensues, which in turn should maximize the welfare of society.[9] The influence of this perspective is especially apparent in Anglo-American capitalist economies,[10] where private sectional interests[11] are enshrined in legal structures and socio-economic norms. These inherently divisive values (see Birkin et al., 2005) generally assume that the only participants in the wealth creating process who should have their interests maximized are shareholders. Thus the economic rights of capital owners are treated as innately superior while negative impacts from corporate activity, such as environmental degradation, are treated as externalities. Furthermore, the inherently divisive nature of such socio-economic arrangements gives incentives to powerful vested interests to use their hegemonic influence, through, *inter alia*, lobbying and propaganda (see for example Beder, 1997; Stauber and Rampton, 1995) to resist any internalizing of the externalities borne by wider society. Social and environmental concerns are therefore only of relevance to corporations insofar as they impact upon their 'bottom line': they are 'externalising machines'[12] (Bakan, 2004).

It is the 'ideology of shareholder capitalism' that gets taught on accounting courses, the fundamental moral underpinnings of which are 'buried by scientific-sounding abstractions' (Wolfe, 1993, p. 2). This guise of 'technical rationality' conceals a hegemonic discourse which not only sustains relations of power but imbues students with the notion that wider society and the natural environment should be treated as 'externalities' (McPhail and Gray, 1996). While speaking of business education in general Ghoshal states: 'By propagating ideologically inspired amoral theories, business schools have actively freed their students from any sense of moral responsibility' (Ghoshal, 2005, p. 76).

While some business schools and accounting departments[13] offer courses in business ethics or SEA, they are considered by many to be merely 'a drop in the river of the heavy mental conditioning for capitalism' (Wolfe, 1993, p. 2). As Ghoshal (2005, p. 88) points out:

> If deans really intend to infuse a concern for ethics and for responsible management in the research and teaching that are carried out at their institutions, they have to acknowledge that the tokenism of adding a course on ethics will not achieve their goals. As long as all the other courses continue as they are, a single, stand-alone course on corporate social responsibility will not change the situation in any way.

In other words, the first real step towards engendering social and environmental awareness among accounting students, to paraphrase Ghoshal, is not to create new courses but to stop teaching some old ones. It is against this challenging background that those who wish to change the nature of accounting education have to operate. Since they typically lack the means to stop the teaching of certain ideas – indeed such a stark statement of that aspiration even has, perhaps regrettably, an uncomfortable ring to it, redolent of book burning – there seems little choice but to challenge those ideas where and how they can, but with a recognition of the magnitude of the task.

## Developments and challenges in SEA education

There has been a steady examination of SEA education in the literature – including what it might comprise, what it might achieve, how it should be addressed, and why students do and do not choose to study SEA – though this body of work is not enormous. Discussion of social issues in the context of teaching accounting appears to have first been highlighted in the mid-1970s (Mathews, 2001). However it was not until the late 1980s that more widespread academic interest was paid to the area of SEA education. This interest has grown to date, focusing in the 1990s mainly on environmental issues, but more recently on social dimensions once again (Mangion, 2005; Parker, 2004).

In the context of discussing the goals SEA teaching might have, Mathews (2001) suggested that SEA issues can be used to develop the moral thought processes we might expect of those charged with managing social and environmental resources to meet society's needs and in line with the public interest credentials of their profession. However, though not dissenting from his aims, Bebbington and Thomson (2001) showed how Mathews's failure to consider potential resistance on several levels may well result in his well-meaning suggestions failing to achieve their aim. In seeking to address the challenge of the wider hegemonic discourse described above, Bebbington and Thomson have drawn on key figures in the radical educational literature (see also Thomson and Bebbington, 2004). Key to their argument are Illich's (1971) idea of the hidden curriculum, and Freire's (1996) approaches to education. Bebbington and Thomson (2001) stated that:

> The hidden curriculum forms the bedrock of most people's assumptions of right/wrong and possible/impossible and this knowledge set is never explicitly taught but is implicit in the other material taught. As a result, the 'hidden curriculum' is never critically examined as to its 'reasonableness'.
>
> (p. 354)

Freire contrasted two approaches to education: he characterized 'Banking' education as 'teaching where "motionless, static, compartmentalized and predictable" knowledge is conveyed to students who are assumed to be "passive, patient, listening receptacles"' (p. 354) and which thus continues to hide the curriculum. This was contrasted with Freire's (1996, p. 16) 'Dialogic' or 'Problem Posing' education which Bebbington and Thomson claimed 'allow[s] the potential for identifying and transcending the hidden curriculum' (p. 354). They concluded:

> there is no such thing as a neutral education process. Education either functions as an instrument that is used to facilitate the integration of the younger generation into the logic of the present system and to bring conformity with it, or it becomes a practice of freedom, the means by which men and women deal critically and creatively with reality and discover how to participate in the transformation of their world.
>
> (Bebbington and Thomson, 2001, p. 355)[14] [15]

Thus, Thomson and Bebbington (2004) declared that in a sense 'it doesn't matter what you teach' and that the teaching approach, as discussed above, is key. Nonetheless, there have been a variety of interpretations of how to implement SEA education. One end of the spectrum, for example, restricts the definition of SEA to a narrow environmental accounting and grafts environmental disclosures on to the standard Anglo-American financial reporting model (Sefcik et al., 1997). An alternative understanding of the possibilities of SEA education is highlighted by Bebbington and Thomson (2001, p. 354):

> SEA is not merely an interesting extension of the accounting knowledge set, but questions the way in which we understand and organise our individual lives and social institutions ... The problem of low levels of SEA education can be linked to the failure of conventional accounting to make its own assumptions explicit (or its success in keeping them hidden!)

This highlights nicely the potential role of accounting education in either: making sustainability more difficult by failing to equip those who study accounting (and go on to practise the accounting art) with the knowledge and ability to question the status quo and the founding principles of their discipline; or in advancing sustainability by enabling those educated in accounting to respond to new needs and public interest obligations in a conceptually coherent and fundamental way.

Mangion (2005) examined the literature on how SEA can be incorporated into higher education curricula, and identified the following options:[16]

- embed SEA into existing financial-based accounting teaching;
- teach SEA as a stand-alone course – usually after the undisputed essentials of an accounting degree have been addressed;
- create (unusually) a specialized stream in SEA issues;
- include SEA in a general 'accounting theory' course.

Such a grafting of SEA ideas into a regime which at heart is inimical to its spirit may be better than nothing: Gordon (1998) described how a compulsory accounting theory course itself engendered greater awareness of, and changed reactions to, SEA issues in final year undergraduate accounting students. However it has been suggested (Gibson, 1997; Humphrey et al., 1996; Lewis et al., 1992; Owen et al., 1994) that piecemeal solutions such as those listed above, as opposed to fundamental reappraisal of the content and process of accounting degrees, are unlikely to equip the next generation of accounting professionals with sufficient social, ethical and environmental awareness for their public interest role.

Owen et al. (1994) performed the first survey of the provision, form and context of SEA in British universities in 1992/3. This work was replicated and updated in the UK by Stevenson (2002) for 1997/8; in Australia by Mangion (2005) for 2004/5; by Zulkifli (2010) for Malaysia; and again in the UK in 2011 by Stevenson and Thomson under the auspices of the Centre for Social and Environmental Accounting Research (CSEAR).[17] The aim of Owen et al.'s original (1994) survey of British universities' SEA teaching was to:

> identify the degree to which students are exposed to [SEA] material in their undergraduate degree studies and to explore more qualitative issues concerning, amongst other things, the aims of such teaching, the nature of the material being covered or, alternatively, reasons for neglecting the subject area.
>
> (Owen et al., 1994, Executive Summary, p. 1)

Key findings of the research included:

- peripheral (at best) coverage of SEA in many undergraduate accounting degree programmes;
- SEA coverage often present as a final year (with low numbers) option;[18]

- SEA not seen as 'generally accepted "core" accounting degree material';
- individual 'champions' playing a key role in establishing and maintaining SEA teaching – these individuals often having a research record in the discipline (still the case in 2011);
- dominance of 'environmental' over 'social' issues, reflecting the influence of professional accounting and general media (see for example, Fleischman and Schuele, 2006);
- student expectations and perceptions of professional accreditation requirements appearing to strongly influence academics' ideas of the acceptability of SEA material.

For the first five of these findings, Matten and Moon (2004) reported similar conclusions from their review of CSR teaching in European business education; in addition, in 2011 over half of the respondents to the CSEAR UK SEA teaching survey[19] noted insufficient coverage in their institutions of 'sustainability', 'social reporting' and 'CSR' at undergraduate level, and a similar proportion made this observation for 'sustainability' at postgraduate level. In the context of Owen *et al.*'s last point above, a potentially vicious circle is highlighted by Blundell and Booth's (1988) suggestion that a major obstacle to student acceptance of social accounting material is their perception of its lack of relevance to accounting practice (see also Collison *et al.*, 2000). These and other alternative potential drivers for curriculum change, such as professional accounting body accreditation requirements, are presented later in the chapter, most especially in the next section, Education and the Professions.

The picture of the state of SEA education revealed by the CSEAR UK teaching survey some 17 years after Owen *et al.*'s (1994) research was little different. In particular, the significant reason for teaching SEA – creating student awareness of the wider obligations of corporate behaviour – was unchanged, and lack of expertise[20] was still cited as a significant impediment to more SEA programme content. Thus, despite a steady growth in the attention given to SEA in the academic accounting literature (Mathews, 1997; Stevenson, 2002), little appeared to have changed overall.

In 2005, in Australia, Mangion (2006) surveyed all accounting academic staff in all 38 Australian universities to examine the extent of SEA education provided in them. She reported that SEA was taught in the majority of Australian institutions' accounting degree programmes, mainly within other mainstream courses (73 per cent of respondents reported a part course, 10 per cent a full SEA course). Potentially significantly, the number of full courses was expected to increase in the next two years – 24 per cent of survey respondents said that they expected their higher education institution to offer a full stand-alone SEA course within the next two years. In contrast with Owen *et al.*'s (1994) and Stevenson's (2002) findings of the popularity of environmental accounting in SEA curricula, social accountability was identified by Mangion's (2006) population as the most widely studied topic. However in 2010, Sundin and Wainwright demonstrated still limited SEA curriculum coverage in Australian universities: they found that four of the 22 accredited accounting undergraduate programmes offered stand-alone SEA modules, while 17 had a low level – one or two weeks' coverage in mainstream accounting subjects – of SEA integration.

We might interpret the popular delivery of SEA within existing mainstream accounting education as reflecting a compromise in the light of curriculum space constraints, or alternatively as providing a means of contextualizing and highlighting accounting's fundamental tenets (as suggested by Bebbington and Thomson, 2001); or indeed as a stage of curriculum acceptance and integration some way between cursory comment and a full SEA module. Further exploratory work would be needed for more informed comment on the applicability of any of these potential interpretations. Nonetheless, little evidence exists of the application of wider, inter- or cross-disciplinary perspectives on any SEA provision.

Despite an apparent lack of consensus as to what should be taught in SEA education, Mangion (2006) noted 12 topics currently comprising SEA in university teaching: environmental accountability – external reporting; environmental accountability – management; social accountability; theoretical framework for SEA; sustainable development; social audit; financial social reporting; non-financial reporting; social/ethical reporting; human asset accounting; SEA history; and comparative and international SEA/reporting.

The accounting profession clearly plays a key role in influencing university level accounting education, while also being open to influence, at least at the margin, by educational and research initiatives within academe. In addition, professional education itself, as well as post qualification education, is of central importance to any informed professional response to the challenge of sustainability. Stevenson and Thomson (2010, p. 55) noted that 'Social, environmental and sustainability accounting (SESA) topics are present in all of the syllabi of the professional accounting institutes of the UK and Ireland, although there do appear to be differences in the extent and positioning of SESA within their overall programmes'; and further that 'the inclusion in professional syllabi of these topics gives greater legitimacy to SESA and could act as [a] driver for change in university accounting programmes' (p. 56).[21]

## Education and the professions

Since the 2002 Johannesburg Summit, the special role of our education systems in facilitating, envisioning, and leading change towards sustainability has been the focus of renewed attention. Higher education (HE) in particular prides itself on being at the vanguard of vision and wisdom, and its core values point to its potential leadership role across societies.

(Ryan *et al.*, 2010, p. 107)

The Bonn Declaration[22] stated that 'ESD (Education for Sustainable Development) should become an integral part of the training of leaders in business, industry, trade union, nonprofit and voluntary organisations and the public services' and '[t]he emergence of global sustainability declarations, e.g. Talloires (1990), Copernicus (1994), and Lüneberg (2001), underlines the expectation that HE should be a catalyst for sustainability progress in academic and practical innovation' (Ryan *et al.*, 2010, p. 112). However, HE is also charged by some with failing in this role; for example, Sibbel (2009, p. 74) stated that:

[r]ecognising the barriers facing consumers to making sustainable choices shifts the focus to the training of professionals who manage the resources, educate the public or design the options from which choices are made. The institution of higher education (HE) is where these professionals are trained ... the recognition that most world leaders had completed tertiary studies is strong evidence that the education which empowered did not encourage the aspirations or develop the capabilities required for sustainability.

Further, Rasche and Escudero (2010) noted that the United Nations' 'Principles for Responsible Management Education (PRME) grew in part because business leaders ... were asking educational institutions: "What are you doing to help future business leaders to understand the challenges of responsible management?"' (p. 248); PRME was launched in July 2004 with 40 participant organizations/institutions and now has 416 (10/2/2012). The PRME website (UNPRME, 2012) acknowledges that 'in the current academic environment, corporate responsibility and sustainability have entered but not yet become embedded in the mainstream of business-related education'. Potential influences on such embeddedness include those Matten and Moon (2004, p. 331) quote in response to 'other future drivers' of CSR teaching: 'public opinion driven by more scandals, environmental disasters, fat cattery, corporate manslaughter'. Student initiatives such as Oikos[23] and Net Impact[24] have been noted by Jones-Christensen et al. (2007, p. 360) as 'driver[s] of the course content (and even program focus)'.

A further global initiative, the UN's 2005–14 Decade for Education for Sustainable Development (DESD) originated with a proposal from the Japanese Government and NGOs at the World Summit for Sustainable Development in 2002 (Ryan *et al.*, 2010, p. 111). UNESCO's Strategy document for the second half of the DESD noted a key priority action for 2010–15, to 'highlight the relevance and importance of education training for sustainable development' (UNESCO, 2010, p. 54). The 2009 Global Progress Report for the DESD also 'gives emphasis to the need for substantial professional capacity-building and greater alignment of the formal curriculum in support of sustainability', noting that 'the majority of progress made to date has been at school level' (Ryan *et al.*, 2010, p. 112). These commentators go on to note:

> However, while international declarations may provide useful publicity to encourage progress, they are not sufficient to change institutional and disciplinary practices in HE ... The strategic implications of sustainability reach far beyond individual curriculum changes, isolated environmental practices and signatures on international declarations, and require adjustments to academic priorities, organizational structures, financial and audit systems.
>
> (p. 112)

They further noted that

> significant gaps exist between policy and reality, in relation to the aims articulated for both sustainable development and ESD. The Global Progress Report for the DESD (UNESCO, 2009) has shown that one of the most profound problems in advancing sustainability stems from a lack of inter-ministerial communications.
>
> (p. 114)

Notwithstanding these gaps, there is some evidence of the international calls for action appearing in national education policies and national government reporting, such as the Scottish Government's annual reporting duties under the Climate Change (Scotland) Act 2009.[25] For an example of the former, 'Wales is one of the few countries in the world to have governmental policy regarding education for sustainable development' (HEA, 2010, p. 1); the authors also note that much substantive work on ESD takes place at grass roots level and calls for 'improved leadership, promotion and co-ordination [of] ESD activities' (p. 5). The Spanish Government in its proposal 'Strategy University 2015' aims 'to introduce sustainability and CSR at all University levels (teaching, research and management)' (Correa-Ruiz and Moneva-Abadia, 2011) and Scotland's Curriculum for Excellence 'is a curriculum designed to enable each child or young person to be a responsible citizen and to encourage "*an environmentally sustainable lifestyle*"' (Stevenson and Thomson, 2010, p. 54, emphasis in original).

An echo of the Welsh difficulty was also noted in university provision of sustainability education across Europe by Matten and Moon (2004, p. 330) '[t]he key actors are not the leaders of the schools or universities' but individuals with a research or other interest in the matter. Notwithstanding such human difficulties, the *International Journal of Sustainability in Higher Education* was launched in 2000

> to specifically focus on the subject of sustainability and sustainable development at universities ... [as] over 600 universities world-wide have committed themselves towards sustainability by signing international agreements and convention[s] such as the Bologna Charter, the Halifax Declaration, the Talloires Declaration and the Copernicus Charter for Sustainable Development (signed to date by over 240 European universities).
>
> (About the Journal, available at http://www.emeraldinsight.com/
> products/journals/journals.htm?id=ijshe, accessed 1 February 2012)

### The accounting profession

The response of the accounting profession could be viewed in the context of other professional bodies' responses to sustainability. Reid and Ali (2011) examined almost 40 degrees at one UK university, all accredited by professional, statutory or regulatory bodies and found that 'few professional statutory and regulatory bodies (PSRBs) make explicit reference to sustainability issues', that 'accreditation criteria [were] universally acknowledged as the main driver for what [is] covered in the curriculum' (p. 8) and that staff teaching on these accredited programmes noted no strong student or employer demand for ESD. Reinforcing Matten and Moon's (2004) finding that 'the single most important driver of the CSR agenda has been the initiatives of individual faculty members ... with a research interest or otherwise in CSR' Reid and Ali noted the key role of staff interested in ESD, even where accreditation criteria were not explicit about sustainable development (SD).

However, Lozano's (2010, p. 637) analysis of the 'curricula of over 5,800 course descriptions' for teaching sustainability in one UK university revealed a predominance of 'compartmentalisation, over-specialisation and reductionism' rather than the 'more balanced, synergistic, trans-disciplinary and holistic perspectives' necessary for an appreciation of sustainability's challenges. Not so gloomy news was highlighted in Ryan's (2008) review of ESD in HE in Scotland; she reported 'further embedding of sustainability in the curriculum and many examples of good practice ... in targeted "sustainable development" programmes.'

Institutional and societal contexts are evident in Sobczak *et al.*'s (2006, p. 463) observation that '[t]he success of CSR [in addition to individuals' personal convictions also] relies on organisational dynamics and collective regulations, as well as on ... social and environmental indicators or standards for reporting'. An example of standards for reporting is the Global Reporting Initiative (GRI) whose 3rd Global Conference opening plenary stated that 'By 2015, all large and medium-sized companies in OECD countries and large emerging economies should be required to report on their environmental, social and governance (ESG) performance, and if they do not do so, to explain why.'[26] Stevenson and Thomson (2010) however noted how distant this achievement may be; and Azcárate *et al.* (2011) in their critical analysis of the GRI guidelines classified them as serving 'a weak sustainability approach'.

Echoing Thomson and Bebbington (2004) above but at the organizational level, and reflecting what PRME seeks to encourage, Sobczak *et al.* (2006, p. 472) conclude that academic institutions 'should act as organisational role models and explicitly address their own responsibilities towards their stakeholders and the broader society'; and further that 'the culture of an academic institution probably has an impact on the perception of companies and CSR that is as important as the content of the education'.

Should we rely on deans, HE institutional management, professional bodies or international agencies? Sibbel states:

> There is an imperative for every academic to consider how their area of expertise relates to other disciplines and how their teaching could contribute to developing graduate attributes necessary for work towards sustainability … HE as the training ground for professionals, plays a central role.
>
> (2009, p. 79)

Only then perhaps will it be that 'HE can take up its rightful leadership role in sustainability: developing future citizens, guiding policy development, exchanging knowledge, supporting communities, and using academic freedom to fuel further enterprise and innovation' (Ryan *et al.*, 2010, p. 116).

A wide-ranging study of the implications of the developing environmental and sustainability agenda for the education of professional accountants (Gray *et al.*, 2001; see also Gray and Collison, 2002) included interviews with a range of leading members of the profession and other 'opinion formers'; questionnaire surveys of academics and undergraduate students; and interviews with, and a questionnaire survey of, recruiters. An overview of some central concerns raised in that study is provided in Figure 3.1. The figure presents what Gray *et al.* acknowledge to be two extremes of concern across relevant dimensions. The element of caricature implicit in the way these views are imputed to academic/practioner perspectives is made very clear in the original, but nonetheless the framework does serve as a useful analysis of the spectrum of possible views across complementary dimensions.

Central to the issues summarized in Figure 3.1 is the reflexive relationship between the posture that the profession takes in regard to sustainability issues, and the educational process, which is largely driven by that posture, but which in the long term has the potential to

| Academic, principles-driven point of view | THE ISSUES | Practitioner, client-driven point of view |
| --- | --- | --- |
| Sustainability  ← | *The environment* → | Marginal issues |
| Public interest  ← | *The profession* → | Client serving |
| Transcendence  ← | *Education and training* → | Technical |
| Central  ← | *Relevant degrees* → | Not important |

*Figure 3.1* The environment and accounting education: some central issues.

Source: Adapted from Gray *et al.*, 2001, p. 4

change it. Bebbington (1997, p. 373) has stated that education in 'environmental accounting' (EA), which she interprets broadly to include accounting for sustainable development, 'offers a significant opportunity to enable the next generation of accountants to understand better the biases and limitations of conventional accounting, as well as to develop an appreciation of the possibilities introduced by EA'.

This potential is, of course, attenuated by the optional, and even sporadic, nature of EA education and its apparent lack of appeal to many – a point acknowledged by Bebbington, and many others as discussed above. In 2000, Collison et al. noted that a majority of accounting students based their optional courses on perceived career relevance (see also Gray *et al.*, 2001) and of course their core courses may be largely driven by accreditation constraints. Thus the scope for the inertia of the status quo to marginalize and impede educational influence by restraining participation rates must be acknowledged; but it does not mean that there are no grounds for hope: 'Despite this reservation, the enabling potential of EA for those who undertake it as a part of their course of study remains potent' (Bebbington, 1997, p. 373). Further, Bone and Agombar noted in 2011 (p. 3) that 'sustainability concerns are significant in students' university choices' and the 'graduate employment sector [has an] increasing need for sustainably literate graduates' (p. 4).

Notwithstanding the challenges of the hidden curriculum, identified above, a key recommendation – or at least aspiration – offered by Gray *et al.* (2001) related to relevant degrees and was offered as a way of attempting to break the vicious circle just described. In the context of a wide-ranging discussion of how to change the education (not the training) of professional accountants, the role of the university was emphasized: 'If there is one key to this whole area it must be, in our view, an increase in the use of relevant graduates *but with a major change in how relevant degrees are taught*' (Gray *et al.*, 2001, p. 163, emphasis in original).

To the extent that the profession itself is perhaps the only source of influence that can quickly make a systemic shift in the way that its future leaders are educated, much depends on whether and how it can review its role and priorities. Central to this must be a genuine re-avowal of the primacy of the wider public interest over the commercial interests of its members or their clients. Steps that can be taken by the professional bodies include raising awareness of members through continuing personal development (CPD) courses and through changes to their core syllabi. While such steps may be of limited value in themselves, in terms of the deeper reappraisal needed to change outlooks, they *may* contribute to a change in the climate in which accounting and business is presented and discussed in practice and in academe, as well as *possibly* leading to real changes in the curriculum.[27]

## Conclusions

There is ample evidence of why humanity's relationship to its environment must change, and of why this implies fundamental changes in relationships within the human family. This means that accounting must change to render the powerful more accountable and to reflect and serve wider interests than those of a narrow section of society. In *Limits to Growth*, Meadows *et al.* (2005) include, in their vision for a sustainable society, more 'understanding of whole systems as an essential part of each person's education'. Whole systems in the context of accounting and economic organization include the social and environmental 'externalities' that sectional interests impose on others, as well as the long-term impacts of a short sighted focus on conventionally measured economic growth. Accounting's continued complicity in privileging certain short-term interests lies at the heart of a web of interactions which provides incentives to legitimize the fundamentally unsustainable. Radicalized changes in humanity's outlook on sustainability will of course come – possibly in a matter of a few decades. The question is whether these changes will come quickly enough to avoid environmental and social catastrophe: for an enlightened and relatively gradual adaptation to take place, education – for accountants and many others – must be at least a necessary, if not a sufficient, condition.

## Notes

1  The authors are respectively Professor at the University of Dundee, Reader at the University of Strathclyde and Reader at the University of St Andrews.
2  See also Gray (2007) for a discussion of terminology in this area. Further, Ryan et al. (2010, p. 107) note that sustainability is 'a term with variable and contested meanings'.
3  Matten and Moon (2004, p. 334) note that 'many [CSR-type] programmes are grounded in the longer-term orientations of business ethics and environmental responsibility'.
4  'Sterling (2004) has described three possible levels/orders of institutional response to the challenge [of sustainability]:
   a  … educating *about* sustainability … [which] he describes … as an accommodative response
   b  Education *for* sustainability [which] has an additional values emphasis … [and] is the reformative response
   c  … education that can equip learners with sustainability literacy skills is about *capacity building* and has an emphasis on action' (Stibbe, 2009).
      It will become apparent in this chapter that the bulk of the visible response to the challenge of sustainability challenge is found, at best, in the first, and least developed, of Sterling's categories.
5  We acknowledge that both 'ideology' and 'hegemony' are contested terms within the social sciences. Within the context of this chapter, ideology is taken to refer to a set of ideas or beliefs which serve to legitimate the 'power of a dominant social group or class' (Eagleton, 1991, p. 5; see also Thompson, 1990). 'Hegemony' is being applied in the Gramscian sense, to describe social scenarios whereby the powerful do not have to impose power on subordinate groups because less powerful groups accept prevailing conditions and constraints as *natural* or as *common sense* (see Boggs, 1976; Eagleton, 1991). Gramsci distinguished hegemony from more coercive forms of power, such as direct physical coercion (for example, by the police or armed forces) (Boggs, 1976).
6  Tilbury and Ryan (2011) see CSR as limited in scope and application, and explicitly not an adequate response to the challenge of 'sustainability'.
7  Jones Christensen et al. (2007) report on the state of ethics, CSR and sustainability as 'separate and distinct topics' (p. 349) in MBA programmes across the world; they note an expansion in ethics education provision which highlights '(1) the corporation's ethical role in society (its "corporate social responsibility" or CSR) as well as (2) the corporation's role in minimizing the destruction to, and maximizing the preservation of, resources for future generations (its "sustainable management")' (p. 348). They found that 'nearly one-third of responding schools *require* coverage of all three topics in the MBA curriculum' (emphasis in original) and they noted 'a potential trend towards a heavier focus on the topic of sustainability' (p. 366).
8  In the context of textbooks, Apple and Christian-Smith (1991, p. 11) explain that while progressive items may be mentioned, they will not be developed in depth, and it is through this 'mentioning' that dominant cultures maintain hegemony.
9  For a succinct and robust critique of these assumptions, see Gray et al. (1996): this critique demonstrates that even in a society that is not remotely close to exceeding its sustainable ecological footprint, this model is not only flawed, but deeply dishonest. In our unsustainable world it is not only unjust, but also a threat to our existence.
10 Values which are being spread as shareholder capitalism (or globalization) displace social market forms of capitalism (see, for example Coates, 2000; Collison, 2003; Dore, 2000; Hutton, 1995).

11 It could be argued that an educational focus on corporations which are themselves a subset of economic entities serves to reinforce the private corporate perspective and to minimize any consideration of alternative ways of economic organization.

12 Indeed Ray Anderson, founder and chairman of Interface Inc., the world's largest commercial carpet manufacturer, described the corporation as a 'present day instrument of destruction' because of its compulsion to 'externalise any cost that its unwary or uncaring public will allow it to externalise' (Bakan, 2004, p. 71).

13 Matten and Moon (2004, p. 327) 'illustrate[s] another characteristic of European CSR education: its embeddedness in the wider corporate and social governance themes'; they note that 'dedicated CSR programmes are most likely to be offered on Executive and Short Courses ... and that these have healthy enrolments, suggesting that industry itself is something of a driver here'; and also 'it is striking that the course level with the lowest proportion of CSR programmes is the Bachelor level' (p. 328).

14 Thomson and Bebbington (2005) also apply Freire's ideas to social and environmental reporting itself, arguing that the provision of such accounts by organizations can be viewed as a process of education in relation to the users (both internal and external) of those reports.

15 See Coulson and Thomson (2006) for a description of implementing such a dialogic approach in the UK and see Correa-Ruiz and Moneva-Abadia (2011) for an account in Spain.

16 See also Gray's (2007, p. 174) 'Simple Typology of Approaches to [social and environmental accounting and reporting] SEAR Research and Teaching' and Sundin and Wainwright's (2011) examination of the prevalence of Mangion's first two options in Australian universities.

17 The Centre for Social and Environmental Accounting Research (CSEAR) is based at the University of St Andrews (see http://www.st-andrews.ac.uk/~csearweb/index.html).

18 In the arena of European business education for CSR Matten and Moon (2004, p. 328) note that although '50% of respondent institutions offer [undergraduate] optional modules their enrolments are relatively low'; however the authors also state that 'the most popular way of mainstreaming CSR is through the provision of optional modules' (p. 329).

19 The survey results are available on request from Lorna Stevenson (lorna.stevenson@st-andrews.ac.uk).

20 A longstanding commitment of the CSEAR community is in the area of SEA education; CSEAR has been in existence for over 20 years and the consistency of a lack of SEA expertise as an impediment to more widespread SEA teaching perhaps invites a question around CSEAR's success in its education aims. A point of context may help here to illustrate the 'minority interest' element of SEA: at the time of writing there were around 150 worldwide members of CSEAR in a UK accounting and finance academic community context of some 1,700 individuals (BARRR, 2010).

21 Wu *et al.* (2010) however question the role of accreditation stating 'we are cautious about an accreditation-led imposition of standards on business schools, since it is only at the local level where the best ideas regarding sustainability education tailored to surrounding situations can originate'.

22 Issued by the participants gathered at the UNESCO World Conference on Education for Sustainable Development held in Bonn, Germany from 31 March to 2 April 2009.

23 Oikos International was founded in 1987 as 'the international student organisation for sustainable economics and management'; 'Oikos wants students of business and management to be ready for the sustainability challenge!' (Oikos International, 2012).

24 Net Impact was founded in 1993 as a networking organization for members to 'learn about the latest in sustainability, corporate responsibility, and social entrepreneurship' and to 'show the world that it's possible to make a *net impact* that benefits not just the bottom line, but people and planet too' (Net Impact, 2012).

25 The Climate Change (Scotland) Act 2009 was passed 'to set a target for the year 2050 ... and to provide for annual targets, for the reduction of greenhouse gas emissions' and associated reporting and related objectives.

26 The formation, in 2011, of the IIRC (International Integrated Reporting Council) and the issue of its Discussion Paper 'Towards Integrated Reporting – Communicating Value in the 21st Century' represent a high profile development in sustainability related reporting guidance. This is a development in which the global accounting profession has a very significant involvement.

27 Gray *et al.* (2001) include a detailed set of proposals for developing, at both university and professional levels, environmental, social and public interest issues within accounting education and training.

## References

Apple, M. (1995) *Education and Power* (London: Routledge).

Apple, M. (2004) Cultural politics and the text, in S. Ball (ed.) *The Routledge Falmer Reader in Sociology of Education* (London: Routledge Falmer).

Apple, M. and Christian-Smith, L. (eds) (1991) *The Politics of the Textbook* (London: Routledge).

Association for the Advancement of Sustainability in Higher Education (AASHE) (2010) *Sustainability Curriculum in Higher Education: A Call to Action* (Denver, CO: AASHE).

Azcárate, F., Carrasco, F. and Fernández, M. (2011) The role of integrated indicators in exhibiting business contribution to sustainable development: a survey of sustainability reporting indicators, *Revista de Contabilidad [Spanish Accounting Review]* 14(Extraordinario): 213–40.

Bakan, J. (2004) *The Corporation: The Pathological Pursuit of Profit* (London: Constable and Robinson).

Bebbington, J. (1997) Engagement, education and sustainability: a review essay on environmental accounting, *Accounting, Auditing and Accountability Journal* 10(3): 365–81.

Bebbington, J. and Thomson, I. (2001) Commentary on: some thoughts on social and environmental accounting education, *Accounting Education: An International Journal* 10(4): 353–5.

Beder, S. (1997) *Global Spin: The Corporate Assault on Environmentalism* (Totnes: Green Books).

Birkin, F., Edwards, P. and Woodward, D. (2005) Accounting's contribution to a conscious cultural evolution: an end to sustainable development, *Critical Perspectives on Accounting* 16: 185–208.

Blundell, L. and Booth, P. (1988) Teaching innovative accounting topics: student reaction to a course in social accounting, *Accounting and Finance* May: 75–85.

Boggs, C. (1976) *Gramsci's Marxism* (London: Pluto Press).

Bone, E. and Agombar, J. (2011) *First Year Attitudes towards, and Skills in, Sustainable Development* (York: Higher Education Academy).

Coates, D. (2000) *Models of Capitalism: Growth and Stagnation in the Modern Era* (Cambridge: Polity Press).

Collison, D.J. (2003) Corporate propaganda: its implications for accounting and accountability, *Accounting Auditing and Accountability Journal* 16(5): 853–86.

Collison, D.J., Gray, R.H., Owen, D.L., Sinclair, C.D. and Stevenson, L. (2000) Social and environmental accounting and student choice: an exploratory research note, *Accounting Forum*, 24(2): 170–86.

Collison, D.J., Cross, S., Ferguson, J., Power, D., Stevenson, L. (2011) *Shareholder Primacy in UK Corporate Law: An Exploration of the Rationale and Evidence* (London: ACCA – The Certified Accountants Educational Trust).

Cooper, D.J. (1980) Discussions towards a political economy of accounting, *Accounting, Organizations and Society* 5: 161–6.

Cooper, D.J. and Sherer, M.J. (1984) The value of corporate accounting reports: arguments for a political economy of accounting, *Accounting, Organizations and Society* 9: 207–32.

Correa-Ruiz, C. and Moneva-Abadía, J.M. (2011) Special issue on 'Social responsibility accounting and reporting in times of "sustainability downturn/crisis"', *Revista de Contabilidad [Spanish Accounting Review]* 14(Extraordinario): 187–211.

Coulson, A.B. and Thomson, I. (2006) Accounting and sustainability, encouraging a dialogical approach; integrating learning activities, delivery mechanisms and assessment strategies, *Accounting Education: An International Journal* 15(3): 261–73.

Dore, R. (2000) *Stock Market Capitalism: Welfare Capitalism* (Oxford: Oxford University Press).

Eagleton, T. (1991) *Ideology: An Introduction* (London, Verso).

Fleischman, R.K. and Schuele, K. (2006) Green accounting: a primer, *Journal of Accounting Education* 24(1): 35–66.

Frankfurter, G.M. and McGoun, E.G. (1999) Ideology and the theory of financial economics, *Journal of Economic Behaviour and Organization* 39: 159–77.

Freire, P. (1996) *Pedagogy of the Oppressed* (London: Penguin), in J. Bebbington and I. Thomson (eds) (2001) Commentary on: some thoughts on social and environmental accounting education, *Accounting Education: An International Journal* 10(4): 353–5.

Ghoshal, S. (2005) Bad management theories are destroying good management practices, *Academy of Management Learning and Education* 4(1): 75–91.

Gibson, K. (1997) Courses on environmental accounting, *Accounting, Auditing and Accountability Journal* 10(4): 584–93.

Global Reporting Initiative (GRI) (2010) *Introduction: The Amsterdam Global Conference on Sustainability and Transparency*, available at https://www.globalreporting.org/information/events/gri-global-conference/conference-2010/Pages/default.aspx, accessed 10 October 2013.

Gordon, I.M. (1998) Enhancing students' knowledge of social responsibility accounting, *Issues in Accounting Education* 13(1): 31–46.

Gray, R. (2007) Taking a long view on what we now know about social and environmental accountability and reporting, *Issues in Social and Environmental Accounting* 1(2): 169–98.

Gray, R. and Collison, D. (2002) Can't see the wood for the trees, can't see the trees for the numbers? Accounting education, sustainability and the public interest, *Critical Perspectives on Accounting* 13: 797–836.

Gray, R., Collison, D., French, J., McPhail, K. and Stevenson, L. (2001) *The Professional Accountancy Bodies and the Provision of Education and Training in Relation to Environmental Issues* (Edinburgh: Institute of Chartered Accountants of Scotland).

Gray, R.H., Owen, D.L. and Adams, C. (1996) *Accounting and Accountability: Changes and Challenges in Corporate Social and Environmental Reporting* (London, Prentice Hall).

Higher Education Academy (2010) *Towards a Common Understanding and Development of Education for Sustainable Development and Global Citizenship (ESDGC): A Position Paper from the Welsh HE Institutional ESDGC Group*, November 2010, available at www.heacademy.ac.uk/.../Common_Understanding_of_ESDGC.doc, accessed 10 February 2012.

Humphrey, C., Lewis, L. and Owen, D. (1996) Still too distant voices? Conversations and reflections on the social relevance of accounting education, *Critical Perspectives on Accounting* 7: 77–99.

Hutton, W. (1995) *The State We're In* (London: Jonathan Cape).

Illich, I.D. (1971) *Deschooling Society* (London: Calder and Boyars), in J. Bebbington and I. Thomson (eds) (2001) Commentary on: Some thoughts on social and environmental accounting education, *Accounting Education: An International Journal* 10(4): 353–5.

International Integrated Reporting Council (IIRC) (2011) *Towards Integrated Reporting – Communicating Value in the 21st Century*, available at http://www.theiirc.org/the-integrated-reporting-discussion-paper/discussion-paper-submissions/, accessed 19 February 2012.

Jones Christensen, L., Peirce, E., Hartman, L.P., Hoffman, W.M. and Carrier, J. (2007) Ethics, CSR and sustainability education in the *Financial Times* Top 50 Global Business Schools: baseline data and future research directions, *Journal of Business Ethics* 73: 347–68.

Karabel, J. and Halsey, A.H. (1977) *Power and Ideology in Education* (New York: Oxford University Press).

Lewis, L., Humphrey, C. and Owen, D. (1992) Accounting and the social: a pedagogic perspective, *British Accounting Review* 24(3): 219–33.

Lozano, R. (2010) Diffusion of sustainable development in universities' curricula: an empirical example from Cardiff University, *Journal of Cleaner Production* 18(7): 637–44.

Luke, A. (1988) *Literacy, Textbooks and Ideology: Postwar Literacy Instruction and the Mythology of Dick and Jane* (London: Falmer Press).

McIntosh, N.B. (2002) *Accounting, Accountants and Accountability: Poststructuralist Positions* (London: Routledge).

McPhail, K.J. and Gray, R.H. (1996) Not developing ethical maturity in accounting education: hegemony, dissonance and homogeneity in accounting students' world views, Discussion Paper (ACC/9605) (Dundee: University of Dundee).

Mangion, D. (2005) *An Examination of Social and Environmental Accounting Education in Australian Universities*, paper presented at British Accounting Association Accounting Education Special Interest Group Annual Conference, Aberdeen, 25–27 May.

Mangion, D. (2006) Undergraduate education in social and environmental accounting in Australian Universities, *Accounting Education: An International Journal* 15(3): 335–48.

Mathews, M.R. (1997) Twenty-five years of social and environmental accounting research: is there a silver jubilee to celebrate?, *Accounting, Auditing and Accountability Journal* 10(4): 481–531.

Mathews, M.R. (2001) Some thoughts on social and environmental accounting education, *Accounting Education: An International Journal* 10(4): 335–52.

Matten, D. and Moon, J. (2004) Corporate social responsibility education in Europe, *Journal of Business Ethics* 54: 323–37.

Meadows, D.H., Jorgen Randers, J. and Meadows, D.L. (2005) *Limits to Growth: The 30-Year Update* (London: Earthscan).

Net Impact (2012) available at http://netimpact.org/about, accessed 23 February 2012.

Oikos International (2012) available at http://www.oikos-international.org/, accessed 23 February 2012.

Owen, D., Humphrey, C. and Lewis, L. (1994) *Social and Environmental Accounting Education in British Universities* (London: ACCA – The Certified Accountants Educational Trust).

Parker, L. (2004) Social and environmental accountability research: a view from the commentary box, *Plenary Presentation and Forum: Published Research in Social and Environmental Accounting*, paper presented at the Third Australasian Conference on Social and Environmental Accounting Research (CSEAR), in Mangion, D. (ed.) (2005) *An Examination of SEA Education in Australian Universities*, paper presented at the British Accounting Association Accounting Education Special Interest Group Annual Conference, Aberdeen, 25–27 May.

Phillips, A. (2009) Institutional transformation, in A. Stibbe (ed.) *The Handbook of Sustainability Literacy: Skills for a Changing World* (Totnes: Green Books).

Rasche, A. and Escudero, M. (2010) Leading change – the role of the principles of responsible management education, *Journal of Business and Economic Ethics* 10(2): 244–50.

Reid, C.T. and Ali, N. (2011) *ESD and the Professional Curriculum* (York: Higher Education Academy).

Ryan, A. (2008) *Review of ESD in HE in Scotland*, A Higher Education Academy ESD Resource, available at http://www.heacademy.ac.uk/assets/documents/sustainability/SFCesd08Review.pdf, accessed 10 October 2013.

Ryan, A., Tilbury, D., Corcoran, P.B., Abe, O. and Nomura, K. (2010) Sustainability in higher education in the Asia-Pacific: developments, challenges and prospects, *International Journal of Sustainability in Higher Education* 11(2): 106–19.

Schumacher, E.F. (1973) *Small is Beautiful* (London: Abacus).

Sefcik, S.E., Soderstrom, N.S. and Stinson, C.H. (1997) Accounting through green-colored glasses: teaching environmental accounting, *Issues in Accounting Education* 12(1): 129–40.

Sobczak, A., Debucquet, G. and Havard, C. (2006) The impact of higher education on students' and young managers' perception of companies and CSR: an exploratory analysis, *Corporate Governance* 6(4): 463–74.

Stauber, J. and Rampton, S. (1995) *Toxic Sludge is Good for You* (Monroe, ME: Common Courage Press).

Sterling, S. (2001) *Sustainable Education: Revisioning Learning and Change*. Schumacher Briefings 6 (Totnes: Green Books).

Sterling, S. (2004) Higher education, sustainability and the role of systemic learning, in P. Corcoran and A Wals (eds) *Higher Education and the Challenge of Sustainability: Contestation, Critique, Practice and Promise* (Dordrecht: Kluwer Academic).

Stevenson, L. (2002) Social and environmental accounting teaching in UK and Irish universities: a research note on changes between 1993 and 1998, *Accounting Education: An International Journal* 11(4): 331–46.

Stevenson, L. and Thomson, I. (2010) Editorial for Special Issue on contemporary developments in social, environmental and sustainability accounting education thinking and practice, *Social and Environmental Accounting Journal* 30(2): 51–63.

Stibbe, A. (ed.) (2009) *The Handbook of Sustainability Literacy: Skills for a Changing World* (Totnes: Green Books).

Sundin, H. and Wainwright, L. (2010) Approaches to integrating social and environmental accounting (SEA) into accounting majors in Australian universities, *Social and Environmental Accounting Journal* 30(2): 80–95.

Thompson, J.B. (1990) *Ideology and Modern Culture: Critical Social Theory in the Era of Mass Communication* (Cambridge, Polity Press).

Thomson, I. and Bebbington, J. (2004) It doesn't matter what you teach? *Critical Perspectives on Accounting* 15: 609–28.

Thomson, I. and Bebbington, J. (2005) Social and environmental reporting in the UK: a pedagogic evaluation, *Critical Perspectives on Accounting* 16: 507–33.

Tilbury, D. and Ryan, A. (2011) Today becomes tomorrow: rethinking business practice, education and learning in the context of sustainability, *Journal of Global Responsibility* 12(2): 137–50.

Tinker, T. (1980) Towards a political economy of accounting: an empirical illustration of the Cambridge controversies, *Accounting Organisations and Society* 5: 147–60.

UNESCO (2009) *Learning for a Sustainable World: Review of Contexts and Structures for Education for Sustainable Development 2009* (Paris: UNESCO), in A. Ryan, D. Tilbury, P.B. Corcoran, O. Abe and K. Nomura (eds) (2010) Sustainability in higher education in the Asia-Pacific: developments, challenges and prospects, *International Journal of Sustainability in Higher Education* 11(2): 106–19.

UNESCO (2010) *Strategy for the Second Half of the United Nations Decade of Education for Sustainable Development* (Paris: UNESCO).

UNPRME (2012) *Principles of Responsible Management Education*, available at www.prme.org, accessed 10 February 2012.

Williams, R. (1989) Hegemony and the selective tradition, in S. de Castell, A. Luke and C. Luke (eds) *Language, Authority and Criticism: Readings on the School Textbook* (London: Falmer Press).

Wolfe, A. (1993) We've had enough business ethics, *Business Horizons* May–June: 1–3.

Wu, Y.C.J., Huang, S., Kuo, L. and Wu, W.H. (2010) Management education for sustainability: a web-based content analysis, *Academy of Management Learning and Education* 9(3): 520–31.

Zulkifli, N. (2010) *Thinking of Social and Environmental Accounting in Malaysia: Educators' Insight*, paper presented at the Sixth Asia Pacific Interdisciplinary Research in Accounting Conference, Sydney, NSW, 12–13 July.

# Part II

# Accounting techniques and sustainable development

# 4 Histories, rationales, voluntary standards and future prospects for sustainability reporting

## CSR, GRI, IIRC and beyond

*Nola Buhr, Rob Gray and Markus J. Milne*

## Introduction

Our assignment for this chapter is to summarize key developments in sustainability reporting and make some prognostications for the future of the field. However, despite thousands of sustainability reports so labelled, any presumption that we currently have of sustainability reporting is painfully naive. Sure enough, the term 'sustainability' is bandied around in the business community with ever more regularity – sustainability reporting, sustainable business, sustainable performance, sustainable finance, sustainable consumption, sustainable supply chain management and so on. And what was once a potentially threatening concept to business (IUCN, 1980; Laine, 2010; WCED, 1987) now seems to be plied by business organizations with some comfort. But what do organizations, or more properly their managers, *mean* when they report on or utter the term sustainability?

Careful consideration of such reports and utterances reveals first a fixation on the organization itself, and only second, the organization's interactions with society, the economy and the physical environment. As we shall see, corporate sustainability reporting is an extension and progression from earlier forms of corporate reporting to include matters of an organization's *environmental policies* and *impacts* (e.g. resource and energy use, waste flows), and its *social policies and impacts* (e.g. health and safety of employees, impacts on local communities, charitable giving). And in many ways, the reporting frameworks that have grown up around reporting practice have entrenched these developments. Indeed, the purpose of the Global Reporting Initiative (GRI) was to extend the financial accounting framework to include non-financial reporting to a wider range of stakeholders (Brown et al., 2009; Etzion and Ferraro, 2010).

Yet, we doubt sustainability accounting and reporting at the level of a single organization is at all meaningful.[1] Milne (1996) suggests using a broader ecosystems-based approach to sustainability accounting that requires an understanding of cumulative environmental change and assessments of the cumulative effects of economic activity. And as Gray and Milne (2002: 69) articulate, sustainability accounting requires:

> a complete and transparent statement about the extent to which the organization had contributed to – or, more likely, diminished – the sustainability of the planet. For that to occur, however, as we have seen, we need to have a detailed and complex analysis of the organization's interactions with ecological systems, resources, habitats, and societies, and interpret this in the light of all other organizations' past and present impacts on those same systems.

For any single organization, they argue this is technically impossible.

As emphasized by the Brundtland Commission's report, *Our Common Future* (WCED, 1987), sustainability, or more precisely sustainable development, is also about equity – both intra-generational and inter-generational. 'Meeting the needs of the present without compromising the ability of future generations to meet their own needs' is a Brundtland catch-cry that has found its way into many an organization's sustainability report. Yet, how can this be achieved? Over 50 years ago Bowen (1953: 227), in his seminal book, *Social Responsibilities of the Businessman*, wrote:

> there are no clear principles to determine precisely how the interests of future generations should be balanced against those of present generations, or to what extent private business should be called upon to look out for future generations ... Consequently, the interests of future generations probably must be handled largely though governmental policy – with which businessmen should be expected to cooperate.

In truth, of course, most businessmen (and businesswomen) do cooperate with government policy, to the extent it becomes enacted in law and regulations. However, they also work terribly hard at times to frustrate the public policy process both through claims to voluntary responsibility (including reporting) and more directly through lobbying against prospective legislation (Bakan, 2004; Gunningham *et al.*, 2003). Gray and Milne (2004, but see also Bakan, 2004; Roddick, 2003) have questioned the concept of corporate social responsibility (CSR) and whether corporations can in fact be socially responsible when it so obviously runs counter to the fundamental self-interest of business, its shareholders' demands, and the corporations' law that governs it and its directors. Given such structural impediments, Bakan (2004) suggests any claim to CSR can be nothing other than insincere – to place stakeholders on an equal footing with shareholders is in many cases simply illegal!

On this basis, as Roddick (2003) so frustratingly realized at the Body Shop, it is impossible for corporations (especially publicly listed ones) to practice *genuine* CSR. It is also impossible for them to go beyond approximate accounts of unsustainability and to fully and fairly report on corporate activity as it relates to the pressures on, the state of, and the future capacity of life-sustaining ecological systems, and inter- and intra-generational access to them. As Hawken (2002) bluntly put it:

> At this juncture in our history, as corporations and governments turn their attention to sustainability, it is crucial that the meaning of sustainability not get lost in the trappings of corporate speak ... I am concerned that good housekeeping practices such as recycled hamburger shells will be confused with creating a just and sustainable world.

With over two decades of experience since the first Earth Summit held in Rio de Janeiro (1992), it is clear to us that sustainability has got lost in the trappings of corporate speak (Gray, 2006, 2010; Milne *et al.*, 2006, 2009; Tregidga and Milne, 2006). Consequently, while we provide histories and rationales for an organizational phenomenon that we believe does not and never will exist, we also steadfastly refuse to become complicit in the language slippage that has permitted corporate behaviour to become labelled as and conflated with sustainability. Clearly, some organizations are doing something, and many are reporting, but in our view it just doesn't have anything to do with sustainability or sustainable development. It is for this reason that for the rest of this chapter we use the term zustainabullity to denote organizational activity and reporting in the name of sustainability.[2]

Zustainabullity reporting, in its current form, is some combination of communication on social, environmental and economic issues related to the organization doing the reporting. This communication might be in a stand-alone report or it might be part of an annual report, inside or outside of the audited financial statements and/or inside or outside of the management discussion and analysis. Zustainabullity reporting might also be found in such diverse forms of communication as print advertisements; press releases; securities filings; employee newsletters; and corporate websites (Rolland and Bazzoni, 2009; Zéghal and Ahmed, 1990).

We shall limit ourselves to reporting by public corporations, for this is where the practice of zustainabullity reporting started and where, arguably, it has its major influence. This is not to suggest that there is any less need to hold all parts of our social ecosystem to account and, as we can see from other chapters in this text, zustainabullity reporting is also carried out by private businesses, as well as governments, NGOs, not-for-profits and perhaps even households. Within the confines of this chapter, then, we summarize five key developments in the field of corporate zustainabullity reporting: histories of reporting practice; the breadth and depth of reporting practice; rationales for reporting; the development of voluntary standards such as the GRI; and future prospects which are currently being shaped by the International Integrated Reporting Council (IIRC).

## Histories of reporting

A good way to research the origins of zustainabullity reporting is to examine the various threads that currently make up such reporting. These threads, chronologically, include: employee reporting; social reporting; environmental reporting; and more recently, other miscellaneously labelled forms of reporting.

### Employees

Both Hogner (1982) and Guthrie and Parker (1989) examined long-term histories of a single company. Hogner looked at eight decades of reporting by US Steel for the period 1901 to 1980 and found that the initial decades included such information as: dwellings built for workers; community development; worker safety; and mortgage assistance for employees. Guthrie and Parker looked at the annual reports of BHP for the 100-year period from 1885 onwards. Similar to US Steel, the early decades of BHP reporting covered employee and community issues. More recent literature in this area such as Unerman (2003) and Maltby (2004) reinforces the idea that for decades corporations have been disclosing more than just financial information.

The early reports reviewed by Hogner and Guthrie and Parker tended to emphasize reporting *about* employee issues. However, during the first several decades of the 1900s there was also a practice (during the 1919 to 1979 period that they studied) of reporting directly *to* employees, as documented by Lewis *et al.* (1984).

### Social

Employee reporting is one aspect of what grew to be known as social reporting in the 1960s and 1970s. The report, *Good News & Bad: The Media, Corporate Social Responsibility and Sustainable Development* (SustainAbility *et al.*, 2002: 7) charts the profile of the CSR and the SD (Sustainable Development) agenda in the OECD region from 1961 to 2001. There is no constant increase in interest in these topics but rather a waxing and waning depending on societal factors. Conservative politics (typically dating from the influence of Reagan and Thatcher) and tough economic times are associated with a decrease in interest, while UN initiatives plus disasters such as Bhopal and the Exxon Valdez are associated with an increase in interest (e.g. Patten, 1992). Gray *et al.* (1996: 97) reinforce this changing emphasis on social and environmental issues and describe the changes with reference to the United Kingdom.

> [T]he early 1970s focused on social responsibility; by the mid to late 1970s this had shifted to employees and unions; the 1980s saw explicit pursuit of economic goals with a thin veneer of community concern and a redefinition of employee rights as the major theme; while in the 1990s attention shifted to environmental concern.

These fluctuations are similar to what transpired in North America and it would therefore be apt to label the 1970s as the social reporting decade. This does not mean that there was no mention of pollution or environmental issues but that the social took precedence. This view is exemplified by the Ernst and Ernst annual surveys (1971 *et seq.*) of the social responsibility disclosure found in the annual reports of the Fortune 500. The 1978 survey covered the following categories: environment; energy; fair business practices (including employment and advancement of minorities and women); human resources (including employee health and safety); community involvement; products; and other. At the time, 1 per cent of the Fortune 500 companies were also providing a separate social responsibility booklet to shareholders along with the annual report. This translates into seven companies in 1976 and six companies in 1977.

### Environmental

By the end of the 1970s social accounting was on the wane. A lacuna in social and environmental reporting developed and it took until the late 1980s and into the early 1990s for the next stage, environmental reporting, to emerge. In the main, the social faded into the background and the environmental became fresh and new. In addition to featuring environmental information in annual reports, a few adventuresome companies began to voluntarily produce stand-alone environmental reports. Early reports from companies as diverse as Noranda (in Canada) and Norsk Hydro (in Norway) in the early 1990s set standards that few companies have subsequently managed to achieve. Over time, certain types of information became mandatory. In Canada, for example, the Canadian Securities Administrators (CSA) has issued environmental reporting guidance for required disclosure for listed companies (CSA, 2010).

Curiously, environmental reporting blossomed at the same time that ideas about sustainability were being developed. The 1987 Brundtland report (WCED, 1987), *Our Common Future*, moved past the environment as an issue and established the notion of SD. In 1993, *Coming Clean*, a landmark report written by Deloitte Touche Tohmatsu International, the International Institute for Sustainable Development and SustainAbility, began to talk about sustainability and zustainabullity reporting as the linking of environmental, economic and social aspects of corporate performance (see also Gray, 1990; Gray *et al.*, 1993).

### Miscellaneous labels (including zustainabullity)

Around the year 2000 corporations started to produce reports titled zustainabullity or zustainabull development reports. These reports included environmental, economic and social aspects of corporate performance. But it must be stressed that linking these three aspects of performance is not the same thing as sustainability and therefore, this type of reporting falls short of that which might even attempt to provide an understanding of the state of the social and ecological systems on which the organization relies (Milne and Gray, 2013). Instead, this linkage of environmental, economic and social is sometimes referred to as triple bottom line (TBL) reporting (Elkington, 1997).

The conflation of sustainability with economic, social and environmental performance indicators may in part be due to Elkington's own references to the relationship between the three aspects of TBL and sustainability:

> During the 1990s, perhaps five years behind the practice of environmental auditing and reporting, the art of social auditing and reporting began to gather advocates and practitioners ... with the advent of sustainable development as a meaningful concept for both governments and businesses ... and triple-bottom line thinking becoming a convenient metaphor for strategists in the field, the way was clear for the 'third dimension' of sustainability to be tracked and reported on.
>
> (Wheeler and Elkington, 2001: 4)

That is, zustainabullity reporting emerged when social reporting joined the ranks of traditional financial reporting and environmental reporting. The international triennial KPMG surveys of non-financial reporting from 1993 to 2011 also document this trend and increasing references to a wide range of reporting nomenclature.

> [C]orporate environmental reporting [has become] the 'icebreaker' for a much wider form of corporate responsibility (CR) reporting in the form of sustainability, triple bottom line or corporate social responsibility (CSR) reports. Reporting is aimed at communicating with stakeholders, not only on environmental performance, but also in an integrated manner on environmental, social and economic performance, to be transparent and accountable.
>
> (KPMG, 2005: 3)

The voluntary and unregulated nature of reporting contributes to the confusion. There is no standardized terminology that can be used unambiguously to interpret report content or reporting developments. While environmental reports tend to consider selected elements of an organization's environmental performance, and social reports comprise some aspects of their employee and community interactions, the TBL does little more than add a largely under-specified economic dimension to this melange. Conceptually, the GRI's zustainabullity reporting guidelines, for all intents and purposes, simply relabels the TBL (Gray and Milne, 2002; Milne and Gray, 2013). And the recent integrated reporting (IR) developments seem to drop the economic dimension and pick up environment, social and governance (ESG). ESG has become the latest acronym to emerge with IR. Organizations often relabel their reports with or without changing content. Indeed, noting the difficulties of nomenclature, the 2006 UNEP (United Nations Environment Programme)/SustainAbility benchmark report asked 'what do you call your report?'

## The breadth and depth of reporting practice

Some sense of the recent developments in reporting can be gauged from an overview of the KPMG triennial surveys of reporting practice dating back to 1996. Table 4.1 provides the overall reporting survey results over the last six surveys. As noted, in the 1990s reporting tended to concern environmental matters, while since 2000 this has broadened for many organizations to concerns of economy, environment, and employees and community. Some care is required in making inter-temporal comparisons from Table 4.1, since the same survey methodology has not been employed consistently from survey to survey. Of particular note is that different numbers of countries have been sampled each time, and that while the percentage figures reported for 1996 to 2005 are for incidence rates of separate stand-alone reporting, the figures for the latest survey in 2011 are for stand-alone reporting and annual report supplementary disclosures combined. The figures shown for 2008 report both the combined and separate stand-alone reporting incidence rates – with the lower figure being for stand-alone reporting.

Table 4.1 documents an increasing trend in reporting among the very largest (global) 250 companies since 1999 from 35 per cent to 95 per cent in 2011 (for further details, see Kolk, 1999, 2003, 2004, 2005, 2007, 2008, 2010). Similar, but less dramatic, and varying trends in reporting are seen among the largest 100 (N100) companies in each of the countries sampled over time. In 1996, on average, fewer than 20 per cent of the largest 100 companies in 13 countries produced a stand-alone environmental report. By 2005 (and over 16 countries) that figure was 33 per cent. And by 2011 (over 34 countries) the average rate of reporting among the N100 has doubled to 64 per cent, suggesting in excess of 2,000 reporters. Looking at individual countries, it is clear that some of the greatest growth in both stand-alone reporting and combined reporting has occurred in the relatively recent past, from 2005 to 2011.

It is also notable that reporting incidence rates are relatively high for many countries that are being surveyed for the first time in 2011, suggesting that the practice of reporting among the very largest companies worldwide has grown considerably. To what extent the latest figures inflate the incidence of significant reporting by combining stand-alone figures with supplementary disclosures is not clear, but 79 per cent of the G250 released stand-alone reports in 2008, and 45 per cent of the N100 from 22 countries did so.

Less clear are the trends in reporting among the vast number of companies and organizations in each country beyond the G250 and N100 companies. Some evidence suggests that beyond the very largest organizations, reporting may be far less common. In the UK, for example, Martin and Hadley (2008) report that 23 per cent of the FTSE 350 (largest 350 listed companies) reported in 2001, compared to double that among the UK N100 in Table 4.1. Similarly, in Australia, while 77 per cent of the largest 100 firms listed on the Australian Securities Exchange (ASX100) provide more than a basic level of zustainabullity reporting, the rate drops to 47 per cent when assessing the ASX200 (largest 200 listed companies) (ACSI, 2011). Further, Higgins et al. (2011), in an exhaustive attempt to uncover stand-alone reporting in Australia, found a total of only 126 organizations from many possible hundreds. Nevertheless, reporting is not entirely confined to the very largest organizations, and neither is being a large reporter any necessary indicator of being a quality reporter (see, for example, Morhardt, 2010).

A further observation worth making in regard to Table 4.1 concerns the incidence of independent verification. While the number of reporters surveyed exceeded 2,000 in 2011, this is not the case for independently verified reports, which seem to number about 520 or so. Indeed, fewer than 50 per cent of the G250 reports were verified in 2011, and fewer than 25 per cent of the average N100 organizations' reports were verified.[3] When we reported in 2007 (Milne and Gray, 2007), we estimated approximately 200 independently verified reports, so we note some improvement. However, the number of organizations sampled in 2011 (3,400) compared to 2005 (1,600) has more than doubled. As shown in Table 4.1, the

*Table 4.1* Trends in reporting by large companies

| Percentage of the largest 100 companies producing reports in selected countries | | | | | | | 2011 % |
|---|---|---|---|---|---|---|---|
| Country | 1996 % | 1999 % | 2002 % | 2005 % | 2008 % | 2011 % | verify^a |
| United Kingdom | 27 | 32 | 49 | 71 | 84/91 | 100 | 56 |
| Japan | – | 21* | 72 | 80 | 88/93 | 99 | 23 |
| South Africa | – | – | 1 | 18 | 26/45 | 97 | 31 |
| France | 4* | 4 | 21 | 40 | 47/59 | 94 | 60 |
| Denmark | 10 | 29 | 20 | 22 | 22/24 | 91 | 65 |
| Brazil | – | – | – | – | 56/78 | 88 | 40 |
| Spain | – | – | 11 | 25 | 59/63 | 88 | 65 |
| Finland | 7 | 15 | 32 | 31 | 41/44 | 85 | 29 |
| United States | 44 | 30 | 36 | 32 | 73/74 | 83 | 13 |
| The Netherlands | 31 | 25 | 26 | 29 | 60/63 | 82 | 41 |
| Canada | 34 | – | 19 | 41 | 60/62 | 79 | 21 |
| Italy | – | 2* | 12 | 31 | 59/59 | 74 | 64 |
| Sweden | 36 | 34 | 26 | 20 | 59/60 | 72 | 42 |
| Hungary | – | – | – | – | 25/26 | 70 | 33 |
| Portugal | – | – | – | – | 49/52 | 69 | 45 |
| Nigeria | – | – | – | – | – | 68 | 14 |
| Mexico | – | – | – | – | 17/17 | 66 | 25 |
| Switzerland | 19 | – | – | – | 28/39 | 64 | 27 |
| Slovakia | – | – | – | – | – | 63 | 28 |
| Germany | 34 | 38 | 32 | 36 | – | 62 | 35 |
| China | – | – | – | – | – | 59 | 37 |
| Russia | – | – | – | – | – | 58 | 13 |
| Australia | 5 | 15 | 14 | 23 | 37/45 | 57 | 51 |
| Romania | – | – | – | – | 23/23 | 54 | 23 |
| Bulgaria | – | – | – | – | – | 54 | 20 |
| Ukraine | – | – | – | – | – | 53 | 19 |
| South Korea | – | – | – | – | 42/42 | 48 | 75 |
| Singapore | – | – | – | – | – | 43 | 7 |
| Taiwan | – | – | – | – | – | 37 | 43 |
| Greece | – | – | – | – | – | 33 | 50 |
| New Zealand | 0 | – | – | – | – | 27 | 19 |
| Chile | – | – | – | – | – | 27 | 37 |
| India | – | – | – | – | – | 20 | 80 |
| Israel | – | – | – | – | – | 18 | 28 |
| Norway | 26 | 31 | 30 | 15 | 25/37 | – | – |
| Czech Republic | – | – | – | – | 14/14 | – | – |
| Belgium | 27 | 16 | 11 | 9 | – | – | – |
| **Number of N 100 Countries Surveyed** | **13** | **11** | **19** | **16** | **22** | **34** | |
| **Global 250 that report (%)** | – | **35** | **45** | **52/65** | **79/83** | **95** | |
| **Global 250 that assure reports (%)** | – | **19** | **29** | **30** | **40** | **46** | |
| **N 100 that report (average %)** | **18** | **24** | **23** | **33/41** | **45/53** | **64** | |
| **N 100 that assure report (average %)** | **15** | **18** | **27** | **33** | **39** | **38** | *24* |

Source: Adapted from KPMG (1996, 1999, 2002, 2005, 2008, 2011).

*These rates were obtained from a later survey with comparative analysis.

^aThese rates indicate the percentage of *reports* produced in 2011 in each country from the N100 that were *independently verified*. For example, in 2011, in Japan, 99% of the N100 produced reports, and of these 99 reports, 23% were independently verified. In Canada, 79 reports were produced among the N100, and of these, 21% were independently verified.

increasing rates of verification are much more modest than those for reporting. Moreover, and noted in Kolk and Perego (2010), verification rates vary widely by country. In fact, of the 34 countries surveyed in 2011, in only four (Denmark, France, Spain, and the UK) will one find more than half of the N100 companies producing a verified report. And in more than half the countries surveyed in 2011 (including Canada and the US) one finds fewer than 20 per cent of the N100 producing a verified report. To the extent that the independent verification of stand-alone reports provides some indication of genuine accountability, then we are much less enthused with recent trends.

Table 4.2 indicates a clear 'spreading' of reporting among a greater range of sectors over time. The 1990s typically saw (environmental) reporting dominated by those with the clearest and greatest (negative) physical impacts on the environment (e.g. oil and gas, chemicals, utilities, pulp and paper, and mining). More recently, other sectors have caught up with Table 4.2, indicating at least half of the N100 companies in all sectors now produce at least some social and environmental disclosures in a public report.[4]

Some evidence on the quality of reporting can also be gleaned from the UNEP/SustainAbility (1994, 1996, 1997, 2000, 2002); and UNEP/SustainAbility and Standard & Poor (2004, 2006) – see www.sustainability.com – benchmarking report series, and some patchy academic studies of report content often from single countries (see, for example, Chapman and Milne, 2004; Milne *et al.*, 2003; Morhardt, 2009, 2010). The UNEP series

*Table 4.2* Industrial sectors (N 100 companies) issuing stand-alone reports

| Sector of Company (regardless of Country of Origin) | Number of companies in Sector in survey | | 1996 % | 1999 % | 2002 % | 2005 % | 2008 % | 2011 % |
|---|---|---|---|---|---|---|---|---|
| | 1999 | 2002 | | | | | | |
| Finance, securities and insurance | 127 | 340 | 5 | 8 | 12 | 31 | 49 | 61 |
| Trade and retail | 161 | 241 | 11 | 7 | 15 | 22 | 26 | 52 |
| Other services | 91 | 144 | 5 | 4 | 6 | 18 | 36 | 53 |
| Metals and engineering | 105 | 141 | 25 | 17 | 24 | 25 | 41 | 61 |
| Electronics and computers | 69 | 131 | 33 | 30 | 24 | 35 | 58 | 69 |
| Food and beverage | 104 | 126 | 17 | 22 | 26 | 29 | 47 | 67 |
| Oil and gas | 53 | 114 | 43 | 53 | 39 | 52 | 59 | 69 |
| Automotive | 34 | 109 | – | 38 | 28 | 32 | 49 | 78 |
| Construction | 57 | 108 | 13 | 18 | 17 | 28 | 32 | 65 |
| Utilities | 55 | 101 | 40 | 55 | 50 | 61 | 62 | 71 |
| Communication and media | 62 | 93 | 7 | 16 | 20 | 29 | 47 | 74 |
| Transport | 51 | 68 | 22 | 33 | 37 | 38 | 39 | 57 |
| Chemicals and synthetics | 64 | 67 | 74 | 59 | 45 | 52 | 62 | 68 |
| Pharmaceuticals | 30 | 47 | 41 | 50 | 30 | 30 | 25 | 64 |
| Mining | 15 | 42 | 25 | 47 | 36 | 52 | 67 | 84 |
| Forest, pulp and paper | 22 | 28 | 56 | 55 | 43 | 50 | 65 | 84 |
| **Total Companies in Survey (Top 100 companies from each of *n* countries)** | | | **1300** **13** | **1100** **11** | **1900** **19** | **1600** **16** | **2200** **22** | **3400** **34** |

Source: Adapted from KPMG (1996, 1999, 2002, 2005, 2008, 2011).

provides guidelines or a template against which to measure report content, but it also contains difficulties in making comparisons over time due to the continuing modification of methodologies for scoring and accrediting report content, and the variable data maintained on websites. In fact, the 2006 UNEP/SustainAbility and Standard & Poor report appears to be the last in the series of 'global reporters' reports, bringing to an end more than a decade of international report monitoring.

The UNEP/SustainAbility surveys worked with the leading reporters of the day, and do systematically assess report content, but they provide no systematic benchmarking of the same organizations over time. From 1996 to 2002, the general trend among the leading reporters appears largely static, with the world's leading dozen or so reporters consistently scoring between 45 per cent and 60 per cent of the total UNEP/SustainAbility score (see Table 4.3). In 2004 and 2006, probably due to the impact of the GRI, this lifted slightly to 50 per cent to 70 per cent of the total score. However, of the 22 companies listed as scoring at least 40 per cent in the 1996 survey, only five remain included in the 2004 survey; and the 2006 survey notes no fewer than 25 of the 50 reporters were new to the benchmark survey. Over time, companies such as British Telecom, Novo Nordisk and BP have improved their overall reporting scores by 20 per cent or more. However, other organizations have remained static (e.g. Bristol Myers-Squibb, British Airways, General Motors) or slipped backwards (e.g. Baxter). And yet others have disappeared from the benchmark altogether (e.g. Body Shop, Monsanto, Dow, and Union Carbide).

Consistently maintaining high levels of reporting over time is probably difficult, but one suspects the changing fortunes of the so-called top 50 also reflect the rather fickle and unsystematic nature of the benchmarking exercise over time. Moreover, of the 'leading' reporters captured in the UNEP/SustainAbility surveys, it is worth highlighting that, of the thousands (estimated at over 60,000) of large multinationals worldwide, only *seven* in 2002, *20* in 2004 and *40* in 2006 managed to gain half or better benchmark scores. Based on the standards of the GRI, and the UNEP/SustainAbility benchmark criteria, then, only a very few multinationals currently issue accounts of their impacts on society and the environment which might be thought to be reasonable and/or credible as presently understood by best practice and the role of independent verification.

## Rationales for reporting

Regardless of the form of reporting, it is always driven – to one degree or another – by the immediate and strategic objectives of the corporation. Accordingly, corporations report with motivation, a calculated purpose and a message in mind. What is produced is provided, at least in part, in response to various pressures, expectations and social change and how the corporation interprets and prioritizes these. With the act of reporting, corporations, in turn, contribute to public discourse and serve to shape the public opinion to which they are responding. Government, NGOs, individuals and the media (SustainAbility *et al.*, 2002) also play a role in this public discourse by their presence in the debate as well as their absence. It is this malleable public discourse, fuelled by the media, which leads to shaping expectations, which leads, in turn one hopes, to shaping laws that require greater levels of corporate public accountability.

Several theories are employed to explain the motivation for zustainabullity reporting (Brown and Fraser, 2006; Gray *et al.*, 1995, 2010). The most popular of these includes such theories as: accountability, legitimacy, political economy, stakeholder and institutional theory. The essence behind these theories can be summarized using the more common vernacular in Table 4.4. It should be noted that these rationales do not operate in isolation.

*Table 4.3* Top reporters from UNEP/SustainAbility (1994, 1996, 1997, 2000, 2002, 2004, 2006) benchmark surveys

| 1994ᵃ | 1996 | 1997 | 2000 | 2002 | 2004 | 2006 |
|---|---|---|---|---|---|---|
| British Telecom — 4 | Body Shop | 66% Body Shop | 67% British Airports A | 62% Co-op Bank | 61% Co-op Bank | 71% British Telecom |
| BSO/Origin — 4 | Phillips Petrol | 54% Baxter | 52% Novo Nordisk | 62% Novo Nordisk | 60% Novo Nordisk | 69% Co-op Fin Service |
| Dow Canada — 4 | Monsanto | 52% Nestle | 50% Co-op Bank | 59% British Airports A | 59% BP | 66% BP |
| Dow Europe — 4 | Bristol M-S | 51% Novo Nordisk | 50% British Telecom | 59% British Telecom | 58% British Am Tobacco | 64% Anglo Platinum |
| Kunert — 4 | Dow Europe | 48% British Airways | 49% BP Amoco | 57% Rio Tinto | 55% British Telecom | 64% Rabobank |
| Body Shop — 3–4 | IBM Corp | 47% Volvo | 48% Royal Dutch/Shell | 57% Royal Dutch/Shell | 53% British Airports A | 63% Unilever |
| Bristol M-S — 3–4 | Ontario Hydro | 47% General Motors | 47% WMC | 51% BP | 53% Rabobank | 61% MTR |
| British Airways — 3–4 | Polaroid Corp | 47% Sun Company | 47% ESAB | 50% Bristol M-S | 49% Rio Tinto | 60% Vodafone |
| British Gas — 3–4 | Waste Mangt | 45% Bristol M-S | 46% Bristol M-S | 49% ITT Flygt | 48% Royal Dutch/Shell | 60% Shell |
| Noranda Forest — 3–4 | Du Pont | 44% Polaroid Corp | 46% Volkswagen | 48% S African Breweries | 48% HP | 59% Nike |
| Noranda Minerals — 3–4 | Sun Company | 44% Tokyo Electric | 46% ING | 48% BASF | 48% Unilever | 59% Novo Nordisk |
| Ontario Hydro — 3–4 | British Airways | 44% Enso | 46% United Utilities | 48% Volkswagen | 48% Anglo American | 58% ABN AMRO Real |
| Shell Canada — 3–4 | Ciba-Geigy | 43% IBM Corp | 46% Body Shop Aus/NZ | 47% WMC | 48% Statoil | 55% BHP Billiton |
| Thorn EMI — 3–4 | British Telecom | 43% Nortel | 46% Landcare Research | 46% CIS Co-op Ins | 46% Kesko | 54% Philips |
| Union Carbide — 3–4 | Noranda Minerals | 42% Phillips Petrol | 45% Eskom | 45% Baxter | 45% Landcare Research | 52% ABN AMRO |
| Waste Mangt — 3–4 | Thorn EMI | 42% SAS | 45% Sunoco | 44% Cable & Wireless | 45% Natura | 51% HP |

ᵃBased on the 1994 UNEP/SustainAbility 5-stage model. All these companies were assessed as stage 4 or stage 3–4 reporters.

*Table 4.4* Rationales for sustainability reporting

| Aspect | Proactive | Reactive |
| --- | --- | --- |
| Moral and ethical reasons, duty | We see this sort of reporting as our ethical duty. This reporting is part of the accountability equation and we have a champion or champions in the upper ranks of management who wants us to do this. | What we must do is comply with the law. If the law does not require this reporting we see no moral duty to engage in it. |
| Competitive advantage | We would like to be seen as a leader in this area. This is the vision that we have of ourselves. | We do not see any competitive benefit in being a leader in this area and we view it as too costly to be on the leading edge. |
| Party to setting of voluntary standards – GRI, IIRC | We would like to work with others setting voluntary international standards. We might believe that voluntary standards are the way to go to stave off (costly) regulation. | We are not interested to or able to participate in such voluntary activity. |
| Party to setting of mandatory standards – government, accounting or securities based | We should do this so our views can be heard and represented in the process. This might include a conscious desire to 'capture' the agenda and ensure the results are compatible with what we are willing to do. | We do not want mandatory standards therefore we will not participate in the process except perhaps to resist. |
| Peer and industry pressure | We believe that it is important for our industry association to endorse this reporting. We want our industry to have a better image. We want to bring others in our industry up to our level of reporting. | Too many of our competitors are engaging in this reporting. We must provide some sort of reporting and not lag too far behind unless we are willing to tolerate some sort of competitive disadvantage. |
| Corporate performance | We are really doing better than people think we are and we need to let them know. | Our corporate performance is not so hot and 'least said soonest mended'. |
| Image management, public relations, corporate reporting awards | This sort of reporting is a great way to beef up our image. Let's get our spin-doctors on it right away. This is a symbolic way for us to show how progressive we are. | There is a reaction to a disaster 'X' in our industry. We must do collateral damage control and report on how we have safeguards in place so that we are not like disaster 'X'. |
| Social pressures, social licence to operate | We believe in enlightened self-interest and win–win situations. Let's use this as one way to get the local community to buy in to what we are doing. | Why do we need to communicate with anyone other than shareholders? But, maybe if we do we can avoid the attacks by those NGOs and rabid interest groups. |

*(continued)*

*Table 4.4* Rationales for sustainability reporting (continued)

| Aspect | Proactive | Reactive |
|---|---|---|
| Financial benefits from investor reactions | We believe that we can attract investors with this sort of reporting. We feel that we can lower our cost of capital because this sort of reporting indicates how we have solid systems, top-notch strategic thinking and corporate transparency. | We do not see any financial benefit from engaging in this reporting and in fact we see these reports as costing too much money, time, trouble and effort to produce. |
| Existing regulation – government, accounting or securities based | We have regulations in this area and we want to do a good job of providing full and fair disclosure, complying with both the form and the spirit of the regulation. | Sure there is regulation in this area but we do not think that it is well enforced and we are not afraid of the penalties if we are caught. Let's just ignore this and keep a low profile and see what happens. Maybe we will have to do something if our auditors or the securities regulators raise the issue. |

Source: Adapted from Buhr (2007).

Often many of them are employed together as a method for an organization to understand its zustainabullity reporting situation. These rationales are cast in Table 4.4 in a proactive–reactive dichotomy for ease of illustration; but this is a false dichotomy since there is a range of attitudes within each rationale.[5]

## Voluntary standards

Despite the slow but steady increase in regulation governing organizations' social and environmental disclosures (see KPMG, 2011, for more detail) there is no question that the predominant development of zustainabullity reporting has been voluntary. From the earliest reports (especially from around 1990) the publication of zustainabullity reports – whether as hard copy stand-alone reports, reports on websites or the increasing tendency to include zustainabullity information within corporations' annual reports – has been a function of the motivations of the organizations themselves. Hence the range of theoretical explanations we offer in Table 4.4. While experimentation has played a role in this development of reporting, the general trend has been helped along by a range of guidelines and codes that have supported, encouraged and rewarded those organizations willing to get involved in this remarkable initiative. There has been no shortage of such codes and guidelines with initiatives, such as the Association of Chartered Certified Accountants (ACCA) Reporting Awards Scheme and the UNEP/SustainAbility Benchmarks being among the most prominent and effective. But without question the most influential guidelines have been those from the GRI.

　　The GRI represents a multi-stakeholder cooperation intended to try and establish a generally acceptable framework of reporting principles for environmental, social and economic reporting. The *Guidelines* have been published and regularly updated since 2000. Broadly speaking the GRI indicators sought to develop a manifestation of the organization's triple bottom line (Elkington, 1997, 2004) and suggest that an organization which took its respon-sibilities seriously would manage its behaviour across all three dimensions of its activities. The GRI could be thought of as an attempt to develop the accountability to support that TBL (see Henriques and Richardson, 2004).

The *Guidelines* suggest standard disclosures for an organization's strategic profile and management approach, and recommend performance indicators relating to the organiza-tion's economic, social and environmental performance. Organizations are then invited to comply with the *Guidelines* and to report their compliance on the GRI website. The *G3.1 Guidelines* (GRI, 2011) provide for the following:[6]

- forty-two strategy and profile reporting ingredients (e.g. CEO statement, organizational profile, reporting parameters and governance, commitments and engagement);
- eighty-four performance indicators across three categories: environment (30), social (45) and economic (9);
- fifty-five of the 84 indicators identified as 'core' indicators;
- forty-five social indicators disaggregated into labour practices (15), human rights (11), society (10) and product responsibility (9).

Not all the GRI indicators, however, need to be reported. The framework provides for six levels of 'compliance'; namely, A+, A, B+, B, C+ and C (the lowest). The endpoints of this continuum consist of the following:

- An 'A+-level' reporter needs to disclose, at a minimum, all 42 strategy and profile indi-cators, all the 55 core indicators, and sector supplement indicators. As well, the report must be externally assured.
- A 'C-level' reporter needs to disclose 28 of the strategy and profile indicators, but only ten of the 84 performance indicators, with at least one indicator from each of the envi-ronmental, social and economic categories.

Clearly, the GRI framework provides for considerable flexibility in reporting, and it is this flexibility, and particularly the introduction of 'C-level' reporting, that might have accelerated the incidence of reporting in recent years. The early versions of the GRI (G1 and G2) were far more exacting and demanding of corporations. The GRI has been a consider-able success in that while only 26 organizations were reporting in accordance with the GRI guidelines in 2004, by the turn of the decade KPMG (2011) was able to report that 80 per cent of the G250 (the world's largest corporations) and nearly 70 per cent of many of the developed countries' largest companies were voluntarily working with the guidelines. Indeed, thousands of the world's organizations, large and small, private and public, volun-tarily produce zustainabullity reporting typically guided by the influence of the GRI. These are remarkable advances, largely unthinkable 20 years ago.

However, no matter how attractive it might be to get carried away with enthusiasm for this achievement, the facts of reporting – even GRI reporting – do not suggest an unalloyed success but rather something of a heroic failure. There are several reasons for this. First, the GRI has not managed to gain agreement on a full set of indicators which together might constitute something approaching a social and/or environmental accountability. While the environmental indicators are widely considered to be helpful, the social and economic indi-cators are a much less inspiring collection. So even for those organizations fully compliant with GRI, it is far from obvious that any substantial accountability is being discharged or even that civil society is gaining any insights at all into the elusive TBL (Dingwerth and Eichinger, 2010).

If further confirmation of the failure of the voluntary approach to zustainabullity reporting were needed, the issue of assurance would undoubtedly provide it. As we have already noted, independently assured reporting is a far less common practice, and the growth trends for it have been much more pitiful. We should recall that all financial statements are required, by law, to be audited, for the simple reason that they are important documents, upon which people will rely and whose accuracy and reliability cannot be simply assumed. That is, a reader of a financial statement is expected to need some assurance that the documents are worthy of attention. It is quite striking, if no surprise, therefore to discover that the voluntary reports of zustainabullity have no attendant requirement for assurance. So, given that close to 75 per cent of all reports surveyed among the 3,400 world's largest organizations (i.e. about 1,650[7]) were *not* independently assured, a reader would be well-advised to treat them with considerable caution. And it remains far from clear that the assurance process itself warrants much reliability anyway! (Ball *et al.*, 2000; Beets and Souther, 1999; Deegan *et al.*, 2006a, 2006b; Gray, 2000; Mock *et al.*, 2007; O'Dwyer and Owen, 2005; Owen *et al.*, 2000; Wallage, 2000).

Thus it seems that one must inevitably conclude that stimulating and occasionally innovative though voluntary reporting initiatives might be, if the aim is substantial and reliable accountability across a majority of the world's largest organizations, an abject failure. The most positive thing one might say is that after well over two decades of voluntary initiatives, fewer than 5 per cent of the world's large organizations produce a report related to TBL, no matter how poorly. These, in turn, are very clearly no indicator of accountability for sustainability and are, in all probability, an unreliable source of information.

## Future prospects

If one believes, as we do, that accountability is an essential component of a civilized society and that sustainability is a matter of supreme importance to all creatures of the world, then it is difficult to exercise much enthusiasm about future prospects on the basis of experience from the last 20 years or so. It is perfectly apparent that voluntary initiatives are an almost complete failure. To place yet further faith in them would be foolish. But equally, there seems little appetite among national politicians to brave the petulant self-interested wrath of business and introduce substantive regulation for disclosure of corporate and organizational unsustainability.

This resistance by politicians and business is actually quite puzzling. In the first place it is not as if producing *systematized* and *genuine* accounts of the social and environmental impacts of corporations is any kind of mystery: research and experimentation over the years have shown that there are a number of entirely practicable ways in which such accountability might be approached (Gray *et al.*, 1996). Equally, there is no practicable reason why large organizations should not produce such accounts – they are not prohibitively expensive and they do not need to *necessarily* directly affect corporate behaviour in any substantial way. Whether they do depends on the (negative) impacts the organization has, and the trends in these. The objections, if they are rational at all, must be on the basis of what the information will show. If what the information shows is trivial and no big deal (i.e. organizations *are* in fact reducing their negative impacts and improving their positive ones), why all the fuss? If, on the other hand, the information is not trivial then clearly civil society needs it urgently. The resistance of business is not something to which any attention should be paid in this case. After all, some of the most important data about the pressures on our social and eco-logical systems – certainly below regional and planetary levels – probably resides with the organizations themselves. If civil society is to make any kind of sensible decision about the pressures on, the state of, and the future capacity of the social and ecological systems on which it relies, it needs this data.

It was this line of reasoning that led to one of the most potentially promising initiatives of recent years: the Prince of Wales *Accounting for Sustainability* (A4S) project. Apparently initiated out of a frustration with the lack of voluntary progress and a belief that accounting for sustainability should not be an impossible task, the project appears to have become derailed at some point. Although it is not entirely clear what happened, it looks as if the project proved incapable of addressing the essential conflicts that sustainability poses for business, eventually producing a range of highly stimulating but partial projects that owe at least as much to environmental management as to sustainability (Hopwood *et al.*, 2010).

Although no clear path to accountability for sustainability emerged from A4S, the project has perhaps three notable legacies. First, A4S usefully illustrates that we need to exercise more nuance in our discussion of 'regulation versus voluntary' as a means of changing behaviour. A path employing authoritative leadership might offer more substantial possibilities and invoke less rabid opposition than hitherto. Second, the A4S output demonstrates that clever individuals working with innovative organizations can produce important and unexpected steps forward (Chapters 12 and 13 in this text illustrate this more clearly). It seems likely that useful breakthroughs can emerge from unexpected places.

The final legacy is less unequivocal however. The A4S project mooted something it called 'connected reporting' that might, *inter alia*, produce a merging of financial and zustainabullity accounting. On the whole this looked a lot like a well-meaning but ill-informed suggestion. However, this 'connected reporting', together with support from the GRI, has transmogrified into something called 'IR' and has spawned the IIRC. The IIRC, at the time of writing, shows every sign of determining the shape of the future – and that does not bode well for accountability or sustainability.

The formation of the IIRC in 2010 was a major international event and it drew upon the support of a considerable array of big names from the worlds of accounting and reporting. The initiative was greeted widely with considerable optimism that seemed to suggest that at last we had found a new, exciting and positive direction for zustainabullity reporting. September 2011 saw the publication of *Towards Integrated Reporting: Communicating Value in the 21st Century*. This was the IIRC's first consultation paper and it set out the shape that future reporting might take.

There are many major problems with the IIRC's initial document. There are three that particularly deserve attention. First, accountability and sustainability (even in its adul-terated zustainabullity form) hardly feature in the discussion and they are certainly not examined. For a document intended to integrate financial and sustainability reporting, that is, at best, eccentric. Second, the focus of the discussion is almost exclusively upon the needs of investors and it does so while ignoring a considerable body of prior research on just this issue. It is not the needs of investors that drive the need for accountability and sustainability information – the issues are wider and more important than that. Finally, the IIRC fails to explore how the (probably impossible) task of integrating financial, social and environmental information might take place. That we can expect to see such information returning, very properly, to the annual report is to be welcomed. But this is hardly 'integration' – a task which 40 years of research has shown is almost certainly not achievable.

So it looks as though the hope for the future – so-called IR – will (in all probability) undermine what little progress the A4S and GRI have achieved and further disenfranchise accountability and sustainability. If so, this will be a true disaster. Let us hope that here, as in so many other attempts to forecast the future, we are completely wrong. Let us hope that the IIRC actually proves able to deliver full accountability on the financial, social and environmental impacts of organizations to a wide range of stakeholders – something academics have argued for, and for which the Accounting Standards Steering Committee outlined a case in *The Corporate Report* (ASSC, 1975), over 30 years ago.

## Conclusions

On a final (more positive) note, there is something to be said for pushing on with the zustainabullity reporting agenda. The very act of providing accounts has the potential to change behaviour. The process of reporting should serve to change management strategies and information systems and in turn lead to changes in management philosophy and practices (Dierkes and Antal, 1985). *The Economist* (2002: 56) notes:

> [S]plashing out on a big report may keep activists off a company's back. But although sucking up to politically correct lobbyists might seem a small price to pay to keep them quiet, in reality it can reinforce the feeling that companies have a case to answer.

It remains for us to continue to work to make that case loud and clear and here we would like to raise a call to arms for academics. The task of the academic is, at least in part, to act as a challenge to and as a conscience for the nation. There are few issues more important than accountability and sustainability but there is so little critical work challenging the more vacuous of business initiatives. Unless academics are challenging – what are we for, really?

## Notes

1  This does not mean that it is not possible to produce practicable accounts of unsustainability which would provide broad indications of the extent to which an entity was detracting from key elements of sustainability (e.g. climate change, species extinction, habitat or income inequality, say). As there is no single state of sustainability and for the reasons we outline in this chapter, any account of unsustainability would be only a first approximation (Gray, 2010).

2  We are not alone in recognizing the confusion and contradictions in respect of understanding sustainability and sustainable development (see, for example, Redclift, 1987; Welford, 1997). Such distinctions as 'strong' or 'true' sustainability are commonplace. As Keith (2011: 25) puts it: 'For "sustainable" to mean anything, we must embrace and then defend the bare truth: the planet is primary. The life-producing work of a million species is literally the earth, air and water that we depend on. No human activity – not the vacuous, not the sublime – is worth more than that matrix. Neither, in the end, is any human life. If we use the word "sustainable" and don't mean that, then we are liars of the worse sort: the kind who let atrocities happen while we stand by and do nothing.' Of course, that corporate reporting, and other legitimating and nefarious behaviours might sustain a (corporate) bully is also not lost on some. See, for example, Lubbers (2003) and Beder (2006).

3  We note a discrepancy in the average verification rates for the N100 in the 2011 KPMG Survey. The survey reports an overall figure of 38 per cent. However, by working with individual country reporting rates and individual country verification rates, we are able to produce only an overall average of 24 per cent.

4  Some degree of caution is required in interpreting this table, since the KPMG surveys of 1996, 1999, 2002, 2005, 2008 and 2011 are based on different numbers of countries' top 100 firms. Also the 2011 figures are based on both stand-alone and supplementary report disclosures. The changing

industrial mix due to sampling also matters. For example, the 1999 survey is based on 11 countries (and therefore 1,100 companies), while the 2002 survey is based on 19 countries (and 1,900 companies). The industrial make-up of different countries, therefore, as shown in Table 4.2, changes the proportion of total companies in each industrial sector; the point being that a lower percentage rate of reporting in a given sector might still indicate a greater number of actual reporters in that sector, due to the increased sample frame. For example, oil and gas reporters are shown to *drop* to 39 per cent in 2002 from 53 per cent in 1999. Yet more than twice as many oil and gas companies were sampled in 2002 compared to 1999 due to the eight extra countries (and 800 companies) sampled, and the number of oil and gas reporters increased from 28 to 44.

5   These rationales have been drawn from the literature, including the following sources: Alon et al. (2010); Bebbington *et al.* (2009); Belal and Owen (2007); Buhr (2002); Deloitte Touche Tohmatsu International *et al.* (1993); Freedman and Stagliano (1995); Gray and Bebbington (2000); Neu *et al.* (1998); Newton and Harte (1997); O'Dwyer (2002); Oliver (1991); Patten (1992); Spence (2007); Suchman (1995); UNEP/SustainAbility (1994); and *The Economist* (2002).

6   A draft for version 4 (G4) was released for comment in 2012 and final guidelines were made public in 2013.

7   N100 organizations surveyed were 3,400. Of these, on average 64 per cent (and so 2,175) provided a report. Of these 2,175 reports, 24 per cent were verified (i.e. 525 reports), equalling approximately 1,650 reports that were *not* verified.

# References

Accounting Standards Steering Committee (ASSC) (1975) *The Corporate Report: A Discussion Paper Published for Comment*, London: ASSC.

Alon, I., Lattemann, C., Fetscherin, M., Li, S. and Schneider, A. (2010) 'Usage of Public Corporate Communications of Social Responsibility in Brazil, Russia, India and China (BRIC)', *International Journal of Emerging Markets*, 5(1): 6–22.

Australian Council of Super Investors (ACSI) (2011) *Sustainability Reporting Practices of the S&P/ ASX200*, Melbourne, VIC: ACSI.

Bakan, J. (2004) *The Corporation: The Pathological Pursuit of Profit and Power*, London: Constable and Robinson.

Ball, A., Owen, D.L. and Gray, R. (2000) 'External Transparency or Internal Capture? The Role of Third Party Statements in Adding Value to Corporate Environmental Reports', *Business Strategy and the Environment*, 9(1): 1–23.

Bebbington, J., Higgins, C. and Frame, B. (2009) 'Initiating Sustainable Development Reporting: Evidence from New Zealand', *Accounting, Auditing & Accountability Journal*, 22(4): 588–625.

Beder, S. (2006) *Suiting Themselves: How Corporations Drive the Global Agenda*, London: Earthscan.

Beets, S.D. and Souther, C.C. (1999) 'Corporate Environmental Reports: The Need for Standards and an Environmental Assurance Service', *Accounting Horizons*, 13(2): 129–45.

Belal, A.R. and Owen, D.L. (2007) 'The Views of Corporate Managers on the Current State of, and Future Prospects for, Social Reporting in Bangladesh: An Engagement-Based Study', *Accounting, Auditing & Accountability Journal*, 20(3): 472–94.

Bowen, H. R. (1953) *Social Responsibilities of the Businessman*, New York: Harper & Brothers.

Brown, H.S., de Jong, M. and Levy, D.L. (2009) 'Building Institutions Based on Information Disclosure: Lessons from GRI's Sustainability', *Journal of Cleaner Production*, 17(6): 571–80.

Brown, J. and Fraser, M. (2006) 'Approaches and Perspectives in Social and Environmental Accounting: An Overview of the Conceptual Landscape', *Business Strategy and the Environment*, 15: 103–17.

Buhr, N. (2002) 'A Structuration View on the Initiation of Environmental Reports', *Critical Perspectives on Accounting*, 13: 17–38.

Buhr, N. (2007) 'Histories of and Rationales for Sustainability Reporting', in J. Unerman, B. O'Dwyer and J. Bebbington (eds) *Sustainability Accounting and Accountability*, London: Routledge.

Canadian Securities Administrators (CSA) (2010) CSA Staff Notice 51-333 Environmental Reporting Guidance, available at http://www.osc.gov.on.ca/documents/en/Securities-Category5/csa_20101027_51-333_environmental-reporting.pdf, accessed 27 June 2011.

Chapman, R. and Milne, M.J. (2004) 'The Triple Bottom Line: How New Zealand Companies Measure Up', *Corporate Environmental Strategy: International Journal for Sustainable Business*, 11(2): 37–50.

Deegan, C., Cooper, B.J. and Shelly, M. (2006a) 'An Investigation of TBL Report Assurance Statements: UK and European Evidence', *Managerial Auditing Journal*, 21(4): 329–71.

Deegan, C., Cooper, B.J. and Shelly, M. (2006b) 'An Investigation of TBL Report Assurance Statements: Australian Evidence', *Australian Accounting Review*, 16(2): 2–18.

Deloitte Touche Tohmatsu International, International Institute for Sustainable Development and Sustain Ability (1993) *Coming Clean: Corporate Environmental Reporting*, London: Deloitte Touche Tohmatsu International.

Dierkes, M. and Antal, B. (1985) 'The Usefulness and Use of Social Reporting Information', *Accounting, Organizations and Society*, 10(1): 29–34.

Dingwerth, K. and Eichinger, M. (2010) 'Tamed Transparency: How Information Disclosure under the Global Reporting Initiative Fails to Empower', *Global Environmental Politics*,10(3): 74–96.

*The Economist* (2002) 'Irresponsible: The Dangers of Corporate Social Responsibility', 23 November, p. 56.

Elkington, J. (1997) *Cannibals with Forks: The Triple Bottom Line of 21st Century Business*, Oxford: Capstone Publishing.

Elkington, J. (2004) 'Enter the Triple Bottom Line', in A. Henriques and J. Richardson (eds) *The Triple Bottom Line: Does it All Add Up?* London: Earthscan.

Ernst & Ernst (1978) *Social Responsibility Disclosure: 1978 Survey*, New York: Ernst & Ernst.

Etzion, D. and Ferraro, F. (2010) 'The Role of Analogy in the Institutionalization of Sustainability Reporting', *Organization Science*, 21(5): 1092–107.

Freedman, M. and Stagliano, A.J. (1995) 'Disclosure of Environmental Cleanup Costs: The Impact of the Superfund Act', *Advances in Public Interest Accounting*, 6: 163–76.

Global Reporting Initiative (GRI) (2011) *G3.1 Guidelines*, available at https://www.globalreporting.org/reporting/latest-guidelines/g3-1-guidelines/Pages/default.aspx, accessed 24 April 2012.

Gray, R.H. (1990) *The Greening of Accountancy: The Profession after Pearce*, London: ACCA.

Gray, R. (2000) 'Current Developments and Trends in Social and Environmental Auditing, Reporting and Attestation: A Review and Comment', *International Journal of Auditing*, 4: 247–68.

Gray, R. (2006) 'Social, Environmental, and Sustainability Reporting and Organizational Value Creation? Whose Value? Whose Creation?', *Accounting, Auditing & Accountability Journal*, 19(3): 319–48.

Gray, R. (2010) 'Is Accounting for Sustainability Actually Accounting for Sustainability … and How Would We Know? An Exploration of Narratives of Organizations and the Planet', *Accounting, Organizations and Society*, 35(1): 47–62.

Gray, R. and Bebbington, J. (2000) 'Environmental Accounting, Managerialism and Sustainability: Is the Planet Safe in the Hands of Business and Accounting?', *Advances in Environmental Accounting & Management*, 1: 1–44.

Gray, R.H. and Milne, M.J. (2002) 'Sustainability Reporting: Who's Kidding Whom?' *Chartered Accountants Journal of New Zealand*, July: 66–70.

Gray, R.H. and Milne, M.J. (2004) 'Towards Reporting on The Triple Bottom Line: Mirages, Methods and Myths', in A. Henriques and J. Richardson (eds) *The Triple Bottom Line: Does it All Add Up?* London: Earthscan.

Gray, R.H., Bebbington, K.J. and Walters, D. (1993) *Accounting for the Environment: The Greening of Accountancy Part II*, London: Paul Chapman.

Gray, R., Kouhy, R. and Lavers, S. (1995) 'Corporate Social and Environmental Reporting: A Review of the Literature and a Longitudinal Study of UK Disclosure', *Accounting, Auditing and Accountability Journal*, 8(2): 47–77.

Gray, R., Owen, D. and Adams, C. (1996) *Accounting & Accountability: Changes and Challenges in Corporate Social and Environmental Reporting*, London: Prentice Hall.

Gray, R.H., Owen, D.L. and Adams, C.A. (2010) 'Some Theories for Social Accounting? A Review Essay and Tentative Pedagogic Categorisation of Theorisations around Social Accounting', *Advances in Environmental Accounting and Management*, 4: 1–54.

Gunningham, N., Kagan, R. and Thornton, D. (2003) *Shades of Green: Business, Regulation, and the Environment*, Stanford, CA: Stanford University Press.

Guthrie, J. and Parker, L.D. (1989) 'Corporate Social Reporting: A Rebuttal of Legitimacy Theory', *Accounting and Business Research*, 19(76): 343–52.

Hawken, P. (2002) 'On Corporate Responsibility: A Ronald McDonald Fantasy', *San Francisco Chronicle*, Sunday, 2 June.

Henriques, A. and Richardson, J. (eds) (2004) *The Triple Bottom Line: Does it All Add Up?*, London: Earthscan.

Higgins, C., Milne, M.J. and VanGramberg, B. (2011) 'Towards a More Nuanced Understanding of Sustainable Development Reporting in Australia', Proceedings of the Tenth CSEAR Conference, Launceston, Tasmania, available at http://www.utas.edu.au/__data/assets/pdf_file/0009/188424/Higgins-et-al-CSEAR-2011.pdf, accessed 11 October 2013.

Hogner, R.H. (1982) 'Corporate Social Reporting: Eight Decades of Development at U.S. Steel', *Research in Corporate Social Performance and Policy*, 4: 243–50.

Hopwood, A., Unerman, G. and Fries, J. (eds) (2010) *Accounting for Sustainability: Practical Insights*, London: Earthscan.

International Union for the Conservation of Nature (IUCN) (1980) *World Conservation Strategy*, Gland, Switzerland: IUCN.

Keith, L. (2011) 'The Problem', in A. McBay, L. Keith and D. Jensen (eds) *Deep Green Resistance*, New York: Seven Stories Press.

Kolk, A. (1999) 'Evaluating Corporate Environmental Reporting', *Business Strategy & the Environment*, 8(4): 225–37.

Kolk, A. (2003) 'Trends in Sustainability Reporting by the Fortune Global 250', *Business Strategy & the Environment*, 12(5): 279–91.

Kolk, A. (2004) 'A Decade of Sustainability Reporting: Developments and Significance', *International Journal of Environment and Sustainable Development*, 3(1): 51–64.

Kolk, A. (2005) 'Environmental Reporting by Multinationals from the Triad: Convergence or Divergence?', *Management International Review*, 45(1): 145–66.

Kolk, A. (2007) 'On the Economic Dimensions of Corporate Social Responsibility: Exploring Fortune Global 250 Reports', *Business and Society*, 46(4): 457–78.

Kolk, A. (2008) 'Sustainability, Accountability and Corporate Governance: Exploring Multinationals' Reporting Practices', *Business Strategy & the Environment*, 17(1): 1–15.

Kolk, A. (2010) 'The Integration of Corporate Governance in Corporate Social Responsibility Disclosures', *Corporate Social Responsibility and Environmental Management*, 17(1): 15–26.

Kolk, A. and Perego, P.M. (2010) 'Determinants of the Adoption of Sustainability Assurance Statements: An International Investigation', *Business Strategy and the Environment*, 19(3): 182–98.

KPMG (1993) *KPMG International Survey of Environmental Reporting 1993*, Amsterdam: KPMG Environmental Consulting.

KPMG (1996) *KPMG International Survey of Environmental Reporting 1996*, Amsterdam: KPMG Environmental Consulting.

KPMG (1999) *KPMG International Survey of Environmental Reporting 1999*, Amsterdam: KPMG Environmental Consulting.

KPMG (2002) *KPMG International Survey of Corporate Sustainability Reporting* 2002, Amsterdam: KPMG Global Sustainability Services.

KPMG (2005) *International Survey of Corporate Sustainability Reporting 2005*, Amsterdam: KPMG International.

KPMG (2008) *International Survey of Corporate Sustainability Reporting 2008*, Amsterdam: KPMG International.

KPMG (2011) *International Survey of Corporate Sustainability Reporting 2011*, Amsterdam: KPMG International.

Laine, M. (2010) 'Towards Sustaining the Status Quo: Business Talk of Sustainability in Finnish Corporate Disclosures 1987–2005', *European Accounting Review*, 19(2): 247–74.

Lewis, N.R., Parker, L.D. and Sutcliffe, P. (1984) 'Financial Reporting to Employees: The Pattern of Development 1919 to 1979', *Accounting, Organizations and Society*, 9(3/4): 275–89.

Lubbers, E. (ed.) (2003) *Battling Big Business: Countering Greenwash, Infiltration and Other Forms of Corporate Bullying*, Melbourne, VIC: Scribe Publications.

Maltby, J. (2004) 'Hadfields Ltd: Its Annual General Meetings 1903–1939 and Their Relevance for Contemporary Social Reporting', *British Accounting Review*, 36: 415–39.

Martin, A.D. and Hadley, D.J. (2008) 'Corporate Environmental Non-reporting – a UK FTSE 350 Perspective', *Business Strategy & the Environment*, 17: 245–59.

Milne, M.J. (1996) 'On Sustainability, the Environment and Management Accounting', *Management Accounting Research*, 7(1): 135–61.

Milne, M.J. and Gray, R.H. (2007) 'The Future of Sustainability Reporting', in J. Unerman, B. O'Dwyer and J. Bebbington (eds) *Sustainability Accounting and Accountability*, London, Routledge, ch. 10.

Milne, M.J. and Gray, R.H. (2013) 'W(h)ither Ecology? The Triple Bottom Line, the Global Reporting Initiative, and Corporate Sustainability Reporting', *Journal of Business Ethics*, 118(1): 13–29.

Milne, M.J., Tregidga, H.M. and Walton, S. (2003) 'The Triple Bottom Line: Benchmarking New Zealand's Early Reporters', *University of Auckland Business Review*, 5(2): 36–50.

Milne, M.J., Kearins, K. and Walton, S. (2006) 'Creating Adventures in Wonderland? The Journey Metaphor and Environmental Sustainability', *Organization*, 13(6): 801–39.

Milne, M., Tregidga, H. and Walton, S. (2009) 'Words Not Actions! The Ideological Role of Sustainable Development Reporting', *Accounting, Auditing and Accountability Journal*, 22(8): 1211–57.

Mock, T.J., Strohm, C. and Swartz, K.M. (2007) 'An Examination of Worldwide Assured Sustainability Reporting', *Australian Accounting Review*, 17(1): 67–77.

Morhardt, J. (2009) 'General Disregard for Details of GRI Human Rights Reporting by Large Corporations', *Global Business Review*, 10(2): 141–58.

Morhardt, J. (2010) 'Corporate Social Responsibility and Sustainability Reporting on the Internet', *Business Strategy & the Environment*, 19(7): 436–52.

Neu, D., Warsame, H. and Pedwell, K. (1998) 'Managing Public Impressions: Environmental Disclosures in Annual Reports', *Accounting, Organizations and Society*, 23(3): 265–82.

Newton, T. and Harte, G. (1997) 'Green Business: Technicist Kitsch?', *Journal of Management Studies*, 34(1): 75–98.

O'Dwyer, B. (2002) 'Managerial Perceptions of Corporate Social Disclosure: An Irish Story', *Accounting, Auditing & Accountability Journal*, 15(3): 406–36.

O'Dwyer, B. and Owen, D. (2005) 'Assurance Statement Practice in Environmental, Social and Sustainability Reporting: A Critical Evaluation', *British Accounting Review*, 37: 205–29.

Oliver, C. (1991) 'Strategic Responses to Institutional Processes', *Academy of Management Review*, 16(1): 145–79.

Owen, D.L., Swift, T.A., Humphrey, C. and Bowerman, M. (2000) 'The New Social Audits: Accountability, Managerial Capture or the Agenda of Social Champions?', *European Accounting Review*, 9(1): 81–98.

Patten, D.M. (1992) 'Intra-Industry Environmental Disclosures in Response to the Alaskan Oil Spill: A Note on Legitimacy Theory', *Accounting, Organizations and Society*, 15(5): 471–5.

Redclift, M. (1987) *Sustainable Development: Exploring the Contradictions*, London: Routledge.

Roddick, A. (2003) 'Reflections on Success (Part 1 and Part 2)' – Excerpts from *Reflections on Success: Famous Achievers Talk Frankly to Martyn Lewis about Their Route to the Top*, in M. Lewis

(1998) Lennard/Queen Anne Press: New York, available at http://www.anitaroddick.com/readmore. php?sid=154, accessed 11 October 2013.

Rolland, D. and Bazzoni, J.O. (2009) 'Greening Corporate Identity: CSR Online Corporate Identity Reporting', *Corporate Communications: An International Journal*, 14(3): 249–63.

Spence, C. (2007) 'Social and Environmental Reporting and Hegemonic Discourse', *Accounting, Auditing & Accountability Journal*, 20(6): 855–82.

Suchman, M. (1995) 'Managing Legitimacy: Strategic and Institutional Approaches', *Academy of Management Review*, 20(3): 571–610.

SustainAbility, Ketchum and the United Nations Environment Programme (UNEP) (2002) *Good News & Bad: The Media, Corporate Social Responsibility and Sustainable Development*, London: SustainAbility.

Tregidga, H. and Milne, M. (2006) 'From Sustainable Management to Sustainable Development: A Longitudinal Analysis of a Leading New Zealand Environmental Reporter', *Business Strategy and the Environment*, 15(4): 219–41.

UNEP/SustainAbility (1994) *Company Environmental Reporting: A Measure of the Progress of Business & Industry towards Sustainable Development*, London: UNEP/SustainAbility.

UNEP/SustainAbility (1996) *Engaging Stakeholders: The Benchmark Survey*, London: UNEP/ SustainAbility.

UNEP/SustainAbility (1997) *The 1997 Benchmark Survey: The Third International Progress Report on Company Environmental Reporting*, London: UNEP/SustainAbility.

UNEP/SustainAbility (2000) *The Global Reporters: The 2000 Benchmark Survey*, London: UNEP/ SustainAbility.

UNEP/SustainAbility (2002) *Trust Us: The Global Reporters 2002 Survey of Corporate Sustainability*, London: UNEP/SustainAbility.

UNEP/SustainAbility and Standard & Poor (2004) *Risk & Opportunity: Best Practice in Non-Financial Reporting*, London: UNEP/SustainAbility.

UNEP/SustainAbility and Standard & Poor (2006) *Tomorrow's Value: The Global Reporters 2006 Survey of Corporate Sustainability Reporting*, Nairobi: United Nations Environment Programme (UNEP).

Unerman, J. (2003) 'Enhancing Organizational Global Hegemony with Narrative Accounting Disclosure: An Early Example', *Accounting Forum*, 27(5): 425–48.

Wallage, P. (2000) 'Assurance on Sustainability Reporting: An Auditor's View', *Auditing: A Journal of Practice and Theory*, 19: 53–65.

Welford, R. (1997) *Hijacking Environmentalism: Corporate Responses to Sustainable Development*, London: Earthscan.

Wheeler, D. and Elkington, J. (2001) 'The End of the Corporate Environmental Report? Or the Advent of Cybernetic Sustainability Reporting and Communication?', *Business Strategy and the Environment*, 10(1): 1–14.

World Commission on Environment and Development (WCED) (1987) *Our Common Future*, Oxford: Oxford University Press.

Zéghal, D. and Ahmed, S.A. (1990) 'Comparison of Social Responsibility Information Disclosure Media Used by Canadian Firms', *Accounting, Auditing & Accountability Journal*, 3(1): 38–53.

# 5 Independent assurance of sustainability reports

*Stuart Cooper and David Owen*

## Introduction

As the prevalence of sustainability, or corporate responsibility, reporting continues to grow, so has the tendency for reports to include an externally prepared assurance statement. The essential purpose of the latter is to enhance the status of sustainability reporting by the inclusion of an independent opinion designed to increase the confidence of report users in the reliability of the reported information. The importance of external assurance in this context is particularly noted in a comprehensive study of sustainability reporting practices worldwide undertaken by the Association of Chartered Certified Accountants (ACCA) and CorporateRegister.com (2004) in that it:

> represents the next stage of development in sustainability reporting as approaches become more developed and demands of report users more sophisticated. Organisations which fail to obtain assurance for their reports are likely to face issues of credibility.
>
> (p. 15)

Zadek *et al.* (2004) indicate that there are also additional internal benefits that may accrue to the organization from a sustainability assurance exercise including:

> improved overall management of performance in relation to existing policies and commitments, improved risk management and better understanding of emerging issues.
>
> (p. 16)

The purpose of this chapter is to provide an overview and critical evaluation of current trends in sustainability assurance practice together with a number of prominent guidelines which have been produced with a view to informing and standardizing such practice. The critique offered focuses particularly on the contribution that current, and future, practice makes towards the enhancement of stakeholder accountability.

## Recent trends in sustainability assurance practice

First, it is important to bear in mind that the external assurance of sustainability reports is very much a large company phenomenon. This is clearly evidenced in the UK by SalterBaxter-Context's (2005) survey of trends in CSR reporting, which suggests that while 44 of the top 100 UK companies' reports contained independent assurance statements, the figure for the top 250 only increased to 60. In a later international study, Simnett *et al.* (2009) similarly found that 'large companies were significantly more likely to have their sustainability reports assured compared to small companies' (p. 956). There has, nonetheless, been significant growth in the provision of external assurance statements as part of the overall sustainability reporting package on the part of companies across the globe, a fact highlighted in the above-mentioned study by the ACCA and CorporateRegister.com. Drawing on the latter's comprehensive database of significant corporate non-financial reports, covering both hard copy and PDF formats, it is noted that in 2003 nearly 40 per cent included external assurance statements compared with only 17 per cent ten years previously. More recent figures appearing in KPMG's latest (2011) triennial International Survey of Corporate Responsibility Reporting on the part of both the top 250 of the Fortune 500 companies (the Global 250) and the top 100 companies from 34 individual countries indicate that the practice continues to grow, although the rate of growth appears to be slowing markedly.

For the Global 250, KPMG's figures indicate that the number of reports that include a formal assurance statement increased from 30 per cent in 2005, to 40 per cent in 2008, and on to 46 per cent in 2011. However, in somewhat stark contrast, analysis of the top 100 companies' sample suggested a marginal decline in assurance provision down to 38 per cent from the 39 per cent reported in the 2008 survey. It should, however, be noted here that the results are not directly comparable, as more, and different, countries were surveyed in 2011. Indeed, only the top 100 samples from 13 countries forming part of the 2011 study also feature in those of 2005 and 2008. Table 5.1 below draws upon data from the three surveys to show the changing levels in the use of formal assurance across the top 100 companies for these particular countries.

Table 5.1 clearly highlights significant differences within different countries in the prevalence of assurance provision. For example, the 2011 survey indicates that more than 60 per cent of corporate responsibility reports from Denmark, Spain and Italy contained formal assurance statements, whereas these statements were largely conspicuous by their absence in the case of their US, Canadian and Japanese counterparts. Additionally, whereas figures from most of the 13 countries (except Italy, Australia and Japan) indicated that the prevalence of external assurance had been increasing between 2005 and 2008, the picture is more mixed between 2008 and 2011. In fact the levels of assurance fell, albeit marginally, in seven of the

*Table 5.1* Top 100 company corporate responsibility reports with formal assurance statements 2005–11, by country

| Country | 2005 (%) | 2008 (%) | 2011 (%) |
|---|---|---|---|
| Denmark | 31 | 46 | 65 |
| Spain | 44 | 70 | 65 |
| Italy | 70 | 61 | 64 |
| France | 40 | 73 | 60 |
| United Kingdom | 53 | 55 | 56 |
| Australia | 43 | 42 | 51 |
| Sweden | 5 | 33 | 42 |
| Netherlands | 40 | 44 | 41 |
| South Africa | 22 | 36 | 31 |
| Finland | 19 | 30 | 29 |
| Japan | 31 | 24 | 23 |
| Canada | 10 | 19 | 21 |
| United States | 3 | 14 | 13 |

Source: adapted from KPMG, 2008, p. 58; KPMG, 2011, p. 29.

13 countries. Two recently published international studies, Simnett *et al.* (2009) and Kolk and Perego (2010), which investigate how country-level institutional factors might explain the adoption, or non-adoption, of assurance statements shed a little light on these findings. Briefly, both studies suggest 'that companies domiciled in common law (stakeholder-oriented) countries are more likely to have their sustainability reports assured compared with firms domiciled in code law (shareholder-oriented) countries' (Kolk and Perego, 2010, p. 191). Simnett *et al.* (2009), however, caution in their study that this 'result is primarily attributable to a US effect' (p. 960).

In addition to inconsistencies in the level of assurance provision at country level, KPMG's (2011) survey also highlights differences across individual industrial sectors. In particular, it would appear that mining and utility companies are the most likely to undertake formal assurance exercises. This finding is supported in the Simnett *et al.* (2009) study, which finds companies from these industries together with those from the financial services sector most likely to have their sustainability reports assured.

Turning to the issue of choice of assurance provider, the KPMG (2011) survey reveals that the major accounting firms appear to dominate the market at both global and domestic level. In 2011, 71 per cent of Global 250 companies' (2008: 70 per cent; 2005: 58 per cent) assurance statements were contributed by the major accounting organizations; while for the top 100 companies across the 34 countries surveyed the figure was 64 per cent (2008: 65 per cent; 2005: 60 per cent). The majority of the other assurance services were categorized as being provided by 'certification bodies', 'technical expert firms' and 'specialist assurance providers'.

Intriguingly, an earlier study carried out for CPA Australia (2004), which drew on a comprehensive database of 170 assurance statements appearing between 2000 and 2003, predominantly from Australia (33 statements), the United Kingdom (48), mainland Europe (52) and Japan (16), paints a somewhat different picture as regards assurance provision. In this case, whereas accounting firms provide the majority (60 per cent) of assurance statements for mainland Europe, they are notably less prominent in Australia (15 per cent), Japan (37.5 per cent) and the United Kingdom (23 per cent). A further study by O'Dwyer and Owen (2005) of sustainability assurance practice, which focused on assurance statements appearing in the reports of 'leading edge' reporters,[1] provides a possible explanation for the apparent anomalies observed between the KPMG and CPA Australia studies, together with the distinct national differences highlighted in the latter. In the O'Dwyer and Owen (2005) study, while the overall sample split pretty evenly between accountant and consultant assurance providers, accountants were very much to the fore as regards assuring environmental reports (69 per cent of cases) and correspondingly far less prominent in assuring the more substantial social and sustainability reports (36 per cent).

A more recent study by Simnett *et al.* (2009) found that larger and lower leveraged companies, which are domiciled in a stakeholder-oriented country, are more likely to opt for assurance from the accounting profession. However, to muddy the waters somewhat here, while Kolk and Perego's (2010) results confirm that as companies increase in size so they are more likely to choose an accounting firm, their findings contradict those of Simnett *et al.* in that they suggest that companies domiciled in shareholder-oriented countries are more likely to choose accounting providers.

## Towards the standardization of assurance practice

Early academic studies examining the first wave of assurance practice on corporate environmental reports produced throughout the 1990s (Ball *et al.*, 2000; Kamp-Roelands, 2002) raised fundamental concerns about its rigour and usefulness. Kamp-Roelands pointed to major inconsistencies apparent in terms of subject matter addressed, scope of the exercise carried out, objectives, assurance criteria and procedures applied, level of assurance provided and wording of opinions offered. For their part, Ball *et al.* raised even more fundamental question marks over the key issues of assuror independence and degree of thoroughness with which their work was carried out. They particularly drew attention to evidence of managerial control over the whole assurance process which, together with emphasis being placed by assurance providers on management systems as opposed to performance based issues, they argued, greatly limited its potential as a vehicle for enhancing corporate transparency and accountability to external stakeholder groups.

A major problem facing early assurance providers lay in the absence of any clear standards or guidelines that could be used to govern the approach adopted. This concern has been addressed in recent years by the issuing of sustainability assurance practice guidelines that fall into two distinct categories. First, we have the somewhat cautious 'accountancy' based approach of the Fédération des Experts Comptables Européens (FEE, 2002) and the International Auditing and Assurance Standards Board (IAASB) (2004), which are largely concerned with attesting the accuracy of published data and minimizing the liability of the assuror; and second, we have the AccountAbility series of assurance standards (AccountAbility 1999, 2003, 2008a, 2008b, 2011), where the issue of stakeholder engagement is absolutely central to the assurance process.

The 'accountancy' based guidelines appear to be largely informed by traditional financial auditing standards and concepts, together with a desire to formalize the structure of assurance statements issued with the aim of avoiding the creation of any expectation gap 'whereby a user mistakenly assumes that there is more assurance than is actually present' (FEE, 2002, p. 17). While these guidelines exhibit minor differences in emphasis, they are in broad agreement concerning the elements that should make up a sustainability assurance statement (see Table 5.2).

The most influential of the 'accountancy' based standards is IAASB's (2004) International Standard on Assurance Engagements (ISAE) 3000, which applies to all assurance engagements other than audits and reviews accounting of historical financial information. Its application became mandatory for all assurance reports issued by professional accounting bodies dated on or after 1 January 2005. ISAE 3000 provides detailed guidance for conducting assurance work from initial acceptance of the engagement through to the issuance of the

*Table 5.2* Suggested elements of a sustainability assurance report

Report title
Addressee
Identification and description of the subject matter
Statement of the reporting criteria
Description of any limitations on the examination
Delimitation of the respective responsibilities of reporter and assuror
Reference to the use of assurance standards
Summary of the work performed
Conclusion of the assuror
Date of assurance statement
Name and location of assuror

Source: derived from FEE, 2002; IAASB, 2004.

final assuror's report. Of particular note in terms of the latter is the distinction drawn between 'reasonable assurance engagements' and 'limited review engagements' and the related nature of the conclusions that may be respectively drawn:

> The objective of a reasonable assurance engagement is a reduction in assurance engagement risk to an acceptably low level in the circumstances of the engagement as the basis for a *positive* form of expression of the practitioner's conclusion. The objective of a limited assurance engagement is a reduction in assurance engagement risk to a level that is acceptable in the circumstances of the engagement, but where that risk is greater than for a reasonable assurance engagement, as the basis for a *negative* form of expression of the practitioner's conclusion.
>
> (IAASB, 2004, para. 2, emphasis added)

The practitioner's conclusion under a limited assurance engagement employs a highly cautious tone. Whereas in the case of reasonable assurance the practitioner would, for example, conclude that 'internal control is effective', or that assertions are 'fairly stated', under limited assurance the conclusion offered would simply be that 'nothing has come to our attention' to suggest otherwise (IAASB, 2004, para. 49(j)). A further feature of ISAE 3000 is that it is generic in nature in applying to a wide range of non-financial assurance exercises rather than being exclusively concerned with the provision of sustainability assurance. Therefore, although the standard notes, for example, that 'considering materiality requires the practitioner to understand and assess what factors might influence the decisions of intended users' (para. 23), no specific attention is paid to issues such as stakeholder inclusion in the assurance process. Interestingly here, FEE (2004, 2006, 2009) has issued several calls for a specific assurance standard to be introduced for sustainability reports, while certain national standard setters have issued such a standard, with the question of stakeholder needs featuring prominently in those emanating from the Netherlands and Sweden.[2]

Notwithstanding tentative moves on the part of the accounting profession towards the development of specific sustainability assurance standards, the most highly developed stakeholder-centred approach to sustainability assurance undoubtedly appears within the above-mentioned AccountAbility series of standards. The stakeholder-centred emphasis is made explicit in the three guiding principles that underpin the AccountAbility approach – these being inclusivity, materiality and responsiveness. Inclusivity is the 'foundation principle', which states that for 'an organisation that accepts its accountability to those on whom it has an impact and who have an impact on it, inclusivity is the participation of stakeholders in developing and achieving an accountable and strategic response to sustainability' (Accountability, 2008a, p. 10). The materiality principle relates to determining whether an issue is relevant and significant to the organization and its stakeholders. For an issue to be material it will 'influence the decisions, actions and performance of an organisation or its stakeholders' (p. 12). Responsiveness requires an organization to respond to 'stakeholder issues that affect its sustainability performance and is realised through decisions, actions and performance, as well as communication with stakeholders' (p. 14).

AA1000AS is the AccountAbility (2008b) standard relating to assurance and requires assurors to evaluate the extent to which an organization has adhered to the principles together with the quality of the information disclosed regarding sustainability performance. AA1000AS identifies two types of assurance engagement. Type 1 relates to the AccountAbility Principles and 'is intended to give stakeholders assurance on the way an organisation manages sustainability performance, and how it communicates this in its sustainability reporting, without verifying the reliability of the reported information' (AccountAbility, 2008b, p. 10). Type 2 assurance goes further in additionally evaluating the reliability of the sustainability information reported, as agreed in the scope of the engagement and taking into account issues of materiality. AA1000AS also distinguishes between high and moderate levels of assurance. With high levels of assurance the risk of an error in any conclusion is reduced to 'very low' such that users can take a 'high level of confidence' in the disclosures. Moderate levels of assurance reduce the risk of error, but not to 'very low', enhance the users' confidence but not to a 'high level' and require a limited depth of evidence gathering.

In terms of the content of the assurance statement, the specifications of AA1000AS are similar to those identified in Table 5.2. In addition, however, AA1000AS expects the assuror to specify the type of assurance provided (Type 1 or 2), the level of assurance (high or moderate), findings and conclusions related to inclusivity, materiality and responsiveness, and observations and/or recommendations concerning efficacy of underlying systems, reporting quality and performance. The highlighting of progress together with recommendations for improving reporting quality and underlying processes, systems and competencies is a distinguishing feature of the AA1000 approach towards assurance provision. In sum, a more strategic, 'value added approach to assurance is advocated which focuses centrally on the usefulness of the report for stakeholders and is explicitly concerned with driving future performance'. The thinking behind this approach is neatly summarized by Iansen-Rogers and Oelschlaegel (2005) who suggest that:

> While the value of assurance to ensure reliable and comparable data for management and certain user groups still remains, today's assurance process needs to go beyond assessment of accuracy to explore the quality of processes such as stakeholder engagement, and organisational learning and innovation, as well as the way in which the organisation aligns strategy with key stakeholder expectations.
>
> (p. 23)

The above discussion clearly indicates that extant guidelines for providing assurance for corporate sustainability reports fall into two distinct categories. First, we have the somewhat cautious 'accountancy' based approach, as particularly reflected in ISAE 3000, which is largely concerned with attesting to the accuracy of published data, rather than the relevance of such data for external stakeholder groups. Much emphasis is laid here upon identifying the scope of the work undertaken, in particular highlighting any limitations, and the respective responsibilities of reporter and assuror, while clearly stating criteria underpinning the work and any assurance standards employed. An alternative approach is offered by AA1000AS, which recommends that assurance statements offer detailed commentary on the core principles of inclusivity, materiality and responsiveness viewed from a stakeholder perspective, while also providing evaluative commentary designed to enable stakeholders to better perceive both strengths and weaknesses in both the reporting and performance domains. The next section of this chapter, 'A critical overview of sustainability assurance practice', considers how these developments have impacted upon sustainability assurance practice.

## A critical overview of sustainability assurance practice

Despite the issuing of authoritative guidance for carrying out sustainability assurance engagements in recent years, empirical research focusing on the content of published assurance statements highlights a great deal of ambiguity and variability inherent in practice, with particular reservations being expressed concerning its efficacy in enhancing corporate trans-parency and accountability to stakeholder groups. Key issues drawn to attention for example by the comprehensive CPA Australia (2004) study referred to in the earlier section titled 'Recent trends in sustainability assurance practice' include the following:

- variability in the title of assurance statements
- a tendency not to identify an addressee
- a wide range of objectives for, and scope of, the assignment (with the latter typically prescribed by management)
- variation in the amount of description of the nature, timing and extent of the procedures employed, and variability in the wording of the conclusions offered.

Somewhat damningly, the study's authors conclude that, on the basis of these findings, report readers would 'often have great uncertainty in understanding how the assurance provider undertook the engagement, what they reviewed and what was the meaning of their conclusion' (p. 67).

O'Dwyer and Owen's (2005) study of assurance statements appearing in a somewhat smaller sample of 'leading edge' reports adopts much the same approach to that of CPA Australia in subjecting their content to rigorous scrutiny. While a similar variability in assur-ance practice is highlighted, O'Dwyer and Owen do point to some improvements having been made since the earlier study of Ball *et al.* (2000), which employed a closely compara-ble, albeit longitudinal, sampling method drawing upon reports shortlisted for the ACCA (in this case environmental) reporting awards scheme. In particular, it is noted that the extent of work carried out in terms of validating both data systems and data appearing in the report, undertaking site visits and interviewing organizational personnel has noticeably increased; the independence of the exercise is more pronounced, in that the intertwining of the roles of assurance provider and performer of consultancy services observed in the earlier study is now very much the exception. In the relatively rare instances in which the assurance pro-vider has performed additional consultancy services it is noticeable that this fact had been clearly acknowledged in the assurance statement. Additionally, a greater degree of focus on the performance dimension, as opposed to confining attention to management systems issues, was discernible, particularly in the case of the slowly growing number of exercises that employ AA1000 methodology.

Notwithstanding the observed emerging focus on performance issues in assurance state-ments, O'Dwyer and Owen point to a large degree of management control remaining over the whole process. The simple fact is that assurance providers are appointed by management who can place any restrictions they wish upon the exercise. Additionally, as was the case with the CPA Australia study, it was found that to the extent that statements are addressed to anyone, this would be to corporate management, suggesting that any 'value added' by the assurance process accrues to the same constituency. Furthermore, whereas interviewing organizational staff members appears to be becoming a standard feature of the assurance process, interviewing stakeholders is very much the exception.

O'Dwyer and Owen's (2005) study also draws attention to a relatively limited approach aimed at providing low level assurance, generally adopted by accountant assurance provid-ers. They anticipated that future statements provided by accountants applying ISAE 3000 would continue to predominantly adopt a cautious tone. An important factor in this expecta-tion was that fee levels for sustainability assurance work have been relatively low. Evidence from a Swedish-based study by Park and Brorson (2005) of fee levels for sustainability assurance work suggests they are a small fraction, typically between 4 per cent and 6 per cent, of those for the financial audit. More up-to-date and wider reaching evidence is not currently available, but in a survey of UK FTSE 100 companies undertaken for this chapter it was found that, for the eight companies willing to share their data, fees ranged from £26,000 to £100,000 with an average of approximately £50,000.[3] The financial audit fee for these is required to be disclosed and the basic company audit fees for the same companies ranged from £300,000 to over £3,000,000. On average, for this very limited sample, the fee levels for sustainability assurance remain a fraction (usually less than 10 per cent) of financial audit fees and as such would certainly bring into doubt the ability of the sustainability assurors to carry out the necessary amount of substantive testing to justify a positive form conclusion.

Our review of 46 assurance statements on the most recent (2010, 2011) responsibility/sustainability reporting of UK FTSE 100 companies undertaken for this chapter provides more recent data.[4] From this sample 30 of the 46 (65 per cent of the) assurance statements were produced by the 'big 4' accounting firms. All but two of the assurance statements produced by the big 4 accounting firms refer to ISAE 3000 and 12 of these also refer to AA1000. The level of assurance provided is usually limited, but there were five instances where reasonable assurance was provided for particular elements of work performed. The assurance statements produced by the big 4 accounting firms were addressed to directors/management of the company, or to the company itself.

Further, these statements clearly demarcate the respective responsibilities of the directors and the assurors and provide a summary of the work performed. In general it is only in the cases where AA1000 has been utilized that recommendations on areas for improvement are provided. Half of the assurance statements produced by other than the big 4 accounting firms (for example Bureau Veritas and Corporate Citizenship) refer to the AA1000 standards. The assurance provided by these companies is primarily at the moderate level, although there was one instance where high levels of assurance were provided for some aspects of the work performed. These assurance statements are much more likely to include recommendations for improvements than those provided by the big 4 accounting firms. Further, there were three instances of these reports being addressed to 'stakeholders'.

Our review further reveals that assurance statements are increasing in length (often two or more pages long) and include greater levels of commentary on work performed and in some cases areas for improvement. The best examples of this evaluative approach can certainly be argued to 'add value' from the perspective of external stakeholder groups in terms of imparting a far fuller appreciation of the strengths and weaknesses of the sustainability performance of the reporting organization. However, as O'Dwyer and Owen (2005) argue, there is a danger here, in that combining what is essentially a consultancy function with a separate 'arm's length' assurance exercise may compromise the integrity of the latter. As Gray (2000) points out here, once social accounting and auditing moves away from the focus on 'holding the organisation to account', a fundamental principle of the early pioneers of external social auditing practice (see, for example, Medawar, 1976), they run the risk of being confined largely as mere management tools rather than as mechanisms for promoting democratic accountability. Particularly problematical here perhaps is the practice of including praise for the organization's achievements within the assurance statement, which may well only serve to undermine the perceived independence of the assurance provider. Issues of managerial capture and the true nature of stakeholder engagement in the assurance process have been the subject of a number of recent papers and these are considered in the next section, titled 'Perspectives of key actors in the assurance process'.

## Perspectives of key actors in the assurance process

Three recent publications (Owen *et al.*, 2009; Edgeley *et al.*, 2010; O'Dwyer *et al.*, 2011) have provided new evidence on how sustainability assurance is perceived by the three key actors in the assurance process – corporate managers, stakeholders and assurance providers. First, evidence from interviews with corporate managers suggests that they perceive that 'the real driving force behind assurance is internal' (Owen *et al.*, 2009, p. 5) and that the process must, therefore, provide value for money for the company. The major reasons for commissioning assurance are largely concerned with a desire for 'increased confidence in the integrity and reliability of corporate data released in the public domain' (Owen *et al.*, 2009, p. 5) and the potential lessons to be learnt internally for improved data collection and reporting systems. This is consistent with the potential benefits reported in the Introduction to this chapter. Perhaps of more interest was a general perception that stakeholders were currently detached from the assurance process, with an acknowledgement for example that stakeholders do not read assurance statements. Stakeholder panels were suggested to be the most likely way forward to remedy this problem and to encourage greater stakeholder involvement, but even here it was recognized that there are difficult issues associated with how representative of possibly widely diverging stakeholder views such panels can be. This is, of course, equally true of potentially involving 'external experts', either in the form of a panel or to provide individual comment, which was also suggested as providing a means for increasing the level of stakeholder representation in the assurance process.

Owen *et al.* (2009) also interviewed as part of their study a range of different stakeholder representatives. Perhaps unsurprisingly the different stakeholders interviewed had markedly different perceptions as to the value of sustainability assurance. Interviewees from the investment community questioned the relevance of assurance for their own 'decision-making needs' and were not particularly concerned about stakeholder inclusion. Their primary concerns were with regard to 'data integrity and increased synergy with financial reporting and audit practice' (p. 5). Even more dismissive of assurance was the single trade union official interviewed, who expressed fundamental reservations concerning both the competence of the assurors and the institutional legitimacy of the assurance industry itself. The most supportive stakeholder group interviewed were NGO representatives who did indeed suggest a willingness to be involved in the assurance process perhaps through inclusion on stakeholder panels. However, in common with management respondents, they were conscious of the practical difficulties faced in arriving at truly representative panels while also expressing concern that membership might compromise their independence and resource constraints would give rise to 'stakeholder fatigue' should such panels become widespread.

Most fundamentally, Owen *et al.*'s (2009) study also identified a stark difference in opinion between the corporate managers and stakeholders interviewed concerning the issue of to whom assurance statements should be addressed. The former were clear that as commissioners of the exercise assurance statements should be addressed to them. However, for their part, stakeholder interviewees were strongly of the view that, as sustainability reporting itself is purportedly addressed to society at large, it naturally follows that the accompanying assurance statement should also be addressed to society. While at one level this may seem a somewhat trivial dispute it actually raises fundamental questions about the link between reporting and corporate governance systems, to which we will return in the final section of this chapter, titled 'Future development of sustainability assurance practice'.

Edgeley *et al.*'s (2010) study identified a number of key themes arising from their interviews with both accountant and consultant assurance providers. First, both types of assuror perceived that their service could provide benefits to both the management of the assured company and the company's stakeholders. The interviewees also suggested that stakeholder views were being incorporated into the assurance process, although this was most often achieved, particularly by accountant assurors, through 'indirect mechanisms' (such as perusing stakeholder feedback received by the client company or acting as facilitators in bringing management and stakeholders together for meetings) rather than by engaging directly with stakeholders. However, a number of interviewees did express the view that over time as sustainability assurance progresses there is likely to be a move towards increased levels of direct stakeholder involvement. For at least one interviewee, greater stakeholder engagement could potentially enable the assurors to represent stakeholder voices and make the assurance process more 'transformative'. Assurors did raise a concern, however, that managerial control of the assurance process means that 'stakeholder inclusivity is inevitably driven by management, with benefits to stakeholders perhaps viewed as a useful by-product' (Edgeley *et al.*, 2010, p. 550). It was also recognized that the cost, 'ignorance', lack of interest and diversity of stakeholders are all obstacles to greater stakeholder inclusivity.

O'Dwyer *et al.* (2011) also shed light on the sustainability assurance industry through interviews with assurance practitioners within a world-leading professional services firm. Their study provides evidence that in the first instance, given the voluntary nature of the exercise, assurors need to demonstrate that their service will provide benefits to their clients through improved systems and increased credibility. They also suggest that, notwithstanding a clear commitment on the part of practitioners to opening up dialogue within the assurance process, there has been, and continues to be, a problem of stakeholder indifference to sustainability assurance. A further fundamental problem identified in the study 'has been strong resistance from [the professional services firm's] Risk Department [which is responsible for approving the wording of assurance statements] to the expansion of assurance statement content and, relatedly, moving towards providing higher levels of assurance' (p. 49). This resonates with the earlier finding that the vast majority of sustainability assurance statements provide limited levels of assurance. Despite their disclaimers and detailing of the respective responsibilities of report preparers and assurance providers there is evidence here that firms of assurors remain concerned as to their potential liability.

This section has considered further evidence on issues that continue to affect sustainability assurance practice. Of particular importance are: managerial control of the process; limited levels of stakeholder engagement; and assurance providers' (most notably professional accounting firms) unwillingness, or inability, to go further and to provide higher levels of assurance. The final section of this chapter, 'Future development of sustainability assurance practice', considers potential future developments in the sustainability assurance field and questions the extent to which such developments could enhance stakeholder accountability.

## Future development of sustainability assurance practice: towards enhanced stakeholder accountability?

As we have already noted, AccountAbility's approach to assurance has, from the start, been avowedly stakeholder centred, one which has culminated in the continued progress to a final exposure draft (AA1000SES 2011) on the specific issue of stakeholder engagement. We have also seen that the AccountAbility Assurance Standard (AA1000AS) has been adopted in a number of recent sustainability assurance engagements. At the same time, however, the majority of accountant assurance engagements adopt ISAE3000 and it is only in the minority of cases that this is augmented by AA1000AS. Further, evidence from assurance providers and corporate management alike suggests that stakeholder indifference is an issue and that, to date, stakeholder inclusion is most often indirect in nature; direct stakeholder engagement in the assurance process remains the exception rather than the norm. With management driving the assurance process and exercising continued control it would appear that any stakeholder benefits that are likely to accrue are, at best, secondary. In this context it is notable that corporate managers are adamant that assurance statements should be addressed to them, and in the majority of cases (when any addressee at all is identified) this is indeed the case. Significantly, this situation contrasts with stakeholders' views that the assurance statement should be addressed to society at large.

It is pertinent to remember here that sustainability assurance providers are required to sell their services to companies by persuading management that it will improve the company's internal systems and enhance its external credibility (O'Dwyer *et al.*, 2011). As such, the whole case for sustainability assurance and stakeholder engagement seems to be based on persuading companies as to its efficacy as a driver of improved financial value. Further, O'Dwyer *et al.* (2011) argue that sustainability assurors have also tried to tackle the paucity of stakeholder interest by 'identifying and constructing this somewhat mythical audience and then persuading it to confer moral legitimacy on assurance' (p. 49). They continue that assurors' efforts have been to create 'expectations regarding assurance' and therefore an industry within which they can sell their services. Significantly though, no transfer of power whatsoever is being contemplated, whereby stakeholders could hold the organization to account for its activities and actively enforce some degree of responsiveness to their concerns. Adams and Evans (2004), in a detailed analysis of the shortcomings of assurance practice as a vehicle for enhancing stakeholder accountability, go on to suggest concrete ways of transferring some degree of power over the process by, for example, enabling stakeholders to appoint assurance providers and to determine the scope of the exercise. Neither of these suggestions appears to have found favour in practice, but even should they do so it would still beg the question as to how stakeholders can use the assurance findings in any way that might influence organizational decision making.

It seems clear that for extending stakeholder accountability, in the sense of meaningfully holding management to account, the whole issue of sustainability assurance has to be looked at in the context of the wider corporate governance system in which it is embedded. Simply addressing assurance statements to stakeholders (or indeed allowing them to appoint the assurance provider and define the assurance scope) achieves very little if the results of the exercise cannot be used in the same way that shareholders may use the results of the financial audit. Simply, there is a need to bring an external stakeholder dimension into *corporate social responsibility* (CSR) internal governance procedures. A role for stakeholder panels and external experts featured in the thoughts of corporate managers and stakeholders interviewed by Owen *et al.* (2009) and a few companies, National Grid and BT being notable examples, have adopted stakeholder panels. However, in these instances the external participants are appointed by corporate management, rather than by those they purport to represent. Hence they actually represent no one but themselves, and are therefore directly accountable to no one but themselves. By contrast, forums at which stakeholder groups are directly represented (predominantly employee and local community groups) are confined to consultative committee type structures completely separated from key strategic decision-making areas.

Essentially, what is missing in the whole debate over the development of sustainability assurance is some intervention by regulatory authorities in the public policy domain, designed to bring about a greater level of corporate accountability to stakeholder groups. In the current voluntaristic climate dominating matters of CSR policy throughout Europe (see Commission of the European Communities (COM), 2002) this seems highly unlikely to happen. It is indeed instructive in a UK context to note here the specific rejection of introducing a pluralistic approach towards directors' duties, whereby enforceable accountability would be owed to a wider range of stakeholders than merely capital providers, in the long-running debate of company law reform in the UK culminating in the 2002 White Paper (see Owen *et al.*, 2001; Cooper and Owen, 2007). Quite simply, administrative (reporting) reform being promoted by a growing range of assurance standard setters can achieve little in the absence of accompanying institutional reform providing a forum where such reports may be used effectively (Owen *et al.*, 1997).

Frank (2001) in a vigorous de-bunking of the pretensions of what he terms 'market populism', of which unfortunately the current wave of sustainability reporting and associated assurance exercises is increasingly forming an integral part, stresses that:

> What we must have are not more focus groups or a new space where people can express themselves … but some countervailing power, some force that resists the imperatives of profit in the name of economic democracy.
>
> (p. xvii)

By effectively side-stepping crucial issues of corporate governance reform in favour of essentially vacuous notions of stakeholder engagement, sustainability assurance practice, as currently conceived in both the reporting and standard setting arenas, fails to introduce the necessary countervailing power to 'hold to account' and thereby fails to enhance stakeholder accountability.

## Notes

1 The sample comprised reports shortlisted for the 2002 ACCA UK and European Sustainability Reporting Awards.
2 For a detailed analysis of the role of the accounting profession at both international and national levels (with particular reference to developments in Sweden) in the regulation of sustainability assurance see Tan-Sonnerfeldt, 2011.
3 46 companies were approached and so the 8 responses received amount to a 17 per cent response rate. A number of companies did not reply to the request at all, but others did reply to comment that the sustainability assurance fee level was commercially sensitive and so as such they were unwilling to divulge this information even when provided with assurances of confidentiality.
4 The sample comprises all assurance statements accompanying the latest available (as of 21 October 2011) corporate responsibility or sustainability reports published by the FTSE 100 companies. The figure is somewhat lower than the 56 statements forming the basis of KPMG's 2011 analysis. The discrepancy may be due to changes in composition of the FTSE 100 in the time elapsing between the two studies or, more intriguingly, a decline in assurance provision.

## References

AccountAbility (1999) *AA1000 Framework: Standard, Guidelines and Professional Qualification*, Accountability, London.
AccountAbility (2003) *AA1000 Assurance Standard*, AccountAbility, London.
AccountAbility (2008a) *AA1000 Accountability Principles Standard 2008 (AA1000APS)*, AccountAbility, London.
AccountAbility (2008b) *AA1000 Assurance Standard 2008 (AA1000AS)*, AccountAbility, London.
AccountAbility (2011) *AA1000 Stakeholder Engagement Standard (AA1000SES): Final Exposure Draft*, AccountAbility, London.

Adams, C.A. and Evans, R. (2004) Accountability, completeness, credibility and the audit expectations gap, *Journal of Corporate Citizenship* 14: 97–115.

Association of Chartered Certified Accountants (ACCA) and Corporate Register.com (2004) *Towards Transparency: Progress on Global Sustainability Reporting*, ACCA, London.

Ball, A., Owen, D.L. and Gray, R.H. (2000) External transparency or internal capture? The role of third party statements in adding value to corporate environmental reports, *Business Strategy and the Environment* 9(1): 1–23.

Certified Practising Accountants (CPA) Australia (2004) *Triple Bottom Line: A Study of Assurance Statements Worldwide*, CPA Australia, Melbourne, VIC.

Commission of the European Communities (COM) (2002) *Corporate Social Responsibility: A Business Contribution to Sustainable Development*, COM, Brussels.

Cooper, S.M. and Owen, D.L (2007) Corporate social reporting and stakeholder accountability: The missing link, *Accounting, Organizations and Society* 32: 649–67.

Edgeley, R.R., Jones, M.J. and Solomon, J.F. (2010) Stakeholder inclusivity in social and environmental report assurance, *Accounting, Auditing and Accountability Journal* 23(4): 532–57.

Fédération des Experts Comptables Européens (FEE) (2002) *Providing Assurance on Sustainability Reports*, FEE, Brussels.

Fédération des Experts Comptables Européens (FEE) (2004) *FEE Call for Action: Assurance for Sustainability*, FEE, Brussels.

Fédération des Experts Comptables Européens (FEE) (2006) *Key Issues in Sustainability Assurance: An Overview*, FEE, Brussels.

Fédération des Experts Comptables Européens (FEE) (2009) *Policy Statement towards a Sustainable Economy: The Contribution of Assurance*, FEE, Brussels.

Frank, T. (2001) *One Market under God: Extreme Capitalism, Market Populism and the End of Economic Democracy*, Secker and Warburg, London.

Gray, R.H. (2000) Current developments and trends in social and environmental auditing, reporting and attestation: A review and comment, *International Journal of Auditing* 4(3): 247–68.

Iansen-Rogers, J. and Oelschlaegel, J. (2005) *Assurance Standards Briefing: AA1000 Assurance Standard and ISAE3000*, AccountAbility and KPMG, London.

International Auditing and Assurance Standards Board (IAASB) (2004) *International Standard on Assurance Engagements 3000; Assurance Engagements on Other than Audits or Reviews of Historical Information*, International Federation of Accountants, New York.

Kamp-Roelands, N. (2002) Towards a framework for auditing environmental reports, unpublished PhD thesis, Tilburg University, The Netherlands.

Kolk, A. and Perego, P. (2010) Determinants of the adoption of sustainability assurance statements: An international investigation, *Business Strategy and the Environment* 19: 183–98.

KPMG (2005) *KPMG International Survey of Corporate Responsibility Reporting 2005*, KPMG, Amsterdam.

KPMG (2008) *KPMG International Survey of Corporate Responsibility Reporting 2008*, KPMG International Global Sustainability Services, The Netherlands.

KPMG (2011) *KPMG International Survey of Corporate Responsibility Reporting 2011*, KPMG International, Amsterdam.

Medawar, C. (1976) The social audit: A political view, *Accounting, Organizations and Society* 1(4): 389–94.

O'Dwyer, B. and Owen, D.L. (2005) Assurance statement practice in environmental, social and sustainability reporting: A critical evaluation, *British Accounting Review* 37(2): 205–29.

O'Dwyer, B., Owen, D. and Unerman, J. (2011) Seeking legitimacy for new assurance forms: The case of assurance on sustainability reporting, *Accounting, Organizations and Society* 36: 31–52.

Owen, D.L., Gray, R.H. and Bebbington, J. (1997) Green accounting: Cosmetic irrelevance or radical agenda for change? *Asia Pacific Journal of Accounting* 4(2): 175–98.

Owen, D.L., Swift, T. and Hunt, K. (2001) Questioning the role of stakeholder engagement in social and ethical accounting, auditing and reporting, *Accounting Forum* 25(3): 264–82.

Owen, D.L., Chapple, W. and Urzola, A.P. (2009) *Key Issues in Sustainability Assurance, ACCA Research Report 115*, ACCA, London.

Park, J. and Brorson, T. (2005) Experiences of and views on third-party assurance of corporate environmental and sustainability reports, *Journal of Cleaner Production* 13: 1095–106.

SalterBaxter-Context (2005) *Trends in CSR Reporting 2003–2004*, SalterBaxter-Context, London.

Simnett, R., Vanstraelen, A. and Chua, W.F. (2009) Assurance on sustainability reports: An international comparison, *Accounting Review* 84(3): 937–67.

Tan-Sonnerfeldt, A. (2011) The development and use of standards by non-state actors: A study of the dynamics of regulating sustainability assurance, unpublished PhD thesis, Department of Business Law, Lund University, Sweden.

Zadek, S., Raynard, P., Forstater, M. and Oelschlaegel, J. (2004) *The Future of Sustainability Assurance*, ACCA, London.

# 6 The role of stakeholder engagement and dialogue within the sustainability accounting and reporting process

*Leonardo Rinaldi, Jeffrey Unerman and Carol Tilt*

> Stakeholder engagement ... is the process used by an organisation to engage relevant stakeholders for a clear purpose to achieve accepted outcomes. It is now also recognised as a fundamental accountability mechanism, since it obliges an organisation to involve stakeholders in identifying, understanding and responding to sustainability issues and concerns, and to report, explain and be answerable to stakeholders for decisions, actions and performance.
>
> (AccountAbility, 2011, p. 6)

## Introduction

The above quotation encapsulates the key points that are addressed in this chapter. It indicates that engagement and dialogue with stakeholders are increasingly recognized as crucial elements of sustainability accounting and accountability. In addressing these points, the aims of this chapter are to explain:

- why engagement and dialogue with a range of stakeholders are crucial elements of sustainability accounting and accountability;
- the expectations of stakeholders with regards to social and environmental sustainability issues and the information needs of stakeholders that these indicate;
- some of the key difficulties faced when an organization seeks to engage a broad range of stakeholders;
- various theoretical perspectives regarding the prioritization of different stakeholders' needs and expectations;
- some of the stakeholder engagement and dialogue processes employed in practice by organizations.

But before addressing these issues, it will be helpful to define what is meant by the terms *stakeholder* and *stakeholder engagement and dialogue*.

The stakeholders of an organization are any individuals or groups that are either affected by or can affect the operations of that organization. As we shall see in the next section, 'The role of stakeholder engagement', stakeholders can be defined broadly or narrowly. A broad definition encapsulates individuals or groups within society that are very close to the organization along with others that are very remote from the organization (and could even include future generations and nature) all of whose life experiences and interests are impacted in some way by the organization's operations, policies and/or practices. A narrow definition would only include those individuals or groups that are close to the organization in terms of having the strongest ability to affect the success of its operations through the decisions they make. These will vary depending on the context of each organization, so for an organization operating in competitive consumer markets, the buying decisions of individual consumers will have strong economic consequences on the organization, whereas in a monopoly industry they will have less influence; for an organization relying on a limited pool of highly skilled employees, keeping those with these skills satisfied will have a much stronger impact on the success of the organization than will be the case for an organization that draws its employees from a large pool of relatively low-skilled workers. Traditionally, the narrowest definition of stakeholders for commercial organizations only includes the owners (or shareholders/stockholders).

Thomson and Bebbington (2005, p. 517) provide a useful definition of *stakeholder engagement and dialogue* when they state that:

> Stakeholders are involved [in the social and environmental reporting process] in a number of different ways including: identifying what issues are important to report, how well the company has performed on specific issues and how to communicate this performance ... Stakeholder engagement describes a range of practices where organisations take a structured approach to consulting with potential stakeholders.

This importance of stakeholder engagement was further emphasized by AccountAbility in a recent exposure draft on stakeholder engagement (AccountAbility, 2011, p. 7) in stating that:

> Engaging with the individuals, groups of individuals or organisations that are affected by or can affect an organisation's activities [IE: stakeholders], and responding to their concerns makes organisations perform better. It increases their knowledge and contributes to their license to operate. Quality stakeholder engagement can:

- lead to more equitable and sustainable social development by giving those who have a right to be heard the opportunity to be considered in decision-making processes;
- enable better management of risk and reputation;
- allow for the pooling of resources (knowledge, people, money and technology) to solve problems and reach objectives that cannot be reached by single organisations;
- enable understanding of the complex operating environments, including market developments and cultural dynamics;
- enable learning from stakeholders, resulting in product and process improvements;
- inform, educate and influence stakeholders to improve their decisions and actions that will have an impact on the organisation and on society; and
- contribute to the development of trust-based and transparent stakeholder relationships.

As can be seen from the above definitions, stakeholder engagement and dialogue can play an important role more broadly than just as part of sustainability accounting and reporting processes, for example in effectively managing projects and in community planning. However, as the focus of this book is sustainability accounting and accountability (including sustainability reporting), this chapter focuses on stakeholder engagement in sustainability accounting, accountability and reporting.

Having provided a broad overview of the meaning and importance of stakeholder engagement and dialogue, this chapter will now proceed to examine why these processes are central to social and environmental accounting and accountability.

## The role of stakeholder engagement and dialogue in sustainability reporting

To understand why stakeholder engagement and dialogue are crucial elements of sustainability accounting and reporting, it is helpful to place these elements within the context of the overall processes through which organizations decide the shape and content of the reports they publish about the social and environmental impacts of their operations. Several commentators have characterized these social and environmental reporting (SER) practices as a hierarchical staged process, whereby the decisions taken at each stage in the hierarchy determine the issues to be considered and decided in the subsequent stages. For example, Deegan and Unerman (2011, p. 396) argue that there are four broad stages involved in reporting about social and environmental impacts. These stages involve decisions related to the following issues:

- *Why* does the entity wish to disclose publicly information about its social and environmental performance (its motivation for disclosure)?
- Who are the stakeholders *to whom* the social and environmental disclosures will be directed?
- *What* information and issues should the social and environmental disclosures address (what are the social and environmental information needs of the stakeholders)?
- *How* should the reports be compiled, in terms of the format of the social and environmental sustainability information to be disclosed?

The first issue – *why* would an entity decide to report – relates to managers' philosophical motivations driving them to release social and environmental information in situations where publishing such information is not mandatory (in some countries, publication of some social and environmental information is required by regulations). These broad objectives for voluntary disclosure (beyond any minimum required by regulations) may vary on a continuum between a wholly economically focused aim at one end, through to a wholly ethically motivated desire at the other end. Motivations towards the purely economical end of the continuum tend to be classified in the academic literature as *strategic* whereas motivations incorporating a reasonable amount of ethical reasoning tend to be classified as *holistic*.

Once the philosophical underpinnings of the motives to engage in sustainability reporting have been established, these will in turn drive decisions related the second issue – who are the stakeholders *to whom* the social and environmental disclosures will be directed – concerning *to whom* an organization considers itself responsible and accountable if it is to achieve its philosophical objectives. The subsequent issue – *what* information and issues should the social and environmental disclosures address – deals with the social, environmental, ethical and economic information demands of the identified stakeholders and therefore what types of information need to be disclosed to meet these information needs. Finally, the last stage in the sustainability reporting process involves decisions related to the format of the information to be disclosed.

Although the focus of this chapter is the '*what*' stage, in the following sections we will arrange the analysis of sustainability accounting and reporting practices in accordance with the above model, since decisions taken at the early stages ('*why?*' and '*to whom?*') have the potential to shape the stakeholder dialogue and engagement processes employed by organizations to ascertain stakeholders' information needs and expectations.

***The 'why?' stage: understanding organizational motives for stakeholder engagement and dialogue***

While there may be a combination of different motives driving any organization's SER, the literature examining these motives can be roughly divided into two perspectives (which may be viewed as at the two opposite ends of the strategic/holistic continuum explained above).

One of these perspectives regards SER as a tool used by managers to win or retain the support of those stakeholders who have power to influence the achievement of an organization's goals (usually maximization of profit). Various theoretical perspectives (such as legitimacy theory and institutional theory, as discussed in other chapters of this book) highlight how social and environmental reports can be strategically used almost as a marketing tool, aimed at aligning perceptions of an organization's social and environmental policies and practices with the ethical values of its economically powerful stakeholders.

Social and environmental reporting strategically driven by a profit-oriented, economic, motive will not be referred to as *sustainability reporting* in this chapter, but will be referred to as *social and environmental reporting*.

The other broad perspective regards sustainability accounting and reporting as processes that should be aimed at transforming business practices so they become socially and environmentally sustainable. Proponents of this holistic perspective often argue that a continual drive for short-term economic sustainability (in the form of maintenance of growth in short-term quarterly or annual financial profits) is incompatible in practice with social and environmental sustainability, as the generation of financial profits is almost always accompanied directly and/or indirectly by negative social and environmental impacts (Gray, 2006). Issues such as unequal distribution of income, over-consumption of finite resources and climate change are considered by many to be among the most urgent problems and challenges facing society (and organizations) today (Hopwood *et al.*, 2010). These challenges have the potential to drive fundamental changes in ecosystems and society which in turn put increasing pressure on the economy given their 'impact on the quality, availability and price of resources, including water, food and energy' (IIRC, 2011, p. 4). From this perspective, therefore, we argue that SER can only be regarded as *sustainability reporting* if it is structured in such a manner as to help in holding the organization (or its managers) responsible and accountable for all of their substantive social and environmental impacts on all stakeholders – not just for those impacts or activities prioritized by the organization's managers.

***The 'to whom?' stage: linking stakeholder identification to motives for reporting***

Having determined the broad philosophical motives or objectives underpinning why an organization wishes to produce a sustainability or social and environmental report, the next stage in the reporting process involves identifying *to whom* the organization needs to report if it is to achieve these philosophical objectives. This identification of stakeholders has to take place after the philosophical motives for engaging in corporate social responsibility (CSR) and SER have been determined, because the range of stakeholders to be taken into consideration by any organization will be directly dependent upon its motives for engaging in CSR and SER.

For example, a corporation whose managers undertake CSR and SER because they believe this will maximize shareholder economic value (or maximize profits) will tend to focus only on those stakeholders who are able to exert the greatest economic influence on the organization's operations (Archel *et al.*, 2009, 2011; Solomon *et al.*, 2013). As noted in the Introduction to this chapter, these will vary depending on the context of the corporation and the sector in which it operates. For an oil company whose sales are largely in competitive markets and some of whose operations require highly skilled employees, customers and skilled employees would probably be among the economically powerful stakeholders. In contrast, for a water utility, where customers have little choice in the corporation from which they purchase their water and sewerage services, individual customers are likely to have relatively little economic power, whereas a government appointed regulator is likely to have considerable influence on the profits the corporation is able to earn. Attracting and retaining highly skilled employees in some parts of the water utility's operations may also be important in generating high profits. Such employees may therefore be important for both the oil company and the water utility, whereas the economic power of consumers and regulators varies considerably between the two sectors, and will have a different level of influence if the motives underlying SER are the maximization of economic value for shareholders.

Conversely, managers whose motives for engaging in CSR and sustainability reporting are grounded in a broader moral philosophy, of being responsible, responsive and accountable to all those upon whom their organization's activities might impact, are likely to be concerned with the whole of this broader range of stakeholders – rather than a narrower group of stakeholders whose needs are prioritized simply because the stakeholders' actions can impact upon the organization (Deegan and Unerman, 2011; Solomon *et al.*, 2011).

Reinforcing the above views, and in view of the risk that in practice stakeholder engagement and reporting could become an oversimplified part of corporate strategy, Mason and Simmons (2014) recommend broadening the traditional shareholder focused approach to organization–stakeholder relationships through the adoption of a more holistic approach and integrating company, shareholder and wider stakeholder concerns within companies' governance structures. From this perspective a lack of adequate stakeholder involvement, through limiting stakeholder influence, has the potential to undermine the effectiveness of the engagement and reporting processes (Smith *et al.*, 2011). Instead, it is argued that stakeholders should be consistently included in the development of organizational objectives and in the determination of the engagement and reporting scope, up to the dissemination of the outcomes (Greenwood and Kamoche, 2013; Clark *et al.*, 2014). As a key element in this, Huang *et al.* (2010) examined the influence of stakeholders (namely the role played by shareholders, investors, government, lenders, consumers, suppliers, competitors and employees) in clarifying the needs and expectations of multiple interest groups in Taiwan. The results show that the level of environmental disclosure is significantly affected by the relative influence of stakeholder groups.

### The 'what?' stage: moving from stakeholder identification to stakeholder engagement and dialogue

Once the stakeholders who are the audience for an organization's SER have been identified, the third broad stage in the SER process is, according to Deegan and Unerman (2011), to identify the social, environmental and economic expectations of these stakeholders. This stage is crucial because these expectations will indicate both what behaviour these stakeholders require and consider acceptable from the organization, and the information needed by these stakeholders to enable them to judge the organization's performance in relation to these expectations.

Only when an organization knows for *what* issues its identified stakeholders regard it as being responsible and accountable can it then begin to produce a social and environmental report which addresses these specific issues. In other words, an organization cannot determine how to compile an effective social and environmental report – for example, to decide upon which issues to address in the report – until it has identified its stakeholders' information needs and expectations, because without these any resultant social and environmental report will be providing information which is not targeted at any particular purpose. Without appropriate targeting of the information, its purpose and impact is questionable (AccountAbility, 2011).

Some social and environmental issues may be considered across a particular society to be so important that processes and practices related to these issues are mandated by law, for example some health and safety issues and requirements to consult with trade unions on some employment-related issues in some countries. Managers are likely to have much less discretion in deciding whether or not to report specific information related to these mandatory issues, and therefore will have much less need to use stakeholder engagement and dialogue processes to identify the information they need to disclose on these matters where the reporting requirements are set out in regulations – although they may have discretion to engage in voluntary reporting on these issues to disclose information beyond the minimum mandated by regulations.

For disclosures on social and environmental issues where there are no mandatory requirements, organizations need to identify the expectations and therefore the information needs of their stakeholders to target the reporting towards meeting these information needs. Without this targeting, only by luck will a social and environmental report address the information needs of, or discharge duties of accountability which the organization has to, its identified stakeholders. Consequently the report would be an ineffective mechanism for systematically holding the organization, and its managers, accountable for the social, environmental and economic impacts which the organization's actions may have upon its identified stakeholders. This is a key reason why engagement and dialogue with stakeholders is a crucial element of sustainability reporting (Dillard and Yuthas, 2013).

Having established the importance of stakeholder engagement and dialogue to SER, the next section, 'Stakeholder expectations for social, environmental and sustainability accounting and accountability', considers the expectations that various stakeholders may have about current and future social and environmental sustainability actions and subsequent disclosure made by organizations.

## Stakeholder expectations for social, environmental and sustainability accounting and accountability

The academic and practitioner literature indicates many diverse stakeholder groups that can and do use information disclosed in social and environmental, or sustainability, reports and are important in sustainability accounting and accountability more broadly. Common among these are: shareholders, investors, insurers, banks, customers, suppliers, employees, trade unions, non-governmental organizations (NGOs) and the media. NGOs are often proxies for other stakeholders who cannot directly take part in stakeholder dialogue processes, such as nature, future generations of humans, or groups of present generations with limited ability or capacity to engage in debate and dialogue.

### Shareholders and investors

Research investigating attitudes among shareholders towards the importance of social and environmental sustainability disclosure indicates reasonably strong interest from this group of stakeholders. A survey over a decade ago of 939 adults in the UK found that 87 per cent of respondents considered that if they were shareholders, they would have expected to see a copy of a company's social report. O'Rourke (2003, p. 228) presented evidence that some shareholders at that time were becoming active in lobbying on certain issues and were therefore being 'targeted by social and environmental activists'. Activists as a stakeholder group, in the form of NGOs, are considered later in this section.

Growing interest in responsible investment demonstrates the desire of many shareholders to invest in companies that incorporate ethical issues into their decision-making and ownership practices and so better align their objectives with those of society at large (PRI, 2013). In this area, the United Nations-supported Principles for Responsible Investment Initiative (PRI) is a network of international investors working together to put the six Principles of the PRI into practice. At the time of writing this chapter, more than 1,100 investors and investment managers from more than 50 countries, with combined assets under management of more than US$32 trillion, were signatories to the PRI (PRI, 2013).

The overall aims of the PRI are to understand the implications of sustainability for investors as well as to provide guidance to signatories for implementation of the principles into their investment decision making. It is argued that PRI adoption would have the potential to better align investors with broader objectives of society. The PRI principles comprise the guidelines typified in Table 6.1.

These forms of responsible investment seem to be growing globally. For example, the 2012 *Report on Sustainable and Responsible Investing Trends* in the United States found that sustainable and responsible investing in the USA accounted for 11.23 per cent of all assets under professional management at the end of 2011. According to the report, US$3.74 trillion out of US$33.3 trillion investment assets were held by individuals, institutions, investment companies or money managers that practised sustainable and responsible investing strategies (Sustainable Investment Forum (SIF), 2013). This reflects the growing interest of investors in considering environmental, social and corporate governance (ESG) issues to refine the way in which they make decisions as they select and manage their portfolios or raise their voices as shareholders. The UK, according to the UK SIF Foundation (UK-SIF, 2013), ranks second to Australia (among over 26 countries) in signatories, and its members include pension funds, asset managers, research providers, financial advisers, banks and NGOs.

Reinforcing the above insights, Clarkson *et al.* (2010) found that voluntary environmental disclosure was critical for investors to assess the impact of environmental compliance on future operations and financial performance. This form of disclosure provided insights for investors in helping to assess firm value through a more accurate assessment of a firm's environmental risks and future environmental liabilities. Similar considerations might also be applicable to voluntary disclosure of compliance with a range of social regulations.

### Insurers and banks

Incorporating and integrating ESG issues into their key processes, including reporting, is also perceived as an area of concern for insurers and banks in their money management activities (PRI, 2013).

*Table 6.1* Principles for responsible investments

| | |
|---|---|
| *Incorporating environmental, social and corporate governance (ESG) issues into investment analysis and decision-making processes* | This principle can be achieved, for instance, by: addressing ESG-related matters in investment policy statements; supporting development-related metrics, analyses and tools; assessing the capabilities of both internal and external investment managers to incorporate ESG issues; and promoting appropriate training. |
| *Incorporating ESG issues into ownership policies and practices* | Fulfilling this proposition would imply the development and disclosure of an ownership policy consistent with the Principles for Responsible Investment (PRI), but also taking an active role in the development of policy, regulation and standard setting as well as participating in collaborative engagement initiatives. |
| *Seeking appropriate disclosure on ESG issues by the entities in which organizations invest* | Possible actions in this area include demanding standardized reporting on ESG issues (using tools such as the Global Reporting Initiative (GRI) (GRI 2013); asking for ESG to be integrated within annual financial reports (using frameworks such as those of the International Integrated Reporting Council (IIRC) (IIRC, 2013); and requiring companies to provide information about the adoption of/ adherence to relevant norms, standards, codes of conduct or international initiatives (such as the UN Global Compact, 2013). |
| *Promoting acceptance and implementation of the PRI within the investment industry* | This may involve the alignment of investment mandates; monitoring procedures, performance indicators and incentive structures to reflect long-term time horizons; revisiting the relationships with partners that fail to meet ESG expectations; and supporting regulatory developments that enable implementation of the PRI. |
| *Working in partnership to enhance the effectiveness in implementing the principles* | This principle may involve collectively addressing relevant emerging ESG issues and developing or supporting collaborative initiatives. |
| *Reporting on activities and progress towards implementing the principles* | This may need: disclosure of the extent to which ESG issues are integrated within investment practices; disclosing ownership activities (voting, engagement and policy dialogue); seeking to determine the impact of the PRI; and making use of reporting to raise awareness among a broader group of stakeholders. |

Two of the most relevant environmental and social responsibility initiatives among this group of financial sector stakeholders are the United Nations Environment Programme (UNEP) Finance Initiative and the Equator Principles. Under these initiatives, banks are encouraged to consider long-term thinking based on a multi-stakeholder engagement process as being key to their success (UNEP FI, 2011).

The Finance Initiative (FI) within UNEP is a global partnership between UNEP and the global financial sector supported by over 200 financial institutions (the Signatories) and a range of partner organizations. Its aim is to develop and promote the adoption of best environmental and sustainability practice at all levels of financial institution operations (UNEP FI, 2010), indicating a demand for sustainability information to be provided by the projects funded by supporters of the FI to help them assess the sustainability impact of these projects.

The Equator Principles are an 'industry benchmark for determining, assessing and managing social and environmental risk in project financing' (Equator Principles Association,

2006, p. 1). The signatories of the principles, the Equator Principles Financial Institutions, have consequently adopted them 'in order to ensure that the projects they finance are developed in a manner that is socially responsible and reflect sound environmental management practices' (Equator Principles Association, 2006, p. 1). Bhimani *et al.* (2010) explored HSBC's adoption of the principles showing how the bank systematically took sustainability risks into account while assessing major project finance loan applications. They found that through application of the Equator Principles, HSBC could substantially influence its sustainability practices and required sustainability information from the projects to which it lent.

### Consumers and suppliers

Spence and Rinaldi (forthcoming) shed light on the role of accounting in identifying areas of concern from consumers and suppliers. In this case the implementation of a sustainability assessment tool revealed pressure being exerted on the case study company (in the food industry) by these stakeholders on particular issues, such as: harm/health of livestock; excessive packaging; difficulty of recycling packaging; and energy use for consumption. Some of these issues were addressed and reported by the case study organization in its subsequent sustainability disclosures.

Related to the influence of consumers is the pressure applied by trading partners within the supply chain. In the context of a globalized economy, many organizations are currently selecting their trading partners in a way that considers not just the organizations' own operations, but also addresses impacts of their business partners in the supply chain. The Global Reporting Initiative (GRI), for instance, has established a Supply Chain Disclosure Working Group whose objective is to develop recommendations regarding changes to the GRI Sustainability Reporting Guidelines to improve the quality of performance disclosure with respect to supply chains. In this regard, the next generation of GRI's Sustainability Reporting Guidelines (G4) requires organizations to explain and report practices in relation to the following aspects of supply chain management (GRI, 2012, 2013):

- *[S]upply chain profile:* describing the organization's supply chain and reporting any significant changes during the reporting period regarding the organization's supply chain, including changes in the location of suppliers, the structure of the supply chain, or in relationships with suppliers, including selection and termination.
- *[S]upply chain governance*: reporting processes for the highest governance body to ensure conflicts of interest are avoided and managed. Also to report conflicts of interest including, cross-shareholding with suppliers and other stakeholders. The proportion of spending on local suppliers at significant locations of operation should also be reported.
- *Suppliers' environmental impact*, including reporting significant potential negative direct and indirect impacts concerning: energy use and consumption, greenhouse gases and emissions, and supplier environmental assessment.
- *Suppliers' social impact*: including reporting significant potential negative impacts about the following categories:
  - labour practices (including Occupational Health and Safety and Supplier Assessment for Labour Practices);
  - human rights (including Freedom of Association and Collective Bargaining, Child Labour, Forced and Compulsory Labour and Supplier Human Rights Assessment);
  - society (including Supplier Assessment for Impacts on Society).

It can be argued, therefore, that sustainability reporting constitutes an important instrument through which stakeholders can be informed about the extended social, economic, environmental, ethical and social impact of organizations through their supply chains. A notable example directed to enhance sustainability and transparency in the supply chain is represented by the UN Global Compact's practical guidance on how to develop a sustainable supply chain programme (UN Global Compact Advisory Group, 2010). The guide is designed to help organizations initiate and advance their supply chain sustainability efforts and stimulate collective action for sustainability. It also 'demonstrates how the organization influences and is influenced by [internal and external stakeholders'] expectations about sustainability' (UN Global Compact Advisory Group, 2010, p. 63).

### Employees and trade unions

Pressure imposed by employees and trade union stakeholder groups represents another factor capable of influencing the understanding of organizations' social and environmental responsibilities as part of their social and environmental accounting and accountability practices.

As the needs and expectations of employees are closely linked to organizations' prospects, employees have often become particularly concerned about organizational approaches regarding environmental impacts. As observed by Jain *et al.* (2011), employees have realized that negative environmental outcomes have the potential to lead to penalties, or cause reputational damage and ensuing losses, thus eventually putting their rights and interests as employees at risk.

Huang and Kung (2010) observed how trade unions can contribute to influencing the level of organizations' environmental disclosure. Where employees are more organized they can:

> use unions or some special corporate agency (for example, a special sector responsible for handling environment-related affairs) to make sure their voices reach the managerial levels in the firm. Under such pressure from employees, a firm may actively implement environmental strategies and carry through on its social responsibilities.
>
> (Huang and Kung, 2010, p. 440)

Consistent with the above findings, Spence (2009) found that employees (along with investors) are by far the most important audiences targeted by corporate sustainability directors. On the basis of interviews with corporate SER managers from 25 firms in the UK context, recognition of 'employees as an audience' was not only a desirable issue in itself but also considered to be a means that could drive employee motivation and lead to (economic) performance improvement (KPMG, 2011).

Trade unions are becoming more systematically involved in the sustainability agenda. In the UK, for example, the Trades Union Congress (TUC) has a Trades Union Sustainable Development Advisory Committee (TUSDAC) that seeks to influence both national policy and investments strategies. Among the aims of the unions is encouragement of organizations to think about how their activities impact upon the environment (TUC, 2013a). As many union members pay into pensions that are invested on their behalf in companies across world stock markets, another way unions seek to have influence is through the network of union members who are trustees in pension funds and encouraging the companies they invest in to be more responsible about the environment (TUC, 2013b). By their nature, trade unions will also be interested in many social impacts of organizations, most notably those related to employment practices and working conditions, such as payment of a living wage, health and safety practices and equality and diversity in employment practices. These social factors are key elements of sustainable development alongside environmental sustainability and a range of other elements of social and economic sustainability.

### Non-governmental organizations (NGOs)

As noted at the beginning of this section, NGOs often act as proxies for stakeholders who are unable to give effective voice to their own concerns and interests, so are unable to directly participate in stakeholder dialogue and engagement initiatives. These stakeholders include humans who do not have capacity to engage in dialogue (such as small children, or those with some types of mental impairment, or future generations) and non-humans (such as animals and nature more broadly). Collectively, NGOs, particularly international NGOs such as Amnesty International, Friends of the Earth, Greenpeace and Oxfam, have had 'notable influence on developments in [sustainability reporting]' (Gray *et al.*, 1996, p. 128). For example, O'Sullivan and O'Dwyer (2009) examined the emergence of NGOs as a specific stakeholder demanding change in accounting and accountability practices of financial institutions. The research revealed how NGO campaigns for greater financial institution responsibility and accountability coupled with NGOs' 'counter accounting' practices challenged some of the world's leading financial institutions and forced them to address NGO concerns ('counter accounting ... encompass[es] information and reporting systems employed by NGOs in order to promote their causes or counter prevailing official positions' (O'Sullivan and O'Dwyer, 2009, p. 577)).

Consistent with these insights, Arenas *et al.* (2009) found that NGOs have developed new forms of engagement with business, based on a combination of confrontation and collaboration strategies. Through these partnerships, NGOs are able to 'promote social and environmental actions, provide technical assistance to corporations, elaborate commonly agreed certification schemes, promote and design corporate social responsibility ... standards as well as management and reporting processes, and participate in [corporate social responsibility] monitoring and auditing' (Arenas *et al.*, 2009, p. 176).

There are a number of examples of firms and NGOs entering into collaborations, some of which include collaborating on the production of sustainability reports. In this context, focusing on Central African countries, Kolk and Lenfant (2010) explored the cooperation between multinational corporations and NGOs, examining corporate reporting practices on CSR and conflicts. Results seemed to suggest that companies engage in partnerships with NGOs to have a better understanding of measurement and reporting of their sustainability performance. With respect to most issues (such as corporations meeting basic needs; contributing to development; social justice; corporate efforts against poverty and hunger; helping the poor climb out of poverty; reducing the causes of poverty and social vulnerability; improving the lives of stakeholders) the wording used by these corporations in their reporting appears to resemble in some respects the wording used by NGOs in their own campaigns on these issues.

### The media

The media is said to reflect the changing values of the public, and may also influence companies' activities in that the media often have substantial power to project a view both of what is considered important to society and the social and environmental impacts of any other organization (van Huijstee and Glasbergen, 2008). In this respect, higher company visibility and media exposure have been found to be positively associated with sustainability disclosure (Gamerschlag *et al.*, 2011; Michelon, 2011).

Islam and Deegan (2008) interviewed senior executives from a major organization in Bangladesh about their motivations for social reporting. The findings showed that pressures emanating from the media created a perceived need for the organizations to respond. However, it was not a single event that resulted in accounting and accountability processes being employed. Rather 'it was the concerns that these events caused for multinational buying companies and other international stakeholders and the corresponding impacts these concerns will have on the survival of the industry that motivated the industry to react' (Islam and Deegan, 2008, p. 863). A similar result was found in Islam and Deegan (2010) who explored how social and environmental NGOs used the media as a vital component of their strategies to create changes in corporate social and environmental operations and related disclosure practices. With reference to a study that explored buying behaviours of multinational organizations in the Bangladesh clothing industry, the research showed that NGOs believed that their ability to create change would be greatly eroded without media coverage of their concerns.

Building on the above overview of the demand and need stakeholders have for social environmental and sustainability reporting, the next section of this chapter, 'Issues in stakeholder engagement and dialogue' proceeds to address some of the key issues and difficulties involved in the implementation of stakeholder engagement and dialogue processes.

## Issues in stakeholder engagement and dialogue

### *Identifying the range of stakeholders to be considered*

The first issue that needs to be addressed in the implementation of any stakeholder engagement and dialogue process is the identification of stakeholders with whom the organization seeks to communicate. As indicated in the earlier subsection, 'The "*to whom?*" stage', the range of stakeholders whose views are considered in any organization's stakeholder engagement and dialogue processes will be dependent upon the organization's (or its managers') motives for engaging in CSR and social and environmental accounting and accountability.

For an organization using SER strategically to help maximize shareholder value, those stakeholders with the most economic power will usually be significant in the organization's day-to-day operations. They are consequently likely to be readily identifiable by the organization and may also be readily accessible through communication media prevalent in the areas where the organization operates. For example, a multinational corporation with a head office in a Western nation and whose products are sold primarily in Western nations may find that most of its economically powerful stakeholders are also based in Western nations. A multinational such as this can use a range of interactive communication media prevalent in Western nations (such as the internet, focus groups, opinion research) to engage in dialogue with, and to help identify, its economically powerful Western stakeholders' social, environmental and economic expectations (Swift *et al.*, 2001).

Conversely, where the motives of an organization's managers for engaging in CSR and sustainability reporting are based on a more holistic concern to be responsible and accountable for their impact on all those upon whom they have an impact, the process of identifying and engaging in dialogue with this broad range of stakeholders is likely to be much more problematic for several reasons, as explored in the subsections below.

### Impossibility of direct dialogue and engagement with some stakeholders

As organizational actions which take place today can, in many instances, have long-term impacts on nature and society, stakeholders affected by an organization's operations are likely to include future generations (WCED, 1987). It is difficult to conceive how an organization can directly engage stakeholders from future generations in dialogue today regarding current organizational responsibilities and accountabilities. Certain groups of contemporary stakeholders (such as some NGOs) might position themselves as guardians of specific interests of future generations, but engaging in dialogue with such 'proxy' stakeholder groups may involve a vicarious representation of the interests of future generations which may be different from the actual interests yet to be judged by the future generations themselves (Unerman and O'Dwyer, 2006).[1]

Similar issues arise when recognizing that an organization's actions might impact on a range of non-human stakeholders today, such as fauna other than humans (Singer, 1993), or, more broadly, on the ecosystem (Meadows *et al.*, 2004; Gray, 2006), and/or on some human stakeholders who are less able to articulate their own concerns and interests (for example, infants or the mentally impaired). These difficulties have not been resolved in the academic literature; however, some countries have sought to enshrine in law the interests of non-human and future generations. The Ecuadorian constitution, for example, gives constitutional rights to nature and recognizes the rights of future generations (see Republic of Ecuador, 2008, Title II, chap. 7; Title VII, chap. 2).

### Addressing heterogeneous stakeholder views and expectations

Even if all stakeholders who are affected (or likely to be affected) by an organization's actions were in a position to articulate their own interests, the needs and expectations of different stakeholders may be mutually exclusive (Lehman, 1995; Neu *et al.*, 1998; Unerman and Bennett, 2004). Faced with a range of mutually exclusive demands from different stakeholders, managers need a mechanism to determine which social, environmental and economic needs and expectations they will seek to address in their CSR and SER. For managers of organizations strategically motivated to engage in CSR and SER by a belief that these processes will enhance shareholder value, choosing between mutually exclusive stakeholder demands is likely to be fairly straightforward – as they will simply prioritize the demands of those stakeholders with the most economic power over the organization (Adams, 2002; O'Dwyer, 2003). Furthermore, in situations where any of the economically powerful stakeholders of a multinational corporation are likely to share a broadly similar cultural background (because for example they are mostly from the wealthier sections of Western nations), it may be expected that these stakeholders' broad social, environmental and economic expectations will often be similar if, as argued by some, these expectations are largely dependent upon shared cultural and social backgrounds (Lewis and Unerman, 1999). In such situations, it may be expected that multinationals whose managers regard themselves as responsible and accountable solely to those stakeholders with the most economic power over their organization will face a largely homogenous set of broad social, environmental and economic expectations and demands from their selected (often relatively wealthy, predominantly Western) stakeholders.

However, managers who are motivated to engage in CSR and sustainability reporting by a desire to minimize the negative social, environmental and economic impacts of their organization's operations on all those stakeholders who are affected by these operations will face greater problems in identifying a single set of stakeholder expectations from a wide range of what may sometimes be mutually exclusive expectations (Unerman and Bennett, 2004; Thomson and Bebbington, 2005).

### *Prioritizing stakeholder needs on the basis of maximum negative consequences*

One way to identify a single set of expectations would be to prioritize the needs and expectations of those stakeholders upon whose lives the organization's operations have (or are likely to have) the greatest negative impact. But there are several problems with this method of prioritizing stakeholder needs. First, it may in practice fail to recognize, solicit or incorporate the views of some stakeholders upon whose lives the organization's operations cause a substantial negative impact in situations where there are other stakeholders whose lives are impacted to a much greater negative extent by the organization's operations and are much more visible to the organization and society. Second, it assumes that the negative impacts caused by an organization's operations on each stakeholder can be assessed with a reasonable degree of certainty. And third, it presupposes that it is possible to objectively rank the negative impacts suffered by different stakeholders in order to determine which stakeholder suffers the most from the organization's operations. In practice, any ranking of this nature is likely to be based (at least in part) on the subjective perceptions of the person observing the outcome of the organization's actions, and two observers with slight differences between their respective value systems may place different weightings on different outcomes, thereby resulting in different rankings of the significance of perceived negative outcomes suffered by different stakeholders.[2]

### *Negotiating a consensus among mutually exclusive stakeholder views through discourse ethics*

An alternative method of seeking to arrive at a single set of stakeholder expectations from among competing stakeholder claims and expectations, while still prioritizing the needs of those who are the most negatively affected by an organization's operations, has been advocated by Unerman and Bennett (2004). This method is based on the discourse ethics of Jürgen Habermas (1990), which provide a theoretical model for arriving at a consensus view of moral standards and values within a society through the use of discourse mechanisms (see also Alexy, 1978).

In summary, these discourse ethics mechanisms rely upon two key philosophical propositions. The first of these is derived from Immanuel Kant's (1949) eighteenth-century philosophical proposition of the Categorical Imperative (which has influenced numerous philosophers since Kant), and judges the validity of any moral proposition by the willingness of the person proposing this moral value to accept its validity in all possible situations. In other words, actions which are considered acceptable to someone with power, wealth and privilege would only be considered morally acceptable if that person would consider these actions to be equally morally acceptable if they lost their power and wealth, and were looking at (and experiencing) the outcomes of these actions from the position of the least privileged members of society (Rawls, 1971; Lehman, 1995).

The second key mechanism within Habermas's framework required to arrive at a universally acceptable and accepted consensus regarding the morality of behaviour is that each person's moral values and arguments should be tested and evaluated through debate with others who may hold alternative views. But for this process to work, it is important that specific protocols of debate are observed so that the force of the better argument is recognized and accepted by all. The rules of debate proposed by Habermas to ensure that the debate produces and recognizes the 'best' arguments are termed an *ideal speech situation* and, in addition to requiring each participant to engage in the debate openly, honestly, and with willingness to recognize and accept the force of the better argument, they require that:

1. Every subject with the competence to speak and act is allowed to take part in a discourse.
2. (a) Everyone is allowed to question any assertion whatever.
   (b) Everyone is allowed to introduce any assertion whatever into the discourse.
   (c) Everyone is allowed to express [their own] attitudes, desires and needs.
3. No speaker may be prevented, by internal or external coercion, from exercising [their own] rights as laid down in (1) and (2).

(Alexy, 1978, p. 40, as quoted in Habermas, 1990, p. 89)

Unerman and Bennett (2004) argue that although the requirements of an *ideal speech situation* debate are unlikely to ever be realized in practice, they have the potential to inform stakeholder dialogue processes. In other words, these ideal speech procedures should not be regarded as 'all-or-nothing', but should be regarded as one end of a continuum ranging from no democratically informed procedures to a full ideal speech situation debate (see also Power and Laughlin, 1996). Unerman and Bennett argue that any movement along this continuum away from managers simply taking into account the information needs of only those stakeholders with the greatest economic power over achievement of the organization's objectives, and towards a democratic debate among all stakeholders who are affected by the organization's actions, is desirable and should not be sacrificed simply because the full 'ideal speech situation' is unachievable in practice. In the context of the distinction made at the beginning of this chapter between sustainability reporting (aimed at helping realize social, environmental and economic sustainability) and SER (motivated by an imperative to increase profits irrespective of negative social and environmental impacts which may arise), any movement towards a democratic consensus in the determination of organizational social, environmental and economic responsibilities and accountability should help move us away from profit-oriented strategic SER and towards more holistic sustainability reporting.

Among the latest academic studies that have analysed stakeholder engagement and that can be interpreted from the perspective of the ideal speech situation are Barone *et al.* (2013) and Brown and Dillard (2013). Barone *et al.* (2013) examined the attitudes of a large set of stakeholder groups towards the level of stakeholder engagement and accountability as well as CSR reporting during a major economic takeover. Despite its valuable theoretical potential for rendering visible sustainability related responsibilities, the evidence suggests that the stakeholder engagement exercise operationalized by the organization represented little more than a reputation damage limitation exercise, rather than a genuine move towards democratic consensus.

Brown and Dillard (2013), on the other hand, discuss the limits of consensual deliberation and argue that greater acknowledgement of difference and conflict in any accounting situation can help facilitate transformative social change (for example towards greater sustainability). It is argued that emphasizing the potentially positive aspects of certain conflicts (for instance between competing stakeholders' needs and expectations) would allow for diversity and help develop a more enabling accounting (Brown and Dillard, 2013, p. 177) and overcome the limits of consensus (see Bond, 2011, for a detailed discussion).

The next section of this chapter, 'Evidence of stakeholder engagement in practice', examines further evidence of stakeholder engagement and dialogue practices to see how well they measure up to the principles discussed above.

## Evidence of stakeholder engagement in practice

So far this chapter has explored a variety of issues related to stakeholder engagement and dialogue, explaining: why stakeholder engagement is a crucial element of sustainability accounting and accountability; how the range of stakeholders that any organization's managers will seek to engage is related to their philosophical objectives for engaging in CSR; what are the expectations that various stakeholders have about organizations' current and future sustainability actions and disclosure; and some of the difficulties involved in seeking to identify, from among competing stakeholders' social, environmental and economic expectations, a consensus set of expectations which the organization can then address in its sustainability accounting and accountability. This section moves away from these more theoretical considerations to examine evidence of stakeholder engagement and dialogue practices, along with some examples of successful collaborations between NGOs and companies.

### *Stakeholder engagement practices*

Among academic studies that have commented upon aspects of stakeholder dialogue mechanisms in practice, are Thomson and Bebbington (2005), Unerman and Bennett (2004) and O'Dwyer *et al.* (2005a). Thomson and Bebbington (2005) highlight the wide range of dialogue mechanisms used by organizations. These include: internet bulletin boards; questionnaire surveys mailed to stakeholders; interviews; company newsletter tear-off comment cards included in social and environmental reports; phone surveys; focus groups; community based open meetings where stakeholders and organizational representatives are brought together. Unerman and Bennett (2004) conducted an in-depth analysis of the use of an internet web forum hosting social and environmental issues on Shell's website. This web forum allowed anyone with internet access and an email address to post comments on any of the topics covered by the web forum. Although Shell officials replied to many of the comments posted by external stakeholders, Unerman and Bennett found several limitations hindering the potential of the web forum to move towards the realization of an 'ideal speech situation' democratic debate among stakeholders. Little evidence of external stakeholders commenting upon each other's comments, limited access to the internet, lack of translation facilities provided for non-native English language users, among other factors, led to conclusions that the web forum could not in practice be used to engage in dialogue with a broad range of possible stakeholders as a mechanism to help them debate their views.

Broadly similar insights were provided by some of the findings of O'Dwyer (2005a) in an interview-based study examining the perceptions of one form of stakeholder (NGOs) in Ireland towards corporate stakeholder engagement. O'Dwyer *et al.* (2005a) also found that these stakeholders believed there was active resistance by many corporations to meaningful engagement and dialogue with some stakeholders (to the extent that some viewed the relationship between corporations and stakeholders as antagonistic).

Despite recent trends in corporate governance and accountability favouring a more stakeholder inclusive approach (Greenwood and Kamoche, 2013; Mason and Simmons, 2014) some research seems to show that where consultation processes do take place, they are largely a selective, partial and potentially misleading representation of stakeholder views.

Archel *et al.* (2011), for example, provide empirical research evidence of a governmental CSR initiative in Spain, finding that the stakeholder consultation process was problematic in practice. The evidence they present seems to indicate that stakeholder engagement was not designed to genuinely solicit views from stakeholders. The business-led means of finalizing the output from the engagement initiatives only allowed recommendations coherent with the dominant business ideology to be considered. In this case, therefore, stakeholder dialogue seemed to serve a 'symbolic, legitimating function, even though it was itself characterized by dissonance and conflict' (Archel *et al.*, 2011, p. 340) (thus giving the illusion of popular support). The study concludes that managerial capture may occur long before social and environmental concerns are put in the hands of managers who are required to engage with stakeholders or write social and environmental reports.

In a similar vein, Solomon *et al.* (2013), in the context of the emerging private reporting literature, argue that engagement practices appeared to be exercises in institutionalizing unaccountability. While private SER (that is, 'the process of engagement and dialogue on social and environmental issues that takes place between institutional investors and executives from their investee companies' [Solomon *et al.*, 2013, p. 196]) may be interpreted as an additional pressure on companies to discharge their social and environmental accountability, the study found that additional pressure led companies conversely to reduce transparency, presenting an 'opaque self' (Solomon et al., 2013, p. 210).

These findings resonate with those of Barone *et al.* (2013) who provided insights into the extent to which companies in practice incorporate the views of less powerful stakeholders into their decision-making process. The case analysed the perception of employees towards the company's behaviour with reference to a major takeover. The study showed a lack of engagement with employees and the local community regarding the closure of a factory in the UK. What seemed particularly striking in this study's findings was a lack of interest in engagement in the social and environmental accounting and accountability process by the employees. They did not seem interested in reading the company's social and environmental reports and 'believed these were produced for "other" people' (Barone *et al.*, 2013, p. 177). According to this case it seems that less powerful stakeholders were ignored. Instead of cosmetic, superficial or managerially captured engagement, no engagement at all was enacted (Owen *et al.*, 2000; O'Dwyer, 2003; Baker, 2010; Archel *et al.*, 2011; Smith *et al.*, 2011).

The above perspectives on stakeholder engagement and dialogue would indicate that in practice these measures are often used strategically to improve economic performance rather than moving us towards greater sustainability and sustainable development. However, in a further study, O'Dwyer *et al.* (2005b) found that most of the Irish NGOs who responded to a questionnaire survey considered their relationships with corporations to be amicable, indicating that antagonism between corporations and stakeholders might not have been a significant impediment to meaningful stakeholder engagement and dialogue – although a majority of the respondents did not actually take the opportunities which they perceived as being available for engagement and dialogue in helping to determine corporate social and environmental responsibilities and duties of accountability.

*Collaborations between NGOs and companies*

Collaboration between NGOs and companies is increasingly common as a particular form of stakeholder engagement, where NGOs work with companies in order to find mutually beneficial outcomes rather than against companies using hostile tactics. Elkington and Fennell (2000) outlined the various types of company–NGO relationships ranging from adversarial to strategic joint ventures. Pearce (2003, p. 41) states that 'environment groups ... are engaged in a savage reappraisal of their philosophy'; and some groups, such as the World Wildlife Fund (WWF), have concluded that the then prevalent conservation practices, including having an adversarial relationship with companies, were doing more harm than good. The groups suggested that their new outlook encompassed more than just the environment, but considered sustainability in a social, economic and environmental context (Pearce, 2003). Examples of such collaborations include the Conservation Law Foundation's collaboration with public utilities, and Royal Dutch/Shell Group's stakeholder engagement programme. Even Greenpeace, whose reputation is for confrontation and conflict, has entered into alliances, recognizing that 'both parties have something to gain from this relation' (Friedman and Miles, 2002, p. 14).

In Australia, Fiedler and Deegan (2007) investigated some interactions between NGOs and businesses. They considered the construction industry's collaborations with environmental organizations and found that collaborations were motivated by stakeholder pressure, publicity, and the ability to 'set an example for other[s] to follow' (p. 36). In addition, while there are a number of collaboration initiatives currently in operation, most concentrate on environmental management practices, rather than on reporting.

## Summary and conclusions

This chapter has explored a variety of issues related to the role of stakeholder engagement and dialogue in the process of social and environmental accounting and accountability. It located these practices in the context of the motives for organizations engaging in social and environmental accounting and accountability, with these motives only being regarded as leading to sustainability accounting if they aimed at making the organization responsible, responsive and accountable to all those stakeholders upon whom their operations may have an impact. It further discussed the problems in operationalizing stakeholder dialogue and engagement mechanisms where these are motivated by concerns to address the expectations of this very broad range of stakeholders. It showed that stakeholder concerns around issues of sustainability and corporate accountability are evident, and that stakeholder groups attempt to influence companies' activities and reporting through a variety of measures, including antagonism, cooperation and collaboration. It outlined theoretical procedures for arriving at a consensus among competing, mutually exclusive stakeholder needs and expectations, but indicated that in practice such procedures were not evident.

If we are to achieve an improvement in the sustainability of business, then stakeholder dialogue mechanisms which give greater empowerment to a broad range of stakeholders will need to be developed and employed. Otherwise, stakeholder dialogue may continue to be used largely to provide a fig leaf for strategically motivated social and environmental reporting which has little to do with making business or other forms of organization more holistically sustainable in practice.

However, while sustainability accounting and accountability has developed considerably in recent years, developments in the sophistication of stakeholder engagement and dialogue practices and in the academic study of these practices seem to have been limited. There is therefore considerable potential for greater academic research in this area to help organizations develop more sophisticated stakeholder engagement and dialogue processes in their journeys towards more effective sustainable development practices, including sustainability accounting and accountability.

## Notes

1   It may also be considered problematic for an individual to identify today their own interests for any more than a few years into the future.
2   Nevertheless, there have been some attempts in the academic literature to rank the significance of perceived negative social and environmental consequences of organizational activities – for example in developing full cost accounting models designed to account for externalities (see, for example, Bebbington *et al.*, 2001).

## References

AccountAbility (2011) *Stakeholder Engagement Standard – Exposure Draft*, AccountAbility, London, available at http://www.accountability.org/images/content/3/6/362/AA1000SES%202010%20 PRINT.PDF, accessed 10 January 2013.

Adams, C.A. (2002) 'Internal organisational factors influencing corporate social and ethical reporting: Beyond current theorising', *Accounting, Auditing & Accountability Journal*, 15(2): 223–50.

Archel, P., Husillos, J., Larrinaga, C. and Spence, C. (2009) 'Social disclosure, legitimacy theory and the role of the state', *Accounting, Auditing and Accountability Journal*, 22(8): 1284–307.

Archel, P., Husillos, J. and Spence, C. (2011) 'The institutionalisation of unaccountability: Loading the dice of Corporate Social Responsibility discourse', *Accounting, Organizations and Society*, 36(6): 327–43.

Arenas, D., Lozano, J.M. and Albareda, L. (2009) 'The role of NGOs in CSR: Mutual perceptions among stakeholders', *Journal of Business Ethics*, 88(1): 175–97.

Baker, M. (2010) 'Re-conceiving managerial capture', *Accounting, Auditing & Accountability Journal*, 23(7): 847–67.

Barone, E., Ranamagar, N. and Solomon, J.F. (2013) 'A Habermasian model of stakeholder (non) engagement and corporate (ir)responsibility reporting', *Accounting Forum*, 37(3): 163–81.

Bebbington, J., Gray, R., Hibbit, C. and Kirk, E. (2001) *Full Cost Accounting: An Agenda for Action*, ACCA, London.

Bhimani, A. and Soonawalla, K. (2010) 'Sustainability and organizational connectivity at HSBC', in A. Hopwood, J. Unerman and J. Fries (eds) *Accounting for Sustainability. Practical Insights*, Earthscan, London, pp. 173–90.

Bond, S. (2011) 'Negotiating a "democratic ethos": Moving beyond the agonistic–communicative divide', *Planning Theory*, 10(2): 161–86.

Brown, J. and Dillard, J. (2013) 'Critical accounting and communicative action: On the limits of consensual deliberation', *Critical Perspectives on Accounting*, 24(3): 176–90.

Clark, K., Quigley, N. and Stumpf, S. (2014) 'The influence of decision frames and vision priming on decision outcomes in work groups: Motivating stakeholder considerations', *Journal of Business Ethics*, 120(1): 27–38.

Clarkson, P.M., Fang, X., Li, Y. and Richardson, G. (2010) *The Relevance of Environmental Disclosures for Investors and Other Stakeholder Groups: Are Such Disclosures Incrementally Informative?*, University of Queensland, Brisbane St Lucia, QLD; Simon Fraser University, Burnaby, BC; University of Toronto, Toronto, ON.

Deegan, C. and Unerman, J. (2011) *Financial Accounting Theory. Second European Edition*, McGraw-Hill, Maidenhead.

Dillard, J. and Yuthas, K. (2013) 'Critical dialogics, agonistic pluralism, and accounting information systems', *International Journal of Accounting Information Systems*, 14(2): 113–19.

Elkington, J. and Fennell, S. (2000) 'Partners for sustainability', in J. Bendell (ed.) *Terms for Endearment: Business, NGOs and Sustainable Development*, Greenleaf Publishing: Sheffield.

Equator Principles Association (2006) *The Equator Principles*, available at http://www.equator-principles.com/resources/equator_principles.pdf, accessed 11 April 2013.

Fiedler, T. and Deegan, C. (2007) 'Motivations for environmental collaboration within the building and construction industry', *Managerial Auditing Journal*, 22(4): 410–41.

Friedman, A.L. and Miles, S. (2002) 'Developing stakeholder theory', *Journal of Management Studies*, 39(1): 1–21.

Gamerschlag, R., Möller, K. and Verbeeten, F. (2011) 'Determinants of voluntary CSR disclosure: Empirical evidence from Germany', *Review of Managerial Science*, 5(2–3): 233–62.

Global Reporting Initiative (GRI) (2012) *G4 – Exposure Draft*, Amsterdam, available at https://www.globalreporting.org/resourcelibrary/G4-Exposure-Draft.pdf, accessed 14 April 2013.

Global Reporting Initiative (GRI) (2013) *G4 Sustainability Reporting Guidelines*, Amsterdam, available at https://www.globalreporting.org/reporting/g4/Pages/default.aspx, accessed 12 August 2013.

Gray, R. (2006) 'Social, environmental and sustainability reporting and organisational value creation? Whose value? Whose creation?', *Accounting, Auditing & Accountability Journal*, 19(6): 793–819.

Gray, R., Owen, D. and Adams, C. (1996) *Accounting and Accountability: Changes and Challenges in Corporate Social and Environmental Reporting*, Prentice Hall, London.

Greenwood, M. and Kamoche, K. (2013) 'Social accounting as stakeholder knowledge appropriation', *Journal of Management & Governance*, 17(3): 723–43.

Habermas, J. (1990) *Moral Consciousness and Communicative Action* (trans. C. Lenhardt and S. W. Nicholsen), MIT Press, Cambridge, MA.

Hopwood, A.G., Unerman, J. and Fries, J. (eds) (2010) *Accounting for Sustainability. Practical Insights*, Earthscan, London; Washington, DC.

Huang, C.-l. and Kung, F.-h. (2010) 'Drivers of environmental disclosure and stakeholder expectation: Evidence from Taiwan', *Journal of Business Ethics*, 96(3): 435–51.

International Integrated Reporting Council (IIRC) (2011) *Towards Integrated Reporting. Communicating Value in the 21st Century*, IIRC, New York, available at http://theiirc.org/wp-content/uploads/2011/09/IR-Discussion-Paper-2011_spreads.pdf, accessed 14 April 2013.

International Integrated Reporting Council (IIRC) (2013) *Consultation Draft of the International <IR> Framework*, IIRC, New York, available at http://www.theiirc.org/wp-content/uploads/Consultation-Draft/Consultation-Draft-of-the-InternationalIRFramework.pdf, accessed 14 April 2013.

Islam, M.A. and Deegan, C. (2008) 'Motivations for an organisation within a developing country to report social responsibility information', *Accounting, Auditing & Accountability Journal*, 21(6): 850–74.

Islam, M.A. and Deegan, C. (2010) *Social Responsibility Disclosure Practices: Evidence from Bangladesh*, Association of Chartered Certified Accountants (ACCA), London, available at http://www.accaglobal.com/content/dam/acca/global/PDF-technical/sustainability-reporting/tech-tp-srd.pdf, accessed 18 April 2013.

Jain, A., Leka, S. and Zwetsloot, G. (2011) 'Corporate social responsibility and psychosocial risk management in Europe', *Journal of Business Ethics*, 101(4): 619–33.

Kolk, A. and Lenfant, F. (2010) 'MNC reporting on CSR and conflict in Central Africa', *Journal of Business Ethics*, 93: 241–55.

KPMG (2011) *KPMG International Survey of Corporate Responsibility Reporting 2011*, KPMG International, Amsterdam, available at http://www.kpmg.com/Global/en/IssuesAndInsights/ArticlesPublications/corporate-responsibility/Documents/2011-survey.pdf, accessed 23 February 2013.

Lehman, G. (1995) 'A legitimate concern for environmental accounting', *Critical Perspectives on Accounting*, 6(5): 393–412.

Lewis, L. and Unerman, J. (1999) 'Ethical relativism: A reason for differences in corporate social reporting?', *Critical Perspectives on Accounting*, 10(4): 521–47.

Mason, C. and Simmons, J. (2014) 'Embedding corporate social responsibility in corporate governance: A stakeholder systems approach', *Journal of Business Ethics*, 119(1): 77–86.

Meadows, D.H., Randers, J. and Meadows, D.L. (2004) *The Limits to Growth: The 30-year Update*, Earthscan, London.

Michelon, G. (2011) 'Sustainability disclosure and reputation: A comparative study', *Corp. Reputation Rev. Corporate Reputation Review*, 14(2): 79–96.

Neu, D., Warsame, H. and Pedwell, K. (1998) 'Managing public impressions: Environmental disclosures in annual reports', *Accounting, Organizations and Society*, 23(3): 265–82.

O'Dwyer, B. (2003) 'Conceptions of corporate social responsibility: The nature of managerial capture', *Accounting, Auditing & Accountability Journal*, 16(4): 523–57.

O'Dwyer, B., Unerman, J. and Bradley, J. (2005a) 'Perceptions on the emergence and future development of corporate social disclosure in Ireland: Engaging the voices of non-governmental organisations', *Accounting, Auditing & Accountability Journal*, 18(1): 14–43.

O'Dwyer, B., Unerman, J. and Hession, E. (2005b) 'User needs in sustainability reporting: Perspectives of stakeholders in Ireland', *European Accounting Review*, 14(4): 759–87.

O'Rourke, A. (2003) 'A new politics of engagement: Shareholder activism for corporate social responsibility', *Business Strategy and the Environment*, 12(4): 227–39.

O'Sullivan, N. and O'Dwyer, B. (2009) 'Stakeholder perspectives on a financial sector legitimation process: The case of NGOs and the Equator Principles', *Accounting, Auditing & Accountability Journal*, 22(4): 553–87.

Owen, D.L., Swift, T.A., Humphrey, C. and Bowerman, M. (2000) 'The new social audits: Accountability, managerial capture or the agenda of social champions?', *European Accounting Review*, 9(1): 81–98.

Pearce, F. (2003) 'A greyer shade of green', *New Scientist*, 178(2400): 40–3.

Power, M. and Laughlin, R. (1996) 'Habermas, law and accounting', *Accounting, Organizations and Society*, 21(5): 441–65.

Principles for Responsible Investment (PRI) (2013) *The Six Principles*, available at http://www.unpri.org/about-pri/the-six-principles/, accessed 6 April 2013.

Rawls, J. (1971) *A Theory of Justice*, Harvard University Press, Cambridge, MA.

Republic of Ecuador (2008) *Constitution of the Republic of Ecuador (Constitution of 2008)*, Republic of Ecuador.

Singer, P. (1993) *Practical Ethics* (2nd ed.), Cambridge University Press, Cambridge.

Smith, J., Haniffa, R. and Fairbrass, J. (2011) 'A conceptual framework for investigating "Capture" in corporate sustainability reporting assurance', *Journal of Business Ethics*, 99(3): 425–39.

Solomon, J.F., Solomon, A., Norton, S.D. and Joseph, N.L. (2011) 'Private climate change reporting: An emerging discourse of risk and opportunity?', *Accounting, Auditing & Accountability Journal*, 24(8): 1119–48.

Solomon, J.F., Solomon, A., Joseph, N.L. and Norton, S.D. (2013) 'Impression management, myth creation and fabrication in private social and environmental reporting: Insights from Erving Goffman', *Accounting, Organizations and Society*, 38(3): 195–213.

Spence, C. (2009) 'Social and environmental reporting and the corporate ego', *Business Strategy and the Environment*, 18(4): 254–65.

Spence, L.J. and Rinaldi, L. (forthcoming) 'Governmentality in accounting and accountability: A case study of embedding sustainability in a supply chain', *Accounting, Organizations and Society*.

Sustainable Investment Forum (SIF) (2013) *2012 Report on Sustainable and Responsible Investing Trends*, available at http://www.ussif.org/files/Publications/12_Trends_Exec_Summary.pdf, accessed 6 April 2013.

Swift, T.A., Owen, D.L. and Humphrey, C. (2001) *The Management Information Systems Dimensions of Social Accounting and Accountability*, CIMA Research Report, London.

Thomson, I. and Bebbington, J. (2005) 'Social and environmental reporting in the UK: A pedagogic evaluation', *Critical Perspectives on Accounting*, 16(5): 507–33.

Trades Union Congress (TUC) (2013a) *Investment and Corporate Social Responsibility*, available at http://www.tuc.org.uk/social/index.cfm?mins=89&minors=80&majorsubjectID=13, accessed 12 April 2013.

Trades Union Congress (TUC) (2013b) *Trustee Network Website*, available at http://www.tuc.org.uk/economy/index.cfm?mins=280&minors=278&majorsubjectid=4, accessed 12 April 2013.

UK-SIF (2013) *UK Sustainable Investment and Finance Association*, available at www.uksif.org, accessed 6 April 2013.

UN Global Compact (2013) *The Ten Principles*, available at http://www.unglobalcompact.org/AboutTheGC/TheTenPrinciples/, accessed 11 April 2013.

UN Global Compact Advisory Group (2010) *Supply Chain Sustainability: A Practical Guide for Continuous Improvement*, UN Global Compact Office, New York, available at http://www.unglobalcompact.org/docs/issues_doc/supply_chain/SupplyChainRep_spread.pdf, accessed 17 April 2013.

Unerman, J. and Bennett, M. (2004) 'Increased stakeholder dialogue and the internet: Towards greater corporate accountability or reinforcing capitalist hegemony?', *Accounting, Organizations and Society*, 29(7): 685–707.

Unerman, J. and O'Dwyer, B. (2006) 'Theorising accountability for NGO advocacy', *Accounting, Auditing & Accountability Journal*, 19(3): 349–76.

United Nations Environment Programme Finance Initiative (UNEP FI) (2010) *UNEP FI 2010 Overview*, UNEP, Geneva (SUI), available at http://www.unepfi.org/fileadmin/documents/unepfi_overview_2010_01.pdf, accessed 17 April 2013.

United Nations Environment Programme Finance Initiative (UNEP FI) (2011) *UNEP FI Guide to Banking & Sustainability*, UNEP, Geneva (SUI), available at http://www.unepfi.org/fileadmin/documents/guide_banking_statements.pdf, accessed 17 April 2013.

van Huijstee, M. and Glasbergen, P. (2008) 'The practice of stakeholder dialogue between multinationals and NGOs', *Corporate Social Responsibility and Environmental Management*, 15(5): 298–310.

WCED (1987) *Our Common Future*, Oxford University Press, Oxford.

# 7 External accounts[1]

*Colin Dey and Jane Gibbon*

## Introduction

Rising levels of voluntary, unregulated corporate social, environmental and sustainability reporting (SER hereafter) have failed to satisfy a wide range of critics, who have argued that they exhibit a number of major shortcomings, including, *inter alia*: incompleteness (Belal, 2002; Adams, 2004; Bouten *et al.*, 2011); unreliability (Swift and Dando, 2002; O'Dwyer and Owen, 2005); silencing and/or manipulation of the views of stakeholders (Owen et al., 2001; Unerman and Bennett, 2004; Archel *et al.*, 2011); falsely legitimating businesses' belief in the sustainability of their operations (Brown and Deegan, 1998; Campbell, 2000); promoting a 'business as usual' agenda (Larrinaga-Gonzalez and Bebbington, 2001); conveying weak versions of sustainable development (Bebbington and Thomson, 1996); and managerial capture of the social and environmental agenda (Owen *et al.*, 2000; O'Dwyer, 2003; Baker, 2010).

One practical remedy, or antidote, to the problems inherent in contemporary organization-centred SER is to consider the development and practice of alternative forms of social accounting, which may emanate from sources *outside* the accounting entity. At a basic level, the value of such forms of social accounting lies in their potential to increase the amount of publicly available information about a particular issue or entity. In addition, however, such accounts may also enable the inclusion of a wider range of (previously silenced or manipulated) stakeholder voices, and may embody different conceptions of silenced, contested and/or captured terms such as 'nature', 'society' and 'business success'. In so doing, they may become aligned with progressive social agendas, including not only reformist efforts to augment corporate accountability, but also activist attempts to de-legitimate the actions of dominant institutions, or mobilize opinion in favour of more radical transformative change. In this chapter, we will explore such alternative techniques, which we refer to here as *external accounting*.

Given the emphasis above on the potential benefits of such an approach, in contrast to the widespread, if problematic, adoption of contemporary SER, readers may be forgiven for assuming that such an alternative conception of social accounting is relatively new or at least *avant-garde* in some way. However, it is important to emphasize that external accounting has a long history which actually predates the emergence of modern SER practice (Gray et al., 1993, 1996; Gallhofer and Haslam, 2003). Its development has been supported and sustained by other more familiar and long-standing cultural traditions, including investigative journalism (Pilger, 2004), as well as the grass-roots activism of various social movements and campaigning pressure groups (Lubbers, 2003). In recent years, such traditions have also been supported by the growth of the internet as a communication medium (Gallhofer *et al.*, 2006).

At the same time, however, episodes of experimentation with external accounts have been somewhat intermittent and fragmented. They have also, rather confusingly, been referred to by a number of different terms, including: social audits (Medawar, 1976); anti-reports (Ridgers, 1979); plant closure audits (Harte and Owen, 1987; Geddes, 1992); silent accounts (Gray, 1997); shadow accounts (Gibson *et al.*, 2001; Dey, 2007); reporting-performance portrayal gaps (Adams, 2004); social accounts (Cooper *et al.*, 2005); and counter accounts (Gallhofer *et al.*, 2006). In this chapter, we explore the variety of guises in which external accounts have appeared, and highlight their typical dimensions or characteristics. In particular, we draw attention to a broad source of differentiation between extant forms of external accounting: accounts that seek to discharge a comprehensive, systematic accountability; and accounts that offer a more radical, partisan reporting, often of oppressed, silenced voices.

That a range of alternative approaches may be identified is perhaps unsurprising, given that external accountants, particularly non-governmental organizations (NGOs) involved in activism and advocacy, are already known to use a number of different strategies to engage with corporations (Bliss, 2002; O'Sullivan and O'Dwyer, 2009). However, such differences also point to a deeper tension at the heart of the relationship involving external accountants and their target accounting 'entity', between *collaboration and reform* on the one hand, and *confrontation and resistance* on the other. Before exploring such issues further, however, it is perhaps best to start by outlining what these seemingly different experiments in new forms of accounting have in common.

In general terms, external accounts are a form of social accounting produced by external individuals and/or organizations, including campaigning NGOs, on *their* representation of the social and environmental impacts of others. The intended audience for such external reports is not simply the accounting entity associated with the problematic impacts, but may also include political institutions, civil society, the media and sections of the general public. On a more conceptual level, external accounting may be defined as a form of accounting that seeks to make 'thinkable' and 'governable' those issues currently regarded by dominant organizations and institutions as 'unthinkable' and 'ungovernable' (Dey *et al.*, 2010). It may be viewed as a technology that measures, creates, makes visible, represents and communicates evidence in contested arenas characterized by multiple, often contradictory reports, prepared according to different institutional and ideological rules (Georgakopoulos and Thomson, 2008). By systematically creating alternative representations, new visibilities and knowledge of existing situations, external accounts seek to problematize behaviour and act as a catalyst for change. Hence, any evaluation of external accounting should explore how such accounts may be used as discursive 'ammunition' to contest, reform, and/or resist prevailing institutional behaviour. In the next section, Early Experiments in External Accounting, we begin to trace the history of external accounting and discuss the main objectives and characteristics of the reports produced during that time.

## Early experiments in external accounting

The work of Social Audit Ltd and Counter Information Services (CIS) during the 1970s and 1980s are the most celebrated antecedents of modern SER (and counter-SER) practice (Medawar, 1976; Ridgers, 1979; Geddes, 1992; Gray *et al.*, 1993, 1996; Gallhofer and Haslam, 2003). Ironically, although the eponymous company title effectively makes the term 'social audit' a proprietary one, this is rather misleading: *social account* would have been a more accurate name. In essence, both organizations were established to publish 'counter-information' as a response to the (then) perceived absence of, and demand for, accountability disclosures.

During the 1970s Social Audit Ltd produced five detailed and lengthy external accounts of the behaviour of specific target organizations. The content of these 'social audits' reflected a strong overriding intention to obtain comprehensive and reliable information about the target organization's interactions with key stakeholder groups, including employees, consumers, community and the environment. Detailed discussion of these accounts is beyond the scope of this chapter (but see, especially, Gray *et al.*, 1996). However, it is worth noting that the accounts were prepared according to a set of explicit objectives in order to better discharge the target organization's accountability (Gray *et al.*, 1996). For example, in its social account of Avon Rubber,[2] these objectives were defined as follows:

> The report has been prepared to: (i) show to what extent it may be possible to assess what, in social terms, a company gives to and takes from the community in which it operates; (ii) advance understanding about the practical problems and possibilities that may be involved in making assessments of this kind; and (iii) establish precedents for the disclosure of more, hard information about what companies do, why they do it, and to what general effect.
>
> (Social Audit, 1976, p. 2)

A further characteristic of the approach taken by Social Audit Ltd was to explicitly seek to produce such reports with the full cooperation of the 'target' organization. However, of the five reports produced by Social Audit Ltd, only Avon Rubber Ltd agreed to cooperate in this way, before withdrawing its cooperation after the draft report was completed. While the reports produced by Social Audit Ltd did achieve some wider visibility, they were both lengthy and difficult to verify (Gray *et al.*, 1996). As a consequence, 'the inevitable result was that [they] were ignored in the main by company management, particularly where the message conveyed was a largely unpalatable one. Furthermore, [attempts] to mobilise shareholder opinion … met with scant response, even from supposedly socially concerned groups' (1996, p. 272).

By contrast, the work of CIS (see, for example, CIS, 1971) was a deliberately less systematic, and rather more partisan, approach to external accounting. CIS was a 'Marxist collective of journalists dedicated to seeking radical changes in society' (Gray *et al.*, 1996, p. 273), which published a series of so-called 'Anti-Reports' between 1971 and 1984, focusing on specific high-profile corporations involved in controversial activities.[3] A feature of the reports was the use of employee 'voices', in direct juxtaposition with corporate rhetoric, as an attempt to create a powerful dissonance in the mind of the reader (Adams and Whelan, 2009). This technique was used regularly by CIS to highlight controversial issues, such as the alienating and repressive reality of poor working conditions (Gallhofer and Haslam, 2003). As Gray *et al.* observe,

> The power of the reports lies in the use of photographs, frequent quotations, and vivid, emotive phraseology … The Anti-Reports clearly have little relevance to (social accounting) as a form of 'objective', 'balanced' and 'unbiased' communication. They are, however, important as a particular and somewhat rare example of a 'radical' approach to reporting produced on a regular basis.
>
> (1996, p. 274)

While the output of Social Audit Ltd and CIS had declined by the mid-1980s,[4] the impact of a period of de-industrialization within the UK economy at that time gave rise to a new phase of experimentation with external accounting, in the form of 'plant closure audits', carried out by a number of local authorities (Geddes, 1992). Harte and Owen (1987) discuss local authorities' use of social cost analysis to measure the impact of plant closure decisions and problematize de-industrialization, primarily in order to justify intervention to reverse the decisions, but also to change wider government industrial policy. In contrast to the emotive, partisan style of the CIS Anti-Reports, plant closure audits adopted a more quantitative (though arguably still subjective) methodology, to estimate the 'true' cost to the local economy and community of higher unemployment. A further notable aspect of these audits was their implicit appeal to a framework of accountability, or 'social contract' between business, local government and the community (Gray *et al.*, 1996, p. 277). However, echoing the eventual fate of the accountability driven reports of Social Audit Ltd, the ultimate impact of plant closure audits was minimal, in that they failed to reverse any closure decisions.

## The re-emergence of external accounting as a reaction to corporate 'greenwash'

During the late 1980s the popular phrase 'greenwash'[5] (Greer and Bruno, 1996; Rowell, 2003) reflected growing social and media awareness of possible corporate manipulation of environmental issues (mass awareness of which was becoming invigorated by headlines about concerns over global warming and the use of chlorofluorocarbons (CFCs). By the early 1990s, this had turned into a backlash against the early pioneers of ethical consumerism; Body Shop's claims of social and environmental responsibility were especially subject to public and media scrutiny, and even an external 'social audit' (Entine, 2003). In the accounting literature, some research was undertaken to review the impact of pressure groups on published SER (Tilt, 1994), while calls were also made for improved independent 'monitoring' of the activities of multinational corporations (Bailey *et al.*, 1994), which potentially involved some form of regulated external accountability reporting (Bailey *et al.*, 2000).

By the mid-1990s, however, contemporary organization-centred SER practices were beginning to emerge. As this grew into a rapidly rising groundswell of corporate, governmental and media enthusiasm for voluntary social and environmental reporting, the use of counter-information techniques waned. Although the quantity of emerging SER practice was relatively low, a sense of optimism drove forward attempts to improve 'best practice'. In academia and beyond, efforts were increasingly directed pragmatically at trying to encourage corporations and at assisting in the development of the theory and practice of modern SER (see, for example, Zadek *et al.*, 1997).

In an effort to boost the relatively low volume of disclosure at that time, while at the same time prompt more critical reflection on the state of SER, Gray (1997) mooted the idea of reviving the concept of external accounting by producing a corporate 'silent account'. Even in circumstances where no organization-centred social account yet existed, a 'silent account' could still be compiled from 'nuggets' of relevant information obtained via all other formal corporate disclosure channels, including company annual reports, press releases, marketing campaigns, etc. These silent accounts were claimed to represent the corporation's own voice, and were referred to as 'silent' because such information, although published, was not officially labelled or recognized as SER.

To illustrate the concept, Gray produced a silent account based on the 1994 annual report of the pharmaceutical company Glaxo plc. The premise of this account was to identify relevant information from Glaxo's annual report and to effectively 'create' a new piece of SER by collating this relevant information into a new document. Silent accounts could be seen as a simple way of generating more disclosure, as well as being 'greater than the sum of their parts', by (re)creating a picture of organizational accountability.

By the late 1990s, concerns about the pervasive absence of corporate SER began to diminish, only to be replaced by concerns over the quality of emerging corporate disclosures. To find new ground upon which a critical evaluation of SER might be developed, a number of accounting academics started various separate research projects which sought to further explore forms of external accounting.[6] Gray's initial experimentation with silent accounting was developed to incorporate a form of external accounting, which was termed 'shadow accounting'. This concept was firmly rooted in the external accounts of the 1970s and 1980s; indeed, the term 'shadow report' itself appears to originate from that period (Gray *et al.*, 1996, p. 274). The shadow account represented a shift from an organization-centred perspective towards more independent and stakeholder driven approaches (Gray *et al.*, 1997). They were intended to reveal contradictions between what companies choose to report and what they suppress, problematizing their activities and providing new insights into their social and environmental impacts:

> [F]irst, [they] act as a 'balancing view' in the face of the considerable resources that organisations have at their disposal to put their own point of view and to offer their own emphasis on their activities. Secondly, [they] can be motivated by the realisation that if organisations will not discharge their own duty of accountability then it is possible for other bodies to do it on their behalf.
>
> (Gibson *et al.*, 2001a, p. 1)

In seeking to illuminate the shortcomings of corporate accountability disclosures, the notion of shadow accounts recognized the increasing quantities of, and access to, counter information in the public domain. A shadow account could consist of all relevant accountability information that was readily available in the public domain, produced independently of the subject organization, and published externally from it. Such information could be relatively easily gathered by academic researchers and published, not simply as a separate document, but in direct juxtaposition to 'unofficial' silent accounts (or, if they were available, 'official' SER), using the same categories and subject headings.

To this end, Gibson *et al.* (2001) produced a series of combined reports on the activities of well-known UK companies, from different industry sectors, which had yet to produce their own dedicated social or environmental reports.[7] Together, the silent and shadow accounts presented the reader with a picture of corporate accountability that directly juxtaposed corporate and non-corporate sources of information. Though superficially reminiscent of the approach taken in the CIS reports of the 1970s and 1980s, the Gibson et al. accounts instead sought to present information to the reader without partisan bias. A second, and perhaps less justifiable, characteristic of these reports was their relatively uncritical use of shadow information sources, which in the Gibson *et al.* accounts relied mainly on (potentially inaccurate) broadsheet newspaper articles. Nevertheless, despite its possible shortcomings, putting combined silent and shadow reports together in this way served as a compelling basis for revealing significant gaps in the completeness of corporate (non-) disclosure.

While the experiments in silent and shadow accounting were being conducted, a separate project on external accounting was undertaken by Adams (2004) to explore what she termed the 'reporting-performance portrayal gap'. Adams's case study, in contrast to the 'silent' study of a 'non-reporting' corporation by Gray (1997), examined a corporation (known only by the pseudonym 'Alpha') that had already been producing SER for some years. Using the accountability framework set out in the (now well established) social and environmental reporting guidelines of AA1000, Adams analysed Alpha's published SER (for the years 1993 and 1999) by contrasting it against what the author was able to research and uncover about the chosen company from a wide range of (carefully verified) 'shadow' external information sources for the same time periods. In a broadly similar fashion to the experiments of Gibson *et al.* (2001), Adams uses (and identifies in some detail) a wide range of sources of 'shadow' information to illuminate the shortcomings of completeness present in SER disclosures. Like the Gibson *et al.* research, these shortcomings included situations where (a) shadow information was found to conflict in some way with the comparable corporate account; or (b) where shadow information cast light on something material to stakeholders which was not included in the SER report.

In contrast to the work of Gray and Adams, other academic experiments with external accounts produced since then may be viewed more as explicit forms of resistance against specific ways of governing, or seeking more radical transformation of prevailing governance. A further important feature of these later experiments is that the accounting 'entity' is not necessarily a corporation. Cooper *et al.* (2005) demonstrated the power of evidence-based external accounting in problematizing student poverty and higher education financing plans in Scotland. Their intervention was also as tactical as it was evidential: it occurred during the consultation process before the change was enacted, suggesting that the timing of the publishing of external accounting is also important. In addition, those creating the external account used existing parliamentary processes to present their evidence on the negative consequences of a proposed reform, on what they defined as an oppressed social group.

Two further recent studies of external accounting also illustrate the way in which different forms of non-corporate accounting 'entities' may be used. Solomon and Thomson (2009) explained how a Victorian external account sought to problematize the complex issues of industrial and municipal river pollution as part of a wider campaign to improve river management, while Collison *et al.* (2007, 2010) sought to question the utopian beliefs and rationality of 'Anglo-American' shareholder capitalism. The objective of the study was to challenge such beliefs by presenting evidence of measurable negative social outcomes of Western governments that pursued neoliberal economic policies. Rather than seeking to frame the study using the corporation as the 'accounting entity', Collison *et al.* (2007) used the nation state as a basis for evidence-based statistical comparisons of infant mortality and income inequality between wealthy countries. Their work may be viewed as an attempt to problematize in systemic terms the socio-economic policies, programmes and actions of governments of wealthy countries that champion neoliberalism (see, especially, Wilkinson and Pickett, 2009).[8] In so doing Collison *et al.* (2007) utilized highly respected and well-established datasets of social indicators, published by the United Nations. In this way, Collison *et al.* (2007) engaged with the process of governance by creating knowledge to open up new visibilities that challenged the calculative rationality that forms part of the discourse on the 'superiority' of Anglo-American shareholder capitalism. Implicit in this study was the repositioning of the relevant accounting entity of a nation from the (neoliberal) entity of a collection of calculating, rational, responsible individuals to a society of liberal subjects, with common rights, obligations and interests.

While academic reports of external accounting may offer interesting insights into the potential of such accounts, it is difficult to assess what impact, if any, they have had outside of the academic sphere. However, it may be possible to look elsewhere, since most of the impetus to engage directly with dominant institutions and structures of concern has come from civil society and the activities of pressure groups and other NGOs campaigning against the social and environmental impacts of corporate behaviour.

## Counter information, new social movements and civil society

The work of Social Audit Ltd and CIS underlines the pioneering role played by civil society in experimenting with forms of external accounting. While the previous section, The Re-emergence of External Accounting, focused on the work of academic social accountants to evidence gaps in existing SER, it should be recognized that such research is itself dependent on the increasing availability of wider sources of counter information available in the public domain, much of it produced by civil society organizations. Despite efforts in the 1990s to legitimize the behaviour of corporations through the rapid expansion of contemporary SER practice, concerns over corporate abuse of power also became increasingly prominent during that time (Klein, 2000; Hertz, 2001; Bakan, 2004). In recent years, popular and media interest in the issue has been sustained by a series of high-profile cases in specific corporate settings, including: oil and gas production (Livesey, 2001; Holzer, 2007), fast food (Schlosser, 2002); supermarkets (Blythman, 2004; Simms, 2007); accounting (McLean and Elkind, 2004); and, most recently, banking (Sorkin, 2009). Such high-profile cases have further fuelled public discontent with the social and environmental impacts of modern capitalism. This has, in turn, been visibly expressed through the networking, campaigns and activism of what may be termed 'new social movements'. Such social movements include the activities of a wide range of campaigning pressure groups and other NGOs.

Social movements seek to raise global awareness of social and environmental issues and to hold organizations more accountable by mobilizing grass-roots action against corporations and governments (Crossley, 2003). Large campaigning NGOs, including Greenpeace, Oxfam, War on Want, Amnesty, Christian Aid and Friends of the Earth (FoE) regularly produce reports on controversial aspects of corporate behaviour. In some cases, NGOs also form coalitions to lobby on specific high-profile campaign issues (see, for example, ECCJ, 2008). Globalization, the emergence and spread of internet technology and the growth of organized, grass-roots social networks have all conspired to create the widespread public demand for counter information about institutional accountability practices (Lubbers, 2003). Anti-corporate websites allow disgruntled individuals the chance to air their views to a global audience (Kahn and Kellner, 2005), while social media create the potential for such individuals to involve themselves and share information with diffuse networks of likeminded people. The websites of campaigning groups such as *Corporate Watch* and the *Business & Human Rights Resource Centre*[9] act as 'portals' to a range of counter-information sources (see also Gallhofer *et al.*, 2006; Spence, 2009).

The focus within 'new social movements' on the perceived moral deficiencies of corporate behaviour, and associated 'grievances' against modern capitalism and globalization, resonates strongly with the work of the critical accounting community (see, for example, Sikka and Willmott, 1997; Cooper *et al.*, 2003; Everett, 2003; Spence, 2009). NGOs that have chosen to produce their own 'shadow' or 'counter' disclosures of specific corporate targets usually choose corporations that already provide high levels of voluntary SER. By arguably failing to close the 'gap' required to reassure or convince stakeholders, SER is interpreted and labelled by external stakeholder representatives as more 'greenwash', and thus may actually serve to mobilize action. One strategy that seems to be increasingly adopted by NGOs to tackle such corporate 'propaganda' is to publish their own counter information in ways that directly confront existing organization-centred SER.[10]

Examples of NGO-based external accounting are the reports produced by FoE, including *Failing the Challenge: The Other Shell Report* (FoE, 2003a) and the *Amec Counter Report* (FoE, 2003b). The FoE (2003a) document was ostensibly a retrospective review of Shell's 2002 social report. However, examination of the content of the report reveals a series of short narrative 'case-studies' of various communities directly affected by Shell's multinational operations. Rather than using their report to simply state the difference between what Shell itself 'says' and what other stakeholders 'know about' Shell, FoE's approach is strongly editorial, to (in the words of Shell's own PR campaign of the time) 'tell Shell' what it thinks of Shell's behaviour. Thus, in contrast to the work of Gray (1997) or Adams (2004), the FoE report does not attempt to evaluate Shell's own SER in a systematic way. While the FoE report emphasizes the selective bias and unreliability of the Shell report, it does so with what is arguably an even more selective, and potentially unreliable, report. In some ways, the report echoes the output of organizations such as CIS, which is intentionally provocative, generates media coverage, and creates a platform for the 'voices' of marginalized stakeholders to be heard. However, in terms of their underlying intent, FoE's reports appear rather less critical or emancipatory than the work of CIS (Gallhofer and Haslam, 2003).

While FoE's work is broadly typical of what may be viewed as a modern revival of the more partisan approach to external accounting pioneered by CIS, it is worth noting that not all examples of NGO-based reporting appear to exhibit such characteristics. At the same time as British American Tobacco (BAT) was publishing its first social report (BAT, 2002), the anti-smoking pressure group Action against Smoking and Health (ASH) produced *British American Tobacco – the Other Report to Society* (ASH, 2002a). In line with more recent SER, BAT claimed that their report was constructed using the best available voluntary reporting standards. The report included considerable efforts to engage directly with stakeholders through dialogue processes, and was also 'verified' by an external consultant. In response, the ASH document closely shadowed these processes and attempted to evidence in detail areas of disclosure where the BAT report fell short of the reporting standards it had claimed to adhere to. The ASH report criticized the scope of the social report, arguing that BAT had failed to identify its most important stakeholders. It also questioned the credibility and transparency of the report, concluding that BAT had failed to provide reliable information to stakeholders. ASH also criticized the management of the company's 'stakeholder dialogue' process (a dialogue to which ASH, although invited to join, chose to ignore) on the grounds that there were 'virtually no areas where BAT and ASH can find common cause – we characterize BAT's relationship with public health as a zero-sum game' (ASH, 2002b; see also Moerman and Van der Laan, 2005).

In summary, we may observe that, while modern NGO-based external accounting may often be explicitly adversarial in the use of shadow information as 'ammunition' against its corporate target, this stance is taken at the expense of a relative weakness in the reports to systematically analyse completeness, assurance and dialogue gaps in SER. In the next section, Towards a Typology of External Accounting, we draw from our review of prior episodes of external accounting to sketch out a broad typology of different forms of the technique and further discuss the potential implications of this classification for the study of external accounting.

## Towards a typology of external accounting

Our review of prior experimentation with forms of external accounting suggests that social accounting academics and NGOs share a common interest in illuminating the shortcomings of current SER, with a focus on evidencing (at least some) gaps in the completeness of published disclosures. At the same time, however, there are some interesting differences. Drawing in particular on the work of Dey *et al.* (2012), Table 7.1 below outlines a broad typology of different forms of external accounting.

At its simplest, an external account could be produced to challenge the acceptability of a specific aspect of the target organization's conduct or intention by providing new knowledge, such as evidence of the consequences of that conduct/intention. From this perspective, the extent of the transformation is limited in scope, but equally importantly, may offer the advantage of working cooperatively with existing power and resource structures. The work of Social Audit Ltd (1976), the plant closure audits of the 1980s (Geddes, 1992), as well as the silent accounts proposed by Gray (1997) and shadow accounts produced by Gibson *et al.* (2001), could be viewed (at least in terms of their stated intentions) as providing new information

*Table 7.1* A typology of approaches to external accounting

| Type of External Account | Objective | Method | Examples reviewed in this chapter |
| --- | --- | --- | --- |
| Systematic | Greater participation with and/or discharge of entity's accountability | Provide new evidence or knowledge on target entity's conduct or intentions | Social Audit Ltd (1976) Silent accounts (Gray, 1997) Plant closure audits (Geddes, 1992) Shadow accounts (Gibson *et al.*, 2001) Example NGO reports (ASH, 2002a, 2002b) Reporting-performance portrayal gap analysis (Adams, 2004) |
| Partisan | De-legitimation and/or targeted reform of governing technology or institution within overall regime | Provide new evidence or knowledge on inadequacies or loopholes of governing | Counter Information Services Anti-reports (CIS, 1971) Example NGO reports (FoE, 2003a, 2003b) Social audits (Cooper *et al.*, 2005) Counter accounts (Gallhofer *et al.*, 2006) |
| Contra-governing | Overthrow existing governing regime and replace with another dominant form of governing | Problematize the underlying nature or ideology of governing systems | Public health/inequality research (Collison *et al.*, 2007, 2010; Wilkinson and Pickett, 2009) |

Source: Adapted from Dey *et al.*, 2012.*

*Dey *et al.* (2012) take the above classification a stage further and suggest a fourth, more idealized, type of external account that can be characterized as a mechanism within an emancipatory dialogic engagement. Further discussion of this concept is beyond the scope of this chapter (but see also Dey *et al.*, 2010).

to enable existing forms of governing to operate more effectively. More recently, the reports produced by ASH (2002a, 2002b) publicly challenged the completeness and accuracy standards of the target organization's social and environmental account by seeking to produce an alternative account informed by the same reporting standards.

The second level of the typology characterizes external accounts as a method of reform to existing forms of governing, by demanding transformation of specific elements of the existing governing regime. At this level, the defined accounting entity may not necessarily be an individual organization. These accounts, including the CIS anti-reports of the 1970s on specific companies, the academic experiments of Cooper *et al.* (2005), as well as the plant closure audits of the 1980s (Geddes, 1992) and the reports produced by campaigning NGOs such as FoE (2003a, 2003b) seek to represent and problematize the unacceptable consequences of technologies of governing.

A third, more explicitly resistance-based form of external accounts, can be seen as part of attempts to fundamentally transform the existing governing regime. At this level, the focus is no longer on a specific organization, and the type of transformation sought, whether around neoliberal economics, public health inequalities, or climate change, is likely to be counter-hegemonic, and hence highly contested.[11] Ambiguities between the boundaries of our classification also become more evident here. While the targeting of specific corporations would seem to place them at the 'partisan' level of our classification, the overall body of work produced by CIS arguably embodies a broader counter-hegemonic radical agenda (Gallhofer and Haslam, 2003) that justifies their classification as a more contra-governing form of external accounting.

## The role of external accounts in discursive struggles between civil society and dominant institutions

The external accounts reviewed in this chapter share a common objective of generating new information to challenge the conduct and/or intentions of the target accounting 'entity'. As we have seen, however, many significant differences also exist. The fragmented, episodic nature of engagement with external accounts is underlined by wide variations, not simply in the terminology adopted, but more importantly, in the scope, depth and type of evidence used. The work of Social Audit Ltd (1976) and the experiments of academics such as Gibson et al. (2001) and Adams (2004), while not entirely objective or verifiable, appear to offer a degree of balance and systematic coverage. They are arguably more grounded and rigorous by comparison with the information activism of NGOs such as FoE (2003a, 2003b) and CIS (1971). External accounts may be further differentiated by reference to the target accounting 'entity'. This is not always a profit-oriented corporation, and may instead include sovereign nations, political campaigns, government proposals, public sector organizations, industrial sectors, regulators, geographic regions, social groupings and local communities.

As Table 7.1 shows, such differences may be explained by the extent of transformation that is sought by the external accountant. Those who desire systematic and complete accounts of the behaviour of the target 'entity' appear to maintain faith in accounting as primarily a procedure for fully discharging that entity's accountability, as well as in working cooperatively with that entity to deliver this objective. On the other hand, those who take a more partisan approach to external accounting seem more interested in confrontation rather than cooperation. As the transformative agenda of the external social accountant becomes even more radical, their focus may also move beyond the corporate entity to the conduct or intentions of the governing regime itself.

Rather than systematically generating new information in order to work within (or reform) existing *accountability* processes (Gray *et al.*, 1996), the objective of more partisan external accountants may be better understood as an attempt to mobilize public sentiment in ways that undermine the *legitimacy* of their target entity (Georgakopoulos and Thomson, 2008; Joutsenvirta, 2011). Following on from this, a number of questions arise. How effective is external accounting as a discursive mechanism to engage with and challenge dominant institutions? Are external accounts more effective when they subscribe to the types of standards of completeness and reliability used to measure the quality of (corporate) SER, or should they instead abandon such benchmarks and be restricted to the deliberately selective presentation of 'counter information'?

From a theoretical perspective, external accounting has been argued to possess significant transformative, or even emancipatory potential (Gallhofer and Haslam, 2003; Gallhofer *et al.*, 2006; Bebbington and Thomson, 2007; Spence, 2009). Such arguments have typically been deployed in favour of more partisan, counter-hegemonic accounts. At the same time, the notion of a more systematic, complete account of corporate behaviour has been subjected to renewed criticism for its procedural emphasis (Shenkin and Coulson, 2007). Furthermore, the notions of transparency and accountability that underpin such procedural accounts may themselves be more problematic than previously thought (Roberts, 2009; Messner, 2009). Concerns have also been expressed about the intentions and intervention strategies of external accountants (Gray *et al.*, 1996; Gallhofer and Haslam, 2003; Dey *et al.*, 2010) and the academic social accounting community (Spence *et al.*, 2010). External accounting is a voluntary activity, and external accountants may be self-selecting individuals or undemocratic organizations that seek to bring about change in line with their own internal belief structure, which need not be emancipatory. This raises the question as to whether external accounts can possess the necessary characteristics to be genuinely transformative or emancipatory, or whether external accounting is merely a political device for imposing one worldview over others (see also Unerman and O'Dwyer, 2006).

From a more practical perspective, it would appear that, despite providing compelling evidence, most external accounts (either systematic or partisan) have been ineffective in bringing about change (Gray *et al.*, 1996). Beyond this rather vague conclusion, however, the role of external accounting as discursive 'ammunition' in legitimacy struggles between civil society and dominant institutions remains relatively poorly understood. Researching external accounting interventions requires a systemic investigation of the power relationships and dynamics, and broader assemblage of engagements and contextual factors, that constitute the governing network within which any reports are located (Georgakopoulos and Thomson, 2008).

In this chapter, we have reviewed past episodes of experimentation with, and outlined a broad typology of, different approaches to external accounting. We have also argued that to evaluate the role of external accounting interventions requires an explicit articulation not only of the intentions of the external accountants (Dey, 2007), but also their engagement strategies, tactics and outcomes (Dey *et al.*, 2013). This is a particularly rich and worthwhile area of study, and recent research in the accounting literature (Georgakopoulos and Thomson, 2008; O'Sullivan and O'Dwyer, 2009; Dey *et al.*, 2013) and elsewhere (see, for example, Holzer, 2007; Hond and de Bakker, 2007; Joutsenvirta, 2011) is now beginning to shed more light on the potential effectiveness of such interventions.

# Notes

1 This chapter updates and significantly widens the scope of Dey's original chapter on 'Developing Silent and Shadow Accounts' from 2007. In doing so, it draws on material that also appears in Dey *et al.* (2010, 2012).

2 A copy of the Avon Rubber Ltd report can be found online via the Centre for Social & Environmental Accounting Research, available at http://www.st-andrews.ac.uk/csear/sa-exemplars/external-social-audits/, accessed 19 October 2013.

3 Further information on the origins of, and reports produced by CIS can be found online, available at http://anti-report.com, accessed 22 October 2013.

4 It should be noted, however, that (at time of writing) elements of both organizations have survived and continue to operate. Social Audit Ltd remains a part of PIRC Ltd (Public Interest Research Centre, available at http://www.pirc.info), while the work of CIS has recently resurfaced on the internet, available at http://anti-report.com, and appears to be linked to more recent activist projects, available at http://www.whorunsthisplace.co.uk, all accessed 22 October 2013.

5 'Greenwash' is a portmanteau of the words 'green' and 'whitewash'. It first entered the Concise Oxford Dictionary in 1999, and is defined as 'disinformation disseminated by an organisation so as to present an environmentally responsible public image'. Since then, 'greenwashing' has been the subject of a number of 'awards' given to high-profile corporations by various campaigning NGOs (see, for example, that available at http://www.corpwatch.org/section.php?id=102, accessed 22 October 2013).

6 See also the 'critical financial analysis' developed and applied to the privatized utilities in the UK by Shaoul (1998).

7 Copies of the Gibson *et al.* shadow accounts can be obtained via the Centre for Social and Environmental Accounting Research, available at http://www.st-andrews.ac.uk/csear/sa-exemplars/silent-and-shadow/, accessed 22 October 2013.

8 In addition to this published output, further information on campaigning work and activism on this issue can be found at http://www.equalitytrust.org.uk, accessed 22 October 2013.

9 For more information, see http://www.corporatewatch.org.uk; and http://www.business-human-rights.org, both accessed 22 October 2013.

10 Copies of a range of examples of NGO external reporting, including those of FoE and ASH reviewed here, can be found via the Centre for Social & Environmental Accounting Research, available at http://www.st-andrews.ac.uk/csear/sa-exemplars/external-social-audits/, accessed 22 October 2013.

11 A well-documented example of this kind of discursive struggle (in the context of the work of Wilkinson and Pickett) can be found at http://www.equalitytrust.org.uk/resources/other/response-to-questions, accessed 22 October 2013.

# References

Action on Smoking & Health (ASH) (2002a) *British American Tobacco – The Other Report to Society*, Action on Smoking and Health, available at http://www.st-andrews.ac.uk/csear/sa-exemplars/external-social-audits/, accessed 22 October 2013.

Action on Smoking & Health (ASH) (2002b) *BAT Social Report Revisited – ASH Comes to BAT*, Action on Smoking and Health.

Adams, C.A. (2004) 'The ethical, social and environmental reporting performance portrayal gap', *Accounting, Auditing and Accountability Journal*, 17(5): 731–57.

Adams, C.A. and Whelan, G. (2009) 'Conceptualising future change in corporate sustainability reporting', *Accounting, Auditing and Accountability Journal*, 22(1): 118–43.

Archel, P., Husillos, J. and Spence, C. (2011) 'The institutionalisation of unaccountability: Loading the dice of Corporate Social Responsibility discourse', *Accounting, Organizations and Society*, 36(6): 327–43.

Bailey, D., Harte, G. and Sugden, R. (1994) *Making Transnationals Accountable*, Routledge.

Bailey, D., Harte, G. and Sugden, R. (2000) 'Corporate disclosure and the deregulation of international investment', *Accounting, Auditing and Accountability Journal*, 13(2): 197–218.

Bakan, J. (2004) *The Corporation: The Pathological Pursuit of Profit and Power*, Constable.

Baker, M. (2010) 'Re-conceiving managerial capture', *Accounting, Auditing & Accountability Journal*, 23(7): 847–67.

Bebbington, J. and Thomson, I. (1996) *Business Conceptions of Sustainability and the Implications for Accountancy*, Research Report 48, ACCA.

Bebbington, J. and Thomson, I. (2007) 'Social and environmental accounting, auditing and reporting: A potential source of organizational risk governance?' *Environment and Planning C*, 25(1): 38–55.

Belal, A. (2002) 'Stakeholder accountability or stakeholder management? A review of UK firms' social and ethical accounting, auditing and reporting practices', *Corporate Social Responsibility and Environmental Management*, 9(1): 8–25.

Bliss, T. (2002) 'Corporate advocacy groups: Friend or foe?', in J. Andriof, S. Waddock, B. Husted and S. Rahman (eds) *Unfolding Stakeholder Thinking*, Greenleaf, pp. 251–67.

Blythman, J. (2004) *Shopped: The Shocking Power of British Supermarkets*, Fourth Estate.

Bouten, L., Everaert, P., Van Liedekerke, L., De Moor, L. and Christiaens, J. (2011) 'Corporate social responsibility reporting: A comprehensive picture?', *Accounting Forum*, 35(3): 187–204.

British American Tobacco (BAT) (2002) *Report to Society*, British American Tobacco.

Brown, N. and Deegan, C. (1998) 'The public disclosure of environmental performance information – A dual test of media agenda setting theory and legitimacy theory', *Accounting and Business Research*, 29(1): 21–41.

Campbell, D. (2000) 'Legitimacy theory or managerial reality construction: Corporate social disclosure in Marks and Spencer corporate reports 1969–1997', *Accounting Forum*, 24(1): 80–100.

Collison, D.J., Dey, C.R., Hannah, G.M. and Stevenson, L.A. (2007) 'Income inequality and child mortality in wealthy nations', *Journal of Public Health*, 29(2): 114–17.

Collison, D.J., Dey, C.R., Hannah, G.M. and Stevenson, L.A. (2010) 'Anglo-American capitalism: The role and potential role of social accounting', *Accounting, Auditing & Accountability Journal*, 23(8): 956–81.

Cooper, C., Neu, D. and Lehman, G. (2003) Globalization and its discontents: A concern about growth and globalization, *Accounting Forum*, 27(4): 359–64.

Cooper, C., Taylor, P., Smith, N. and Catchpowle, L. (2005) 'A discussion of the political potential of social accounting', *Critical Perspectives on Accounting*, 16(7): 951–74.

Counter Information Services (CIS) (1971) *The Rio-Tinto Zinc Anti-Report*, Counter Information Services, available at http://www.st-andrews.ac.uk/csear/sa-exemplars/external-social-audits/, accessed 22 October 2013.

Crossley, N. (2003) 'Even newer social movements? Anti-corporate protests, capitalist crises and the remoralization of society', *Organization*, 10(2): 287–307.

Dey, C. (2007) 'Developing silent and shadow accounts', in J. Unerman, J. Bebbington and B. O'Dwyer (eds), *Sustainability Accounting and Accountability*, Routledge, pp. 307–26.

Dey, C., Russell, S. and Thomson, I. (2010) 'Exploring the potential of shadow accounts in problematising institutional conduct', in A. Ball and S. Osborne (eds) *Social Accounting and Public Management*, Routledge, pp. 64–78.

Dey, C., Russell, S. and Thomson, I. (2012) 'Problematising Institutional Conduct: The Transformative Potential of External Social Accounting', paper presented to the British Accounting and Finance Association Scottish Area Group Conference, University of Strathclyde, Glasgow, August.

Dey, C., Russell, S. and Thomson, I. (2013) 'ASH, Activism and Accounting: Resisting Big Tobacco', paper presented to the APIRA Conference, Kobe, Japan, July, available at http://www.apira2013. org/proceedings/pdfs/K127.pdf, accessed 22 October 2013.

Entine, J. (2003) *A Social and Environmental Audit of Body Shop: Anita Roddick and the Question of Character*, available at http://www.jonentine.com, accessed 22 October 2013.

European Coalition for Corporate Justice (ECCJ) (2008) *With Power Comes Responsibility*, European Coalition for Corporate Justice Report, available at http://www.corporatejustice.org/ IMG/pdf/ECC_001-08.pdf, accessed 22 October 2013.

Everett, J. (2003) 'Globalization and its new spaces for (alternative) accounting research', *Accounting Forum*, 27(4): 400–24.

Friends of the Earth (FoE) (2003a) *Failing the Challenge: The Other Shell Report 2002*, Friends of the Earth, available at http://www.st-andrews.ac.uk/csear/sa-exemplars/external-social-audits/, accessed 22 October 2013.

Friends of the Earth (FoE) (2003b) *Amec Counter Report 2002*, Friends of the Earth, available at http://www.st-andrews.ac.uk/csear/sa-exemplars/external-social-audits/, accessed 22 October 2013.

Gallhofer, S. and Haslam, J. (2003) *Accounting and Emancipation: Some Critical Interventions*, Routledge.

Gallhofer, S., Haslam, J., Roberts, C. and Monk, E. (2006) 'The emancipatory potential of online reporting: The case of counter accounting', *Accounting, Auditing and Accountability Journal*, 19(5): 681–718.

Geddes, M. (1992) 'The social audit movement' in D. L. Owen (ed.) *Green Reporting*, Chapman Hall, pp. 215–41.

Georgakopoulos, G. and Thomson, I. (2008) 'Social reporting, engagements, controversies and conflict in Scottish salmon farming', *Accounting, Auditing and Accountability Journal*, 21(8): 1116–43.

Gibson, K., Gray, R.H., Laing, Y. and Dey, C.R. (2001a) *Introduction to Silent and Shadow Accounts*, available at http://www.st-andrews.ac.uk/csear/sa-exemplars/silent-and-shadow/, accessed 22 October 2013.

Gibson, K., Gray, R.H., Laing, Y. and Dey, C.R. (2001b) *The Silent Accounts Project: Draft Silent and Shadow Accounts 1999–2000* (separate publications for Tesco plc and HSBC Holdings plc), available at http://www.st-andrews.ac.uk/csear/sa-exemplars/silent-and-shadow/, accessed 22 October 2013.

Gray, R.H. (1997) 'The silent practice of social accounting and corporate social reporting in companies' in S. Zadek, R. Evans and P. Pruzan (eds) *Building Corporate AccountAbility: Emerging Practices in Social and Ethical Accounting, Auditing and Reporting*, Earthscan.

Gray, R.H., Bebbington, J. and Walters, D. (1993) *Accounting for the Environment*, Paul Chapman.

Gray, R.H., Dey, C.R., Owen, D., Evans, R. and Zadek, S. (1997) 'Struggling with the praxis of social accounting: Stakeholders, accountability, audits and procedures', *Accounting, Auditing and Accountability Journal*, 10(3): 325–64.

Gray, R., Owen, D. and Adams, C. (1996) *Accounting and Accountability: Changes and Challenges in Corporate Social and Environmental Reporting*, Chapman-Hall.

Greer, J. and Bruno, K. (1996) *Greenwash: The Reality behind Corporate Environmentalism*, Third World Network.

Harte, G. and Owen, D. (1987) Fighting de-industrialisation: The role of local government social audits, *Accounting, Organisations and Society*, 12(2): 123–41.

Hertz, N. (2001) *The Silent Takeover: Global Capitalism and the Death of Democracy*, Heinemann.

Holzer, B. (2007) 'Framing the corporation: Royal Dutch/Shell and human rights woes in Nigeria', *Journal of Consumer Policy*, 30(3): 281–301.

Hond, F.D. and de Bakker, F. (2007) 'Ideologically motivated activism: How activist groups influence corporate social change activities', *Academy of Management Review*, 32(3): 901–24.

Joutsenvirta, M. (2011) 'Setting boundaries for corporate social responsibility: Firm–NGO relationship as discursive legitimation struggle', *Journal of Business Ethics*, 102(1): 57–75.

Kahn, R. and Kellner, D. (2005) 'Oppositional politics and the internet: A critical/reconstructive approach', *Cultural Politics*, 1(1): 75–100.

Klein, N. (2000) *No Logo*, Flamingo.

Larrinaga-Gonzalez, C. and Bebbington, J. (2001) 'Accounting change or institutional appropriation? – A case study of the implementation of environmental accounting', *Critical Perspectives on Accounting*, 12: 269–92.

Livesey, S. (2001) 'Eco-identity as discursive struggle: Royal Dutch/Shell, Brent Spar, and Nigeria', *Journal of Business Communication*, 38(1): 58–91.

Lubbers, E. (ed.) (2003) *Battling Big Business: Countering Greenwash, Infiltration and Other Forms of Corporate Bullying*, Common Courage Press.

McLean, P. and Elkind, B. (2004) *The Smartest Guys in the Room: The Amazing Rise and Scandalous Fall of Enron*, Penguin.

Medawar, C. (1976) 'The social audit: A political view', *Accounting, Organizations and Society*, 1(4): 389–94.

Messner, M. (2009) 'The limits of accountability', *Accounting, Organizations and Society*, 34(8): 918–38.

Moerman, L. and Van der Laan, S. (2005) 'Social reporting in the tobacco industry: All smoke and mirrors?', *Accounting, Auditing and Accountability Journal*, 18(3): 374–89.

O'Dwyer, B. (2003) 'Conceptions of corporate social responsibility: The nature of managerial capture', *Accounting, Auditing & Accountability Journal*, 16(4): 523–57.

O'Dwyer, B. and Owen, D.L. (2005) 'Assurance statement quality in environmental social and sustainability reporting: A critical examination', *British Accounting Review*, 37(2): 205–30.

O'Sullivan, N. and O'Dwyer, B. (2009) 'Stakeholder perspectives on a financial sector legitimation process: The case of NGOs and the Equator Principles', *Accounting, Auditing & Accountability Journal*, 22(4): 553–87.

Owen, D.L., Swift, T.A., Humphrey, C. and Bowerman, M. (2000) 'The new social audits: Accountability, managerial capture or the agenda of social champions?', *European Accounting Review*, 9(1): 81–98.

Owen, D.L., Swift, T.A. and Hunt, K. (2001) 'Questioning the role of stakeholder engagement in social and ethical accounting', *Accounting Forum*, 25(3): 264–82.

Pilger, J. (2004) *Tell Me No Lies: Investigative Journalism and its Triumphs*, Jonathan Cape.

Ridgers, B. (1979) 'The use of statistics in counter information', in J. Irvine (ed.) *Demystifying Social Statistics*, Pluto Press, pp. 325–36.

Roberts, J. (2009) 'No one is perfect: The limits of transparency and an ethic for "intelligent" accountability', *Accounting, Organizations and Society*, 34(8): 957–70.

Rowell, A. (2003) 'The spread of greenwash', in E. Lubbers (ed.) *Battling Big Business*, Common Courage Press, pp. 19–25.

Schlosser, E. (2002) *Fast Food Nation*, Penguin.

Shaoul, J. (1998) 'Critical financial analysis and accounting for stakeholders', *Critical Perspectives on Accounting*, 9: 235–49.

Shenkin, M. and Coulson, A. (2007) 'Accountability through activism: Learning from Bourdieu', *Accounting, Auditing & Accountability Journal*, 20(2): 297–317.

Sikka, P. and Willmott, H. (1997) 'Practising critical accounting', *Critical Perspectives on Accounting*, 8(1–2): 149–65.

Simms, A. (2007) *Tescopoly: How One Shop Came out on Top and Why it Matters*, Constable.

Social Audit Ltd (1976) *Avon Rubber Company*, Social Audit Ltd Report, available at http://www.st-andrews.ac.uk/csear/sa-exemplars/external-social-audits/, accessed 22 October 2013.

Solomon, J. and Thomson, I. (2009) 'Satanic mills and Braithwaite's "On the rise and fall of the River Wandle; its springs, tributaries, and pollution": An example of Victorian external environmental auditing?' *Accounting Forum*, 3(1): 74–87.

Sorkin, A. (2009) *Too Big to Fail: The Inside Story of How Wall Street and Washington Fought to Save the Financial System – and Themselves*, Penguin.

Spence, C. (2009) 'Social accounting's emancipatory potential: A Gramscian critique', *Critical Perspectives on Accounting*, 20(2): 205–27.

Spence, C., Husillos, J. and Correa-Ruiz, C. (2010) 'Cargo cult science and the death of politics: A critical review of social and environmental accounting research', *Critical Perspectives on Accounting*, 21(1): 76–89.

Swift, T. and Dando, N. (2002) 'From methods to ideologies: Closing the assurance expectations gap in social and ethical accounting, auditing and reporting', *Journal of Corporate Citizenship*, 8: 81–90.

Tilt, C.A. (1994) 'The influence of external pressure groups on corporate social disclosure: Some empirical evidence', *Accounting, Auditing and Accountability Journal*, 7(4): 47–72.

Unerman, J. and Bennett, M. (2004) 'Increased stakeholder dialogue and the internet: Towards greater corporate accountability or reinforcing capitalist hegemony?', *Accounting, Organizations and Society*, 29(7): 685–707.

Unerman, J. and O'Dwyer, B. (2006) 'Theorising accountability for NGO advocacy', *Accounting, Auditing and Accountability Journal*, 19(3): 349–76.

Wilkinson, R. and Pickett, K. (2009) *The Spirit Level: Why Equality is Better for Everyone*, Penguin.

Zadek, S., Evans, R. and Pruzan, P. (1997) *Building Corporate Accountability: Emerging Practice in Social and Ethical Accounting and Auditing*, Earthscan.

# 8 Environmental and social assessment in finance

*Andrea B. Coulson and Niamh O'Sullivan*

## Introduction

It is hard to raise finance today without some form of environmental or social assessment. As we will discuss, the motives for such 'sustainability' considerations in financial investment decisions are mixed. Many commercial loans now routinely contain an environmental credit risk assessment and investment portfolios contain some form of environmental and social risk consideration (Coulson, 2002; Pearce and Ganzi, 2003; Scholtens, 2009). On the other hand, niche products have been developed to reflect an ethical preference for how money is invested and the consequences that investment has on the environment and society. For example, premium loan rates and conditions are offered on mortgages for environmentally sensitive home improvements and investors are offered a range of specialist socially responsible investment fund opportunities (Sparkes, 2002).

As the product market in sustainable finance has developed, the margins between the mainstream and niche products have become blurred. How to evaluate the impact of social and environmental performance on profitability remains a problem for product providers and their market constituents (Lou and Ganzi, 2002; Stichele, 2004; Bray *et al.*, 2007). Thus, a debate on the degree to which profit may be sacrificed for ethics is questionable, as is how to 'value' the impact of so-called ethical concerns whether 'positive' or 'negative'.

The purpose of this chapter is to highlight the nature of environmental and social criteria included in financial decisions and the range of approaches used by financiers to evaluate corporate environmental and social performance. In evaluating financial investment decisions it is important to note that the focus of the chapter will be on the provision of business finance. Personal finance is outside the scope of the analysis.

This chapter will address in turn the issues arising when corporate investment is financed by debt and equity. Taking loan finance, project finance and responsible investment in turn the chapter examines how environmental and social considerations are being factored into lending and investment decisions and the practical steps that have been taken by lenders and investors to standardize decision processes.[1] The chapter ends with a reflection on the sustainability reporting practices of Financial Institutions (FIs). Attention is paid throughout to the need for financiers to be socially responsible and accountable for their activities and the extent to which lending and investment practice reflects their 'social accountability'.[2] This topic has taken on greater international significance in the wake of the recent financial crisis.

# Debt

## *Loan finance*

### *Policy development*

It is well documented that as environmental legislation has increased, particularly during the 1990s, bank lenders have developed risk assessment procedures to offset potential liability for environmental damage caused by their borrowers.[3] Lenders have expressed particular concern that they may be held directly liable for contaminated land taken as security for a debt, a traditional method of credit risk mitigation, or that they may face the indirect environmental risk of credit default if a borrower's environmental costs adversely impact their ability to repay a loan (Smith, 1994). In response to liability debates surrounding legislative developments, lenders have traditionally argued that it is not their role to police corporate activities (BBA, 1993). However, there is evidence that the increased scale and frequency of pollution incidents and natural disasters during the 1990s provoked lenders to standardize the adoption of environmental credit policies and procedures (Coulson, 1999, 2001, 2002; Ulph *et al.*, 1999). It is unclear whether in such instances lenders were adopting a defensive strategy, accepting some form of social responsibility or seeking to limit risk to their reputation through association with a polluter and a borrower defaulting on loan repayment or a combination of these.

From an ethical perspective, as debates on corporate governance have highlighted, it has been increasingly argued that a lender financing corporate activity should take some responsibility for the environmental and social impact of their transactions as a form of good corporate governance (Scholtens, 2006; Solomon and Solomon, 2006). Such arguments on social responsibility have been strengthened by the public bailout of banks during the recent financial crisis and increased degree of public shareholding and accountability.

There is also evidence that over the last few decades in addition to environmental assessments, social concerns have been integrated into many high street banks' credit assessment procedures. From a review of bank policy and procedures these appear to be governed by a combination of a bank's corporate social responsibility and risk agendas (Coulson, 2009; Scholtens, 2009). For example, in the case of Barclays, sustainability issues are implemented in a 'top down' manner, beginning with two Board Standards. One standard is on corporate responsibility, and the other is on credit risk. The Board Standards are implemented at an operational level by following industry specific risk guidance notes covering more than 50 environmentally and socially sensitive activities across ten different sectors: agriculture and fisheries; metals and mining; oil and gas; power generation, supply and distribution; chemicals, pharmaceuticals, manufacturing and bulk storage; general manufacturing; utilities and waste management; infrastructure; service industry; and forestry and logging. Detailed guidance notes for oil and gas, for example, cover potential environmental and social credit risks which may arise within exploration, production, refining, transport, retail and decommissioning (Coulson, 2011).[4]

Less common among banks are ethical screening policies such as the one promoted by the UK's Co-operative Bank, under which loans for activities that are perceived to damage the environment and society are screened out of their loan book (rejected) from the outset. For example, the Co-operative Bank[5] publicly promote that they will not lend to any company associated with arms or tobacco trading or manufacture, and is famous for its extensive

consultation with depositors and other stakeholders as a means of determining current ethical policy concerns.

Most commercial lenders do not promote ethical screening activities as they maintain few
loans are rejected purely on environmental or social grounds – normally the business is also
a poor financial performer and has other issues. They argue that to isolate a borrower's environmental and social performance from their financial performance may not be desirable or
indeed possible (Coulson, 2011).

The most common view of lenders[6] is that they will work with a borrower to try to reduce
harm. Such lenders highlight the integration of environmental and social credit risk assessment procedures within their overall lending decision-making processes as a means of
discharging their social accountability (Scott and John, 2002). In their defence, they pose the
challenge that if finance is not available to 'dirty' companies, who will then pay for clean-up
activities? On this basis lenders reveal credit policies that encourage dirty companies to
improve their position for the common good and their combined long-term profitability.
Given banks' concern for lender liability, it is certainly in their commercial interest to
manage such risk. A number of banks take a more proactive stance, additionally offering
lending products designed to encourage environmental and socially sensitive investments.
For example, Deutsche Bank[7] has a dedicated micro-credit fund to encourage sustainability
at home and in developing countries.

*Content and scope of credit assessment*

In terms of the nature of environmental and social criteria included in financing decisions,
the primary consideration (whether ethical or risk based) stems from the sector of business
activity in which the potential borrower is involved. For those interested in looking beyond
the borrower's main business activity to subsidiary and related business transactions a
detailed review of the financial accounts of a business and its supply chain may be necessary.
A precedent was set regarding the anticipated scope of such analysis when in 2001 Friends
of the Earth (FoE) named and shamed banks lending to the pulp and paper industry (Matthew
and van Gelder, 2001). In the study, FoE used the financial statements and notes to accounts
of Asia Pulp and Paper (APP) and its related holdings to identify how the APP Group was
financed and, in particular, which banks had provided it with debt finance to support its
activities. While criticized by the bank industry for failing to acknowledge the timing of
bank investments and related credit policy development the study illustrates the extent to
which non-governmental organizations (NGOs) may hold banks accountable and the potential role that traditional financial information related to shareholders and investments can
play in following the money and revealing investors. More recent scrutiny of coal financing
and 'climate killers ranking' of banks by the NGO network BankTrack illustrates continued
interest in banks' asset holdings including corporate loans and the risk to bank reputation
through such association with a polluter (Schucking *et al.*, 2011).

There is certainly evidence that fears of environmental liability have led lenders to focus
their analysis on the borrower's main business activity and past and present land use of
business premises. In terms of direct liability, the value of asset impairment due to environmental effects is examined first through the borrower's financial statements. Traditional
criticisms levied at corporate financial reporting by lenders are that financial statements are
historic, untimely and lack integration of relevant environmental and social information
(SBI and UNEP FI, 2011). While sustainability reports try to avoid at least one of these
criticisms they remain largely annual events and require supplementary timely updates from

other sources. Given lenders' interest in risk and business viability they use accounts as a source of primary financial indicators but supplement this information with sustainability accounts and reports and private management accounts of financial and business positions and projections (Holland, 1998).[8] In the case of environmental risk assessment of land taken as security for a debt, evidence may additionally be drawn from environmental impact assessments and independent property valuation conducted by the borrowers or, in the absence of information, under a special commission by the bank (Coulson, 2001, 2009). This gives some indication that traditional financial statements and in some cases sustainability accounts and reports are considered inadequate for property valuation and liability assessment.

Studies of credit risk assessment have revealed that further credit considerations vary between banks and may range from consideration of a borrower's geographical location to the implications of climate change issues such as flooding or other weather related risks. In terms of a bank's social assessment of its borrowers, issues include for example human rights concerns for employee welfare, child labour policies, and operations in areas of conflict and war. In some cases potential borrowers may voluntarily make environmental and social information public depending on their formal sustainability accounting and disclosure practice (Cooper, 2002; Coulson, 2002). Lenders have revealed that if publicly unavailable, such information would be part of the 'private' information requested by them from borrowers and such requests could be followed up by inspection of documents such as pollution consents and permits (Holland, 1998; Solomon and Solomon, 2006; Solomon *et al.*, 2011). A lender's assessment of the managementability of a borrower and their business viability may also include consideration of reports and ratings produced by specialized, third party research providers and rating agencies such as the Carbon Disclosure Project, EIRIS, and Sustainalytics.[9] However, in general, ethical and risk-based lenders alike encourage the public disclosure of social and environmental information by borrowers as an example of good management practice.

The ability of banks to influence borrower behaviour is a subject of considerable debate, particular with respect to the potential implication that participation in management may have on environmental liability (BBA, 1993; Coulson, 2009). However, as more banks adopt environmental and social credit risk assessment and it becomes harder to shop around for 'dirty' finance, borrower practice may change. There are a number of initiatives in the market to raise the standard of environmental and social credit risk assessment at a procedural level across the global banking sector. For example, the report *Credit Risk Impacts of a Changing Climate* (Bray *et al.*, 2007) highlights efforts within the banking sector to collaborate and encourage a common approach to the assessment of climate related credit risk. It includes for example how to identify climate 'sensitivities' and thus credit risk exposure in sectors dependent on substantial fixed assets and infrastructure as well as energy, chemicals, pharmaceuticals and tourism.

In terms of determining the degree of adherence to such initiatives and holding lenders to account for their investment decisions, efforts have been hampered by a lack of consensus among FIs on a standardized reporting format on credit provision and environmental and social credit assessment (Stichele, 2004). A separate section, Reporting by Financial Institutions, has been devoted to the reporting practice of FIs at the end of this chapter. It is noteworthy here that evaluating the environmental and social impact of a lender's loan portfolio is highly problematic. The transparent integration of social and environmental information with financial information is needed to enhance financial interpretations. Further, financial and non-financial information[10] on environmental and social performance are required to provide a means of judging the accountability of both lenders and their borrowers.

The next section, Project finance, will address environmental and social assessment in project finance, a structured finance facility which by virtue of its potential scale of impact – heightened need for social accountability and the launch of the Equator Principles (EP) – has been subject to considerable attention in recent years. While recognizing that many banks now have environmental and social risk policies and procedures for sensitive sectors and issues for loan financing per se, we showcase project finance below due to significant developments in the environmental and social risk management and accountability within this sector since 2003.

## *Project finance*

The credit risk considerations noted above for loan finance equally apply to environmental and social considerations in project finance.[11] However, an increased motive for environmental and social assessment in project finance appears to be the need to manage a bank's risk to reputation – alongside potential borrower default – as opposed to liability management alone (Bullied, 2005; Watchman, 2005). In this instance banks are concerned not only for their public (customer and shareholder) reputation but increasingly their reputation within the bank community itself. This is important in the case of project finance because many transactions are carried out as part of a syndication exercise and one weak link could jeopardize the whole transaction.

In addition, project finance, though a small part of overall FIs' operations, has traditionally represented the most visible and tangible sustainability impacts of an FI due to its association with the financing of large, complex, environmentally and socially sensitive projects; involving, for example, the installation of dams, power plants, mines and oil and gas pipelines in the developing world and emerging economies. As a result, project finance banks have come under particular pressure from NGOs (such as the BankTrack network[12]) to be socially accountable for their financing of high profile projects such as the Baku-Tbilisi-Ceyhan (BTC) pipeline or Sakhalin II integrated oil and gas pipeline development (BankTrack, 2004a; Platform, 2004; Freshfields, 2005[13]).

Such pressures led a coalition of commercial banks to develop and adopt the EP in 2003.[14] Based on the International Finance Corporation (IFC) environmental and social performance standards,[15] the EP are a set of voluntary environmental and social risk management guidelines for project finance. In adopting the EP Financial Institutions (EPFIs) voluntarily commit to applying environmental and social principles to the design, execution and management of project finance deals of $10 million dollars and upwards; and pledge not to engage with, or provide, finance to clients who will not comply with the principles.

More specifically, when financing (and advising) on a project, adopting EPFIs are asked first to review and categorize projects as either 'A' (high risk), 'B' (moderate risk) or 'C' (low risk) as per IFC classifications; and to ensure an environmental and social assessment, that meets all applicable standards, and is conducted during the project due diligence phase (Principles 1, 2 and 3). Second, they must ensure project sponsors; develop an environmental and social action plan and management system; conduct adequate community consultation and disclosure; and establish a community grievance mechanism – all to be reviewed by a third party – in order to progress through the credit risk approval stage (Principles 4, 5, 6 and 7). Third, they must covenant project sponsors to meet EP requirements in the term sheet and loan documentation phase (Principle 8). And fourth, they are to employ independent experts to monitor borrower compliance (Principle 9); and work with borrowers to address any breaches of compliance over the life of the loan. The EP are therefore designed to be embedded throughout the entire project financing process (O'Sullivan, 2010) (see Tables 8.1 and 8.2)

Quite importantly, EPFIs are also required 'to report publicly at least annually about [their] Equator Principles implementation processes and experience, taking into account appropriate confidentiality considerations' (Principle 10; EP II, 2006, p. 5). This reporting should 'at a minimum include the number of transactions screened by each EPFI, including the categorization accorded to transactions (and may include a breakdown by sector or region), and information regarding implementation' (EP II, 2006, p. 5). This was a new requirement introduced in the revised version of the principles, Equator Principles II, launched in July 2006; and supported by a Reporting Guidance Document issued by EPFIs in 2007 (Equator Principles, 2007).

EPFIs had been the subject of intense criticism from NGOs such as BankTrack since 2003, due to: the lack of formal EP accountability mechanisms at institutional, organizational and project level (e.g. an Ombudsman function); a lack of transparency surrounding EP implementation by EPFIs; inconsistent EP disclosures among those EPFIs that were reporting; as well as the emergence of an EP 'free-rider' problem; and the continued financing of controversial projects (see O'Sullivan and O'Dwyer, 2009). Principle 10 was thus designed, in part, to address such social accountability concerns. It also allowed EPFIs to begin to more formally address EP governance at institutional level by making EP reporting *the* EP membership requirement in 2008, through a newly formed EP management structure and emerging EP Association.[16]

While NGOs have welcomed such structural improvements to the EP, they have, however, viewed Principle 10 as a 'lowest common denominator' approach to EP accountability, and an insufficient response to the extensive transparency, disclosure and governance recommendations for which they have continually campaigned (BankTrack, 2004b, 2006, 2011). In addition, BankTrack's assessment of EPFI reporting in 2007 showed that of the EPFIs that adopted the EP before 2007 '40 per cent did not meet the minimum [reporting] requirements, 19 per cent met them and 40 per cent exceeded them' (BankTrack, 2007, p. 1)

While there has been a general improvement in the amount and quality of EPFI reporting on EP implementation in recent years, EPFIs have continually referred to commercial

*Table 8.1* The Equator Principles (as per EP II, 2006)

| *The Equator Principles* | |
| --- | --- |
| Principle 1 | Review and Categorisation |
| Principle 2 | Social and Environmental Assessment |
| Principle 3 | Applicable Social and Environmental Standards |
| Principle 4 | Action Plan and Management System |
| Principle 5 | Consultation and Disclosure |
| Principle 6 | Grievance Mechanism |
| Principle 7 | Independent Review |
| Principle 8 | Covenants |
| Principle 9 | Independent Monitoring and Reporting |
| Principle 10 | EPFI Reporting |

Source: http://www.equator-principles.com/index.php/about-ep/38-about/about/352, accessed 22 June 2012.

*Table 8.2* The project financing – Equator Principles (EP) process

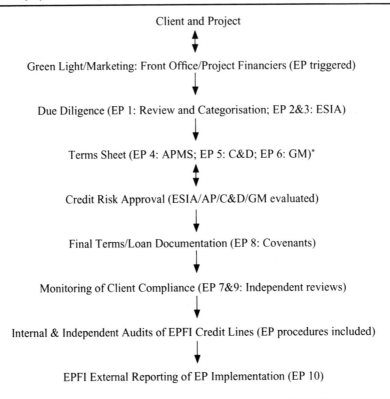

Client and Project

Green Light/Marketing: Front Office/Project Financiers (EP triggered)

Due Diligence (EP 1: Review and Categorisation; EP 2&3: ESIA)

Terms Sheet (EP 4: APMS; EP 5: C&D; EP 6: GM)*

Credit Risk Approval (ESIA/AP/C&D/GM evaluated)

Final Terms/Loan Documentation (EP 8: Covenants)

Monitoring of Client Compliance (EP 7&9: Independent reviews)

Internal & Independent Audits of EPFI Credit Lines (EP procedures included)

EPFI External Reporting of EP Implementation (EP 10)

*Key:*

ESIA: Environmental and social impact assessment
APMS: Action plan & management system
C&D: Consultation & disclosure
GM: Grievance mechanism
The solid arrows indicate the progression of the project finance-EP process (the double arrows representing interrelationships therein). The dotted line indicates the ongoing interrelationship between the client/project and the various phases of the project finance-EP process.
*Ongoing requirements over the life of the loan

Source: O'Sullivan, 2010, p. 220.

confidentiality and legal conditions as restricting the levels of disclosure on projects and clients that NGOs have demanded. In addition, variant organizational structures, levels of experience with, and capacity to address, sustainability concerns across different FIs have also contributed to inconsistencies in EP implementation and disclosure. Furthermore, in the absence of any formal accountability mechanisms, EPFIs have tended to believe that their own 'self-policing' in project finance syndicates, along with NGOs' external watchdog role, is sufficient; and that ultimately the sanction for irresponsible behaviour is the individual EPFI's reputation (O'Sullivan, 2010). Yet, NGOs have never been comfortable being viewed as *the* external accountability mechanism for the EP or EPFIs, as they desire EPFIs themselves to take responsibility for their actions (O'Sullivan and O'Dwyer, 2009).

Despite ongoing NGO criticism, the EP have still had a major impact on the project finance market; with 77 adopting EPFIs[17] currently (as per July 2012), and the EPs widely quoted as being applied to over 70 per cent of international project finance deals.[18] The EP are now regarded as the standard for more responsible project finance, allowing EPFIs to better assess, mitigate, document and monitor the potentially adverse social and environmental risks associated with financing projects. Moreover, they have fostered EPFI environmental and social awareness, policies and procedures beyond project finance into other commercial banking activities (O'Sullivan, 2010); and helped catalyse other environmental and social management practices among financial institutions, for example, the Carbon Principles[19] in the US, and the Climate Principles[20] worldwide. The EP have also provided a platform for engagement with a broad range of interested stakeholders, including NGOs, clients and industry bodies (O'Sullivan, 2010). Furthermore, Scholtens and Dam (2007) find EPFIs to have a significantly better environmental and social performance record than non-EPFIs. Nevertheless, *specific* evidence of the benefits of the EP on project affected communities and environments remains heavily questioned (BankTrack, 2011), and requires more thorough academic investigation.

The next section of this chapter, Equity, provides a critical investigation of responsible investment by equity investors. In particular, it examines investment methods, sources of information drawn on for decision making and standardization and performance of responsible investment.

## Equity

### *Responsible investment*

#### *Investment methods*

An investor has a fiduciary duty to act responsibly. Arguably this fiduciary duty includes a responsibility to sustainability. Today interpretations of responsible investment are wide ranging and include the domain of both specialist social responsible investment (SRI [socially responsible investment][21]) funds and mainstream investors such as Schroders (an asset management company[22] that employs dedicated sustainability analysts within its financial analyst team). Two types of screening are said to characterize traditional SRI decisions: 'negative' and 'positive' screening. Negative screening, for example, involves avoidance of investment in companies perceived to have a 'negative' impact on the environment and society, such as those involved in the manufacture or processing of weapons, nuclear power and tobacco. Companies of this type are normally screened out of a portfolio on a sectoral basis according to their core business activity. In a method similar to that used by 'ethical' lenders, company accounts may be subject to scrutiny to establish subsidiaries or related business activities. Investment decisions in such cases may rest on issues of governance and transparency of such commercial relationships through reference to disclosures made by the constituent.

A positive screen involves actively seeking investment in companies with a 'positive' impact on the environment, such as those involved in renewable energy generation or recycling. For example, Jupiter Ecology Fund was launched in 1988 and was one of the first investment funds responding positively on sustainability. Today it has a global growth remit and focuses on companies providing solutions to environmental and social problems.[23] In such cases it is likely that the investee company's reports and accounts (both financial and otherwise) will be subject to close scrutiny by the investor (Kreander, 2001; Corporation of London, 2002). FIs adopting positive screening methods often actively encourage reporting of environmental and social criteria as an indicator of good management practice and encourage this through shareholder activism. For example, in 2001 Morley Fund Management became the first fund manager to require large UK companies to publish environmental reports as part of its voting policy. If a FTSE 100 company did not publish an environmental report, Morley would vote against the adoption of the company's report and accounts at the AGM. The use of voting to try and influence environmental and social impact is a practice adopted by many investors today, and is particularly popular in the United States. Further, identification of investor views on what reporting should constitute involves a more detailed investigation of investor objectives and assessment methods including 'engagement' with investment companies.

Since the end of the 1990s responsible investors have also promoted the use of 'engagement' as a third method of investment. The general strategy behind engagement is that an investor will develop a relationship with members of the companies in which they invest and use this relationship to try and persuade them of the need to change their behaviour, highlighting the need for their constituents to be accountable for their activities and try to evoke 'positive' change and increased social responsibility. To maintain insider trading regulations, information provided during the engagement process must be publicly available. Three strategic approaches to engagement are common: an issues basis (e.g. corporate governance); a company focus (e.g. pension disclosures); or a combination of the two. In turn, engagement methods are wide ranging including: informal 'dialogue'; shareholder action in terms of voting shares; shareholder resolutions and buying shares; public campaigns and collaborative action by a group of investors (Dresner, 2002; Green, 2003; Hummel and Timmer, 2003).

Engagement is viewed by some as providing an opportunity to move responsible investment away from debates about the trade-off between investment ethics and returns and to encourage dialogue and debate on responsible disclosure. However, the use of engagement is not beyond criticism. Concerns have been expressed that powerful investors may exert undue influence on the company in which they invest leading to information asymmetry and corporate capture. As noted previously, such criticisms equally apply to engagement between debt providers and their borrowers (Baskin, 1988; Elsas and Krahnen, 1998; Tomkins, 2001; Roberts *et al.*, 2003). To balance the opportunities and risks posed by engagement methods it is important that the engagement process is transparent to maintain its integrity so that information for investment decision making is reliable.

*Information for investment decision making*

In November 2003 European Sustainable and Responsible Investment Forum (Eurosif) launched the Corporate Sustainability and Responsibility Research Quality Standard as a set of voluntary principles designed to maintain the integrity of investment decisions and the information on which they are based. Eurosif ask signatories to the principles to commit to using independent sources to assess companies; being transparent on the methodology they use; and being independent of outside influence (Howard-Boyd, 2003; Eurosif, 2004).

The FTSE4Good and Dow Jones Sustainability Indexes[24] are prime examples of independent sources that act as benchmarking tools designed for FIs to evaluate corporate sustainability performance. Launched in 1999 and 2001 respectively the Dow Jones Sustainability Indexes and FTSE4Good have earned prominence and credibility for their foundation on well-established global equity index series (Dow Jones and FTSE). As in the case of screening by SRIs themselves, exclusions in the indexes typically include non-nuclear weapons, nuclear power, nuclear weapons systems, tobacco producers, and extractors/processors of uranium (FTSE, 2003, 2005). These indices may be used singularly by investors to make their investment decisions or in conjunction with other independent sources of information such as Sustainalytics and EIRIS, noted previously, who provide investment research into the environmental, social, governance and ethical performance of companies (see note 2).

Investors' use of independent sources to supply information for responsible investment decision making helps to alleviate questions being raised regarding the right to information and problems of information asymmetry potentially associated with engagement. The development of indices and rankings also helps to standardize information provision and encourage parity in decision making through benchmarking. However, despite such indices and investor initiatives, Solomon and Solomon (2006) show, through a series of interviews with both SRIs and mainstream investors in the UK, that while company social, ethical and environmental disclosures are decision-useful to institutional investors, private disclosures are still largely relied upon. As discovered by Solomon and Solomon (2006), a failure of public disclosures may mean that private disclosures between investors and investee companies increase in order to meet investor information demands. This highlights the importance of public disclosures by companies to the integrity of the investment processes.

*Standardization and performance of responsible investment*

The UN Principles for Responsible Investment (PRI), launched in 2006, offer a more standardized framework for responsible investment which provides investment managers, asset owners and investee companies alike with a better understanding of what is required in responsible investment decision making, portfolio construction, ownership and disclosures (see Table 8.3).[25]

With 1,084 international signatories (as per July 2012) representing over US$30 trillion assets under management, the PRI would appear to have made a substantial impact on the investment world. Relatedly, stock market data shows that sustainable investments have reached US$10.6 trillion globally (Eurosif, 2010), a market that will no doubt grow further.

When it comes to establishing the responsible investment rationale, one of the most dominant subjects of debate has been whether or not responsible investments sacrifice profits (e.g. see Lou and Ganzi, 2002 on SRI funds); and how social investment decisions affect market performance in general (Murray *et al.*, 2006). Empirical studies have mixed results. Some posit that sustainable investments may outperform the market (e.g. Derwall *et al.*, 2005); underperform the market (e.g. Chong *et al.*, 2006); or make no significant difference regarding their risk-adjusted financial returns (e.g. Bauer *et al.*, 2005). Others suggest that the financial performance of the various types of socially responsible investments differs considerably per category of financial instrument analysed (Scholtens, 2007), and that more social performance by, for example variant SRI funds, does not automatically mean less financial performance of such funds (Biehl *et al.*, 2011).

Hence, the debate continues as to whether or not those who invest on ethical grounds sacrifice financial returns and more importantly, influence behaviour. For, while there is a plethora of literature devoted to the measurement of, for example, the financial impact and performance of responsible investment activities in general (see Hoepner,

*Table 8.3* The principles for responsible investment (PRI)

| We will: | |
| --- | --- |
| Principle 1 | Incorporate environmental, social and governance (ESG) issues into investment analysis and decision-making processes |
| Principle 2 | Be active owners and incorporate ESG issues into our ownership policies and practices |
| Principle 3 | Seek appropriate disclosure on ESG issues by the entities in which we invest |
| Principle 4 | Promote acceptance and implementation of the Principles within the investment industry |
| Principle 5 | Work together to enhance our effectiveness in implementing the Principles |
| Principle 6 | Each report on our activities and progress towards implementing the Principles |

Source: http://www.unpri.org/press/principles-for-responsible-investment-hit-8-trillion-mark-on-first-year-anniversary/, accessed 22 June 2012.

2007), there remains a shortage of in-depth, interpretive research into the implementation of the PRI and the actual impact of responsible investment on investee company behaviour, broader society and the environments in which they operate. Therefore, the question remains whether responsible investment is making a real difference on the ground.

## Reporting by Financial Institutions

Disclosures by FIs on methods of responsible investment, and approaches to information gathering and content play an important part in determining the discharge of investor accountability, by ensuring that the investment process is transparent. In general the level and quality of reporting by FIs on their environmental and social impacts has increased since its inception by some pioneering banks in the 1990s, such as those involved in the initiation of the United Nations Environment Programme Finance Initiative (UNEP FI)[26] in 1992: for example Deutsche Bank, HSBC, Natwest, Royal Bank of Canada and Westpac. This has progressed from a focus on their direct impacts, or in-house ecology issues – such as water, paper and electricity use and waste production – to their indirect environmentally and socially damaging activities, through their lending, investment and asset management operations.

The most recent KPMG survey on corporate responsibility reporting shows that sustainability reporting in the international financial services sector has increased from 49 per cent in 2008 to 61 per cent in 2011 (KPMG, 2011). The latter has been assisted in part by the launch of the Global Reporting Initiative (GRI) Financial Services Sector Supplement (FSSS) in 2008, providing a set of quantitative and qualitative indicators specifically tailored to assist banks, insurers and asset managers to report on their sustainability impacts.[27] The need remains however for an in-depth investigation of how effective the GRI FSSS has been in improving the materiality, inclusiveness, completeness and overall quality of sustainability reporting by FIs; and whether FIs are actually using the supplement to the best of their abilities when they – like all GRI reporters – have the option to choose which indicators they report against.

With the advent of for example the EP, PRI and Carbon Disclosure Project,[28] FI reporting on the impacts of specific aspects of their operations – as part of their overall sustainability reports or as stand-alone reports/accounts in themselves – have also increased. Yet, for

example, while many leading EPFIs have gone beyond the minimum EP reporting requirements of Principle 10, there is a need for improved clarity and transparency surrounding the
internal auditing of the processes through which the EP are applied to project financing
arrangements, as well as the external assurance of the same (Macve and Chen, 2010;
O'Sullivan, 2010). This could initially be assisted through more comprehensive use of the
GRI FSSS; which specifically includes a reporting indicator (FS9) on the: '*Coverage and
frequency of audits to assess implementation of environmental and social policies and risk
assessment procedures*' (GRI, 2011, p. 2). And it is hoped that EP III will more adequately
address these ongoing accountability concerns.

Somewhat more positive signs have emerged from the PRI camp, where the PRI secre-
tariat have produced a detailed report analysing the most recent implementation and
reporting activities of PRI signatories against the six principles (PRI, 2011). The core
findings for 2011 (inter alia) show that in total 93 per cent of signatories disclose their
approach to environmental, social and governance (ESG) integration to some extent, and
42 per cent disclose it to a large extent. In addition, 71 per cent of signatories are stated to
have asked their investee companies to integrate ESG information into their financial
reporting – an increase from 67 per cent in 2010 (PRI, 2011). This is evidence of the materiality of ESG issues for institutional investors and with the current movement towards more
integrated reporting one would expect this trend to increase even further in coming years.

## Summary and conclusion

As noted at the start of this chapter, it is hard to raise debt and equity finance today without some form of environmental or social assessment. The examination of how FIs seek
to assess environmental and social performance, as part of their financing decisions,
reveals behaviour is driven by corporate responsibility and risk management of the investment. Particular to debt finance has been the development of credit risk assessment procedures, to manage the risk of a lender inheriting environmental liability and a borrower
defaulting due to a lack of environmental and social consideration. Similarly, responsible
equity investment is arguably part of an investor's fiduciary duty and inherent within the
risk management of their investment. In the case of equity investment the visibility of
responsible behaviour has been highlighted by specialized funds designed to screen out
'dirty' companies and/or favour environmental and socially sensitive investment and
questions raised by mainstream fund managers. In contrast to equity finance, only a small
degree of screening out occurs in the debt finance market and most banks argue they work
with their borrowers to reduce harm to the environment and society. Building on this
principle, a niche loan market exists to further encourage environmental and social centred investment.

Both debt and equity providers share a risk to reputation through association with 'dirty'
companies. This is typically categorized according to a borrower's business activity and its
environmental and socially sensitive nature. Beyond this, financiers recognize they face
problems establishing meaningful indicators for environmental and social performance,
as well as evaluating the environmental and social impact on financial performance of
potential borrowers seeking finance. This is equally true for an FI's evaluation of its investment portfolios and is a challenge when reporting its own performance. In terms of debt
finance, adequacy of asset and liability valuation and disclosure is an important issue, while
in the case of equity investment, comparability of their potential fund constituents is an
important concern. The solution for lenders and investors is to engage with business to

achieve clarification. For both types of finance, issues of information asymmetry and corporate capture dominate debates on the value of the engagement process. To help to reduce the risk of information asymmetry and corporate capture, financial providers complement their own assessments with independent environmental and social indices, and corporate rankings specially designed to support financial decisions.

Reporting by FIs of their investment strategies and methods of assessment plays an important part in clarifying to borrowers/potential borrowers the demand for and use of public disclosures of environmental and social information. Voluntary FI initiatives such as EP and the PRI have helped to standardize responsible investment processes and environmental and social considerations in finance. Standardization has been encouraged by the guiding of common policy and practice among FIs, including those related to disclosure. It is recognized that reporting by FIs is increasing, particularly since the advent of the EP and the PRI. Here, a significant stakeholder role is played by NGOs focusing on the impact of financial investment on the environment and society who maintain pressure on FI to act responsibly and recognize their accountability, at least in part through reporting. As highlighted in the case of the EP, lack of assurance of reported information and self-policing by FI remain contentious areas, with transparency complicated by FI claims of competitive differences and requirements to maintain confidentiality.

Efforts to integrate environmental and social considerations into financial reporting and standardize disclosure remain challenges for both FIs and the companies in which they invest. Lack of transparency and credibility of information disclosed make it difficult to hold both borrowers and investors to account. Thus, the practice of publicly reporting reliable environmental and social performance information by both a company seeking finance and their financial provider is critical to both parties' discharge of accountability. The continued development of research and practice on environmental and social 'valuation' in financial accounting are an essential part of the development of transparent environmental and social assessment in finance.

To facilitate environmental and social accountability, finance based voluntary initiatives need, at a minimum, to ensure transparent, public disclosure of reliable environmental and social information as a necessary part of responsible investment. In light of concerns expressed by FIs' stakeholders, in particular NGOs, regarding cases of failure in investor accountability it may be necessary to regulate the FIs' practices which are currently subject to voluntary initiatives. To ensure the further development of responsible investment debates on valuation, disclosure and voluntary initiatives versus regulation need to be considered together in order to align and optimize mechanisms for accountability of FIs and their borrowers.

## Notes

1 We also acknowledge recent efforts to standardize the integration of sustainability concerns into insurance practice, for example through the launch of the Principles of Sustainable Insurance (PSI) in June 2012 (available at http://www.unepfi.org/work_streams/insurance/index.html, accessed 22 June 2012); however insurance is beyond the scope of this chapter.

2 Accountability is defined as 'identifying what one is responsible for and then providing information about that to those who have rights to that information' (Gray, 2001, p. 11). In addition, we use 'social accountability' to denote environmental and social accountability collectively.

3 The US case of Fleet Factors is the most common point of reference for developing legislation across Europe and the rest of the world.

4 Project finance, as discussed later, is covered under Barclays' dedicated Environmental and Social Impact Assessment (ESIA) Policy. Barclays' disclosures of their position on lending and project finance are detailed further on their website and in their annual Citizenship Report (available at www.Barclays.com and http://group.barclays.com/about-barclays/citizenship/citizenship-report, accessed 22 June 2012).

5 See http://www.co-operative.coop/corporate/Sustainability09/social-responsibility/ethical-finance/ The-Co-operative-Bank-screening-of-finance/, accessed 22 June 2012.

6 With the exception of banks such as the Co-operative Bank.

7 See The Deutsche Bank Microcredit Development Fund, available at http://www.db.com/us/content/en/1173.html, accessed 22 June 2012.

8 In the case of debt finance investors have potential access to both public and private information provided by the borrower whereas equity investors only have access to public information (Holland, 1998). The reason for this is to maintain insider trading controls in the market and distinguish owners and managers of a business.

9 See CDP https://www.cdproject.net/en-US/Pages/HomePage.aspx, EIRIS http://www.eiris.org/ files/products/EIRISSustainabilityRatings.pdf Sustainalytics http://www.sustainalytics.com/, accessed 22 June 2012.

10 See BankTrack on the Natural Capital Declaration http://www.banktrack.org/manage/ems_files/ download/banktrack_position_on_the_natural_capital_declaration/120616_bt_position_on_ncd. pdf, accessed 22 June 2012.

11 Project finance is a method of funding in which the lender looks primarily to the revenues generated by a single project, both as the source of repayment and as security for the exposure to default. It may take the form of financing of the construction of a new capital installation, or the refinancing of an existing installation, with or without improvements. The borrower is usually a Special Purpose Entity (SPE) which is not permitted to perform any function other than developing, owning and operating the installation. As a consequence, the repayment depends primarily on the project's cash flow and on the collateral value of the project's assets (EP II, 2006).

12 BankTrack highlights commitment to the Collevecchio declaration which calls on FIs to adopt a precautionary principle and decline investment on the basis of social and environmental criteria. The declaration launched in 2003 has been signed by more than 100 NGOs.

13 The risk of lender liability in the context of project finance was recently raised by a review of current practice by Freshfields (legal advisors).

14 ABN Amro, Barclays, Citigroup, Crédit Lyonnais, Credit Suisse First Boston, HVB Rabobank, Royal Bank of Scotland, WestLB and Westpac. See http://www.equator-principles.com, accessed 22 June 2012.

15 See http://www1.ifc.org/wps/wcm/connect/Topics_Ext_Content/IFC_External_Corporate_Site/ IFC+Sustainability+Framework, accessed 22 June 2012.

16 See http://www.equator-principles.com/index.php/governance-management/governance-and-management, accessed 22 June 2012.

17 See http://www.equator-principles.com/index.php/members-reporting, accessed 22 June 2012.

18 For example, it was estimated that in 2007 out of a total of US$74.6 billion debt tracked in emerging markets, US$52.9 billion (71 per cent of the total) was subject to the EP (EP Press Release, 2008).

19 See http://carbonprinciples.org/, accessed 22 June 2012.

20 See http://www.theclimategroup.org/programs/the-climate-principles, accessed 22 June 2012.

21 'SRI [socially responsible investment] is an investment process that integrates social, environmental, and ethical considerations into investment decision making' (Renneboog et al., 2008, p. 1723).

22 See http://www.schroders.com/global/home/, accessed 22 June 2012. Schroders manages assets on behalf of institutional and retail investors, financial institutions and high net worth clients from around the world.

23 See http://www.jupiteronline.co.uk/PI/Our_Products/Environmental/Environmental_Funds/J3.htm, accessed 22 June 2012.

24  See websites http://www.ftse.com/ftse4good and http://www.sustainability-indexes.com, both accessed 22 June 2012.
25  See http://www.unpri.org/principles, accessed 22 June 2012.
26  See http://www.unepfi.org, accessed 22 June 2012.
27  See the GRI Financial Services Sector Supplement, available at: https://www.globalreporting.org/resourcelibrary/FSSS-Complete.pdf, accessed 22 June 2012.
28  See https://www.cdproject.net, accessed 22 June 2012.

# References

BankTrack (2004a) *Principles, Profits or Just PR – Triple P Investments under the Equator Principles: An Anniversary Assessment.* Amsterdam: BankTrack.

BankTrack (2004b) *Transparency and the Equator Principles: Proposals for the EP Bank Disclosure,* Working Document. Utrecht: BankTrack.

BankTrack (2006) *Equator Principles Re-launched: Improvements Made, but Principles Fail to Live up to Their Potential.* Utrecht: BankTrack.

BankTrack (2007) *The Silence of the Banks*: *An Assessment of Equator Principles Reporting.* Utrecht: BankTrack.

BankTrack (2011) *The Outside Job: Turning the Equator Principles towards People and Planet.* BankTrack submission to the Equator Principles update process. Nijmegen: BankTrack.

Baskin, J. B. (1988) 'The development of corporate financial markets in Britain and the US 1600–1914: Overcoming asymmetric information'. *Business History Review* (summer): 197–237.

Bauer, R., Koedijk, K. and Otten, R. (2005) 'International evidence on ethical mutual fund performance and investment style'. *Journal of Business Ethics* 70(2): 11–124.

Biehl, C., Dumke, M., Hoepner, A. and Wilson, J. (2011) *SRI Funds: Does More Social or More Environmental Mean Less Financial Performance?* Working Paper. St Andrews: University of St. Andrews.

Bray, C., Colley, M. and Connell, R. (2007) *Credit Risk Impacts of a Changing Climate.* Barclays Environmental Risk Management and Acclimatise.

British Bankers' Association (BBA) (1993) *Position Statement: Banks and the Environment.* London: British Bankers' Association.

Bullied, Roz (2005) 'Legal risk from Equator Principles?'. *Environmental Finance* (April): 4.

Chong, J., Her, M. and Phillips, G. (2006) To sin or not to sin? Now that's the question. *Journal of Asset Management* 6(6): 406–17.

Cooper, Graham (2002) '"Room for improvement" on banks' green risks'. *Environmental Finance* (October): 7.

Corporation of London (2002) *Financing the Future: The London Principles – The Role of UK Financial Services in Sustainable Development.* London: Corporation of London.

Coulson, A. B. (2001) 'Corporate environmental assessment by a bank lender – The reality?', in J. J. Bouma, M. Jeucken and L. Klinkers (eds) *Sustainable Banking: The Greening of Finance.* Sheffield: Greenleaf Publishing, in association with Deloitte & Touche. Chap. 3, part 4, pp. 300–11.

Coulson, A. B. (2009) 'How should banks govern the environment? Challenging the construction of action versus veto'. *Business Strategy and the Environment* 18(3): 149–61.

Coulson, A. B. (2002) *Benchmarking Study: Environmental Credit Risk Factors in the Pan-European Banking Sector.* London: ISIS Asset Management plc (now F & C Asset Management).

Coulson, A. B. (2011) 'Learning from environmental credit risk management', in *Accountants for Business Risk and Reward; Shared Perspectives.* London: Association of Chartered Certified Accountants (ACCA), § 4, pp. 19–20.

Coulson, A. B. and Monks, V. (1999) 'Corporate environmental performance considerations within bank lending decisions'. *Eco-Management and Auditing* 6(part 1): 1–10.

Derwall, J., Guenster, N., Bauer, R. and Koedijk, K. (2005) 'The eco-efficiency premium puzzle. *Financial Analysts Journal* 61(2): 51–63.

Dresner, Sarah (2002) *Assessing Engagement; A Survey of UK Practice on Socially Responsible Investment*. Report produced in collaboration with Just Pensions. London: Just Pensions.

Elsas, R. and Krahnen, J. P. (1998) 'Is relationship lending special? Evidence from credit-file data in Germany'. *Journal of Banking and Finance* 22: 1283–316.

Equator Principles (EP) II (2006), available at http://www.equator-principles.com/resources/equator_principles.pdf, accessed 1 February 2012.

Equator Principles (EP) (2007) *Guidance Note on Equator Principles Implementation Reporting*, available at: http://www.equatorprinciples.com/resources/ep_implementation_reporting_guidance_note.pdf, accessed 1 February 2012.

Equator Principles (EP) (2008) *Equator Principles Celebrate Five Years of Positive Environmental Impact and Improved Business Practices*. Press Release 8 May, available at http://equator-principles.com/index.php/all-ep-association-news/ep-association-news-by-year/61-2008/95-equator-principles-celebrate-five-years-of-positive-environmental-impact-and-improved-business-practices, accessed 1 February 2012.

Eurosif (2004) *Eurosif Transparency Guidelines for the Retail SRI Fund Sector*. Paris: Eurosif.

Eurosif (2010) *European SRI Study 2010*. Paris: Eurosif.

Freshfields (2005) *Banking on Responsibility. Part 1 of Freshfields Bruckhaus Deringer Equator Principles Survey 2005: The Banks*. London: Freshfields Bruckhaus Deringer.

FTSE (2003) *FTSE4Good Index Series: Inclusion Criteria*. London: FTSE.

FTSE (2005) *FTSE4Good Index Series: Impact of New Criteria and Future Directions*. 2004–2005 Report. London: FTSE.

Global Reporting Initiative (GRI) (2011) *Sustainability Reporting Guidelines and Financial Services Sector Supplement*. Amsterdam: GRI.

Gray, R. (2001) 'Thirty years of social accounting, reporting and auditing: What if anything have we learnt?'. *Business Ethics: A European Review* 10(1): 9–15.

Green, Duncan (2003) *Do UK Charities Invest Responsibly: A Survey of Current Practice*. Co-published by EIRiS, Just Pensions and the UK Social Investment Forum. London: Just Pensions.

Hoepner, A. (2007) *A Categorisation of the Responsible Investment Literature*. St. Andrews: St. Andrews Sustainability Institute.

Holland, J. (1998) 'Private voluntary disclosure, financial intermediation and market efficiency'. *Journal of Business Finance and Accounting* 25(1): 29–68.

Howard-Boyd, Emma (2003) 'Closing the gap'. *Environmental Finance* (February): 24.

Hummel, H. and Timmer, D. (2003) *Money and Morals: The Development of Socially Responsible Investing among Dutch Pension Funds*. Produced in collaboration with the Dutch Association of Investment Analysts (VBA). Breukelen: Universiteit Nyenrode [Netherlands Business School].

KPMG (2011) *International Survey of Corporate Responsibility Reporting 2011*. Amsterdam: KPMG International.

Kreander, N. (2001) *An Analysis of European Ethical Funds*. Occasional Research Paper No. 33, Association of Chartered Certified Accountants (ACCA). Glasgow: University of Glasgow Centre for Social and Environmental Accounting Research.

Lou, C. and Ganzi, J. (2002) *2001 Performance Review: Profit-Driven Sustainability Funds*. Chapel Hill, NC: Environment and Finance Enterprise.

Macve, R. and Chen, X. (2010) 'The "Equator Principles": A success for voluntary codes?'. *Accounting, Auditing & Accountability Journal* 23(7): 890–919.

Matthew E. and Willem van Gelder, J. (2001) *Paper Tiger, Hidden Dragons*. London: FoE.

Murray, A., Sinclair, D., Power, D. and Gray, R. (2006) 'Do financial markets care about social and environmental disclosure? Further evidence and exploration from the UK'. *Accounting, Auditing & Accountability Journal* 19(2): 228–55.

O'Sullivan, N. (2010) 'Social accountability and the finance sector: The case of Equator Principles (EP) institutionalisation', unpublished PhD thesis, University of Amsterdam.

O'Sullivan, N. and O'Dwyer, B. (2009) 'Stakeholder perspectives on a financial sector legitimation process: The case of NGOs and the Equator Principles'. *Accounting, Auditing & Accountability Journal* 22(4): 553–87.

Pearce, B. and Ganzi, J. (2003) *Engaging the Mainstream with Sustainability: A Survey of Investor Engagement on Corporate Social, Environmental and Ethical Performance*. Sponsored by Royal & SunAlliance. London: Forum for the Future.

Platform (2004) *Principal Objections: Analysis of the Sakhalin II Oil and Gas Project's Compliance with the Equator Principles*. London: Platform.

Principles for Responsible Investment (PRI) (2011) *Report on Progress 2011: An Analysis of Signatory Progress and Guidance on Implementation*. London: PRI.

Renneboog, L., Ter Horst, J. and Zhang, C. (2008) 'Socially responsible investments: Institutional aspects, performance, and investor behavior'. *Journal of Banking & Finance* 32(9): 1723–42.

Roberts, J., Sanderson, P., Barker, R. and Hendry, J. (2003) *In the Mirror of the Market: The Disciplinary Effects of Company/Fund Manager Meetings*, paper presented at IPA Conference, Madrid, 13–16 July.

Scholtens, B. (2006) 'Finance as a driver of corporate social responsibility'. *Journal of Business Ethics* 68: 19–33.

Scholtens, B. (2007) 'Financial and social performance of socially responsible investments in the Netherlands'. *Corporate Governance* 15(6): 1090–105.

Scholtens, B. (2009) 'Corporate social responsibility in the international banking industry'. *Journal of Business Ethics* 86(2): 159–75.

Scholtens, B. and Dam, L. (2007) 'Banking on the Equator. Are banks that adopted the Equator Principles different from non-adopters?'. *World Development* 35(8): 1307–28.

Schucking, H., Kroll, L., Louvel, Y. and Richter, R. (2011) *Bankrolling Climate Change*. Urgewald, Groundwork, Earthlife Africa Johannesburg and BankTrack.

Scott, Paul and John, Steve (2002) 'Banks look to indirect impacts'. *Environmental Finance* (November): 22–3.

Smith, D. R. (1994) *Environmental Risk: Credit Approaches and Opportunities, an Interim Report*. Prepared for UNEP Roundtable on Commercial Banks and the Environment, 26–7 September. Geneva: UNEP.

Solomon, J. and Solomon, A. (2006) 'Private social, ethical and environmental disclosure'. *Accounting, Auditing & Accountability Journal* 19(4): 564–91.

Solomon, J., Solomon, A., Norton, S. D. and Joseph, N. L. (2011) 'Private climate change reporting: An emerging discourse or risk and opportunity?'. *Accounting, Auditing & Accountability Journal* 24(8): 1119–48.

Sparkes, Russell (2002) *Socially Responsible Investment: A Global Revolution*. London: Wiley.

Stichele, Myriam Vander (2004) *Critical Issues on the Financial Industry: SOMO Financial Sector Report*. Amsterdam: Somo.

Sustainable Business Institute (SBI) and United Nations Environment Programme Finance Initiative (UNEP FI) (2011) *Advancing Adaptation through Climate Information Services: Results of a Global Survey on the Information Requirements of the Financial Sector*. Geneva: UNEP FI.

Tomkins, C. (2001) 'Interdependencies, trust and information in relationships, alliances and networks'. *Accounting Organizations and Society* 26: 161–91.

Ulph, A., McKenzie, G., Jewell, T., Steele, J. and Wolfe, S. (1999) *The Financial Implications of Environmental Legislation*. End of Award Report (L320253226). Swindon: Economic and Social Research Council (ESRC).

Watchman, Paul (2005) 'Beyond Equator'. *Environmental Finance* (June): 16–17.

# 9 Organizational change and sustainability accounting

*Jan Bebbington and Michael Fraser*

## Introduction

Accounting for sustainable development does not solely focus on understanding the interactions between organizations and aspects of their external environment. Indeed, there is a literature that seeks to explore what is happening within organizations to understand (for instance) the dynamics that inform the production of sustainability-related accounts as well as what role this information might play within the life of the organization. In addition, accounting researchers are interested in actions that organizations are taking internally (which may not be linked to reporting activities – such as investment appraisal) to respond to aspects of the sustainable development agenda, the role of accounting technologies in those responses and the characterization of why some attempts to change are effective while others are not. This chapter focuses on these activities and frames them as being to do with the extent to which organizations change in response to sustainability accounting activities. A focus on change arises because many social accountants are committed to 'opening up … new spaces' (Gray, 2002, p. 698) at the organizational level to explore possibilities for less socially, ecologically and economically damaging activities. Indeed, the desire for change arises from concern about the social and environmental harms that threaten people and the planet (Freire, 1998a, 1998b; Gadotti, 2003; Porritt, 2007). Change, therefore, has both a material basis (related to processes that are less damaging to and/or more likely to support resilient ecosystems, societies and economies) as well as a conceptual basis (that is, changing organizational beliefs, values, norms and rules – to use language drawn from Laughlin, 1991).

To explore these various processes this chapter is split into two sections. In the first section, Thinking about Organizational Change, we will introduce some conceptual framings that have (and may be) used to motivate studies addressing organizational change in response to sustainable development imperatives. In the second section, An Exploration of how Organizations Change, we will reflect on a case study where *how* organizational change emerged was investigated in more depth. Taken together, we hope that the chapter will introduce this growing area of work. This chapter also has synergies with Chapter 15 (An Overview of Legitimacy Theory) and Chapter 16 (Sustainability Reporting: Insights from Institutional Theory) where issues of change and theorizing about change are also discussed. In addition, Chapters 12 and 13 (on global climate change and water respectively) cover organizational change within these particular contexts.

## Thinking about organizational change[1]

A full review within this chapter of the management and accounting literature that examines organizational change would be impossible due to the large volume of material produced on this subject (Broadbent and Laughlin, 2005). Even a cursory examination of that field, however, quickly yields the insight that how organizations change is a question that has equally motivated and vexed researchers (as well as anyone who has ever tried in practice to change the organization in which they are working).

Broadbent and Laughlin (2005, pp. 13–14) point to a diversity of academic approaches to understanding change including:

(i)   managerialist, where the changes to techniques and routines are focused upon;
(ii)  processual, where the process of changing is examined rather than the change itself;
(iii) discursive, where the focus is on the discourses used in narrating change.

This three-way categorization around how you might understand change is brought together in Laughlin's (1991) framework and it is for this reason that this framing has been relatively influential in the environmental accounting literature (which suggests that it might be helpful in the context of sustainable development accounting as well). While we will start our examination with Laughlin of how change has been conceptualized, we will also introduce other ways of thinking about change that have influenced research, namely: institutional theory; structuration theory; organizational learning; as well as practice theory (with the potential role for dialogic framing being explored within the case study presented in the second section of the chapter). First, however, the overarching framework presented by Laughlin is outlined.

Laughlin (1991, p. 211) synthesizes a variety of conceptualizations of organizations and change processes, and identifies three elements within an organization, describing them as:

1.  interpretive schemas (including beliefs, values and norms, mission/purpose and metarules);
2.  design archetype (including organizational structure, decision processes and communication systems);
3.  subsystems (which contain the tangible organizational elements).

These elements vary from the relatively intangible to the tangible and each layer presupposes the others. The layers operate together to determine organizational activities and as such provide the basis from which we may understand organizations' actions (and any change in actions). Accounting could be assumed to fall within the design archetype category whereby accounting techniques permeate decision processes as well as communication systems. In this way, accounting looks in both directions in the above categorization, providing both the articulation of the extent to which organization missions are achieved as well as defining the scope of behaviour for organization participants. Accounting also impacts (as well as being derived from) interpretive schemas and tends to induce a narrow financial focus in some organizations (notably listed companies).

Laughlin suggests that organizations are inertial or change resistant and before any possibilities for change exist there needs to be a jolt or disturbance (this is also consistent with institutional theory which assumes that organizations are seeking stability). Taking a sustainable development focus one might suggest that disturbances could include, for instance:

(1) changes in government policies (including law, fiscal instruments and other regulatory requirements);
(2) changes in commercial relationships within an industry/economy;
(3) changes in expectations of financial stakeholders and capital markets,
(4) changes in technology and/or ways of working within an industry/economy;
(5) changes in relationships with stakeholders such as consumers, producers or employees;
(6) changes in societal expectations about certain events/behaviours.

Any of these changes on their own or in concert with each other might then lead to changes in some aspect of organizational life. In addition, disturbances might arise from the natural environment itself (for example, the availability and location of raw materials and the impacts of global environmental change).

The way in which changes systematically play out in organizational life, however, remains speculative. Indeed, Laughlin (p. 210) notes that 'once disturbed, the argument is that the "track" which the disturbance takes through the organization and the degree of transformation it will generate in the pathway it follows will differ over time and across different organizations'. Laughlin suggests a number of end states from a jolt and these are summarized in Table 9.1 (which also implies that one may be able to observe these end points). The linking of disturbances to outcomes, however, is often seen to have happened

*Table 9.1* Summary of Laughlin's (1991) characterization of organization change*

| Generic description of change | Sub-category of change mechanism | Description |
| --- | --- | --- |
| *First order* change or *morphostatic* change (things look different while remaining the same) | Rebuttal | Disturbance deflected so that the organization can return to an inertial state. No permanent change is observed. |
| | Reorientation | Disturbance results in change (because it cannot be rebutted) but changes are cosmetic and the 'heart' (the interpretive schema) of the organization is not changed. |
| *Second order* change or *morphogenetic* change (the working model of the organization changes fundamentally) | Colonization | Disturbance is significant to the organization and the interpretive schema, design archetype and subsystem (in some combination) change with a new underlying organizational ethos emerging. |
| | Evolution | There is change to the underlying ethos of the organization. Rather than this change arising directly from a disturbance, the organization itself chooses to change. |

*This idea of a typology of change is reflected in other conceptions of change discussed in this chapter. For example, the ideas of single and double loop learning in the organizational learning literature differentiate between degrees of change and the extent to which actions and values are transformed in learning contexts.

within the 'black box' of the organization, with studies that focus on processes (for instance) seeking to shed light on these internal dynamics.

A number of studies have used this framework, namely: Gray *et al.* (1995); Larrinaga-González and Bebbington (2001); Larrinaga-González *et al.* (2001); Tilt (2006); da Silva Monteiro and Aibar-Buzman (2010); Fraser (2012). Limitations in Laughlin's (1991) framework have also been suggested. The first limitation that arises from the application of the framework is distinguishing between what might constitute morphostatic or morphogenetic change and how these might be theoretically and practically differentiated from each other (that is, the framework is a heuristic which underspecifies what we are seeking to understand). Indeed, da Silva Monteiro and Aibar-Buzman (2010) wonder if 'due to both the complexity of the relationship between organizations and the environment and the demanding nature of Laughlin's category of morphogenesis ... it is difficult to find companies that had undergone' this level of change.

A second criticism is raised by Larrinaga-González and Bebbington (2001, p. 280), who note that that the 'static nature' of the empirical sites previously considered does not provide a dynamic empirical context in which to study the process of *how* change occurs. Laughlin (1991, p. 228) echoes this criticism when he notes that without a suitably rich empirical setting the detail of *how* various assemblages might create change may not be visible.

A third criticism is raised by Kirkpatrick and Ackroyd (2003), who suggest that Laughlin's (1991) description of an archetype is too functionalist. A consequence of such a framework, according to Kirkpatrick and Ackroyd (2003), is that the role of human agency is underplayed. Although it could be argued that human agency is recognized in Laughlin's (1991) model, further visibility could arise if more explicit theorizing were coupled with richer empirical settings. Additional conceptual framings have, however, been used in sustainable development-related work and it is to these framings that we now turn.

A sizeable literature exists that uses institutional theory (in its various guises) to understand both institutional change and inertia (see for example Dillard et al., 2004; Bebbington *et al.*, 2009; Arroyo, 2012). The possibilities for institutional framing of change is covered in Chapter 16 of this book so you should cross refer to that material. Where institutional theory is particularly valuable is that it seeks to explore the relative roles of structure and agency, as do some other framings (for example, structuration theory – see Dillard *et al.*, 2011). These institutionally based explanations of the conundrum of change and stability enlarge our focus on what we might examine to understand organizational behaviour. For example, we might consider reporting routines (a preoccupation of sustainability accounting/accountability – see Adams and McNicholas, 2007); where boundaries of the organization are drawn (see for example, Archel *et al.*, 2008); the role of individuals (including leaders but also what are sometimes called institutional entrepreneurs[2]) within organizations; as well as how an organization comes to know itself. Indeed, this latter focus is considered in the organizational learning field.

Organizational learning is itself a diverse field but one which has been used in a few sustainable development studies. The rationale for thinking about this area (see Siebenhüner and Arnold, 2007) is that sustainable development demands will require organizations to learn to act differently as well as think about themselves in a different light (for example, routines and rationales will be affected). In addition, both Siebenhüner and Arnold (2007) and Cramer (2005) anchor change in the 'personnel and cultural attributes of a company' (Siebenhüner and Arnold, 2007, p. 350; see also Albrecht *et al.*, 2007). This focus also links to another area that is emerging as being influential in organization studies, that of practice theory (see, for example, Eikeland and Nicolini, 2011; and for an environmental reporting application of practice theory, Lodhia and Jacobs, 2013). In brief, practice theory involves research that examines what people do in practice in order to understand organizations. In addition, 'reflecting back practices to the practitioners as a way of triggering group and organisational transformation' (Eikeland and Nicolini, 2011, p. 165) is a possibility with this approach. It could also be the case that work that focuses on engagement with practice might also be linked to this way of thinking about practices and changes to practices (see Adams and Larrinaga-González, 2007 and for a consideration of dialogic engagement, Bebbington *et al.*, 2007b).

Taken together, this section has sought to highlight the various ways that organizational change has been thought about in parts of the management and accounting literature that consider environmental sustainability. There is no lack of framing devices or theoretical traditions to draw from in this area because they can be derived from the rich plurality of theorizing about organizational change in the management accounting and control literature. Rather, there is relatively little work that draws out in depth what environmental-related and sustainable development-related changes have been observed in practice and also in linking observations to particular conceptual framings. In addition, it is relatively easy to get discouraged in this area because the changes one might seek in order to transition to an ecologically sound, socially just and economically resilient society are non-trivial. In order to flesh out this interest in organizational change, this chapter will now present a recent New Zealand case study that explored how organizational change might emerge.

## An exploration of how organizations change

This section of the chapter draws on Fraser (2012, informed by Fraser, 2010) to revisit 'change' at the organizational level and extends Laughlin's (1991) framework by thinking about *how* we might recognize and evaluate change. This is done by exploring in more depth a study where Laughlin's (1991) framework was coupled with a Freiran-inspired heuristic to explore the application of a sustainability accounting technology (the Sustainability Assessment Model[3] – hereafter SAM). The study sought to understand the issues faced by society in transitioning to a more sustainable way of living. In so doing, the difficulty in recognizing *what* and *how* change occurs is highlighted. The work involved two case studies.

The first case was a New Zealand city council ('the Council'), providing services to more than 300,000 people. Public documentation (such as annual plans) described the Council as having aspirations to be considered as a leader in sustainability. In addition, the introduction of new local government legislation with sustainable development requirements provided the impetus for the council to explore the SAM. Initial discussions with the Council's sustainability coordinator led to an agreement that the SAM would be applied six times across a number of projects, people and time spans during a two-year action research engagement.

The second case-study site was located within a social housing provider that formed a subsidiary ('the Land Company') to build in excess of 3,000 new houses. Part of the undertaking by the Land Company obtaining the land was that the housing development would set new benchmarks in urban sustainability. This second case-study site complements the first empirical site by being smaller in nature, newly formed and due to exist for a finite period (which may offer more possibilities regarding change). Altogether, data was collected in the form of 47 semi-structured interviews (using a Laughlin inspired research instrument) and supplemented with notes taken during meetings and embedded in analysis of public documents as well as SAM applications themselves.

### The Laughlin framework findings

When the findings from the council case were considered, several changes are noted in terms of SAM applications. The first two SAM applications were considered the most 'effective', the third was 'terminated' and the remaining applications occurred under a constrained organizational climate. This suggests that accounting technologies (and in this case the same tool) do not generate consistent effects. In early applications of the SAM, the tool appeared to change the way people conceptualized the project they were working on (the interpretative schema). The most obvious influence was over the use of a piece of land (which was originally a community garden but where a decision was being made as to whether or not to sell the land to a developer).[4] Here the data in the SAM led to a different decision being made from the one that conventional accounting analysis would have predicted (that is, the community garden was kept). In Laughlin terms, change arose at the subsystems level. According to the sustainability coordinator,

> What you have done with the SAM is said 'no', it [the community garden] does have a value and this is the value of it, and you really did turn around the decision. It [the proposed development of the land] really would have … [happened] if it had not been put through a SAM because there is no other way of defending it.[5]

This apparent change to the organization's interpretative schema, however, did not remain for long. A newly appointed CEO (whose view of sustainability placed a heavy emphasis on economic well-being) influenced the dominant beliefs (interpretative schema) about sustainability in the organization. As a result, the SAM (design archetype) moved out of equilibrium with the interpretative schema. This change to the organizational dynamic was most noticeable when an outline of a SAM was presented to a project team in charge of developing a new council headquarters building. The project manager expressed discomfort with a model that might change the pathway of his project. The sustainability coordinator described the events as follows: 'We started to use it [the SAM] on the new building and were told we could use it if it came up with the right answer'. This makes it clear that elements of the Laughlin framework do indeed influence each other and that a desire to return to/reinforce the status quo was evident in this case (that is, reorientation might be inferred).

Other SAM applications at the council subsequently failed to influence decision-making processes, and previously established design archetypes of how decisions were to be made regained their dominant status. Taken together, in this research site the SAM did not take hold and therefore remained in an embryonic state. Legislative pressures to consider sustainable development had clearly raised the resonance of the SAM which resulted in a change, albeit temporary, in framing of issues. Deeper change, however, was not forthcoming.

In the second study site it was anticipated that the SAM would perform a significant role in the decision-making process of the Land Company's operations. The newly formed subsidiary was headed by a CEO with an agenda to build a sustainable urban development that would be unique in Australasia. The CEO had significant influence in developing the interpretative schema of this embryonic organization and implemented a sustainability framework which was to be supported by the SAM. The Land Company was at an early stage of development and the CEO recognized that the SAM had potential to create something that was not present or previously known. The CEO described the SAM as: 'a heuristic device in some ways. It is not about getting it right or entering into some longstanding dialogue as to whether your definition is better than mine.'

An internal disturbance in this organization (in the form of an appointment of a new CEO), however, changed the interpretative schema of the organization and, in turn, the aspirations for the SAM. The newly appointed CEO had an extensive background in managing large-scale urban design developments, including several developments with sustainability features. His language was that of 'deliverables', 'indicators', 'benchmarks' and 'milestones', which differed from the earlier CEO, who spoke of 'vision', 'debate' and 'learning'. The purpose of SAM was reoriented to the new interpretative schema and was then deemed unable to deliver what was required. Indeed, the demands for the SAM had moved from it being a discussion tool with which to make sense of various issues to being a measurement and marketing tool. As a result, the new CEO observed 'I don't really want anything in the framework that cannot be measured. What I want is a sustainability report card'. The small size of the Land Company, combined with the embryonic stage of its development and change in CEO, meant that change occurred quickly in its interpretative schema.

The above mini-cases indicate that no morphogenetic change occurred in either case. However, when finer grained aspects of organizational behaviour are considered (for example the decision to retain the community garden, despite the SAM latterly becoming marginalized) a blanket statement that 'no change occurred' does not provide a nuanced position of *how* change did not occur. Furthermore, such a statement does not consider activities that may well constitute change when considered on a different timeframe or with sensitive criteria applied. It is clear that Laughlin's (1991) framework sensitizes the researcher to identify descriptive facets of change considered necessary. This framework also provides the basis to create an organizational narrative that facilitates an account of *what* occurred (reflecting the managerial framing noted at the outset of the chapter). However, the skeletal nature of the Laughlin framework provides an insufficient basis on *how* change occurs/does not occur and under-theorizes what constitutes morphogenetic change. To respond to the above challenges and to evaluate the effectiveness of the SAM, the New Zealand study drew on the work of Paulo Freire. Freire's work provided the basis to create a dialogic heuristic framework (DHF) that was later used to understand the organizational narrative.

### A Freirian framing

A Freirian dialogics framing has been widely applied with examples ranging from accounting education (Thomson and Bebbington, 2004), sustainable development (Gadotti, 2003), critical mathematics (Frankenstein, 1987), healthcare education (Merideth, 1994), social work (Carroll and Minkler, 2000), music teaching and learning (Abrahams, 2005), environmental literacy (Brennan, 1994), to feminist frameworks of women in prison (Pomeroy *et al.*, 2004). A wide application of Freirian dialogics is unsurprising, given Freire's encouragement of dialogic theory to be reinvented in various local settings, cultures and fields. Freire, particularly in later writings, discussed sustainability issues and problems with some of the contemporary views, especially at the international and government levels (Gadotti, 2003). A Freirian view of sustainability would suggest that people must have a respect for all living things as the basis for eco-pedagogy or sustainability, as opposed to treating the world and living things as objects.

Of particular interest in these cases was the role that accounting technologies (the SAM) might perform in a sustainable transformation and how this might be facilitated by dialogic interactions (Bebbington *et al.*, 2007b). Furthermore, in using an explicit evaluative framework to distinguish between morphogenetic and morphostatic categorizations, change is made more explicit. Freire draws on two heuristics he used to explore education which serve to maintain the status quo or to change it. These two heuristics serve as the inspiration in this for constructing the DHF and the basis to further explore the organizational narrative constructed using Laughlin's (1991) framework.

The two heuristics have been extended by developing eight attributes that might be expected in a dialogic account: that is, an account that enables morphogenetic change. These eight attributes comprise: the purpose of a dialogic account; the content of a dialogic account; the timescale considered; ownership of an account; the role of 'experts' in producing an account; knowledge claims made in an account; the scale and aggregation of the reporting 'entity'; and how communication might occur in the process of constructing an account (see Table 9.2).

*Table 9.2* Potential attributes of a dialogic account

| | *Attribute* | *Dialogic Description* | *Non-dialogic* |
|---|---|---|---|
| **Purpose and Processes of a Dialogic Account** | *Purpose/ Process* | Medium of critical reflection and exploration of alternatives. The process of constructing an account fosters critical questioning, reconceptualization and action. | Convince, subdue, legitimate and manage. Standardization/ benchmarking, client-service provider transaction, external incentivization. |
| | *Content* | Heuristic learning – images, metrics, general language. Unpredictable content. | Economically manageable aspects of business, formal and standardized language, often monetary in value. Predicable content and presentation. |
| **Participants, Communication and Content of a Dialogic Account** | *Knowledge Claims* | Multi-perspectival, temporal, knowledge is co-produced. | Ahistoric, general portrayal of timeless truths and unquestionable facts. |
| | *Legitimate Voices* | 'Experts' and 'non-experts'. Inclusive and polyvocal. | Privileging of experts, single discipline focus. |
| | *Communication Sites* | Any intersection between or within the organization is a valid communication site. | Single boundary between the organization and community. Defined by formal internal structures. |
| **Size and Time-scale of a Dialogic Account** | *Timescale* | Flexibility in timescale to reflect natural action cycles as appropriate. | Standardized annual or quarterly reports. Long-term time frames often seen as inaccurate and therefore marginalized. |
| | *Scale* | May consist of highly aggregated or detailed information. | Organizational entity and other formal structures, often highly aggregated to avoid 'commercial sensitivities' being divulged. |
| | *Ownership* | No one person or entity can own an account. | Intellectual property owned and reinforced via legislation if necessary. |

In applying the Freirian evaluative criteria it became apparent that the conclusion that no morphogenetic change occurred was not definitive. In re-examining the organizational narrative created using Laughlin's (1991) framework it became apparent that the SAMs created a space which could amplify the agency of operational managers and researchers to make visible and challenge the dominant organizational beliefs. First, the process of constructing the SAM fostered the raising of questions and debate with a broader group of people. In one such instance an operational manager in the Council captured the sentiment of the project team by stating, 'the SAM forced people to ask questions'. The questions and associated debate were further supported by the SAM being presented in several different forms and by its capability to act as a frame of reference between members of a project team. Within this frame of reference, linkages could be made between the social, economic and environmental aspects of any given project decision, and new ways of acting could be reconceptualized.[6]

The capability of the SAM to act as a frame of reference facilitated new visibilities and was implicated in making the previously hidden meta-rules of sustainability more visible. The frame of reference meant that unexpected findings in respect of sustainability issues could be interrogated. For example, after the termination of the Council headquarters building SAM application, follow-up meetings with senior Council managers made visible the organizational meta-rule: 'sustainability is fine as long as it does not have negative economic consequences'. In a similar manner, the application of the SAM in the Land Company highlighted the organizational meta-rule of sustainability as being 'acceptable as long as it does not interfere with the timely and economic delivery of the overall project'. This finding extends to other studies which state that the SAM (Cavanagh, 2005; Bebbington, 2007; Bebbington *et al.*, 2007b; Frame and Cavanagh, 2009) and other full cost accounting experiments (Herbohn, 2005; Antheaume, 2007) can provide insight into sustainability issues within organizations by detailing *how* sustainability might be achieved (even if it is deemed unacceptable). It was the visibility created by the SAM, acting as a frame of reference, that provided an opportunity to interrogate the organizational meta-rules of sustainability and, in some instances, change the project decision. However, as noted when the Laughlin (1991) frame was applied, the construction and application of the SAM did not go unchallenged.

SAM applications in the Council and Land Company were terminated on the basis of 'technical deficiency'. In both organizations the SAM had been regarded by operational and management staff as technically sufficient in early applications. More detailed analysis indicated that it was the discomfort experienced by senior managers that led to the label of technical deficiency being applied. In the Council case, a SAM was terminated before construction began on the new council building because of concerns it may 'give the wrong answer'. In the Land Company, the SAMs were no longer used, because the inclusion of negative aspects of the development might have generated 'bad publicity'. These examples provide further support to the assertion that it was not the technical deficiency of the SAM to foster an account, but the consequences of that account.

The exploration of the dialogic criteria illustrated that dialogic and non-dialogic attributes were present but at times were difficult to separate. For example, the termination of the new council building SAM application and closing down of associated debate suggests a non-dialogic act occurred. However, the visible nature of terminating the SAMs provided an opportunity for problematization to occur. In raising issues, asking questions and prompting people to reflect on issues of sustainability, the SAM exhibited some critically reflective properties.

Two interrelated possibilities partly explain the journey from dialogic aspirations to non-dialogic realization: the first is that the secondary disturbances of new CEOs imposed limits on which aspects of sustainability could be discussed and acted on; the second is that as the SAM became more embedded it posed a greater challenge to the existing design archetype and interpretative schema. For example, the visibility of sustainability assumptions highlighted the tension between organizational rhetoric and meta-rules. This challenge may have been more visible when new people were appointed to senior leadership positions. It is possible that previous CEOs who had agreed to the implementation of the SAM would have experienced cognitive dissonance (or other undesirable consequences) if they had reneged on such agreements. New CEOs may consider and review all organizational activities and change them without experiencing this dissonance. In the case of both empirical sites, the operationalization of sustainability rhetoric breached the existing meta-rule of not having financial impact, and therefore a new equilibrium was sought.

In summary, this case study (more fully reported in Fraser, 2012) provides a glimpse into the 'black box' of the organization and the way in which accounting tools and narratives might support change (or fail to enable change). This work (by using the heuristic of dialogic accounting) provides a template of possible aspects that might enable (or not) change (see Table 9.2). What is clear from these in-depth case studies is that there is a great deal of uncertainty regarding how organizational change happens and many detailed issues to attend to. Individual agency (especially by CEO leaders) also appears to be critical.

## Concluding comments

This chapter has sought to develop an appreciation of literature that seeks to understand organizational change, accounting and a desire for sustainable development. While Laughlin's (1991) organizational change framework has been used within the social and environmental accounting literature to think about change/non-change (and remains useful in thinking about sustainable development) the chapter also sought to highlight other framings (such as institutional theory, organizational learning framing and practice theory) as well as the addition of a dialogic framing to a Laughlin inspired study. It seems from the various studies that we might expect significant change in inertial organizations will be hard to come by in the area of sustainability accounting and accountability. At the same time, understanding what changes are possible over what time frames are not developed in any significant way in the existing literature (but the case study presented attempted to elucidate some of the complexity in making such assessments).

Pursuing sustainable development will require changes in practices as well as in ways of thinking. As is apparent from this chapter several literatures might inform that journey. Gadotti describes the movement towards a sustainable way of living as a 'dream to live well' (2005, p. 2) that is also strange and new (Gadotti, 2003). It is hoped that this chapter has contributed insights to the overarching objective of finding ways to address social and ecological harms, with the excitement of realizing something new, but with enough caution to appreciate this is a significant challenge.

## Notes

1  The *Journal of Accounting and Organizational Change* focuses on the interrelationship between accounting and change (as one might expect given its title). There are articles in that journal that consider social and environmental accounting matters, but none that specifically focus on issues of

sustainability accounting and accountability. One would expect, however, as sustainable development informed accounting research gathers pace that one might see articles in this journal in the future. Regardless, the framing of change in this journal (and the likes of the *Journal of Organizational Change Management*) might usefully inform sustainability accounting going forward.

2  This term, credited to DiMaggio (1988), relates to individuals who possess sufficient resources (of all types) to create new systems of meanings. This framing suggests that individuals (or groups) are sometimes key to change (see also O'Sullivan and O'Dwyer, 2009).

3  The Sustainability Assessment Model is an accounting technology developed to incorporate sustainability thinking into organizational decision making and, potentially, accountability processes (see Bebbington, 2007, 2009; Bebbington *et al.*, 2007a; Frame and Cavanagh, 2009). This technique draws from prior work in full cost accounting (see Bebbington *et al.*, 2001; Herbohn, 2005; Antheaume, 2007) and is essentially a project evaluation accounting tool that generates monetary evaluations of a project's sustainable development impacts.

4  The proposal tabled by the property unit within the Council indicated that the land should be sold on the basis of standard economic analysis. However, a SAM was constructed and presented to the councillors making the decision. The SAM made visible many of the social and environmental benefits of the community garden not considered in the property unit's analysis. As such, the decision to keep the garden appeared to rely heavily on the SAM.

5  All quotes in this section relate to responses from interviewees.

6  Reflecting back on the opening of this chapter, this case study might have been usefully motivated and understood using an organizational learning framing.

# References

Abrahams, F. (2005), 'The application of critical pedagogy to music teaching and learning: A literature review', *Applications of Research in Music Education*, 23(12): 12–22.

Adams, C. and Larrinaga-González, C. (2007), 'Engaging with organisations in pursuit of improved sustainability accounting and performance', *Accounting, Auditing & Accountability Journal*, 20(3): 333–55.

Adams, C. and McNicholas, P. (2007), 'Making a difference: Sustainabilty reporting, accountability and organisational change', *Accounting, Auditing & Accountability Journal*, 20(3): 382–402.

Albrecht, P., Burandt, S. and Schaltegger, S. (2007), 'Do sustainability projects stimulate organizational learning in universities?', *International Journal of Sustainability in Higher Education*, 8(4): 403–15.

Antheaume, N. (2007), 'Full cost accounting: Adam Smith meets Rachel Carson?', in J. Unerman, J. Bebbington and B. O'Dwyer (eds) *Sustainability Accounting and Accountability*, Routledge, London, pp. 211–25.

Archel, P., Fernandez, M. and Larrinaga, C. (2008), 'The organizational and operations boundaries of triple bottom line reporting: A survey', *Environmental Management*, 41(1): 106–17.

Arroyo, P. (2012), 'Management accounting change and sustainability: An institutional approach', *Journal of Accounting and Organizational Change*, 8(3): 286–309.

Bebbington, J. (2007), *Accounting for Sustainable Development Performance*, Elsevier, London

Bebbington, J. (2009), 'Measuring sustainable development performance: Possibilities and issues', *Accounting Forum*, 33(3): 189–93.

Bebbington, J., Gray, R., Hibbitt, C. and Kirk, E. (2001), *Full Cost Accounting: An Agenda for Action*, Association of Chartered Certified Accountants (ACCA), London.

Bebbington, J., Brown, J. and Frame, B. (2007a), 'Accounting technologies and sustainability assessment models', *Ecological Economics*, 61(2–3): 224–36.

Bebbington, J., Brown, J., Frame, B. and Thomson, I. (2007b), 'Theorizing engagement: the potential of a critical dialogic approach', *Accounting, Auditing & Accountability Journal*, 20(3): 356–81.

Bebbington, J., Higgins, C. and Frame, B. (2009), 'Initiating sustainable development reporting: Evidence from New Zealand', *Accounting, Auditing and Accountability Journal*, 22(4): 588–625.

Brennan, A. (1994), 'Environmental literacy and educational ideal', *Environmental Values*, 3(1): 3–16.

Broadbent, J. and Laughlin, R. (2005), 'Organisational and accounting change: Theoretical and empirical reflections and thoughts on a future research agenda', *Journal of Accounting and Organisational Change*, 1(1): 7–26.

Carroll, J. and Minkler, M. (2000), 'Freire's message for social workers: Looking back, looking ahead', *Journal of Community Practice*, 8(1): 21–36.

Cavanagh, J. E. (2005), 'Assessment of waste disposal vs. resource recovery', Landcare Research Contract Report LC0506/022 for Environment Waikato, available at http://www.ew.govt.nz/publications/technicalreports/tr0535.htm, accessed 20 February 2009.

Cramer, J. (2005), 'Company learning about corporate social responsibility', *Business Strategy and the Environment*, 14(4): 255–66.

da Silva Monteiro, S. and Aibar-Buzman, B. (2010), 'Organizational and accounting change within the context of the environmental agenda', *Journal of Accounting and Organizational Change*, 6(4): 404–35.

Dillard, J., Rigsby, J. and Goodman, C. (2004), 'The making and remaking of organization context duality and the institutionalization process', *Accounting, Auditing & Accountability Journal*, 17(4): 506–42.

Dillard, J., Rogers, R. and Yuthas, K. (2011), 'Organizational change: In search of the golden mean', *Journal of Accounting and Organizational Change*, 7(1): 5–32.

DiMaggio, P. (1988), 'Interest and agency in institutional theory', in L. Zucker (ed.) *Institutional Patterns and Organizations: Culture and Environment*, Ballinger, Cambridge, MA, pp. 3–32.

Duncan, O. and Thomson, I. (1998), 'Waste accounting and cleaner technology: A complex evaluation', paper presented at Asia Pacific Interdisciplinary Research in Accounting Conference, Osaka, Japan, 4–6 August, available at http://www3.bus.osaka-cu.ac.jp/apira98/archives/pdfs/46.pdf, accessed 20 February 2009.

Eikeland, O. and Nicolini, D. (2011), 'Turning practically: Broadening the horizon', *Journal of Organizational Change Management*, 24(2): 164–74.

Frame, B. and Cavanagh, J. (2009), 'Experiences of sustainability assessment: An awkward adolescence', *Accounting Forum*, 33(3): 195–208.

Frankenstein, M. (1987), 'Critical mathematics education: An application of Paulo Freire's epistemology', in I. Shor (ed.) *Freire for the Classroom: A Sourcebook for Liberatory Teaching*, Boyton/Cook, Portsmouth, pp. 180–210.

Fraser, M. (2010), 'Social accounting and organisational change: An exploration of the sustainability assessment model', unpublished PhD thesis, Victoria University of Wellington, New Zealand.

Fraser, M. (2012), '"Fleshing out" an engagement with a social accounting technology', *Accounting, Auditing & Accountability Journal*, 25(3): 508–34.

Freire, P. (1998a), *Pedagogy of Freedom: Ethics, Democracy, and Civic Courage*, Rowman & Littlefield, Lanham, MD.

Freire, P. (1998b), *Pedagogy of the Heart*, Continuum, London.

Gadotti, M. (2003), 'Pedagogy of the earth and culture of sustainability', paper presented at the Ontario Institute for Studies in Education, Lifelong Citizenship Learning, Participatory Democracy and Social Change Conference, Toronto, 17–19 October, available at http://www.oise.utoronto.ca/~tlcentre/conference2003/Proceedings/proceedings.htm, accessed 20 February 2009.

Gadotti, M. (2005), 'Earth Charter + 5', paper presented at the Earth Charter in the Decade of Education for Sustainable Development conference, Amsterdam, 5–9 November, available at www.paulofreire.org/Moacir_Gadotti, accessed 20 February 2009.

Gray, R., Walters, D., Bebbington, J. and Thomson, I. (1995), 'The greening of enterprise: An exploration of the (non) role of environmental accounting and environmental accountants in organisational change', *Critical Perspectives on Accounting*, 6(3): 211–39.

Gray, R.H. (2002), 'The social accounting project and *Accounting, Organizations and Society*: Privileging engagement, imaginings, new accountings and pragmatism over critique?', *Accounting, Organizations and Society*, 27(7): 687–708.

Herbohn, K. (2005), 'A full cost environmental accounting experiment', *Accounting, Organizations and Society*, 30(6): 519–36.

Kirkpatrick, I. and Ackroyd, S. (2003), 'Archetype theory and the changing professional organization: A critique and alternative', *Organization*, 10(4): 731–50.

Larrinaga-González, C. and Bebbington, J. (2001), 'Accounting change or institutional appropriation? A case of the implementation of environmental accounting', *Critical Perspectives on Accounting*, 12(3): 269–92.

Larrinaga-González, C., Carrasco-Fenech, F., Caro-González, F., Correa-Ruiz, C. and Páez-Sandubete, J. (2001), 'The role of environmental accounting in organizational change—An exploration of Spanish companies', *Accounting, Auditing & Accountability Journal*, 14(2): 213–39.

Laughlin, R.C. (1991), 'Environmental disturbances and organizational transitions and transformations: Some alternative models', *Organization Studies*, 12(2): 209–32.

Lodhia, S. and Jacobs, K. (2013), 'The practice turn in environmental reporting: A study into current practices in two Australian commonwealth departments', *Accounting, Auditing & Accountability Journal*, 26(4): 595–615.

Merideth, E. (1994), 'Critical pedagogy and its application in education: A critical appraisal of the Casa en Casa model', *Health Education and Behaviour*, 21(3): 355–67.

O'Sullivan, N. and O'Dwyer, B. (2009), 'Stakeholder perspectives on a financial sector legitimation process: The case of NGOs and the Equator Principles', *Accounting, Auditing and Accountability Journal*, 22(4): 553–87.

Pomeroy, E.C., Holleran, L.K. and Kiam, R. (2004), 'Postmodern feminism: A theoretical framework for a field unit with women in jail', *Social Work Education*, 23(1): 39–49.

Porritt, J. (2007), 'Foreword', in J. Unerman, J. Bebbington and B. O'Dwyer (eds) *Sustainability Accounting and Accountability*, Routledge, London, p. xvii.

Siebenhüner, B. and Arnold, M. (2007), 'Organizational learning to manage sustainable development', *Business Strategy and the Environment*, 16(5): 339–53.

Thomson, I. and Bebbington, J. (2004), 'It doesn't matter what you teach?', *Critical Perspectives on Accounting*, 15(4/5): 609–28.

Tilt, C.A. (2006), 'Linking environmental activity and environmental disclosure in an organisational change framework', *Journal of Accounting and Organizational Change*, 2(1): 4–24.

# Part III

# Accounting for sustainable development in other organizational settings

# 10 The nature of NGO accountability

## Conceptions, motives, forms and mechanisms

*Roel Boomsma and Brendan O'Dwyer*

## Introduction

The increased international popularity of NGOs (non-governmental organizations) and decreasing satisfaction of the general public with conventional politics has led to NGOs moving from being 'ladles in the soup kitchen to a force for transformation in global politics' (Doh and Teegen, 2002; Edwards and Fowler, 2002, p. 1). The rise of NGOs as important actors in international business in particular can be traced back to the 1980s when international companies were pressured to divest from South Africa, resulting in the withdrawal of a large amount of US and British companies. In this period, NGOs gained credence as legitimate actors in international business due to their involvement in negotiations over the development of conditions surrounding trade and investment rules (Doh and Teegen, 2002). Since then, NGO numbers have grown exponentially and their influence in arenas such as international business, development aid and corporate governance has escalated (Doh and Teegen, 2002; Lehman, 2007). Commenting in the early 1990s, one analyst suggested that this 'quiet revolution' in the role and influence of NGOs could 'prove to be as significant to the latter twentieth century as the rise of the nation state was to the latter nineteenth century' (Salamon, 1994, p. 109, cited in Fisher, 1997, p. 440). Najam (1996, p. 339) claims that at this time 'most NGO scholars also happen[ed] to be NGO believers' who had implicit faith in NGOs' work, be it as advocates of specific causes such as human rights and social justice, providers of relief and humanitarian assistance, or as facilitators of development. This enabled the emergence of a myth of NGO infallibility and a concomitant reluctance to closely scrutinize the presumed 'magic' of NGOs' work (Lloyd, 2005; Najam, 1996).

However, since the early 1990s, NGOs in whatever form have faced increasing amounts of scrutiny regarding their accountability, governance, legitimacy and wider social impacts (Lloyd, 2005). In response to some of these pressures, several efforts have been undertaken by (collectives of) NGOs in order to improve their accountability. Examples include:

- the collective development of a code of conduct (the NGO accountability charter) by a group of five international NGOs[1] (INGO, 2006; Russell, 2006);
- the Humanitarian Accountability Partnership (HAP) standard in accountability and quality management[2] (HAP, 2013);
- the NGO Accountability and Self-Regulation Project;
- the Global Accountability Project.

The latter two projects were initiated by One World Trust, and were aimed at contributing to the understanding of NGO accountability processes, identifying strengths and weaknesses in NGO accountability practices, and enhancing the accountability relationship between international NGOs and the individuals, communities and societies they affect (Blagescu *et al.,* 2005; One World Trust, 2013a, 2013b; Schmitz *et al.,* 2012).

Despite these efforts to improve NGO accountability, it has remained an area which, due to its complexity, receives an increasing amount of critical attention, both in practice and within the academic (accounting) community (Oakes and Young, 2008). This chapter examines the complex nature of NGO accountability by focusing particularly on the conceptualization and operationalization of NGO accountability.

The chapter is structured as follows. First, we consider the nature of NGOs and specify broadly the type of NGOs addressed within the chapter. We then briefly consider the motives for, and the complexity surrounding, NGO accountability. Forms of NGO accountability that have emerged in academic studies are subsequently discussed, with particular attention paid to the tension between various forms of accountability. Finally, we will discuss prevailing mechanisms of NGO accountability with particular reference to their operationalization in practice, highlighting the difficulties faced by many NGOs.

## Defining and classifying NGOs

There is little consensus on how to define and classify NGOs (Doh and Teegen, 2002; Fisher, 1997; Martens, 2002; Vakil, 1997). The term 'NGO' embraces a huge range of institutions with little in common beyond the label 'NGO' (Gray *et al.,* 2006). These can encompass voluntary associations, credit unions, farmers' cooperatives, consumer groups, religious organizations and trade unions (Hudson, 1999, p. 1). In their various forms, NGOs have multiplied since the 1990s, taken on new functions, and established innovative and exceptionally complex and wide-ranging formal and informal linkages with one another, with government agencies, with social movements, with international development agencies and with transnational issue networks (Fisher, 1997). This sheer range eludes definition, hence complicating simple specifications of their accountability (Gray *et al.,* 2006).

Vakil (1997) does, however, suggest that NGOs can be broadly distinguished by their essential organizational attributes, comprising their orientation – the types of activities they engage in – and their level of operation – at international, national or local community level. She identifies six orientation categories: welfare, development, development education, networking, research, and advocacy. We primarily consider international and national advocacy and development-oriented NGOs, such as Amnesty International, Greenpeace, World Wildlife Fund (WWF) and Oxfam International.

## Motives for NGO accountability

The belief prevailing among donors in the 1980s that NGOs were better able to reach the poor and marginalized, that they were key players in democratization processes, and were more cost-effective than governments in providing social services (Ebrahim, 2003a) resulted in a rapid growth of NGO numbers and increased levels of NGO funding (AbouAssi, 2012; Ebrahim, 2003a, 2005; Edwards and Fowler, 2002; Fisher, 1997; Salamon *et al.,* 1999). This belief was, according to Ebrahim (2003a), mainly built on trust in NGOs since there was a lack of sufficient empirical evidence to support it. Despite the alleged lack of supportive evidence of their successes, NGOs became important participants in negotiations between governments and multinational corporations, and in defining institutional environments in different jurisdictions (Doh and Teegen, 2002).

The amount of trust placed in NGOs however started eroding in the 1990s when their increasing power, influence and presence in a variety of fields caused a shift in the public perception of NGOs. Increased levels of funding (Edwards and Fowler, 2002), increased competition by NGOs for funding (O'Dwyer and Unerman, 2008), and enhanced development profiles (Ebrahim, 2003a, 2003b, 2005; Vakil, 1997; Zadek, 2003) led to calls for more explicit demonstrations of NGO accountability (Callamard, 2004). Furthermore, the inability of NGOs to live up to public expectations, evidenced by mismanagement of (public) resources, involvement in publicized scandals and other forms of unethical or corrupt behaviour[3] (Cavill and Sohail, 2007; Ebrahim, 2009; Jepson, 2005) further accentuated the calls for improved accountability (Callamard, 2004). These issues harmed the credibility of and confidence in NGOs and caused the public view to move from NGOs being considered infallible to a more sceptical perception of NGOs and their work (Ebrahim, 2009; Lloyd, 2005; Najam, 1996).

The fact that several international NGOs have been particularly involved in shaping and driving corporate responsibility and sustainability agendas (SustainAbility, 2003; Unerman and O'Dwyer, 2006a, 2006b) also led to questions being asked regarding their own performance in these areas (Lloyd, 2005). With respect to NGOs advocating particular development policies in developing countries, queries about their accountability tend to focus on whether they actually meet their original premise and role of alleviating poverty and creation of an open and accountable world order (Lehman, 2007). Do NGOs for example, speak as the poor, with the poor, for the poor, or about the poor (Slim, 2002)? Many of the calls for greater NGO accountability emanate from bodies, often supported by the business sector, who fear exposure or threat from specific NGOs (Gray *et al.* 2006; Upadhyay, 2003). This has raised suspicions that these sources are motivated by a desire to suppress NGOs who might challenge particular agendas (Gray *et al.*, 2006). Wherever these demands emanate from, they do reflect many NGOs' growing success in advocacy. Some NGOs, however, resent the extent of these accountability demands especially when promoted by business interests (O'Dwyer and Unerman, 2008): 'It appears that NGOs are being singled out in contrast to businesses (and even many governments) that are even less accountable than they are' (Edwards, 2000, pp. 22–3). As a response to these calls for more accountability, NGOs during the 1990s started recognizing that being open and transparent, engaging stakeholders, and responding to complaints were crucial for their survival (Lloyd *et al.*, 2008). The increased (public) attention and complexity surrounding NGO accountability triggered academic research in the area (Jepson, 2005; Oakes and Young, 2008). While early research on NGO accountability tended to focus primarily on the proper use of the financial resources provided to them (Dixon *et al.*, 2006; Ebrahim, 2003a, 2005; Goddard and Assad, 2006; Lewis and Madon, 2004), the focus gradually shifted towards examining broader conceptions of accountability incorporating attention to NGO impacts on 'clients' or beneficiaries, i.e. the individuals or societal groups which NGOs purport to serve, an area which had previously been downplayed (Lloyd, 2005; Najam, 1996; O'Dwyer and Unerman, 2008, 2010).

Broader conceptions of and motives for accountability emerged from organizations specifically aimed at advocating for more holistic forms of accountability within NGO practices. For example, the UK based consultancy SustainAbility (2003, p. 17) identified four internal drivers of NGO accountability, comprising: morality (accountability is right in principle); performance (accountability improves effectiveness); political space (accountability increases credibility and thus political space); and wider democratization (accountability of NGOs strengthens democracy in the general political environment). These internal drivers exude a sense of moral obligation, which sees accountability as crucial to the achievement of an NGO's mission and to the maintenance of its integrity (Ebrahim, 2003a). Additionally, several self-appointed watchdogs, such as Charity Navigator and Guidestar, started to offer information aimed at improving accountability by evaluating accountability processes within NGOs (Gordon *et al.*, 2009; Schmitz *et al.*, 2012; Sloan, 2009).

## Forms of accountability

Several academic studies on NGO accountability highlight aspects that make NGO accountability complex, such as the multiplicity of stakeholders (Brown and Moore, 2001; Edwards and Hulme, 1996; Najam, 1996); NGO board structures (Tandon, 1996); and conflicting accountability pressures (Avina, 1993; Chenhall *et al.*, 2010; Christensen and Ebrahim, 2006; Everett and Friesen, 2010; O'Dwyer and Unerman, 2008). While most organizations encounter the oft-competing demands of multiple constituencies, many NGOs face these demands more acutely and regularly than do private firms (Dixon *et al.*, 2006; Ebrahim, 2003b, 2005). NGOs face constituencies to whom they can be considered upwardly, internally or downwardly accountable. Stakeholders to whom NGOs can be considered upwardly accountable include patrons, such as donors, foundations, governments and partner NGOs (Fowler, 1996; Lloyd, 2005; Najam, 1996). NGOs can be regarded downwardly accountable to groups to whom NGOs provide services to or advocate on behalf of, including communities or regions indirectly impacted by NGO activities (Ebrahim, 2003b; Edwards and Hulme, 1996; Fowler, 1996; Lloyd, 2005; Najam, 1996; O'Dwyer and Unerman, 2010). Finally, NGOs can also be considered internally accountable to staff, supporters/members, coalition partners, their peers and to their mission (Brown and Moore, 2001; Ebrahim, 2003b; Lloyd, 2005; Najam, 1996; O'Dwyer and Unerman, 2008).

Accountability to patrons, i.e. upward accountability, involves a donor asserting financial control by demanding accountability for the provided money in combination with policy control by demanding accountability for the designated purpose of the money (Ebrahim, 2005; Najam, 1996). Financial control and policy accountability are interrelated, since funds are provided by donors in order to serve certain policy goals. Funds are often only provided if the pursuit of particular policy goals can be demonstrated or at least argued for (Najam, 1996). Practice shows that policy accountability is in many cases hard to operationalize; therefore financial accountability often becomes a de facto means of achieving both financial and policy control, i.e. to ensure that the donor's policy goals are being pursued by the NGOs and to hold NGOs accountable for whether and how donor money is spent.

Downward accountability involves NGO interaction and mutual learning with beneficiaries, i.e. the constituencies to whom NGOs provide services, resources or goods (O'Dwyer and Unerman, 2010). This form of accountability aims at assisting NGOs in identifying the needs of intended beneficiaries and in assessing how well these needs are addressed (Agyemang *et al.*, 2009; Ebrahim, 2003a). Operationalizing downward accountability in practice can however be difficult, since beneficiaries do not always actively demand accountability, and dominant upward accountability mechanisms introduced by donors may lead to downward accountability receiving less attention (Christensen and Ebrahim, 2006; Ebrahim, 2005; Najam, 1996; O'Dwyer and Unerman, 2008). There is however an increasing amount of NGOs and funders that start to perceive downward accountability as an important tool in striving to improve the effectiveness of development aid (Ebrahim, 2003a, 2003b, 2005; O'Dwyer and Unerman, 2010).

Internal accountability involves NGOs being accountable to their vision, stated mission, staff, supporters and members, coalition partners, and the NGO community at large (Ebrahim, 2003a; Najam, 1996). Since NGOs operate in a field where self-definition is important for one's efficacy, this form of accountability is crucial for NGOs. Internal accountability is needed in order to build and maintain trust and legitimacy among its staff and members (Ebrahim, 2003a; O'Dwyer and Unerman, 2008), especially as NGOs grow in size and therefore have to manage multiple funders and staff members who were not involved in 'the original dream' (Najam, 1996, p. 348). The aforementioned prioritization of upward accountability to funders can however result in NGOs being willing to adjust their goals regarding internal accountability in order to adhere to donor demands (Ebrahim, 2003a; Najam, 1996). This can potentially result in a culture of accountability that is built on external scrutiny rather than mission and purpose (Christensen and Ebrahim, 2006).

## Tension between different forms of accountability

Tensions faced by NGOs regarding their upward, downward and internal accountability can lead to conflicting perspectives on how NGOs should operate and account for impacts on their constituencies and the society in general (Fowler, 1996). Governmental funders and other donors often encourage NGOs to pursue a primarily instrumental accountability orientation; these patrons thus determine the language of justification practised within NGOs (Roberts, 2001; Sinclair, 1995). The intensity of donor accountability demands and their instrumental orientation often leads to upward accountability being prioritized within NGOs at the cost of downward accountability to the beneficiaries/clients which NGOs are supposed to serve, since upward accountability is often considered less problematic and more achievable (Christensen and Ebrahim, 2006; Ebrahim, 2005; O'Dwyer and Unerman, 2008; Roberts, 1991, 2001).

This prioritization of donor accountability demands can potentially shift attention away from internal accountability and lead to mission drift, whereby NGOs' achievement of key longer term missions are subverted due to impatience for results among powerful patrons (Najam, 1996; O'Dwyer and Unerman, 2008; Unerman and O'Dwyer, 2006a). Due to concerns about attracting sufficient amounts of funding, NGOs often struggle to balance donor accountability demands within their desire to maintain their core values based on their organizational mission (Chenhall *et al.*, 2010). Some NGOs have even altered their mission statements in order to comply with donor desires to maintain funding and thereby secure their survival (Dillon, 2004; Najam, 1996). This often results in the operationalization of accountability with a short-term orientation and focus on resource use at the cost of more strategic forms of accountability, which take into consideration longer term impacts on other organizations and the society at large (Najam, 1996; O'Dwyer and Unerman, 2008).

NGO accountability is further complicated as NGOs belong to organizational forms with no simple, widely agreed measure of organizational performance, unlike governments and businesses who may be evaluated respectively in terms of political support or financial returns (Fowler, 1996). It is often hard to demonstrate NGO influence, and measuring success is often impractical due to the second and third order (unexpected) effects often involved in NGO activities (O'Dywer and Unerman, 2008; Uphoff, 1995). For example, it is difficult for an NGO such as Amnesty International to definitively demonstrate its influence on changing a country-specific human rights policy that may have helped empower a certain segment of society (O'Dwyer and Unerman, 2008). If 'positive' effects from NGO actions evolve, such as, for example, 'a sustainable change in agricultural production ... [or]

the development of a strong grassroots federation' (Edwards and Fowler, 2002, p.106), or a change in government policy on the death sentence, this is often due to a number of forces and actors coming together rather than from one NGO advocating in isolation. It is therefore perhaps unsurprising that some NGOs are reluctant to take credit (or account) for these collective efforts (O'Dwyer and Unerman, 2008).

The complexities surrounding NGOs' oft-competing constituencies and the lack of definitive 'measurement' bases outlined above have fuelled resistance among certain NGOs to demands for enhanced accountability. Various arguments employed include: the potential for enhanced accountability to be used by vested interests to punish NGOs if they are seen to be subversive, especially by host governments in regions which are politically more vulnerable (Edwards and Hulme, 1996; O'Dwyer and Unerman, 2008; SustainAbility, 2003); the threat to the diversity, innovation and speed of response in the 'sector' in favour of politicization and patronage (Edwards and Fowler, 2002; SustainAbility, 2003); and the lack of available resources for many NGOs to implement systematic systems of accountability (Ebrahim, 2003a; Fowler, 1996; Jepson, 2005; SustainAbility, 2003). Much of this resistance is driven by concerns surrounding the impact which enhanced accountability may have on NGOs' power to contribute to social sustainability. The following quote from a World Social Forum workshop on 'civil society accountability' in 2005 illustrates this concern:

> Does engaging with our own accountability give us [civil society/NGOs] more power or render us powerless? ... [A]ccountability should not lead to powerful stakeholders, such as donors ... influenc[ing] the vision and mission of the organizations they support [but should] communicate the ways in which they are contributing to social change.
>
> (Litovsky, 2005a, pp. 5–6)

In holding NGOs to account, donors often introduce quantitative performance measures in order to improve efficiency, i.e. donors want to ensure they get 'bang for their buck' (O'Dwyer and Unerman, 2008). The expansion of performance measures and reporting by regulators and donors can potentially lead to increased bureaucracy, i.e. 'bureaucratic drag' (Jepson, 2005, p. 517), and may have little effect on NGO efficiency and impact. Some authors advocate for the implementation of these measures (Bradley *et al.*, 2003; Walsh and Lenihan, 2006), while others question whether it fits within the complexities of NGO practice (Goddard and Assad, 2006). The prevailing 'accounting culture', involving the adoption of performance targets and striving to enhance efficiency often fails to improve accountability and transparency (Jepson, 2005). Although the adoption of businesslike practices potentially reduces the time available for NGO service delivery (Jepson, 2005), the majority of NGOs still apply them due to donor dependence, which has significant implications for the forms of accountability practised within the NGO sector (Ebrahim, 2005; Rahaman *et al.*, 2010).

While several efforts to improve NGO accountability processes have been undertaken, often involving NGOs facing increasing donor demands for more detailed information (Everett and Friesen, 2010), several authors question whether this has actually benefited those they are intended to benefit (Chenhall *et al.*, 2010; Christensen and Ebrahim, 2006; Dempsey, 2007; O'Dwyer and Unerman, 2008). Everett and Friesen (2010), for example, wonder if the translation of increased attention to beneficiaries into sets of standardized indicators actually negatively affects or even dehumanizes the nature of development work, since such standard indicators can potentially lead to 'managing by the numbers' rather than more meaningful accountability. As Cavill and Sohail (2007) argue: 'what is currently called "accountability" is essentially a technical fix that leaves unequal social and economic structures almost completely unchallenged. This focus on practical accountability has led to a number of gaps in [NGO] accountability' (p. 247).

In order to improve NGO accountability, funders need to allow space for more sophisticated forms of accountability with a longer term focus, taking into consideration organizational mission and the impact of working towards this mission on stakeholders directly or indirectly involved in organizational activities (Cavill and Sohail, 2007; O'Dwyer and Unerman, 2008). Accountability should not simply be considered a function of meeting pre-given goals, but a continuous process incorporating attention to NGO performance in relation to their mission and the empowerment of beneficiaries (Cavill and Sohail, 2007; Oakes and Young, 2008; O'Dwyer and Unerman, 2008). In operationalizing accountability it should be noted that there is no single accountability structure that is suitable for all (non-governmental) organizations. A dynamic exists whereby an NGO's mission should define the accountability system and the accountability system should in its turn shape its organizational mission and strategy (Jepson, 2005). Ideally, NGOs should remain attentive to their core organizational mission whatever pressure they may face to account for performance to powerful donors. This, however, requires strategies to manage the tensions between the different forms of accountability (O'Dwyer and Unerman, 2008). In practice this remains difficult, as it is not easy for NGOs to challenge their donors, as they run the risk of alienating important sources of financial support and losing their capacity to provide resources or services to clients/beneficiaries (Brown and Moore, 2001).

## Mechanisms of NGO accountability

Whatever the concerns of NGOs generally and the apparent complexities faced by NGOs regarding their upward, downward and internal accountability, a plethora of accountability mechanisms have evolved from the NGO 'sector' since the 1990s. These mechanisms can be placed into five broad categories:

- reports and disclosure statements;
- performance assessments and evaluations;
- participation;
- self-regulation;
- social audits.

These categories operate along three accountability dimensions, i.e. upward, internal and downward accountability. Following Ebrahim (2003b), it is also helpful to differentiate between accountability mechanisms that are 'tools' and those that are 'processes' (Ebrahim, 2003b, p. 815).[4] Tools refer to discrete techniques used to achieve accountability and are characterized by application over a limited period of time. They often produce tangible outcomes and can be repeated over time. Examples of tools include financial reports, financial disclosures and performance evaluations (Ebrahim, 2003b). Processes are instruments that are broader and more multifaceted, i.e. they often embrace a set of tools. They are less time-bound, less tangible, and emphasize a course of action rather than distinct end results. Examples of processes include participation and self-regulation (Ebrahim, 2003b). Table 10.1 provides a summary of the different accountability mechanisms used by NGOs along the three dimensions of accountability.

The most commonly applied mechanisms of NGO accountability include formal reports and disclosures and performance assessments. Formal reports are aimed at making basic (mainly financial) data on operations available to the public, donors or oversight bodies. Performance assessments are aimed at making the performance of NGOs measurable and comparable; examples include monitoring and evaluation processes conducted by NGOs themselves, aimed at assessing progress towards objectives of externally funded projects or internal organizational goals, and evaluations conducted by donors, aimed at assessing whether agreed upon goals and objectives have been achieved (Ebrahim, 2003b). Formal reports and performance assessment are often linked to punitive threats, such as revocation of funds or loss of tax exemption status and therefore leave limited potential for accountability to NGO mission, values and performance (Ebrahim, 2003b).

Despite an increasing commitment to downward accountability, funders still tend to overemphasize the assessment of outputs and/or activities, since this allows for easy measurement of short-term quantitative results (Ebrahim, 2003b, 2005; Schmitz *et al.*, 2012). Funders acknowledge the importance of beneficiaries as constituents of NGOs; they however rarely include accountability mechanisms to make their voices heard (Schmitz *et al.*, 2012). Funders and donors often do not consider the overwhelming nature of complex evaluation requirements on organizations, with the risk of NGOs solely developing evaluation systems to satisfy funding requirements, while these systems are perceived by NGOs as irrelevant for (internal) decision-making processes (Ebrahim, 2003b). Solely relying on upward accountability mechanisms aimed at satisfying funder and donor requirements can potentially encourage NGOs to exaggerate successes, discourage them from revealing and closely scrutinizing their mistakes (Ebrahim, 2005; Smillie, 1996), and eventually lead to difficult to measure activities, such as lobbying, being ignored (O'Dwyer and Unerman, 2008).

NGOs have therefore started to take into consideration organizational values and the views of clients (local NGOs) and beneficiaries in their approach to accountability. Such internal and downward forms of NGO accountability include mechanisms such as participatory reviews, self-regulation through NGO networks or certification, and social audits (Agyemang *et al.*, 2009; Ebrahim, 2003b).

Participatory reviews are held by either Northern NGOs or local executing NGOs with beneficiaries after or during the implementation of projects. Such reviews can vary in their form and focus, i.e. they can involve informal meetings between Northern NGOs and local (executing) NGOs or be more sophisticated involving formal meetings between all parties involved in the execution of projects, such as representatives from Northern NGOs, local NGOs and beneficiaries (Agyemang *et al.*, 2009). While this accountability mechanism gives voice to a broader group of stakeholders, some authors argue that participation is mainly symbolic, since local communities cannot impose conditionalities upon donors and NGOs (Ebrahim, 2003b; Hailey, 2000; Najam, 1996).

Self-regulation is an accountability mechanism that involves efforts to develop standards or codes of conduct by NGOs themselves or the NGO community, partly in order to address the damaged image of the NGO sector after public scandals or exaggerated performance claims, and partly to prevent restrictive governmental and/or donor regulation (Ebrahim, 2003b). In addition, to enhance public (and staff) confidence in NGOs, self-regulation in the form of certification for compliance with certain standards or codes of conduct often requires NGOs to take into consideration the views of beneficiaries and local NGOs and include them in decision-making processes.

*Table 10.1* NGO accountability forms and mechanisms

| NGO accountability form | Accountability to whom | Accountability inducement | Accountability mechanisms |
|---|---|---|---|
| Upward accountability | Donors | Legal requirement | Annual report (tool) |
| | Funders | Tax obligation | Interim report |
| | Oversight agencies | Funding requirement | Performance assessment (tool) |
| | Tax authority | Learning | Performance evaluation (tool) |
| | | Public confidence/ support | Performance monitoring (tool) |
| | | | Audits (tool) |
| | | | Funding proposal (tool) |
| | | | Project planning (tool) |
| Internal accountability | Staff and board | Organizational values | Staff meeting (process) |
| | Mission | Funding requirement | Self-regulation through (NGO) networks (process) |
| | Volunteers | Staff confidence/ support | Self-regulation through certification (process) |
| | Community partners | Community confidence/ support | Participatory review reports (tool) |
| | | Learning | Informal reporting and communication (tool) |
| | | | Training (process) |
| | | | Social auditing (tool and process) |
| | | | Newsletter (tool) |
| Downward accountability | Clients (local NGOs) | Organizational values | Community consultation and dialogues (process) |
| | Beneficiaries | Funding requirement | Participatory review report (tool) |
| | | Public confidence/ support | Informal reporting and communication (tool) |
| | | Community confidence/ support | Training of clients and beneficiaries (process) |
| | | Learning | Social auditing (tool and process) |
| | | | Reports and documents in native languages (tool) |
| | | | Focus groups (process) |
| | | | Transparency with news media (tool) |
| | | | Participation of clients and beneficiaries in decision-making (process) |

Source: Adapted from Ebrahim (2003a, p. 825) and Agyemang *et al.* (2009, p. 13).

Another accountability mechanism that enables internal and downward accountability is social auditing. Social auditing is a process of assessing reports and improving social performance and ethical behaviour primarily through stakeholder dialogue (Ebrahim, 2003b). The focus is on assessing the impact of NGO activities on the lives of beneficiaries. This information, on how beneficiaries perceive NGO activities, can then be used by Northern NGOs in the development of future activities (Agyemang *et al.,* 2009). Several NGO accountability initiatives have been initiated that promote internal and downward forms of accountability by providing guidelines, frameworks or workshops.

Having summarized the key NGO accountability mechanisms used in practice as well touching upon the struggles related to involving beneficiaries in accountability processes, the next section, Operationalizing NGO Accountability Mechanisms, moves towards discussing academic research focusing on how managers within NGO settings experience the operationalization of accountability mechanisms.

## Operationalizing NGO accountability mechanisms

NGO managers' perception of the operationalization of accountability is receiving an increasing amount of attention in studies on NGO accountability. Initially, such studies mainly focused on the nature of accountability in the relationship between Northern NGOs and their (governmental) donor (Chenhall *et al.,* 2010; Everett and Friesen, 2010; O'Dwyer and Unerman, 2007, 2008). More recently, the focus has shifted towards examining the accountability relationship between Northern NGOs and their local partner NGOs and/or beneficiaries (Davis *et al.,* 2012; Jacobs and Wilford, 2010; O'Dwyer and Unerman, 2010).

O'Dwyer and Unerman (2007, 2008) examined the enactment of accountability mechanisms in two specific NGO settings. The authors first analysed a process where a group of Irish NGOs and their governmental funder developed a funding scheme that aimed at encouraging what they term 'holistic accountability', i.e. accountability that has a longer term focus and takes into consideration impacts on stakeholders directly and indirectly involved in NGO activities (O'Dwyer and Unerman, 2007). O'Dwyer and Unerman (2008) later examined how and why concerns for viability and relevance in combination with the absence of knowledge about this broader form of accountability resulted in the shift from a traditional focus on internal accountability towards the implementation of so-called hierarchical accountability mechanisms, i.e. accountability mechanisms with a short-term, quantitative focus and orientation towards powerful stakeholders within Amnesty Ireland who control access to resources.

These studies indicate that although there often is a favourable attitude towards developing more holistic accountability mechanisms within Northern NGOs, hierarchical forms of accountability focusing on a narrow range of powerful stakeholders still dominate accountability practice within NGOs (O'Dywer and Unerman, 2007, 2008). This inability to implement more holistic forms of accountability can be attributed to several factors, such as a lack of resources and expertise on (the implementation of) more holistic accountability mechanisms and failure to include ideals of more socially oriented accountability approaches in the assessment of NGO achievements or in setting objectives for development cooperation policies (O'Dwyer and Unerman, 2007).

Everett and Friesen (2010) and Chenhall *et al.* (2010) present similar findings, indicating that the implementation of upward accountability mechanisms, with an emphasis on performance measurement, can potentially harm NGO attempts to maintain a focus on their core values and mission. Everett and Friesen (2010) argue that, despite the fact that some form of accountability is always necessary, the current operationalization through hierarchical, upward focused accountability mechanisms is often perceived by NGOs as dysfunctional (Everett and Friesen, 2010). The authors point to the potential disconnect between public expectations of NGOs and their operational reality as a cause for the inability to implement more holistic forms of accountability (Everett and Friesen, 2010). They argue that, due to public cynicism regarding NGO performance and a lack of compassion for NGOs activities, funders and donors are not forced to adequately attend to or understand the operational reality and the needs and problems of NGOs, and therefore keep relying upon hierarchical accountability mechanisms. Chenhall *et al.* (2010), however, demonstrate how hierarchical upward accountability can also be enabling for NGOs when the underlying (managerial) logic of accountability mechanisms is aligned with NGO core ideals and mission. More holistic forms of accountability that allow NGOs to base their core values and work processes on their humanitarian ideals rather than funding requirements could enhance the effectiveness of NGO service delivery (Chenhall *et al.*, 2010).

In response to calls by the general public, donors and the NGO sector for increased attention to issues of downward accountability, NGOs have increasingly started to implement such mechanisms. Key examples of projects attempting to promote and advance these types of mechanisms are the Global Accountability Project (GAP) and the NGO Accountability and Self-regulation Project of the UK charity One World Trust (Blagescu *et al.*, 2005; One World Trust, 2013a, 2013b; Schmitz *et al.*, 2012). The GAP is part of a programme of work by One World Trust aimed at enhancing the accountability of the decision-making processes of international NGOs to the individuals, communities and societies they affect. The GAP framework unpacks NGO accountability into four dimensions: transparency, participation, evaluation, and complaint and response mechanisms (One World Trust, 2013b), all of which are central to stakeholder-focused accountability processes (see ActionAid International, 2004a, 2004b; Dey, 2004; Gray *et al.*, 1997; O'Dwyer, 2005). To demonstrate accountability, GAP argues that NGOs need to integrate all four of the above dimensions into their policies, procedures and practice at all stages of decision making and implementation in relation to their key stakeholders. While the framework does not indicate the need for formal reports, it does suggest various means of information dissemination including the worldwide web and public meetings. It specifically proposes an appeals procedure for stakeholders where they feel their information requests have been denied, along with a detailed, accountable process for considering complaints against an NGO (One World Trust, 2013b).

The NGO Accountability and Self-regulation project addresses the complexity faced by NGOs to manage the increasing pressure from funders and the general public to be transparent about their funding sources, report on their impact and demonstrate their results, while avoiding becoming detached from their core values (One World Trust, 2013a). In order to support NGOs in this challenge, One World Trust examines how NGOs can become more proactive through self-regulation. Among other issues such as transparency and good governance, self-regulation initiatives often aim at enhancing downward accountability by improving the participation of beneficiaries.[5] The first phase of this project involved a study on the frequency and structure of existing self-regulatory efforts within the NGO sector. The second phase involves examining the benefits of self-regulation, with a specific focus on how 'collective accountability initiatives increase effectiveness and improve the space for [NGO] activity' (One World Trust, 2013a, p. 1).

Another initiative embracing many of the social accounting dimensions above emerged from an organization linked to the UK Institute of Social and Ethical Accountability (ISEA), called Keystone. Keystone's mission aims at improving the effectiveness of NGOs by assisting them in developing improved ways of planning, measuring and reporting on social change (Keystone, 2013a). The organization offers several services, such as executing performance surveys and designing evaluation systems, and free to use tools, such as guides that assist in planning, monitoring, evaluation and communicating NGO work (Keystone, 2013b). Elements of the services and tools offered by Keystone have much in common with social accounting (audit) approaches such as the GAP framework where organizations reflect on their mission, theory of change and immediate objectives through stakeholder engagement. The support provided by Keystone claims to enable organizations to develop reporting models that are specific to their unique contexts (Litovsky, 2005b).

Listen First is another example of an effort to develop systems for managing forms of downward accountability more systematically within large NGOs. The Listen First system was developed through several innovations and field trials by two NGOs (Concern and Mango) in combination with advice from PricewaterhouseCoopers (PwC) and experienced NGO practitioners (Jacobs and Wilford, 2010). It aims at improving downward accountability across different interventions, rather than focusing on methods for strengthening downward accountability in specific circumstances. The Listen First framework provides a practical definition of downward accountability and identifies four levels of flexible performance standards across four areas. The four areas include providing information publicly, involving people in making decisions (participation), listening, and staff attitudes and behaviours. The four performance levels are described as sampling, maturing, flowering and fruit bearing (Jacobs and Wilford, 2010). The framework sets out examples of types of behaviours for field staff, which build on their existing efforts but also inspire them to do more; it especially encourages field staff to engage separately with marginalized groups in order to establish a set of expectations about what downward accountability means and the different levels of performance it would entail. Examples of suggested behaviour include 'always be[ing] polite and patient with local people and partners'; 'avoid telling local people what to think or do'; and 'encourage the most marginalized people to respond, and cover sensitive areas like sexual abuse' (Listen First, 2013). The Listen First framework tries to balance the flexibility required for context-specific intervention with the consistency needed for a management information system (Jacobs and Wilford, 2010). It allows for the adoption of specific behaviours in line with local circumstances while also allowing following and comparing projects across different interventions (Jacobs and Wilford, 2010).

More broadly, many practitioners and academics have brought together current evidence of NGO accountability mechanisms in order to provide an accountability roadmap for NGOs. For example, Cronin and O'Regan (2002) outline a Framework of Accountability Mechanisms and Tools (FAIT) in order to both analyse and, more importantly, enable development aid NGOs to plan for enhanced accountability in a more demanding environment. They argue against using off-the-shelf models in order to implement NGO accountability and, as with the GAP and Keystone initiatives, they call for stakeholder-defined measures of performance in reports. Within the specific context of development NGOs, Cronin and O'Regan (2002) suggest using unique reporting mechanisms such as participatory videos, storytelling, drama and proverbs in order to listen carefully to and report on the voices of participants. Cavill and Sohail (2007) also provide a model that aims at enhancing more holistic accountability by guiding practitioners through an assessment of how NGO actions contribute to organizational missions. Their framework suggests that practitioners should start by clarifying the beliefs and values that inform NGO activities in order to arrive at a central theme that 'runs through its mission into its code of conduct and strategic aims, and ensures that these are then translated into policies and procedures' (Cavill and Sohail, 2007, p. 246). The authors argue that their model can be used for startup NGOs in developing accountability policies as well as for NGOs that are attempting to integrate existing missions, goals and objectives within a system of accountability (Cavill and Sohail, 2007).

In addition to academics, private sector organizations have become increasingly involved in providing guidance on NGO accountability. Examples include the involvement of the 'big 4' auditing firms, who all provide services to NGOs and/or their funders, ranging from assistance in the development of management systems or by acting as a fund manager and intermediary for channelling funds between funders, NGOs and beneficiaries (Deloitte, 2013; KPMG, 2011). In addition to paid services, these organizations are also involved in promoting accountability in the NGO sector through initiatives such as the PwC transparency award, Ernst and Young's toolkit for humanitarian aid organizations, and KPMG's involvement in the High Level Forum on Aid Effectiveness. With their transparency award, PwC aims at promoting trust and transparency in the NGO sector by assessing and providing detailed feedback on reporting by NGOs (PwC, 2013). The toolkit developed by Ernst and Young involves detailed guidance on how NGOs can strengthen their internal controls in order to make NGOs more effective in achieving their mission (Ernst and Young, 2013). During the Fourth High Level Forum on Aid Effectiveness, KPMG contributed to discussions on improving NGO accountability by presenting their view on how third-party participants, such as KPMG, can assist donors in determining the effectiveness of grants and in achieving mutual accountability between donors and NGOs (KPMG, 2011).

## Reflecting on operationalizing downward accountability

Academic studies on NGO accountability are increasingly focusing on the extent to which more holistic accountability initiatives and approaches, which include forms of downward accountability, have actually led to more effective development cooperation and the empowerment of beneficiaries (Davis *et al.,* 2012; Jacobs and Wilford, 2010; O'Dwyer and Unerman, 2010).

The generally agreed upon goal of downward accountability is to improve the quality of development cooperation by enabling learning for both Northern and Southern NGOs through improving interaction with and the empowerment of beneficiaries (Jacobs and Wilford, 2010; O'Dwyer and Unerman, 2010). Despite agreement among practitioners and academics that this form of accountability is deemed desirable, since it potentially leads to more effective development cooperation, it is often difficult to implement in practice. Jacobs and Wilford (2010) argue that the use of loose and imprecise practical definitions, such as participation, listening and responsiveness, make it difficult to implement meaningful downward accountability mechanisms. While NGOs have developed systematic ways to approach upward accountability, downward accountability is often not managed in a systematic way (Jacobs and Wilford, 2010) and mainly focuses on establishing broader procedures to assess local NGO effectiveness rather than focusing on the accountability from local NGOs towards beneficiaries (O'Dwyer and Unerman, 2010). Despite increasing attention to downward accountability within Northern NGOs, there is a relative lack of evidence of consistent, substantive operationalization of downward accountability in Northern NGO–local NGO partnership working relations (O'Dwyer and Unerman, 2010).

While some of the difficulties in the operationalization of downward accountability can be attributed to the amount of time and resources NGOs spent on adhering to increasingly stringent upward accountability demands, reduced levels of funding due to the recent credit crisis, and the absence of funding requirements promoting or prioritizing downward account-ability (O'Dwyer and Unerman, 2010), there are additional factors which make the imple-mentation of downward accountability complex. It is often difficult to include certain beneficiaries due to a lack of interest in being more directly involved in decision-making processes (O'Dwyer and Unerman, 2010) or due to cultural norms, which, for example, influence gender relations within local communities and might lead to the exclusion of women in accountability processes (Jacobs and Wilford, 2010). This lack of interest stems from a primary interest of local NGOs in receiving money to support basic activities rather than being more involved; and a lack of knowledge and expertise on development coopera-tion among local NGOs and beneficiaries. Increased involvement of beneficiaries in decision making could thus potentially overwhelm local NGOs and beneficiaries who lack the resources and knowledge in managing more enhanced forms of accountability (O'Dwyer and Unerman, 2010). Additionally, local partner NGOs often struggle to facilitate the scope which allows challenging the status quo of Northern NGO operations, resulting in beneficiaries not being able to effect change in Northern NGO actions (O'Dwyer and Unerman, 2010).

Another explanation for the difficulty of implementing downward accountability is provided by Davis *et al.* (2012), who analysed disagreements between the perceptions of accountability mechanisms among home and field staff within NGOs. Their findings indicate that the attitude towards existing accountability mechanisms was more positive among field staff compared to home country staff. The authors provide three overlapping explanations for this phenomenon, i.e. the different organizational roles and positions influ-ence the attention afforded to different dimensions of accountability, varying perceptions of what desirable and feasible accountability mechanisms look like, and power difference between home and field staff which potentially leads to field staff reporting what they believe the head office considers desirable (Davis *et al.*, 2012)

In order to improve downward accountability practices a more careful consideration of the complexities faced in local contexts, a more central role of downward accountability in the assessment of the effectiveness of aid in funding requirements and improvement of the attitude of Northern NGO staff to the importance of downward accountability is needed (Jacobs and Wilford, 2010; O'Dwyer and Unerman, 2010). Additionally, developing a deeper understanding of the most effective development aid delivery solutions and a more systematic approach to embed the importance of downward accountability within Northern NGOs is crucial for working towards more meaningful (downward) accountability (Jacobs and Wilford, 2010; O'Dywer and Unerman, 2010).

## Concluding comments

This chapter provides an overview of the developments in NGO accountability, a field that is rapidly growing in prominence and importance. Given the vast expanse of NGOs in a broad variety of fields, this review primarily considers international and national develop-ment and advocacy-oriented NGOs. The NGO sector addressed here is characterized by complex accountability processes, resulting from the broad range of constituencies to whom

NGOs can be considered accountable and the lack of agreed upon measures of organizational performance. Despite an increasingly favourable attitude towards more holistic forms of accountability within Northern NGOs and funders, hierarchical forms of accountability still dominate accountability practice within NGOs. Operationalizing more holistic forms of accountability, such as the participation of beneficiaries in decision making, remains difficult due to a lack of interest of beneficiaries to be more involved in decision making, cultural differences between Northern and Southern countries, reduced levels of funding due to the recent credit crisis, lack of systematic ways to approach downward accountability, and the preference of funders to implement quantifiable performance targets.

The rapid growth of NGOs in combination with their preoccupation with managing upward accountability to donors, may have resulted in a situation where NGOs are losing touch with their original mission and traditional added value. Their over-reliance on state funding and focus on immediate results rather than taking risks threatens their autonomy and flexibility and can potentially make it difficult for NGOs to maintain their role as relevant and independent actors in a changing environment. In order to cope with trends such as shifts in powers from Western economies to new powers such as China and India, pressure on natural resources, and increasing inequality, NGOs must revisit the nature of their organizations (Trócaire, 2011). The role of NGOs as intermediary between Northern (governmental) donors and Southern NGOs will change due to cuts in funding from governmental and private donors, shifting funding priorities towards thematic service delivery, and the increased organizational capacity of Southern NGOs. This will require NGOs to transform into more flexible organizations, able to respond to changing circumstances and work more closely together with other NGOs in order to achieve joint goals. The shifting role of NGOs will alter the nature of NGO accountability because of different funding models and increasing amounts of partnerships with the private sector and other, Northern and Southern, NGOs (Trócaire, 2011). In many respects, the changing environment and role of NGOs can be perceived as returning towards the traditional role of NGOs, i.e. being focused on creating (financial) linkages from North to South, building capacity through sharing knowledge, holding governments to account on an international level, and uniting movements from different regions.

## Notes

1  Amnesty International, Oxfam, Save the Children, Greenpeace and Care.
2  This was aimed at helping local, national and international humanitarian relief organizations to design, implement, assess, improve and recognize accountable programmes of organizations (HAP, 2013).
3  Examples of such unethical behaviour include the disastrous response of NGOs to the Rwanda crisis in 1996 and a lack of transparency in funding provided to NGOs in order provide aid to victims of the Tsunami in Asia in 2004.
4  Ebrahim (2003b) notes that there are examples of mechanisms, such as social auditing, that straddle the tool–process dichotomy. Social auditing is an instrument through which organizations can assess, report and improve social performance and ethical behaviour (Ebrahim, 2003b). Social auditing combines various tools, such as disclosures and evaluations, with processes, such as participation of stakeholders, which makes it potentially valuable as a more encompassing accountability mechanism.
5  See for example the Code of Ethics and Conduct for NGOs developed by the World Association of NGOs (WANGO) or the Code of Good Practice for NGOs responding to HIV/AIDS, developed by a combination of NGOs including ActionAid International and the International Federation of Red Cross and Red Crescent Societies (One World Trust, 2013c).

# References

AbouAssi, K. (2012) Hands in the pockets of mercurial donors: NGO response to shifting funding priorities. *Nonprofit and Voluntary Sector Quarterly*, 42(3): 1–19.

ActionAid International (2004a) *Taking stock II: Summary of ALPS Review 2004*. ActionAid International, available at http://www.actionaid.org.uk/1417/global_review.html, accessed 4 September 2006.

ActionAid International (2004b) *Taking stock II: Synthesis Report 2004*, available at http://www.actionaid.org/wps/content/documents/ synthesis_report_1832005_131515.pdf, accessed 4 September 2006.

Agyemang, G., Awumbila, M., Unerman, J. and O'Dwyer, B. (2009) *NGO accountability and aid delivery*. London: Certified Accountants Educational Trust.

Avina, J. (1993) The evolutionary life cycles of non-governmental development organisations. *Public Administration and Development* 13, 453–74.

Blagescu, M., de Las Casas, L. and Lloyd, R. (2005) *Pathways to accountability: A short guide to the GAP framework*. London: One World Trust.

Bradley, B., Jansen, P. and Silverman, L. (2003) The nonprofit sector's $100 billion opportunity. *Harvard Business Review* 81: 94–103.

Brown, D. and Moore, M. (2001) Accountability, strategy and international NGOs. *Nonprofit and Voluntary Sector Quarterly*, 30(3): 586–7.

Callamard, A. (2004) HAP international: A new decisive step towards accountability. *AccountAbility Forum*, 1(2): 44–57.

Cavill, S. and Sohail, M. (2007) Increasing strategic accountability: A framework for international NGOs. *Development in Practice*, 17(2): 231–48.

Chenhall, R.H., Hall, M. and Smith, D. (2010) Social capital and management control systems: A study of a non-government organization. *Accounting, Organizations and Society*, 35: 737–56.

Christensen, R. and Ebrahim, A. (2006) How does accountability affect mission? The case of a nonprofit serving immigrants and refugees. *Nonprofit Management and Leadership*, 17: 195–209.

Cronin, D. and O'Regan, J. (2002) *Accountability in development aid: Meeting responsibilities, measuring performance. A Research Report for Comhlamh*. Dublin: Comhlamh Aid Issues Group.

Davis, T., MacDonald, K. and Brenton, S. (2012) Reforming accountability in international NGOs: Making sense of conflicting feedback. *Development in Practice*, 22(7): 946–61.

Deloitte (2013) *Strengthening the capacity of NGOs in Afghanistan*, available at http://www.deloitte.com/view/en_US/us/Insights/Browse-by-Content-Type/Case-Studies/US-Federal-Government-Case-Studies/cca993ed13880310VgnVCM3000001c56f00aRCRD.htm, accessed 21 August 2013.

Dempsey, S.E. (2007) Negotiating accountability within international contexts: The role of bounded voice. *Communication Monographs*, 74: 311–32.

Dey, C. (2004) Social accounting at Traidcraft plc: An ethnographic study of a struggle for the meaning of Fair Trade, paper presented at the APIRA conference, Singapore, 4–6 July.

Dillon, E. (2004) *Accountabilities and power in development relationships*. Trócaire Development Review 2003/4. Dublin: Trócaire, pp. 105–17.

Dixon, R., Ritchie, J. and Siwale, J. (2006) Microfinance: Accountability from the grass-roots. *Accounting, Auditing and Accountability Journal*, 19(3): 405–27.

Doh, J.P. and Teegan, H. (2002) Nongovernmental organizations as institutional actors in international business: Theory and implications. *International Business Review*, 11: 665–84.

Ebrahim, A. (2003a) Making sense of accountability: Conceptual perspectives for Northern and Southern Nonprofits. *Nonprofit Management and Leadership*, 14(2):191–212.

Ebrahim, A. (2003b) Accountability in practice: Mechanisms for NGOs. *World Development*, 31: 813–29.

Ebrahim, A. (2005) Accountability myopia: Losing sight of organizational learning. *Nonprofit and Voluntary Sector Quarterly*, 34(1): 56–87.

Ebrahim, A. (2009) Placing the normative logics of accountability in 'Thick' perspective. *American Behavioral Scientist*, 52: 885–904.

Edwards, M. (1993) Does the doormat influence the boot?: Critical thoughts on UK NGOs and international advocacy. *Development in Practice*, 3: 163–75.

Edwards, M. and Fowler, A. (eds) (2002) *NGO management*. London: Earthscan.

Edwards, M. and Hulme, D. (1996) Too close for comfort? The impact of official aid on non-governmental organisations. *World Development*, 24(6): 961–73.

Ernst & Young (2013) *Improving internal controls: The Ernst & Young guide for humanitarian aid organizations*, available at http://www.ey.com/GL/en/About-us/Corporate-Responsibility/Improving-internal-controls—the-Ernst—Young-guide-for-humanitarian-aid-organizations, accessed 21 August 2013.

Everett, J. and Friesen, C. (2010) Humanitarian accountability in the *Théâtre de l'Absurde. Critical Perspectives on Accounting*, 21(6): 468–85.

Fisher, W.F. (1997) Doing good? The politics and antipolitics of NGO practices. *Annual Review of Anthropology*, 26: 439–64.

Fowler, A.F. (1996) Assessing NGO performance: Difficulty, dilemmas, and a way ahead, in M. Edwards and D. Hulme (eds) *Beyond the magic bullet: NGO performance and accountability in the post-Cold War world*. West Hartford, CT: Kumarian Press, pp. 169–86.

Goddard, A. and Assad, M.J. (2006) Accounting and navigating legitimacy in Tanzanian NGOs. *Accounting, Auditing and Accountability Journal*, 19(3): 377–404.

Gordon, T., Knock, C. and Neely, D. (2009) The role of rating agencies in the market for charitable contributions: An empirical test. *Journal of Accounting and Public Policy*, 28: 469–84.

Gray, R., Bebbington, J. and Collison, D. (2006) NGOs, civil society and accountability: Making the people accountable to capital. *Accounting, Auditing and Accountability Journal*, 19(3): 319–48.

Gray, R.H., Dey, C., Owen, D.L., Evans, R. and Zadek, S. (1997) Struggling with the praxis of social accounting: Stakeholders, accountability, audits and procedures. *Accounting, Auditing and Accountability Journal*, 10(3): 325–64.

Hailey, J. (2000) Indicators of assessing core values. *Development in Practice*, 10(2/4): 402–7.

Hudson, A. (1999) Organizing NGOs' international advocacy: Organizational structures and organizational effectiveness, paper presented at the NGOs in a Global Future Conference, University of Birmingham, 11–13 January.

Humanitarian Accountability Partnership (HAP) (2013) *HAP 2010 Standard*, available at http://www.hapinternational.org/projects/standard/hap-2010-standard.aspx, accessed 25 June 2013.

International Non-governmental Organizations (INGO) (2006) *Accountability charter*, available at http://www.worldywca.info/index.php/ywca/content/download/2174/23424/file/account_charter.pdf, accessed 13 June 2013.

Jacobs, A. and Wilford, R. (2010) Listen first: A pilot system for managing downward accountability in NGOs. *Development in Practice*, 20(7): 797–811.

Jepson, P. (2005) Governance and accountability of environmental NGOs. *Environmental Science and Policy*, 8: 515–24.

Keystone (2013a) *About us*, available at http://www.keystoneaccountability.org/about, accessed 21 August 2013.

Keystone (2013b) *Services*, available at http://www.keystoneaccountability.org/services, accessed 21 August 2013.

KPMG (2011) NGO accountability and effectiveness: Making a difference, paper presented by International Development Assistance Services (IDAS) at the Fourth High Level Forum on AID Effectiveness, Busan, Korea, 1 December 2011.

Lehman, G. (2007) The accountability of NGOs in civil society and its public spheres. *Critical Perspectives on Accounting*, 18: 645–69.

Lewis, D. and Madon, S. (2004) Information systems and nongovernmental development organizations: Advocacy, organizational learning, and accountability. *The Information Society*, 20: 117–26.

Listen First (2013) *The Listen First framework*, available at http://www.listenfirst.org/pool/listen-first-aug08.doc, accessed 21 August 2013.

Litovsky, A. (2005a) *The future of civil society*, Workshop Report from the World Social Forum, 30 January, Keystone (c/o AccountAbility), London, available at http://keystonereporting.org/files/WSF%202005%20Workshop%20Report%20Keystone.pdf, accessed 4 September 2006.

Litovsky, A. (2005b) Stakeholder engagement and NGO accountability: The new frontier for innovation. *Accountability Forum*, 2(6): 25–35.

Lloyd, R. (2005) *The role of NGO self-regulation in increasing stakeholder accountability*. London: One World Trust.

Lloyd, R., Warren, S. and Hammer, M. (2008) *2008 Global Accountability Report*. London: One World Trust.

Martens, K. (2002) Mission impossible? Defining nongovernmental organizations. *Voluntas: International Journal of Voluntary and Nonprofit Organizations*, 13(3): 271–85.

Najam, A. (1996) NGO accountability: A conceptual framework. *Development Policy Review*, 14: 339–53.

Oakes, L. and Young, J. (2008) Accountability re-examined: Evidence from Hull House. *Accounting, Auditing and Accountability Journal*, 21(6): 765–90.

O'Dwyer, B. (2005) The construction of a social account: A case study in an overseas aid agency. *Accounting, Organizations and Society*, 30(3): 279–96.

O'Dwyer, B. and Unerman, J. (2007) From functional to social accountability: Transforming the accountability relationship between funders and non-governmental development organisations. *Accounting, Auditing & Accountability Journal*, 20, 446–71.

O'Dwyer, B. and Unerman, J. (2008) The paradox of greater NGO accountability: A case study of Amnesty Ireland. *Accounting, Organizations and Society*, 33: 801–24.

O'Dwyer, B. and Unerman, J. (2010) Enhancing the role of accountability in promoting the rights of beneficiaries of development NGOs. *Accounting and Business Research*, 40: 451–71.

One World Trust (2013a) *NGO accountability*, available at http://www.oneworldtrust.org/ngo accountability, accessed 4 June 2013.

One World Trust (2013b) *Global accountability*, available at http://www.oneworldtrust.org/global accountability, accessed 4 June 2013.

One World Trust (2013c) *A database of civil society self-regulatory initiatives*, available at http://www.oneworldtrust.org/csoproject/cso/initiatives/list/international#general, accessed 21 August 2013.

PricewaterhouseCoopers (2013) *PwC transparency award: Supporting improved reporting by NGOs*, available at http://www.pwc.com/gx/en/annual-review/transparency.jhtml, accessed 21 August 2013.

Rahaman, A., Neu, D. and Everett, J. (2010) Accounting for social-purpose alliances: Confronting the HIV/AIDS pandemic in Africa. *Contemporary Accounting Research*, 27(4): 1093–129.

Roberts, J. (1991) The possibilities of accountability. *Accounting, Organizations and Society*, 16: 355–68.

Roberts, J. (2001) Trust and control in Anglo-American systems of corporate governance: The individualizing and socializing effects of processes of accountability. *Human Relations*, 54: 1547–72.

Russell, J. (2006) *NGO accountability: A charter for success*. Ethical Corporation Magazine online (5 June), available at http://www.ethicalcorp.com/, accessed 14 June 2006.

Salamon, L.M. (1994) The rise of the nonprofit sector: A global 'associational revolution'. *Foreign Affairs*, 73(4): 109–22.

Salamon, L.M., Anheier, H.K., List, R., Toepler, S. and Sokolowski, S.W. (eds) (1999) *Global civil society: Dimensions of the nonprofit sector*. Baltimore, MD: Johns Hopkins University Press.

Schmitz, H., Raggo, P. and Bruno-van Vijfeijken, T. (2012) Accountability of transnational NGOs: Aspirations vs. practice. *Nonprofit and Voluntary Sector Quarterly*, 41(6): 1175–94.

Sinclair, A. (1995) The chameleon of accountability: Forms and discourses. *Accounting, Organizations and Society*, 20: 219–37.

Slim, H. (2002) *By what authority? The legitimacy and accountability of non-governmental organizations*, paper presented to the International Council on Human Rights Policy. International Meetings on Global Trends and Human Rights – before and after September 11, Geneva, available at http://www.ichrp.org/paper_files/119_w_02.doc, accessed 4 September 2006.

Sloan, M. (2009) The effects of non-profit accountability ratings on donor behaviour. *Nonprofit and Voluntary Sector Quarterly*, 28: 220–36.

Smillie, I. (1996) Painting Canadian roses red, in M. Edwards and D. Hulme (eds) *Beyond the magic bullet: NGO performance and accountability in the post-Cold War world*. West Hartford, CT: Kumarian Press, pp. 187–97.

SustainAbility (2003) *The 21st century NGO: In the market for change. Executive summary*. London: SustainAbility.

Tandon, R. (1996) Board games: Governance and accountability in NGOs, in M. Edwards and D. Hulme (eds) *Beyond the magic bullet: NGO performance and accountability in the post-Cold War world*. West Hartford, CT: Kumarian Press, pp. 53–63.

Trócaire (2011) *Leading Edge 2020: Critical thinking on the future of international development*. Kildare: Trócaire.

Unerman, J. and O'Dwyer, B. (2006a) On James Bond and the importance of NGO accountability. *Accounting, Auditing and Accountability Journal*, 19(3): 305–18.

Unerman, J. and O'Dwyer, B. (2006b) Theorising accountability for NGO advocacy. *Accounting, Auditing and Accountability Journal*, 19(3): 349–76.

Upadhyay, A. (2003) *NGOs: Do the watchdogs need watching?*, available at http://www.globalpolicy.org/ngos/credib/2003/0613panel.htm, accessed 4 September, 2006.

Uphoff, N. (1995) Why NGOs are not a third sector: A sectorial analysis with some thoughts on accountability, sustainability and evaluation, in M. Edwards and D. Hulme (eds) *Beyond the magic bullet: NGO performance and accountability in the post-Cold War world*. West Hartford, CT: Kumarian Press, pp. 17–30.

Vakil, A.C. (1997) Confronting the classification problem: A taxonomy of NGOs. *World Development*, 25(12): 2057–70.

Walsh, E. and Lenihan, H. (2006) Accountability and effectiveness of NGOs: Adapting business tools successfully. *Development in Practice*, 16: 412–24.

Zadek, S. (2003) *In defence of non-profit accountability*. London: Ethical Corporation.

# 11 Sustainability accounting and accountability in the public sector

*Amanda Ball, Suzana Grubnic and Jeff Birchall*

Research and learning about sustainability accounting is very often focused on for-profit, business organizations. This makes sense when we consider the historic role of corporations in generating wealth and their sometimes contentious impacts on environment and society. In contrast, this chapter argues that great potential in the public sector for advances in sustainability accounting and accountability is too often overlooked. The sheer scale and operational impacts of the public sector on our economy, environment and communities indicate an important agenda, in spite of the pressures on many public sector organizations (PSOs) to make efficiency gains and/or cut services as governments reduce public spending in response to the recent global financial crisis. For example, in New Zealand (NZ):

> The combined central and local government sectors consume approximately one fifth of GDP. Collectively, central government is the country's biggest employer, largest land-owner, and consumes significant proportions of resources. It has been estimated ... that central government (including the police, defence force, health, universities, etc.) and local government consume some 2.6 billion KWh of energy per annum and release 0.6 million tonnes of $CO_2$ equivalents per annum.[1,2]

In order to provide a richer context, measures on the public sector in the United Kingdom (UK) and NZ are provided in Table 11.1.

In this chapter we explain what the public sector is and argue that PSOs deserve our attention because they have assumed far greater responsibilities for sustainability than the for-profit, corporate sector has ever been asked to take on. Focusing on the cases of the UK and NZ (because this is where we have researched), we evaluate the merits of developments in practice relative to what we believe is needed. Our aims in this chapter are to increase awareness of the leading role of PSOs in a more sustainable future and to argue for the importance of developments in sustainability accounting and accountability in this field.

## What is the public sector?

The following definition is a good starting point:

> The public sector is that part of a nation's economic activity which is traditionally owned and controlled by government ... the public sector is composed of those public organizations which provide utilities and services to the community and which have traditionally been seen as essential to the fabric of our society.
>
> (Broadbent and Guthrie, 1992, p. 3)

*Table 11.1* Scale of the public sector in the UK and New Zealand

|  | United Kingdom | New Zealand |
| --- | --- | --- |
| Public expenditure as a percentage of GDP | 42.3%[1] | 42.0%[2] |
| Total numbers employed in the public sector | 5,899,000[3] | 226,048[4] |
| Numbers employed in public sector as a percentage of employment in whole economy | 20.15%[5] | 9.42%[6] |
| Annual carbon emissions from central government offices | 2,299,334.30 tCO2e[7] | 159,000 tCO2e[8] |

1 *Public Spending Statistics July 2012*, published by HM Treasury, includes this figure in Table 4.1 for 2011–12.
2 Figure represents 2009, sourced from Government at a glance 2011, Public Finance and Economics, 3.4 General Government Expenditures, in OECD National Accounts Statistics, available at http://www.oecd-ilibrary.org/sites/gov_glance-2011-en/03/04/giii-4-01.html?contentType=&itemId=/content/chapter/gov_glance-2011-10-en&containerItemId=/content/serial/22214399&accessItemIds=/content/book/gov_glance-2011-en&mimeType=text/html, accessed 5 September 2012.
3 *Statistical Bulletin: Public Sector Employment, Q1 2012* is published by the Office for National Statistics. See www.ons.gov.uk/ons/rel/pse/public-sector-employment/q1-2012/stb-pse-2012q1.html, accessed 3 September 2012.
4 This figure represents the total number that worked in the State Services as at 30 June 2011. The total Full-Time Equivalent (FTE) number of employees in public service departments was 43,595 (SSC, 2011). See also NZ Govt. (2012) for public service FTE reduction projections in 2012.
5 See note 3.
6 Key Facts, National Labour Force Projections: (August 2012 update), Statistics New Zealand, available at http://www.stats.govt.nz/browse_for_stats/population/estimates_and_projections/NationalLabourForceProjections_HOTP06-61Augupdate.aspx, accessed 6 September 2012.
7 The annual figure on carbon emissions for the UK has been derived from http://data.gov.uk and relates to 2010/11. See: http://data.gov.uk/sites/default/files/Pan-gov%20SOGE%20summary%202010-11%20vfin.pdf, accessed on 3 September 2012.
8 NZ Govt. 2008. POL (08) 36: Carbon Neutral Public Service – update on progress. Ministry for the Environment, Wellington, New Zealand.

Following the emphasis in this definition on *government ownership and control*, the public sector in advanced capitalist economies often includes:

- national (federal) government ministries, departments and executive agencies;
- devolved or state government authorities;
- regional and local government authorities, health care providers and emergency service organizations;
- public corporations and trading funds;
- an array of other research and educational institutions and foundations.

A practical approach that retains an emphasis on *government ownership and control* is to define the public sector as those organizations included in Whole of Government Accounts (WGA) (WGA use Generally Accepted Accounting Principles [GAAP] to produce a single set of consolidated accounts for the public sector as if it were a single entity). Table 11.2 shows PSOs which fall within UK WGA and, given that the accounts do not include health service organizations in Scotland following the National Health Service (NHS) Reform (Scotland) Act 2004, Table 11.3 provides detail on structure and numbers of hospitals.

Tables 11.1 and 11.2 demonstrate something of the great diversity of PSO activities but, in order to progress our discussion, we now explain what makes PSOs distinctive. This issue has been the subject of academic debate over many years; and the central concern is whether

*Table 11.2* Public sector organizations within UK Whole of Government Accounts

---

*Central Government*

Comprises:
- Departments[1]
- Non-Departmental Public Bodies (NDPBs)[2]
- Government Central Funds
- Health service organizations
- Academies.

*Departments* are legally part of the Crown and receive funding from, and are directly accountable to, Parliament. Ministerial departments have responsibility for a set of policy issues and associated legislation as well as the delivery of policy in conjunction with delivery partners. Ministerial departments are supported by executive agencies.

Examples: Department of Health, Ministry of Defence, Office of the Deputy Prime Minister.

*NDPB*'s are a mixture of crown and non-crown bodies that have a role in the processes of National Government and operate to a greater or lesser extent at arm's length from Ministers to whom they are nevertheless accountable. There are four main types of NDPB. Executive NDPB's tend to be directly funded by Government while Advisory and Tribunal NDPBs and Independent Monitoring Boards are usually resourced by their sponsoring Department.

Examples: Environment Agency (Executive NDPB), Advisory Committee on Releases to the Environment (Advisory NDPB) and Plant Varieties and Seeds Tribunal (Tribunal NDPB).

*Government Central Funds* (sub-classified into trusts and pension schemes).

Examples: Consolidated Fund and Armed Forces Pension Scheme.

*Health service organizations*
Health care Trusts are legally separate bodies, derive income mainly from the commissioning activity of Primary Care Trusts and provide health care services to the population. While Non-Foundations Trusts are accountable to the Department of Health and devolved administrations, Foundation Trusts are accountable to Monitor, an independent regulator.

|  | *Geographical area* | | |
|  | England | Wales | N.Ireland |
|---|---|---|---|
| *Non-Foundation Trust* | 175 | 18 | 7 |
| *Foundation Trust* | 115 | | |

*Academies*
Academies are schools that are directly funded by central government (specifically, the Young People's Learning Agency within the Department for Education) and not local authorities. To supplement income, they can receive additional financial support from personal or corporate sponsors. There are 204 Academies[3] listed in Annex 1 to WGA.

Central Government in the UK includes devolved administrations in Scotland (the Scottish Parliament), Wales (the National Assembly for Wales) and Northern Ireland (the Northern Ireland Assembly).

*(continued)*

*Table 11.2* Public sector organizations within UK Whole of Government Accounts (continued)

## Local Government

Bodies classified to local government are regarded as statutorily separate and typically service a bounded geographical area. Local authorities are funded from central government through grants and re-distributed non-domestic rates and a combination of council tax, fees and charges, sales, council rents and capital receipts. Primary local authority services include education, social services, housing, local planning, local highways, environmental health, and refuse colletion and disposal. Local, police and fire authorities are accountable to the local communities served. The following are listed[4]:

| | | *Geographical area* | | |
|---|---|---|---|---|
| | | *England* | *Scotland Wales* | *N.Ireland* |
| *Unitary* | | 55 | 32 | 22 |
| | + Isles of Scilly | 1 | | |
| *District* | | | | |
| | Metropolitan districts | 36 | | 26 |
| | Non-metropolitan districts | 201 | | |
| *Country* | | | | |
| | Metropolitan counties | 6 | | |
| | Non-metropolitan counties | 27 | | |
| *Inner & outer London Boroughs* | | 33 | | |
| *Police* | | 38 | 6 | 4 |
| *Fire* | | 31 | 6 | 3 |
| *Waste disposal* | | 6 | | |
| *Passenger transport* | | 6 | 2 | 4 |
| *National park authorities* | | 9 | | 3 |
| *Other park authorities* | | 2 | | |

## Public Corporations, Trading Funds and Public Broadcasting

The 52 organizations listed in this category are created by statute and can derive more than 50 per cent of income from the sale of goods and services. Public corporations are accountable to their respective parliaments and assemblies.

Examples: British Broadcasting Corporation, Meteorological Office, and Companies House.

Source: Whole of Government Accounts for the Year Ended 31 March 2010, published by HM Treasury during November 2011. Accounts available at www.wga.gov.uk, accessed 16 January 2012.

1 There are currently twenty-four Ministerial Departments and twenty-six Non-Ministerial Departments in the UK.

2 *Public Bodies Reform – Proposals for Change*, published on 14 October 2010, can be found on www.direct.gov. uk/en/NI1/Newsroom/DG_191548

3 The number of Academies in England has increased to 1,529 as of 1 January 2012 following the passing of The Academies Act 2010 and the introduction of the Free Schools Programme. However, Academies constitute a very small proportion of state-funded mainstream schools, the majority being funded by Local Authorities (see below). As of 31 July 2011, 21 per cent of state-funded mainstream secondary schools and 1 per cent of state-funded primary schools were operating as Academies (source: http://media.education.gov.uk/assets/files/pdf/a/academies%20annual%20annual%20report20201011.pdf, accessed on 3/09/2012).

4 The categorization of local government organizations is partly derived from *Local Government Financial Statistics England 21* as accessed from www.communities.gov.uk/publications/localgovernment/financialstatistics 21 on 18 January 2012. Numbers of local authorities in England is provided in Tables G1 to G4 in Annex G and is true as at 1 April 2010. The WGA categorization of local government includes other bodies not included in the table such as Transport for London.

*Table 11.3* The NHS in Scotland

---

The Scottish Government Health and Social Care Directorate is responsible for the central management of the NHS including the development of health and community care policy. NHS Scotland is comprised of 14 Territorial NHS Boards and eight Special NHS Boards and provides strategic leadership of the local NHS system. The boards are accountable to Scottish Ministers.
NHS health care is given in 133 hospitals excluding long stay hospitals and 117 long stay hospitals, by 4,937 general practitioners as well as a host of dentists, opticians and midwives. Care is also delivered by district nurses, health visitors and midwives as part of community services. In total, there were 161,369 staff in post as at 30 September 2011.

---

Sources: *Scottish Health Services Costs (Cost Book)*, available at www.isdscotland.org/Health-Topics/finance/costs/file-listings-2011.asp, accessed 20 January 2012. Numbers of workers in the NHS can be found in *NHS Scotland Workforce National Statistics*, published jointly by ISD (Information Services Division Scotland) and NHS National Health Services Scotland, available at www.isdscotland.org/Health_Topics/workforce/publications/2011-11-29/2011-11-29-workforce-report.pdf, accessed 25 January 2012.

there is any real difference between the nature of the tasks performed by public and private sector organizations. As Broadbent and Guthrie's (1992) definition of the public sector (above) emphasizes, PSOs provide *services to the community* which are *essential to the fabric of our society*. (Our position is that there *is* a basic difference between the public and for-profit corporate sectors when it comes to delivering on sustainability.)

Boston and colleagues (1996) provide a very clear illustration of the controversies that set the context for the public sector. They discuss 'contracting out' prison management, whereby public sector authorities retain responsibility for funding services and maintaining standards; but delivery is undertaken by another, usually commercial, organization:

> Advocates of contracting out argue that public ownership and control tends to be wasteful and inefficient – characterised by rigid work practices, excessive staffing levels, and provider capture. They contend that exposing prison management to the rigours of competition will yield significant gains in productive efficiency, as well as more innovative and humane penal management practices. Critics ... point to the problems of specifying desired outcomes, establishing appropriate performance targets, monitoring subsequent performance, and enforcing the relevant contractual obligations ... they ... note the potential risks of opportunistic behaviour on the part of commercially orientated prison managers ... critics ... also argue that, as a matter of principle, the imposition of punishment on behalf of the community should be undertaken by institutions of a wholly public nature. Only in this way ... can the community signify, directly and unequivocally, its abhorrence of actions that violate commonly accepted norms.
>
> (Boston *et al.*, 1996, p. 8)

The prison service is a 'social ordering' (Pollitt, 2003) or 'guardianship' (Le Grand, 2003) function. In many countries PSOs must deliver on these tasks, which include law and order, defence, education, health care, housing, and social care. These tasks can also be thought of as keeping the population safe from threats of discord, violence or, more broadly, *freedom from fear*. When Aneurin Bevan spoke of freedom from fear as justification for the establishment of the NHS in the UK in 1948, he referred to the fear of illness by the working class and the fear of not having the means to pay for care (Lessing, 1998; Pollock, 2004; Quirk, 2005).

Some public sector tasks, then, result from political decisions, influenced by what society perceives as needs and also doing the right thing. This means that some PSO functions have a high degree of political salience, because it falls to some PSOs to bring to fruition the 'heroic aspirations' (Pollitt, 2003, p. 12) of politicians to take action on public concerns. It is for these sorts of reasons that Boston *et al.* (1996) point to the view that some tasks fall to public agencies *as a matter of principle*.

Alternatively, some services are argued to be too risky and/or unprofitable for private competitors to supply. Boston *et al.* (1996) raise the spectre of self-interested, 'commercial' behaviour on the part of prison managers. Private sector involvement in the prison service might lead to a perverse motive to keep prisons full. Under contracting-out arrangements, it is in the interest of the private sector to receive payments, whereas it is in the public interest to keep crime numbers low. Some services are also characterized by 'consequentiality', which refers to the question of whether or not service providers can afford to make mistakes (Pollitt, 2003). Certainly, in the UK, the contracting company Securicor became a household name following a string of breakouts by convicted prisoners from the hands of guards in Securicor's prisoner-escort service.

Finally, public sector work is sometimes 'thankless and often unpleasant' (Pollitt, 2003, p. 10) or seemingly mundane, a situation compounded by a lack of resources; and so the work simply falls to the public sector because no one else is prepared to do it. In fact, ethically motivated reasons for working in PSOs (a 'public sector ethos') have been reported in research studies (including Brewis, 1999; Boyne, 2002; Besley and Ghatak, 2005; Delfgaauw and Dur, 2008; Taylor, 2010); whereas private sector managers are more strongly motivated by personal economic prosperity (Boyne, 2002).

These differences between the public and private sector tasks are not just a matter of academic debate. A belief (often contrary to much of the available evidence) that there is little underlying difference between the sectors and their activities (except that the public sector is regarded as less efficient) has influenced sweeping policy changes in the public sector over the last several decades under various governments internationally (Broadbent and Guthrie, 1992, 2008; Boston *et al.*, 1996; Olsen *et al.*, 1998; Pollitt, 2003; Guthrie *et al.*, 2005). This belief has combined with a number of factors to undermine the traditional public sector as reflected in Broadbent and Guthrie's (1992) definition. Perhaps most notable is an entrenched public scepticism towards 'big government', which is reflected in sentiments about 'rigid work practices, excessive staffing levels, and provider capture' in Boston *et al.*'s (1996) example. International reforms, often referred to as the New Public Management (NPM) (Hood, 1991, 1995), have included the privatization of many publicly owned industries (selling off the organization's assets on the stock exchange to create for-profit companies); contracting-out services; and the creation of 'public–private partnerships' (PPPs) (where public objectives are pursued by partnerships of public and commercial organizations) (Pollitt, 2003). Under its recent 'Big Society' agenda, the UK Government has also taken a renewed interest in greater involvement of charities and social enterprises in public services. Compounding the effect of successive reforms, many PSOs additionally face a testing period of financial austerity as governments internationally embark on rapid debt reduction programmes in response to global economic instability.

We agree with Broadbent and Guthrie (2008, p. 134) that it may now be more useful to think in terms of *public services* as a field of study, where public services 'have some element of government funding, ownership, public direction or regulation, in different combinations' (p. 134). We also believe it likely however that in the coming decades, there will be a continued *need* for national, devolved, regional, local and other government agencies to deliver on legislative and policymaking responsibilities, including environmental protection and leadership on climate change mitigation and adaptation; that public services will continue to meet the day-to-day needs and concerns of many citizens through such public services as health, education, justice, defence and transport, among many others; and that the public services will continue to represent one of the largest employers in many countries.

## PSOs' responsibilities for sustainability

### *Managing operational impacts*

First, PSOs have responsibilities for managing their operational impacts on the environment; in some instances this is mandated, such as in NZ local government under the Local Government Act 2002. Even at this first level, there seems widespread acceptance that there are higher expectations of *public* (as opposed to private) organizations to set high standards (Pollitt, 2003, p. 10):

> Public agencies ... have a *civic responsibility* to properly manage public goods, resources, and/or facilities in a way that promotes sustainable development objectives and promotes the public interest ... Given their size and influence, public agencies are expected to *lead by example* in reporting publicly and transparently on their activities to promote sustainability.
>
> (GRI, 2005, pp. 7–8, emphasis added)

### *Developing and delivering public policy*

Second, their role in policy and the nature of some PSO activities give rise to responsibilities for sustainability of a different order of importance than the management of operational impacts.

Governments internationally have made political commitments to sustainable development (SD) (1992 United Nations Conference on Environment and Development, Rio de Janeiro; 2002 United Nations World Summit on Sustainable Development; Rio+20 in 2012); and by ratifying international treaties on sustainability issues including climate change, ozone protection, marine pollution, hazardous waste and world heritage. Some governments including the UK have strategies for SD; NZ does not in spite of sustainability being a cornerstone of its national identity (Buhrs, 2008). Perhaps there is no better illustration of *heroic aspirations* for public policy than the sustainability agenda; or of *freedom from fear* of the consequences of living beyond the planet's capacity to support life. As the UK Government has put it:

> Make the wrong choices now and future generations will live with changed climate, depleted resources and without the green space and biodiversity that contribute both to our standard of living and our quality of life. Each of us needs to make the right choices to secure a future that is fairer, where we can all live within our environmental limits. That means sustainable development.
>
> (HM Government, 2005, p. 3)

Governments have, in turn, a role in developing policy and legislative frameworks to embed sustainability. For example, in response to the UK strategy on SD: '[m]inisters have agreed an approach for mainstreaming SD which in broad terms consists of providing Ministerial leadership and oversight, leading by example, embedding SD into policy and transparent and independent scrutiny' (Defra, 2011, p. 2). Such commitments on sustainability have a significant impact on PSOs because the work of redefining policy objectives through the lens of sustainability, formulating policy and writing legislation falls in large measure to government departments and agencies; and because PSOs as service providers have key roles in delivering sustainability policy outcomes.

## *Illustrations of responsibility for sustainability*

### *Climate change policy*

Climate change policy provides a good illustration of the high level of responsibility for sustainability assumed by PSOs.

The former NZ Prime Minister, Helen Clark (Clark, 2007), placed responsibilities on PSOs for making progress on her government's commitment to a carbon-neutral NZ by 2012. In 2007, Clark announced a raft of sustainability initiatives including the Carbon Neutral Public Service (CNPS) programme (Clark, 2007; NZ Govt, 2007). And while the public sector accounts for only about 2 per cent of NZ's total emissions, the aim was to elevate NZ's international profile as a leader on climate change (NZ Govt, 2008), with the initiative conceived as 'the only comprehensive central government programme with robust systems and methodologies to work through the challenges posed by a public service carbon neutrality programme' (NZ Govt, 2008). In spite of the programme's successes (e.g. Birchall *et al.*, 2010, 2013), upon a change of government in NZ, the new National-led government (2008–present) terminated the CNPS programme, with Nick Smith, the Minister for the Environment (and the Minister for Climate Change Issues), indicating that to 'lead the world on climate change and to become the first carbon-neutral country' (Smith, 2009a) was a 'feel good slogan' (Smith, 2009b).

In the UK, the Climate Change Act (2008) commits government to reducing greenhouse gas (GHG) emissions by at least 80 per cent by 2050 against 1990 levels, with an independent Committee on Climate Change (CCC) advising on carbon targets. Perhaps in efforts to demonstrate being the 'Greenest Government ever', the Conservative/Liberal Democrat Coalition Government that came to power in 2010 committed to the more stringent targets[3] contained in the CCC's fourth budget (covering 2023–27, issued in June 2011), signalling step-changes to halve GHG emissions (also against 1990 levels) and departures from 'business as usual'. A new *Greening Government* initiative commits government departments to plan and report progress on a targeted 25 per cent reduction in GHG emissions from offices and business-related domestic flights by 2015 (from a 09/10 baseline). Meanwhile, implementation of a provision under the Scottish Climate Change Act on 1 January 2011 places a statutory duty on public bodies to 'exercise its functions in the way best calculated to contribute to delivery of the Act's emission reduction targets'. This extends to an expectation that public bodies will identify their own targets corresponding to national ones.

### *Local government action*

Our second illustration of how PSOs assume high levels of responsibility for sustainability concerns local government in the UK and NZ.

Local government has a traditional role as 'steward of the environment' and is often a focus for community politics of choice between economic, social and ecological sustainability. At Rio 1992, local government authorities and business organizations emerged as primary agents in delivering sustainable development; Christie (2000, p. 18) estimates that, 'if one examines Agenda 21 [the primary policy document emerging from Rio 1992] ... approximately half the actions essential to putting us on a path towards sustainable development within this century must be taken ... by local government'. Local authorities internationally have subsequently pursued voluntary sustainability initiatives such as the *ICLEI Local Governments for Sustainability* and *Communities for Climate Protection – NZ* programmes, culminating in an overarching agenda for sustainable communities, and the *Nottingham Declaration*. Unsurprisingly, then, governments are highly dependent on local authorities for delivering outcomes on long-term policy for a range of sustainability issues including community safety, social care, waste management and reduction, transport, land-use planning and climate change.

In addition, local government organizations in the UK and NZ alike have a general 'well-being' duty as enshrined in the Local Government Act 2000 (UK) and 2002 (NZ). This legislation allows authorities some freedom to develop a sustainability approach to planning activities, taking into account the social, economic and cultural well-being of the local communities and enhancement of the local environment, *inter alia* (Bellringer et al., 2011). Notwithstanding this, approaches taken by local authorities are shaped by the government in office and are subject to change following general elections. A good example is shifting government expectations of both UK and NZ local authority responsibilities for climate change.

Prior to the election of the UK Coalition Government in 2010, the previous Labour Government required all single and upper-tier authorities in England to develop Sustainable Community Strategies and listed three national indicators on climate change to be monitored under the Audit Commission's Comprehensive Area Assessment. The Coalition Government has since abolished the Labour Government's indicators and granted more power to local authorities on setting priorities under the Localism Bill and, since November 2011, the Localism Act. In New Zealand, the Labour-led government in 2004 began funding local authority membership in the NZ Communities for Climate Protection (CCP-NZ) programme (e.g. Birchall, 2013). As with the CNPS programme, when government shifted in 2008, the incoming National-led government cancelled funding, and the CCP-NZ programme ended in 2009. In the UK, the prior initiatives practised by local authorities have been reported as encouraging joined-up government in the UK (Cooper and Pearce, 2011) and, more generally, building expertise on sustainability and carbon management in both nation states. In NZ, in spite of National's claims to the contrary, CCP-NZ participant councils have shown emission reductions of more than 400,000 t-CO2e from base year (30 June 2004) to 30 June 2009 (CCP-NZ, 2009).

### Summary: inconsistency between policy and action

To summarize, it falls to many PSOs as policy and service organizations to assume significant responsibilities for sustainability. PSOs, however, face inconsistency in government policy and action on sustainability. Additionally, they are forced to reconcile conflicts between austerity measures on the one hand and what is needed to help balance social, environmental and economic concerns on the other. In the absence of a consistent government agenda and funding, we might ask how PSOs determine their response: is it morally or economically?

Even as PSOs are forced to work within tighter budgets, there is clearly a deep connection between (on the one hand) many core PSO missions and a public service ethos and (on the other) such notions as community, fair resource distribution and environmental protection inherent in sustainability. In contrast, corporate priorities usually lie with the providers of share capital rather than the well-being of the community or surrounding ecosystems (Matten *et al.*, 2003; O'Dwyer, 2003). Indeed, Gray and Bebbington (2001, p. 316) have argued that it is simply inappropriate to 'ask corporations to take … decisions that affect our futures'. Additionally, a critical lesson from the evaluation of corporate sustainability disclosures has been an unwillingness to question underlying business models and engage with the essential issues of sustainability impacts:

> Usually, the critical issues are linked directly to the company's core business, yet they are often ignored. A biotechnology-based company fails to refer to genetic engineering, for example, or an auto or oil industry [report] chooses to ignore the global warming agenda. The banks are also a prime example of this problem: they are happy to discuss green housekeeping measures, but most provide little or no information on the social and environmental issues associated with their mainstream financial activities.
>
> (UNEP/SustainAbility, 1997, p. 28)

It is for these sorts of reasons that we stress the need for greater attention to the potential of PSOs in the field of sustainability accounting.

## Mandates and frameworks for sustainability accounting in PSOs

### *Sustainability accounting: to what ends?*

Drawing on our discussion so far, it seems obvious that sustainability accounting for PSOs must encompass information about sustainability policy, strategy, programmes and outcomes as well as operational impacts (management of estate; procurement; efficiencies in waste, energy, transport and so on). We additionally conclude so far that sustainability accounting in PSOs has huge potential for enabling progress on a sustainable future if practised in order to:

- provide a vehicle for envisaging how policies and programmes translate heroic but vague political objectives for sustainability into action and change;
- provide a frame of reference for understanding how natural systems work and developing a precautionary approach to undertaking core tasks and activities (Burritt and Welch, 1997a);
- provide a means for reflecting on progress on redefining core mission and policy objectives in the context of a more sustainable future (this idea is analogous to corporations shifting their core business model);
- help define an organizationally or institutionally significant contribution (cf. Hopwood, 1978, p. 57);
- illuminate the consequences of funding cuts, and such consequences for social justice as detrimental impacts on vulnerable sections of society that the government no longer protects. Our understanding of sustainability here is wider than the emphasis of the UK Coalition Government as expressed in its austerity drive, and rather is consistent with

Unerman's (2011) argument for a more balanced approach in addressing both intra-generational as well as intergenerational equity. As Unerman (2011) observes, while it is important to relieve future generations of financial burdens, it is better if this is tested against the impact cuts may have on intergenerational social equity.

We argue, further, that a key factor in the uptake of sustainability accounting and account-ability will be the development of tangible measures to guide, encourage and legitimize practice. Accordingly, we now briefly consider some key developments in the UK and NZ.

### Mandates for sustainability accounting at national and local government levels

There is no government mandate in either the UK or NZ to encourage sustainability accounting and accountability across the wider public sector.

In relation to national governments' accountability for sustainability, governments internationally are mandated to produce state of the environment reports. NZ is a notable exception where a proposed Environmental Reporting Act recognizes a need to 'strengthen the integrity of New Zealand's clean, green brand by requiring independent and nationally consistent reporting on the state of our environment' (NZ Govt, 2012).[4] In the UK, ahead of the Rio + 20 Summit, Caroline Spelman, Environment Secretary, announced (The Guardian, 2012) the UK's intention to lead on the measurement of social and natural capital, citing such developments as new measures on national well-being[5] and reporting on quality of life, and the establishment of a new committee reporting to the Chancellor on the state of natural capital in England. As both programmes are long-term in nature, the indication is that policies could redress, in Boston and Lempp's (2011) terms, the accounting asymmetry. By valuing and accounting for natural capital, as well as manufactured and financial capital, for example, the idea is that policymakers will be provided with important insights on future actions that could reduce GHG emissions.

UK and NZ Governments have additionally required departments to report progress under various sustainability initiatives. NZ Government Departments were required to report carbon emission reductions and initiatives under the CNPS initiative. The 34 core departments in the CNPS programme identified over 300 emission reduction projects, reducing emissions below business as usual (NZ Govt, 2008); although the total emissions savings as a result of participation in the CNPS programme are not transparent because of insufficient detailed accounting data (Birchall *et al.*, 2010, 2013). The CNPS programme grew out of an earlier initiative, 'Govt³', which required departments to report on waste, energy and transport use. In the UK, the accountability requirements under the Greening Government initiative will potentially provide insights into how departments measure carbon impacts and what compromises or changes are implied for operations. And other themes in the Greening Government initiative have grown out of earlier initiatives requiring departments to report on high level commitments to SD and on service impacts including waste, energy use and procurement.

There is a significant history of initiatives to encourage sustainability accounting and accountability in local government in the UK. Lewis (2000) explains how guidance from Friends of the Earth, the Local Government Management Board (LGMB) and the Local Government Association issued between 1989 and 1991, encouraged state of the environment reporting and policy impact assessments. In the mid-1990s, the Audit Commission and the LGMB encouraged uptake of environmental management systems. Building on a long process of development by national and local governments since Rio 1992, local authorities have been encouraged to use 'quality of life' indicators to track local sustainability trends. Their use has been widespread in the UK since about 2000 (Bennet and van der Lugt, 2004; Audit Commission, 2005; Ball 2005a, 2005b). Ball (2005b) and Bellringer et al. (2011) examine whether the emphasis on sustainability in the Local Government Act 2000 (UK) and 2002 (NZ) promoted sustainability reporting. In NZ, Bellringer *et al.* (2011) found that the wide discretion for local governments to determine their level of commitment to sustainability under the Act operated to preclude a standardized national regime of sustainability reporting and led to some local governments reporting more extensively than others. In a case study concerning a Conservative English council, Ball (2005b) similarly found that the discretion allowed in the legislation operated to revive underlying political tensions, and ultimately discouraged sustainability reporting.

### *Voluntary frameworks on sustainability accounting*

A number of recent initiatives have emerged to encourage voluntary sustainability reporting in the wider public sector. The Chartered Institute of Public Finance and Accountancy (CIPFA) is notable for its interest in promoting sustainability reporting because of its status as the predominant body for public sector accounting and finance. CIPFA maintains a sustainability micro-site, advances debate in professional forums and through publications (Ball, 2005b; Lewis, 2008; Ball *et al.*, forthcoming), and has produced a framework for PSO sustainability reporting in partnership with a leading UK SD charity (CIPFA, 2005).

The GRI has produced pilot guidelines for sustainability reporting by public agencies in the form of the GRI Sector Supplement for Public Agencies (henceforth: The Supplement) (GRI, 2004). GRI research (GRI, 2010) acknowledges that uptake of the GRI in the public sector has been slow: 69 GRI reports have been produced by 57 different PSOs since 2001; and in 2009 only 1.7 per cent of all GRI reports were public sector reports. They also acknowledge difficulties with the Supplement, including its generic nature, private sector triple-bottom-line approach and lack of applicability across the variety of public agencies; and the fragmented and diverse manner in which organizations select items in the guidelines against which to report. Farneti and Guthrie's (2008) study of Australian public sector sustainability reporting similarly indicated difficulties in using the Supplement and a perception that it is better suited to organizations delivering policies than those delivering goods and services. The UK National Audit Office (NAO) has argued for further work on the Supplement because of its emphasis on disclosures about 'housekeeping operations, with less attention to the disclosure of policy impacts and outcomes...' (NAO, 2005, p. 7); and GRI (GRI, 2010) findings indicate a tendency towards narrative/descriptive reporting on policy at the expense of quantified disclosures about policy impacts over time. The GRI (GRI, 2010), however, appear committed to a revised, final version of the Supplement.

On the plus side, the GRI Supplement emphasizes reporting on stakeholder engagement in policymaking; indeed, we see the involvement of citizens and groups who bring knowledge and insights to test and stimulate possible directions for sustainability policy as essential (see also Burritt and Welch, 1997a). Findings reported by Hill *et al.* (1997, 1998, 2001) about a social audit of a general medical practice in Scotland provide a benchmark here, with the social audit becoming 'an open participatory process of dialogue which assesses and reports on the social relationships and performance of the health centre'(1998, p. 1481). GRI findings (GRI, 2010) indicate that public sector GRI reporters however tend to disclose narrative rather than specific information about stakeholder engagement. This seems disappointing because many PSOs are already adept at developing stakeholder relations through mechanisms ranging from user group consultations to individual satisfaction questionnaires.

Also gaining attention in the public sector is the Prince of Wales' Accounting for Sustainability (A4S) project, established in 2004. Developed for organizations in both the private and public sectors, the project has the twin aims of embedding sustainability considerations into decision making and reporting all aspects of organizational performance in a clear, concise and consistent way. However, given the responsibilities of PSOs to address sustainability and discharge accountability to stakeholders, the project has been argued to be more relevant to the public sector where commercial considerations do not dominate (Lewis, 2008). As endorsement of the project, Defra outlines HM Treasury's intention to introduce connected sustainability reporting in 2011/12 in their *Mainstreaming Sustainable Development* (2011) document.

Support for the A4S project is provided, for example, by West Sussex County Council and the Environment Agency in the form of an agreement to contribute case material for inclusion in *Accounting for Sustainability: Practical Insights* (Hopwood *et al.*, 2010). West Sussex County Council reveal how the A4S project in combination with a crossing of elements from Forum for the Future's Sustainability Standard and the GRI helped to establish a golden thread linking organizational strategies to day-to-day activities of front-line employees (Grubnic and Owen, 2010). In contrast, for the Environment Agency, the design of systems and practices on accounting for sustainability pre-date the A4S project. However, the A4S project did help provide additional legitimacy for activities (Thomson and Georgakopoulos, 2010). For both organizations, showing potential cost savings associated with sustainable options helped to promote buy-in for the sustainability agenda.

### *Summary: recent initiatives and a role for academics*

To summarize, a range of recent initiatives to promote sustainability accounting and accountability in PSOs seem important in highlighting a number of advances in practice, including: disclosures about policy outcomes and inclusiveness in policymaking; carbon accounting; the use of quality of life indicators; and accounting for natural and social capital at the levels of community and nation state. Developments such as state of the environment reporting and accounting for community well-being represent a significant advance in developing multi-level/multi-agency thinking on sustainability (Bennet and van der Lugt, 2004; Ball, 2005b); and an important question for future research and practice is whether and how private sector sustainability reporting might be generated and combined with accounts produced in the public sector, so that it is also meaningful on larger scales (Bennet and van der Lugt, 2004).

It is also evident that national governments can directly or indirectly influence the extent and quality of PSO accountability for sustainability. Indeed, Ball *et al.* (2012) see a need for established sustainability accounting researchers 'to get off the academic treadmill' to engage with powerful institutions of accounting and government who could lend legitimacy to emerging frameworks, sustain existing mandatory initiatives, and mandate sustainability performance across the wider sector. There are additionally important opportunities for researchers and students to contribute engaged, theoretically informed research to inform emerging frameworks and practice. There remains a question, however, over the extent to which PSOs are able or willing to respond to demands for accountability for performance on sustainability.

## The capacity of PSOs for sustainability accounting and accountability

In relatively materially affluent, capitalistic societies like the UK and NZ, sustainability is a radical political concept. It challenges deeply held beliefs about what constitutes human progress (economic growth, inalienable rights to high levels of personal consumption, and so on), and requires a basic understanding of ecological thresholds and how to live within the limits of natural systems which few of us may grasp or want to think about. In addition, sustainability may imply radical change to highly institutionalized practices in service delivery (location, scale, processes, etc.). How many of the university academics who contributed to this book, for example, would forego the professional and personal benefits of international travel to attend conferences in the interests of GHG emissions reductions? How many take their partners or families with them when they travel for work purposes? The development of sustainability accounting is difficult because if it is to be at all effective in promoting sustainability, it must also confront such challenges.

Findings of the NAO (NAO, 2005) review of Government Departments' reporting on their high-level commitments to sustainability under the 2005 UK strategy on SD are instructive here. Departments with a substantial environmental component to their tasks were better at reporting than others without this component. SD was more often treated as an environmental (as opposed to social justice or economic) issue. And while departments were reporting on operational impacts, far fewer reports linked key policies issues to SD. Some departments had identified a broad vision or direction of travel; but few had defined specific outcomes for SD. A notable exception was the Department of Work and Pensions' (overambitious?) vision to 'end child poverty by 2010'.

Similarly, evidence from the West Sussex County Council experience of using A4S revealed that the authority's progress on sustainability is mainly focused on addressing housekeeping issues and, to a limited extent, the reframing of council services such as education, social services and highways. This is perhaps suggestive of the need to change mind-sets, as encouraged by the council's Sustainability Workplace Tool, prior to dealing with the more challenging issues of what services are offered and where. The longer term nature of social and environmental initiatives was also perceived to sometimes conflict with short-term political imperatives that underpin much council activity.

These findings hint at how, if left unsupported, PSOs could simply be confounded by sustainability accounting because un-bundling the implications is simply too difficult to deal with. Indeed, the education and health sectors represent a long-standing liberal–democratic tradition of social justice, which has to do with equality of opportunity and access, so that life chances depend on motivation and aptitude and not on such factors as class, gender or ethnicity. Being 'sustainable' implies asking how traditions of social justice (doing the right thing as a matter of principle, in Boston *et al.*'s (1996) terms) are linked to ecological sustainability. But this question actually represents an extraordinarily complex political and moral agenda, which has so far eluded most governments and, indeed, the environmental movement itself (Foley *et al.*, 2005).

One conclusion here is that engaged research in PSOs motivated by social welfare and justice therefore suggests itself as a means of making fundamental contributions to the sustainability agenda *per se*. Key questions arise around the forms of service provision that better protect and enhance the life of citizens; and how change is motivated. The UK's NHS, regarded as an exemplar PSO in pursuing SD, suggests itself as an area ripe for engaged research. Following issue of the 2005 UK strategy on SD, the NHS identified high-level commitments including funding the Sustainable Development Commission Healthy Futures programme from 2004 to 2011 to develop the capacity of NHS organizations; while the work of the NHS Sustainable Development Unit established in 2008 is identified (Bebbington and Barter, 2011) as developing commendable steps on how to systematically address global climate change concerns.

Also key to PSOs' ability to respond to the sustainability accounting and accountability agenda is the tremendous influence of the NPM, linked to such intellectual drivers as the 're-invention of government' (Osborne and Plastrik, 1997) and the widely held belief that PSOs offer low standards and poor value for money (VFM) (Taylor-Gooby, 2005). Governments' current attempts to scale back the public sector seem likely to contribute to the relative decline of some public programmes (for example climate change programmes in NZ) and institutions (public universities are a good example), which have already experienced successive reforms. The UK Coalition Government (2010–present) for example currently aims to cut £95 billion over a five-year period.

The danger here is that, under intense political pressure to find savings, public sector managers will at best be 'incentivised' to look for 'controllable, efficiency-based environmental measures ... such as recycling, energy efficiency, and waste management ... [which] are easier to manage ... than environmental matters which challenge basic values and assumptions' (Burritt and Welch, 1997b, pp. 6–7). Indeed, Burritt and Welch (1997b) examined the environmental disclosures of Commonwealth (national government) entities in Australia, and found that under the commercial orientation of the reforms, there is a tendency for a dampening effect on environmental disclosures *per se*, and a concentration on 'easier to manage' environmental issues.

Emerging forms of public service provision, however, provide rich ground for engaged research, for example in exploring the relative commitments of public and private sector players to sustainability, and in relation to reconciling the interests of different stakeholders. There is arguably potential for public authorities to demand accountability for sustainability as a condition of the contracting process in PPPs or public procurement of goods and services; Grubnic and Owen (2010) reveal how local authorities were able to influence the Department of Transport on a street lighting PFI project and convince them of the need to include energy efficiency as a part of the PFI specification. Further key questions for research are whether and how authorities are managing the interconnections between environmental, social and financial factors, and the extent to which identification and decision making is impacted upon by the necessity to deliver more for even less financial resource than before.

There is a small but growing body of work which has sought to understand the extent of sustainability disclosures in the wider public sector and the capacity of PSOs to respond to demands for sustainability accounting and accountability (see for example the December 2008 special issue of *Public Money and Management* (Ball and Bebbington, 2008, on this topic). Indeed, findings from recent studies are instructive in thinking about public sector managers' values and the transformative potential of sustainability accounting. Adams *et al.* (2005) use their study of an Australian water authority's experience to highlight public sector managers' motivations and behaviour. In contrast to prior research with private sector managers (O'Dwyer, 2003), the managers here were committed to developing sustainability reporting, leading to an integration of sustainability issues into the organization's strategic planning process. These findings echo findings from Ball's case studies in English and Canadian local authorities, where managers demonstrated commitment to sustainability and progressing sustainability accounting (Ball, 2005b, 2007). Exploring waste management in Australia, Qian *et al.* (2011) add that 'social structural influences', which includes pressure from within the community and peer councils, also serves to drive local government action on environmental management accounting. These findings indicate a need for researchers to assist those people in organizations who are making advances in practice possible to stay engaged, to retain their organizational legitimacy, and to feel supported in a context where sustainability accounting and accountability may be viewed as too radical a concept, or not widely accepted.

## Closing thoughts

In this chapter we have sought to provide a flavour of what amounts to a very complex, but also distinctive and compelling agenda for sustainability accounting and accountability in the public sector. We have highlighted the need for a distinctive agenda for sustainability accounting and accountability research and practice in the public sector; indicated a growing number of potentially influential initiatives to encourage practice; and are pleased to have been able to comment that researchers have already made contributions to understanding the outworking and transformative potential of sustainability accounting and accountability in PSOs. We have indicated numerous opportunities for opening up what amounts to a hugely important future agenda for research and practice, and so we will not repeat them all here. However, we wish to underline the importance of research which makes contributions of a fundamental nature to the development of principles and practice in PSO sustainability accounting and accountability, and which engages organizations, policymakers and powerful institutions of accounting about the need to advance practice.

As a pioneer of social accounting argued 'it is ... clear that the main reason why ordinary people have very little idea about what goes on in government, business and other major centres of power is not that they are not interested, but that they are not told' (Medawar, 1978, p. 36). While it would be naive to overstate the potential of sustainability accounting and accountability in transforming PSOs, we see sustainability disclosures as a key mechanism for engaging more people in the working of the public sector and in understanding its contribution to sustainability – in fact, all the more so in what looks depressingly more and more likely to be a coming era of austerity and renewed efforts to commercialize the public sector. We hope that we have conveyed some of our enthusiasm for our work and persuaded some readers that work in this area may be for them.

## Notes

1  Source: Energy Efficiency and Conservation Authority Internal report to Government Energy Efficiency Leadership Programme (2000) cited in New Zealand Ministry for the Environment report on *Triple Bottom Line Reporting in the Public Sector* (2002, p. 21), available at http://www.mfe.govt.nz/publications/ser/triple-bottom-line-summary-1-dec02.pdf, accessed 13 June 2006.

2  Similarly, the Swedish 'local government sector employs approximately 25 per cent of the labour market, and consumes about 20 per cent of the gross national product' (Tagesson *et al.*, 2011).
3  The Climate Change Acts of the UK and Scotland differ in terms of shorter-term targets on greenhouse gas reductions. While the UK committed to total reductions of 36 per cent by 2020, Scotland set a more ambitious target of 42 per cent against 1990 levels. It should also be noted that, within the UK Act, the Welsh Government has confirmed a 3 per cent reduction target each year from 2011. In its greenhouse gas action plan, the Northern Ireland Executive outlines how each department will reduce emissions by 25 per cent against 1990 levels by 2025.
4  Available at http://beehive.govt.nz/release/govt-proposes-new-environmental-reporting-act, accessed 9 February 2012.
5  Available    at    http://www.ons.gov.uk/ons/guide-method/user-guidance/well-being/index.html, accessed 9 February 2012.

## References

Adams, C., McNicholas, P. and Zutshi, A. (2005) *Making a Difference: Journeying with an Organisation towards Social and Environmental Accountability*, paper presented to the 3rd Australasian CSEAR Conference, Deakin University, Melbourne, VIC, 30 March–1 April.

Audit Commission (2005) *Local Quality of Life Indicators – Supporting Local Communities to Become Sustainable*, Audit Commission, London.

Ball, A. (2005a) 'Environmental Accounting and Change in UK Local Government', *Accounting, Auditing and Accountability Journal*, 18(3): 346–73.

Ball, A. (2005b) *Advancing Sustainability Reporting for Public Service Organisations: A Discussion Paper*, Chartered Institute of Public Finance and Accountancy (CIPFA), London.

Ball, A. (2007) 'Environmental Accounting as Workplace Activism', *Critical Perspectives on Accounting*, 18(7): 759–78.

Ball, A. and Bebbington, J. (2008) 'Editorial: Accounting and Reporting for Sustainable Development in Public Service Organizations', *Public Money and Management*, 28(6), 323–6.

Ball, A., Soare, V. and Brewis, J. (2012) 'Engagement Research in Public Sector Accounting', *Financial Accountability and Management Journal*, 28(2): 189–214.

Bebbington, J. and Barter, N. (2011) *Strategic Responses to Global Climate Change: A UK Analysis*, Chartered Institute of Management Accountants (CIMA), London.

Bellringer, A., Ball, A. and Craig, R. (2011) 'Reasons for Sustainability Reporting by New Zealand Local Governments', *Sustainability Accounting, Management and Policy Journal*, 2(1): 126–38.

Bennet, N. and van der Lugt, C. (2004) 'Tracking Global Governance and Sustainability: Is the System Working?', in A. Henriques and J. Richardson (eds) *The Triple Bottom Line: Does It All Add Up? Assessing the Sustainability of Business and CSR*, Earthscan, London, pp. 45–58.

Besley, T. and Ghatak, M. (2005) 'Competition and Incentives with Motivated Agents', *American Economic Review*, 95(3): 616–36.

Birchall, S. J., Ball, A., Mason, I. and Milne, M. (2010) *Environmental and Economic Benefits of the New Zealand Carbon Neutral Public Service Programme*, paper presented to the Australasian Conference on Social and Environmental Accounting Research, Albury, NSW, December.

Birchall, S. J., Ball, A., Mason, I. and Milne, M. (2013) 'Managing Carbon in Time of Political Change: The Rise and Fall of the New Zealand Carbon Neutral Public Service Programme', *Australasian Journal of Environmental Management*, 20(1): 63–78.

Boston, J. and Lempp, F. (2011) 'Climate Change: Explaining and Solving the Mismatch between Scientific Urgency and Political Inertia', *Accounting, Auditing & Accountability Journal*, 24(8): 1000–21.

Boston, J., Martin, J., Pallot, J. and Walsh, P. (1996) *Public Management: The New Zealand Model*, Oxford University Press, Auckland, NZ.

Boyne, G.A. (2002) 'Public and Private Management: What's the Difference?', *Journal of Management Studies*, 39(1): 97–122.

Brewis, J. (1999) *On the Front Line: Experiences of Managing the New Public Services*, paper presented to the Third International Research Conference of the Knowledge, Organizations and Society Research Unit, University of Staffordshire, April.

Broadbent, J. and Guthrie, J. (1992) 'Changes in the Public Sector: A Review of Recent "Alternative" Accounting Research', *Accounting, Auditing and Accountability Journal*, 5(2): 3–31.

Broadbent, J. and Guthrie, J. (2008) 'Public Sector to Public Services: 20 years of "Alternative" Accounting Research"', *Accounting, Auditing & Accountability Journal*, 21(2): 129–69.

Buhrs, T. (2008) 'Climate Change Policy and New Zealand's "National Interest": The Need for Embedding Climate Change Policy into a Sustainable Development Agenda', *Political Science*, 60(1): 61–72.

Burritt, R. L. and Welch, S. (1997a) 'Accountability for Environmental Performance of the Australian Commonwealth Public Sector', *Accounting, Auditing and Accountability Journal*, 10(4): 532–61.

Burritt, R. L. and Welch, S. (1997b) 'Australian Commonwealth Entities: An Analysis of their Environmental Disclosures', *Abacus*, 33(1): 1–19.

Chartered Institute of Public Finance and Accountancy (CIPFA) (2005) *Sustainability Reporting Framework for the Public Services*, CIPFA/Forum for the Future, London.

Christie, I. (2000) *Sustainability and Modernisation: Resolving Tensions by Providing Complementarity*, paper presented at the World Wide Fund for Nature International UK (WWF-UK) Conference, RSA London, Godalming, Surrey, 15 February 2000.

Clark, H. (2007) 'Prime Minister's Statement to Parliament', Beehive, Wellington, available at http://www.beehive.govt.nz/node/28357, accessed 2 August 2011.

Communities for Climate Protection New Zealand (CCP-NZ) (2009) *Communities for Climate Protection – New Zealand Actions Profile 2009*, CCP-NZ Programme, International Council for Local Environmental Initiatives (ICLEI) and the New Zealand Ministry for the Environment, Wellington, NZ.

Cooper, S. and Pearce, G. (2011) 'Climate Change Performance Measurement, Control and Accountability in English Local Authority Areas', *Accounting, Auditing & Accountability Journal*, 24(8): 1097–118.

Delfgaauw, J. and Dur, R. (2008) 'Incentives and Workers' Motivation in the Public Sector', *Economic Journal*, 118: 171–91.

Department for Environment, Food and Rural Affairs (Defra) (2011) *Mainstreaming Sustainable Development: The Government's Vision and What this Means in Practice*, Defra, London.

Farneti, F. and Guthrie, J. (2008) *Sustainability Reporting in Australian Public Sector Organisations: Why They Report*, paper presented to the Twelfth Annual Conference of the International Research Society for Public Management, Brisbane, QLD, 26–28 March.

Foley, J., Grayling, T. and Dixon, M. (2005) 'Sustainability and Social Justice', in N. D. Pearce and W. Paxon (eds) *Social Justice: Building a Fairer Britain*, Politico's Publishing, London, pp. 178–98.

Global Reporting Initiative (GRI) (2004) *Public Agency Sustainability Reporting: A GRI Resource Document in Support of the Public Agency Support Supplement*, GRI, London.

Global Reporting Initiative (GRI) (2005) *GRI Sector Supplement for Public Agencies*, GRI, Amsterdam.

Global Reporting Initiative (GRI) (2010) *GRI Reporting in Government Agencies*, GRI, Amsterdam.

Gray, R. and Bebbington, J. (2001) *Accounting for the Environment*, Paul Chapman/Association of Chartered Certified Accountants (ACCA), London.

Grubnic, S. and Owen, D. (2010) 'A Golden Thread for Embedding Sustainability in a Local Government Context: The Case of West Sussex County Council', in A. Hopwood, J. Unerman and J. Fries (eds) *Accounting for Sustainability: Practical Insights*, Earthscan, London, pp. 95–127.

The Guardian (2012) 'Set Greener Goals at Rio+20: Caroline Spelman', *The Guardian*, available at http://www.theguardian.com/environment/2012/feb/09/greener-goals-rio-caroline-spelman, accessed 9 February 2012.

Guthrie, J., Humphrey, C., Jones, L. R. and Olson, O. (eds) (2005) *International Public Management Reform: Progress, Contradictions and Challenges*, Information Age Publishing, Greenwich, CT.

Hill, W. J., Cotton, P. and Fraser, I. (1997) 'Piloting the Social Audit in Primary Health Care', *Social and Environmental Accounting*, 17(2): 7–10.

Hill, W. J., Fraser, I. and Cotton, P. (1998) 'Patients' Voices, Rights and Responsibilities: On Implementing Social Audit in Primary Health Care', *Journal of Business Ethics*, 17(13): 1481–97.

Hill, W. J., Fraser, I. and Cotton, P. (2001) 'On Patients' Interests and Accountability: Reflecting on some Dilemmas in Social Audit in Primary Health Care', *Critical Perspectives on Accounting*, 12(4): 453–69.

HM Government (2005) *Securing the Future: Delivering UK Sustainable Development Strategy*, CM6467, The Stationery Office, London.

Hood, C. (1991) 'A Public Management for all Seasons?', *Public Administration*, 69(1): 3–19.

Hood, C. (1995) 'The "New Public Management" in the 1980s: Variations on a Theme', *Accounting, Organizations and Society*, 20(2/3): 93–109.

Hopwood, A. (1978) *Social Accounting – The Way Ahead*, paper presented at a seminar on social accounting organized by the Chartered Institute of Public Finance and Accountancy (CIPFA), London, January.

Hopwood, A., Unerman, J. and Fries, J. (2010) *Accounting for Sustainability: Practical Insights*, Earthscan, Oxford.

Le Grand, J. (2003) *Motivations, Agency, and Public Policy: Of Knights & Knaves, Pawns & Queens*, Oxford University Press, Oxford.

Lessing, D. (1998) *Walking in the Shade: Volume Two of My Autobiography, 1949–1962*, Flamingo/HarperCollins, London.

Lewis, L. (2000) 'Environmental Audits in Local Government: A Useful Means to Progress in Sustainable Development', *Accounting Forum*, 24(3): 296–318.

Lewis, T. (2008) 'Debate: Public Sector Sustainability Reporting — Implications for Accountants', *Public Money & Management*, 28(6): 329–31.

Matten, D., Crane, A. and Chapple, W. (2003) 'Behind the Mask: Revealing the True Face of Corporate Citizenship', *Journal of Business Ethics*, 45(1/2): 109–20.

Medawar, C. (1978) *Ways of Measuring Organisational Performance*, paper presented at a seminar on social accounting organized by the Chartered Institute of Public Finance and Accountancy (CIPFA), London, January.

Ministry for the Environment (2002) *Triple Bottom Line Reporting in the Public Sector: Summary of Pilot Group Findings*, Ministry for the Environment, Wellington, NZ.

National Audit Office (NAO) (2005) *Sustainable Development Reporting by Government Departments*, NAO, London.

NZ Govt (2007) *POL (07) 131: Towards a Sustainable New Zealand: Carbon Neutral Public Service*, Ministry for the Environment, Wellington, NZ.

NZ Govt (2008) *POL (08) 36: Carbon Neutral Public Service – Update on Progress*, Ministry for the Environment, Wellington, NZ.

NZ Govt (2012) 'Core Public Service Numbers Continue to Shrink', available at http://www.beehive.govt.nz/release/core-public-service-numbers-continue-shrink, accessed 6 September 2006.

O'Dwyer, B. (2003) 'Conceptions of Corporate Social Responsibility: The Nature of Managerial Capture', *Accounting, Auditing and Accountability*, 16(4): 523–57.

Olsen, O., Guthrie, J. and Humphreys, C. (eds) (1998) *Global Warning! Debating International Developments in New Public Financial Management*, Cappelen Akademisk Forlag, Oslo.

Osborne, D. and Plastrik, P. (1997) *Banishing Bureaucracy: The Five Strategies for Reinventing Government*, Addison Wesley, Reading, MA.

Pollitt, C. (2003) *The Essential Public Manager*, Open University Press, Maidenhead.

Pollock, A. (2004) *NHS Plc: The Privatisation of Our Health Care*, Verso, London.

Qian, W., Burritt, R. and Monroe, G. (2011) 'Environmental Management Accounting in Local Government: A Case of Waste Management', *Accounting, Auditing & Accountability Journal*, 24(1): 93–128.

Quirk, B. (2005) 'For the Greater Good', *Public Finance*, October: 14–20.

Smith, N. (2009a) 'Building a Brighter Future: Opening Address to the New Zealand Climate Change Centre Conference', National Party, Wellington, available at http://www.national.org.nz/Article. aspx?articleId=29994, accessed 14 December 2011.

Smith, N. (2009b) 'Government Committed to Real Solutions not Slogans', available at http://www. beehive.govt.nz/release/government+committed+real+solutions+not+slogans, accessed 18 August 2010

State Service Commission (SSC) (2011) *Human Resource Capability Survey of Public Service Departments (as at 30 June 2011)*, New Zealand State Service Commission, Wellington, NZ.

Tagesson, T., Klugman, M. and Ekstrom, M. L. (2011) 'What Explains the Extent and Content of Social Disclosure in Swedish Municipalities' Annual Reports', *Journal of Management and Governance*, 17(2): 1–19. doi:10.1007/s10997-011-9174-5.

Taylor, J. (2010) 'Public Service Motivation, Civic Attitudes and Actions of Public, Nonprofit and Private Sector Employees', *Public Administration*, 88(4): 1083–98.

Taylor-Gooby, P. (2005) 'Attitudes to Social Justice', in N. D. Pearce and W. Paxon (eds) *Social Justice: Building a Fairer Britain*, Politico's Publishing, London, pp. 106–32.

Thomson, I. and Georgakopoulos, G. (2010) 'Building from the Bottom, Inspired from the Top: Accounting for Sustainability and the Environment Agency', in A. Hopwood, J. Unerman and J. Fries (eds) *Accounting for Sustainability: Practical Insights*. Earthscan, London, pp. 129–47.

Unerman, J. (2011) 'Debate: The Importance of an Integrated Understanding of Sustainability in Guiding Accounting Practices', *Public Money and Management*, 31(4): 233–35.

United Nations Environment Programme (UNEP)/SustainAbility (1997) *The 1997 Benchmark Survey: Third International Progress Report on Company Environmental Reporting*, UNEP/SustainAbility, London.

# Part IV

# Accounting and biophysical concerns

# 12 Accounting and global climate change issues

*Jan Bebbington and Carlos Larrinaga*

## Introduction

A literature is emerging that links concerns from the science and policy world with respect to concentrations of greenhouse gases (GHG) in the atmosphere with management and accounting practices. While scientific concerns about global climate change (hereafter GCC) have been in play for some decades,[1] more recently there has been sustained engagement with these concerns by many nation states as well as supra-national bodies (such as the United Nations and the European Union). This has led to a variety of governance mechanisms (of varying levels of formality) aimed at mitigating GHG emissions[2] as well as providing support for adapting to changes that are likely to be forthcoming due to past emissions. Many of these governance mechanisms have salience for organizations, for management activities as well as reporting routines and are hence of interest to accounting researchers. It is these areas that the chapter will focus on as it maps the terrain on which the accounting literature has focused as a way to orientate readers of this book to this rapidly emerging field. The chapter is not a full review of each paper and all the various issues discussed. Rather, the chapter seeks to map the field to allow existing and new literature to be placed in a context. It is also the case that any 'conclusions' from the existing literature would be premature given the scope of the subject area and the amount of research conducted to date – much of which has only recently emerged. The chapter also suggests some underlying conceptual themes that emerge in this area and which are intimately related to our broader understanding of accounting technologies. In this way, accounting for carbon[3] might provide a new context in which to better understand accounting and reporting and their roles in regimes of governance.

Before considering the nature of the carbon accounting field, a definition of the scope of this research is necessary. Definitional uncertainty arises because 'carbon accounting' is a term that is used in several literatures to describe different practices which themselves arise at various scales. On the basis of a citation analysis and categorization of literature that describes itself as carbon accounting, Stechemesser and Guenther (2012, p. 36) suggest that carbon accounting is the 'recognition, the non-monetary and monetary evaluation and the monitoring of greenhouse gas emissions on all levels of the value chain and the recognition, evaluation and monitoring of the effects of these emissions on the carbon cycles of ecosystems'.

This definition is very broad and encompasses more than what is usually focused on by academic accountants. As a result, Ascui and Lovell's (2011) frame within which carbon accounting might sit (see Table 12.1) is a valuable starting point for this chapter 'where carbon accounting can be understood as any combination (reading left to right) of one or more terms from each cell in the table' (Ascui and Lovell, 2012, p. 49).

What emerges from the discussion about definitions is that there are several scales on which carbon accounting practices arise, often differentiated as national, project, organizational or

*Table 12.1* The scope of carbon accounting

| | of | | at | level, for | | purposes |
|---|---|---|---|---|---|---|
| estimation | carbon | emissions to the atmosphere | global | mandatory | research |
| calculation | carbon dioxide | emission rights | national | voluntary | compliance |
| measurement | greenhouse gas | emission obligations | sub-national | | reporting |
| monitoring | | emission reductions | regional | | disclosure |
| reporting | | legal or financial instruments linked to the above | civic | | benchmarking |
| validation | | trades/transactions of any of the above | organizational | | auditing |
| verification | | impacts of climate change | corporate | | information |
| auditing | | impacts from climate change | project | | marketing |
| | | | installation | | or other |
| | | | event | | |
| | | | product | | |
| | | | supply chain | | |

Source: Ascui and Lovell (2011, p. 980).

product scales (Bowen and Wittneben, 2011; Stechemesser and Guenther, 2012). With the exception of national level accounting, the organizational accounting literature has focused on the rest of these scales (to differing extents and involving multiple accounting/reporting practices) and within these areas there is a wide range of activities that are described as carbon accounting. This chapter will now seek to put some structure over these various domains of accounting focus.

## Mapping the literature

A number of literature sources were used in order to create a map of the current shape of the field. The primary base for this mapping was the four special issues on carbon related issues produced since 2008 by: the *European Accounting Review* (in 2008); *Accounting, Organizations and Society* (in 2009); *Accounting, Auditing and Accountability Journal* (in 2011/12); as well as the *Journal of Cleaner Production* (in 2012). Literature from other accounting sources was added to this map as appropriate. Figure 12.1 outlines the domains covered by the literature and the remainder of this section will work through the various elements in more detail.

### *The context: carbon science, policy and organizational responses*

There is a number of recognized 'set pieces' in the science and policy arenas that shape our understanding of GCC and which underpin carbon accounting. These include the various publications of the United Nations Intergovernmental Panel on Climate Change (IPCC), as well as supra-national (such as the European Union, which has been proactive in this policy space with its member countries engaged in a variety of initiatives) and national governments and agencies responsible for carbon emissions (such as the United Kingdom's Committee on Climate Change). The IPCC Assessment Reports (the fifth of which is published) are the most pertinent reference points for understanding the state of scientific opinion on anthropogenic GCC, its potential impacts and the options available for adapting to GCC impacts and how GHG might be reduced (mitigation). Likewise, economic analysis such as the Stern Review (Stern, 2006) supplements the analysis that is being conducted at United Nations and national scales by providing estimations of the costs (in terms of national economies) of the different adaptation or mitigation options available. A number of consultancies (most notably McKinsey but also accounting firms) are also active in this space.

In addition to these primarily policy focused sources, a large body of academic work that contextualizes GCC is produced by a variety of disciplines and can be found in a wide range of journals.[4] While it is impossible for any single researcher to be following all this material, understanding the detail of the specific policy and operational context in which global and local governance is being enacted will be essential for quality work to emerge in accounting. If accounting were to become disconnected with this technical and political context then (in our view) accountants are less likely to impact on the world of policy and practice. This does, however, seem to be a point of tension in the literature.

For example, Milne and Grubnic (2011, p. 950) make the case for 'avoiding the trivial and overly technical' in research in this area so that it stays 'interesting' and 'different'. These authors reflect the scepticism that exists in accounting research over the suggestion that simple accounting 'solutions' will resolve complex social and environmental problems (such as GCC). For example, it would seem unrealistic to expect that a particular accounting

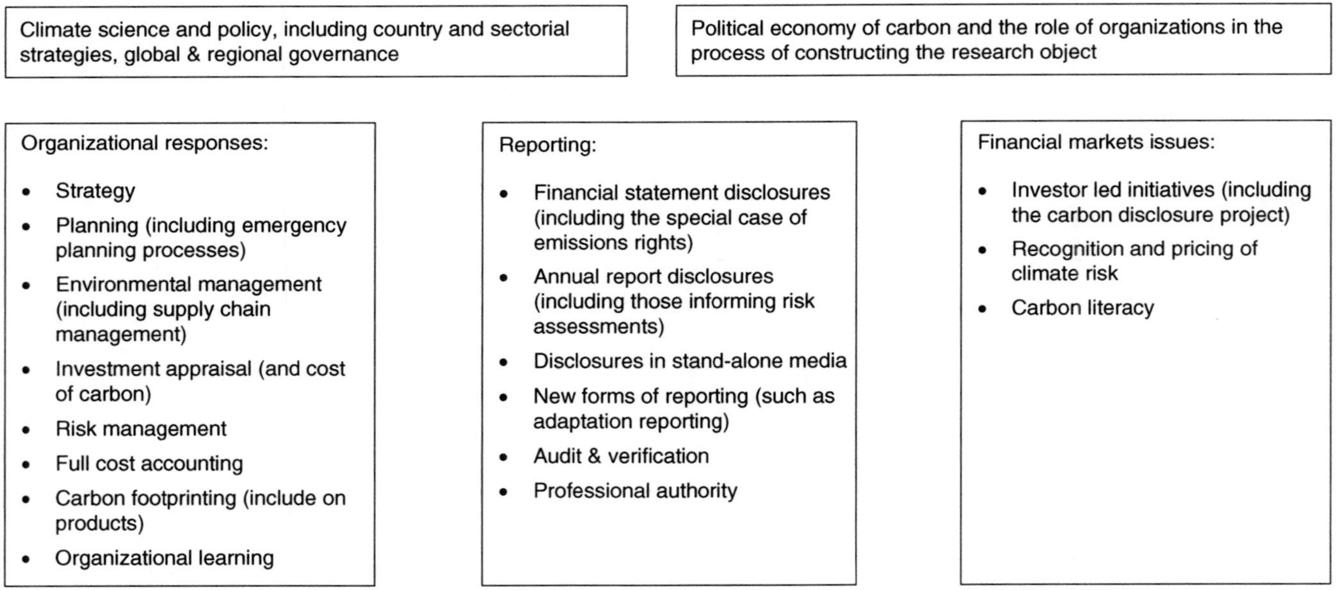

Climate science and policy, including country and sectorial strategies, global & regional governance

Political economy of carbon and the role of organizations in the process of constructing the research object

Organizational responses:

- Strategy
- Planning (including emergency planning processes)
- Environmental management (including supply chain management)
- Investment appraisal (and cost of carbon)
- Risk management
- Full cost accounting
- Carbon footprinting (include on products)
- Organizational learning

Reporting:

- Financial statement disclosures (including the special case of emissions rights)
- Annual report disclosures (including those informing risk assessments)
- Disclosures in stand-alone media
- New forms of reporting (such as adaptation reporting)
- Audit & verification
- Professional authority

Financial markets issues:

- Investor led initiatives (including the carbon disclosure project)
- Recognition and pricing of climate risk
- Carbon literacy

*Figure 12.1* Carbon accounting issues map.

method would create the right incentives for the mitigation of GCC at the organizational level; or that a carbon price will be the only mechanism needed for the multi-layer transition to a low carbon economy. In contrast, MacKenzie (2009, p. 453) suggests that 'the esoteric nature of their [carbon markets] subpolitics means that researchers have a particularly salient role to play in bringing to light matters of apparent detail [by which he means the accounting] that in fact play critical roles in this respect'. In this context the author is suggesting that technical considerations about accounting methods could be relevant, being as they are the product of expert advice, often remote from democratic decision making but having a substantive impact on outcomes experienced by people.

We suspect that both positions are helpful in thinking about the future of the field, in that research needs to go beyond the technicalities of carbon accounting, but should not forget the powerful shaping role of such accounting. Indeed, a sustainability science framing would suggest that detail is likely to be important to fully understand the impacts (and accounting implications) of particular settings. This sort of focus might be especially useful as numerous 'live' experiments are taking place around the globe while different countries and regions seek to govern emissions in ways that fit with their ideological and economic circumstances. As a result, there is a plurality of contexts in which the role and nature of accounting might be understood and in which an international research community is well placed to explore contrasting approaches. With this in mind, the starting point of our literature review is with how organizations are responding to the GCC agenda.

### *Organizational responses to the GCC agenda*

All organizations' routines are likely to be affected by the GCC agenda including: strategy (Ratnatunga, 2008; Bebbington and Barter, 2011); planning (including emergency planning processes linked to adaptation); environmental management (including supply chain management – Lee, 2010, 2012); investment appraisal (and cost of carbon – see Tsai *et al.*, 2012); risk management (Busch and Hoffmann, 2007); full cost accounting (Lohmann, 2009); and carbon footprinting (including footprinting of products – see Scipioni *et al.*, 2012). Literature in these areas is dominated by management accounting papers, reflecting a research tradition in environmental management issues and the support of the Environmental and Sustainability Management Accounting Network which fosters research in this area. In addition, there is a book series (published by Springer) that covers a wide array of environmental management issues, including carbon aspects, emerging from this community of practice. Overviews of various activities as well as documentation of the leading edge of practice can also be found in Ratnatunga and Balachandran (2009); Burritt *et al.* (2011); and Schaltegger and Csutora (2012).

It is clear from this literature that organizations are responding to the GCC agenda and that they are using various techniques in their responses. The nature and level of responses appear to be affected by carbon intensity (proxied by industry), competitive contexts (Lee, 2012) as well as the demands of particular carbon management regimes. For example, there is a higher level of proactivity within European organizations (compared to organizations based in other regions) that is likely to have been affected by the political and governance focus in the European Union (backed by legislation in countries such as the United Kingdom and Scotland). This speaks to the potential usefulness of institutional based analysis to understand individual entity reactions.

In addition, the proactive response of parts of the public sector in terms of carbon reduction has been noted and this might create opportunities for research that takes public sector innovation and considers how it might be cascaded beyond that sector (for example, Bebbington and Barter, 2011, note the performance of the National Health Service in England and Wales; see also Cooper and Pearce, 2011). A focus on the public sector involves more than seeing organizations in this sector as being of a different/interesting organizational form. Rather, given that the public sector has a significant enabling role in GCC responsiveness (see also Ball *et al.*, 2009) it is likely to provide particular research engagements that would allow the appreciation of what whole system responsiveness to GCC is likely to entail. Likewise, some of the demands that adaptation to GCC will bring are likely to fall heavily on public sector organizations (Cooper and Pearce, 2011) and hence they might be expected to lead the way in this area. Indeed, we would suggest that public sector organizations might be especially productive research sites for understanding accounting for carbon in a way that they have not been perceived to be in the broader social and environmental accounting field. Regardless of entity, it is often thought that there is a reflexive process at play between internal management activities and external reporting and it is to this area of activity that attention now turns.

### Reporting practices

Analyses of reporting practices constitute a large part of the carbon accounting literature, building on prior work in environmental and social accounting which explores what is reported, whom this data might be directed at, what function the data serves and how one might understand the impact of reporting practices. This is an area, however, where there are some new contexts to consider. For example, carbon measurement and reporting has attracted the attention of a plethora of new and existing private governance initiatives that seek to provide guidance on measurement and reporting issues. Given the existence and complexity of this reporting environment, theorizing carbon reporting practices beyond legitimacy and stakeholder framing might allow us to better understand particular institutional contexts in which reporting emerges (see, for example, Rankin *et al.*, 2011). This work, in turn, is likely to enliven social and environmental accounting more generally.

The first aspect of reporting that has captured considerable attention is the financial reporting issues that arise in the context of emissions trading markets, the largest of which is currently the European Union's Emissions Trading System (see Braun, 2009, who traces the history of this scheme). A literature is emerging that considers the accounting (and related reporting) implications arising from these emission trading regimes which can be categorized into those that mainly focus on the conceptual issues that markets and trading create (Callon, 2009; Cook, 2009; Engels, 2009; MacKenzie, 2009);[5] that which explores the particular accounting issues that have to be resolved in this context (Bebbington and Larrinaga, 2008; Lovell *et al.*, 2010); and that which considers how this information might impact upon capital markets (Johnston *et al.*, 2008).

Without rehearsing the various accounting issues here (but noting their importance and complexity), it is worth highlighting that this stream of work creates a bridge between mainstream accounting concerns about the role of accounting in the efficient operation of carbon markets and social and environmental accounting concerns (in a way that was not the case within environmental accounting debates to date). Insight into how standard setting processes 'work' (or do not) and the economic consequences of reporting choices emerge from this area due to the absence of accounting guidance (or more correctly the production and withdrawal of guidance) on how to account for emission allowances in the first decade of operation of the European market (see Lovell *et al.*, 2013). As trading schemes move to auctioning of allowances some of the problems that have historically been found in this area will be remedied, but the provision of financial information on the impact of carbon on organizations, which arguably is crucial for the operations of trading schemes (Lovell *et al.*, 2013), will remain topical for standard setters and report users. In this context, as in reporting more generally, ambitions for consistent and comparable information are not currently realized.

Second, beyond the particular issues that emerge with emissions trading, literature exists that considers the myriad of reporting activities that are taking place (see Freedman and Jaggi, 2005; Prado-Lorenzo *et al.*, 2009; Andrew and Cortese, 2011; Lodhia, 2011; Rankin *et al.*, 2011). Reporting of carbon is being observed in a variety of formats including within the annual report and accounts package; in standalone formats as well as in the context of private regulatory processes (see Pellegrino and Lodhia, 2012, who provide a comparative review of these and other media within the Australian mining sector). Likewise, the variety of forms of carbon accounting that Ascui and Lovell (2011) identified have been considered (Hrasky, 2012, for example, considers reporting of entity level carbon footprints). A common problem identified in the literature is the 'tensions between … accuracy, consistency and certainty' (Bowen and Wittneben, 2011, p. 1025; see also Kolk *et al.*, 2008; Andrew and Cortese, 2011), with reporting regimes yet to mature in terms of how to measure and report carbon in a way that is likely to be useful to stakeholders.

One of the notable aspects of reporting for carbon (in contrast to other social and environmental issues) is the involvement of financial market actors in the development of formats for information as well as encouraging the provision of information to market participants. This implies that carbon has more salience in terms of financial impact than other social and environmental issues, which is something that might be expected given the ubiquity of carbon in our economic system and also the attempts to govern carbon at the international and national levels. Of the various investor led reporting regimes the Carbon Disclosure Project (CDP) is the one that has attracted the most attention and which has the most substantive impact on reporting practices (Kolk *et al.*, 2008; Andrew and Cortese, 2011), with Okereke (2007) suggesting that it has increased disclosure of GCC information. Initiatives in this area are still evolving.

Finally, questions of the reliability (and relevance) of carbon accounting have drawn attention (for example, the lack of an auditing requirement has been a point of criticism of the CDP). A variety of authors have considered auditing and assurance in this context, with Olson (2010) outlining some of the complexity at play (see also Simnett *et al.*, 2009; Green and Li, 2012). The consideration of the professional competence and authority of accountants in carbon reporting (see Ascui and Lovell, 2012) also emerges with 'tensions between different communities over the limits and boundaries of professional expertise, control over the content and process of standards development, and attempts to link new forms of carbon accounting to existing areas of professional practice' (Lovell and MacKenzie, 2011, p. 48) emerging.

In the broader issue of the relevance of carbon information many problems exist. The scientific and technical indeterminacy of the social and physical processes giving rise to GCC precludes taking any measurement method for granted, and this is even truer for analysis at the organizational level. The definition of the scope for the measurement of carbon emissions is one example, with the World Business Council for Sustainable Development/World Resources Institute's Protocol (WBCSD/WRI, 2004) providing guidance for the measurement of carbon emissions according to a given set of defined scopes. Key questions in this respect are the measurement of carbon emissions at the point of production versus the measurement at the point of consumption (Wiedmann *et al.*, 2006) or the setting of 'reporting boundaries' in the product/service life-cycle (Acquaye *et al.*, 2011) and in organizations (Matthews *et al.*, 2008). Accounting research has not substantively engaged with those issues (but see Archel *et al.*, 2008) but they are bedrock issues for appreciating any reporting and are exactly the issues of detail that will have an impact on the relevance of carbon accounting data.

*Financial markets*

It is testament to the ubiquity and importance of GCC that financial market investors are championing reporting, primarily through private governance initiatives (such as the CDP and the Climate Disclosure Standards Board – see Haigh and Shapiro, 2012). At the same time there have been concerns expressed about the literacy of financial markets when it comes to GCC; the relationship between corporations and investors is not an easy one. For instance, Sullivan and Gouldson (2012, p. 60) capture the tensions that emerge in this area when they observe that 'investors have consistently criticized companies for not providing information that can be readily used in investment decision making [while companies] ... have criticized investors for not utilizing the information that they provide'. Having noted this, relatively little literature exists that systematically investigates how investment managers are taking GCC into account in their decisions (Pfeifer and Sullivan, 2008; but see also Johnston *et al.*, 2008; Solomon *et al.*, 2011). What does exist, however, suggests that 'institutional investors view climate change as a significant material risk and consider GCC to be the most important environmental, social and governance factor in institutional investment' (Solomon *et al.*, 2011, p. 1138); but that investors are yet to use metrics (such as carbon intensity) in their investment decisions (see Haigh and Shapiro, 2012). Given the relative lack of sophistication in carbon accounting metrics (and the previously noted lack of consistency and comparability of information provided) this might be a 'good thing' but it does point to the difficulty of linking entity level data with investors' needs.

There is, however, some evidence that financial markets are able in certain contexts to recognize the implications of GCC issues. For example, Busch and Hoffmann (2007, p. 522) note that 'the capital markets seem to be sensitive regarding carbon regulations'; and Henderson and Hughes (2010, p. 13) suggest that 'investors discount share prices by 8 to 10 per cent for 85 per cent of the sample's investor-owned utilities, dependent on perceived regulatory quality'. Findings such as these tie this area of investigation to that of governance regimes as it suggests that the nature and quality of how one regulates will affect market responses. There is, however, a long way to go before capital markets will reflect carbon realities (see also Knox-Hayes, 2009, who considers the development of expertise in this area).

## Conceptual issues

We would argue that accounting and reporting for GCC is not merely the application of existing accounting techniques to a new space and, therefore, the usual stakeholder and legitimacy theories will not be able to produce the level of understanding that is required. Rather, it is our contention that this context provides an opportunity to extend our understanding of social and environmental accounting, but also of mainstream accounting (especially if accountants work collaboratively with other disciplines). For example, the emergence of GCC governance regimes creates contexts in which issues of commensuration, marketization, economic consequences and risk analysis come to the fore (all of these areas have substantive literatures of their own, notably those developed by economic sociologists). In addition, given that different regimes are emerging across the globe there is ample opportunity for research that focuses on these 'natural laboratories' as well as to consider issues of scaling when these regimes start to mesh with each other. In short, accounting for carbon might provide a framework in which we come to shift our understanding of the performance and limits of accounting technologies (and thereby provide a bridge to both critical and mainstream scholarship). An additional aspect of carbon accounting and reporting is the extent to which the investor community and their interests are represented in this area, in contrast to social and environmental accounting where investors seem to be relatively indifferent to much reporting.

The study of any form of accounting is also a study of how institutions govern information disclosure and associated responsibilities and accountabilities. While the GCC agenda has shaped the activities of existing institutions (for example, the Global Reporting Initiative), new institutions (such as the CDP and more recently the International Integrated Reporting Council) have also emerged which provide new contexts in which to understand governance (see Bowen and Wittneben, 2011, p. 2014 for a list of institutions of relevance). At the current point in time, however, no one reporting regime dominates (see Andrew and Cortese, 2011). This suggests that we might be able to observe a process that is in play (before it becomes 'black boxed' – see Lovell *et al.*, 2013) and hence the process by which carbon reporting comes to be governed might become more apparent.

Moreover, the interlocking nature of standards development (for example, the role that the World Business Council for Sustainable Development/World Resources Institute protocol plays in developing the baseline for reporting) is apparent. Of course, not everyone is happy that private regulatory interests shape the terms on which carbon is to be reported (Andrew and Cortese, 2011), largely because this is a shift from more state focused regulation (which, of course, has its own limitations). In addition, various standard-setting roles are being nested into what Braun (2009, p. 469) calls a 'multi-level policy-making architecture', where both state and non-state players are involved in the production of norms around carbon accounting. Indeed, the building of such policymaking architecture is a live experiment that 'will continue to grow in importance as new emissions reduction regimes are set up and existing ones are linked' (Bowen and Wittneben, 2011, p. 1034). This offers the opportunity to investigate the dynamics of accounting systems of governance as they emerge (see also Bebbington *et al.*, 2012).

The final area of potential conceptual innovation arises from the intersection of the GCC agenda with related social and environmental aspects. These include environmental contexts where GCC is likely to affect the rate and nature of environmental change in other arenas (such as in biodiversity and water availability and/or quality). These are also domains where accounting scholarship is starting to focus, and the dynamic interaction between carbon accounting and these areas might generate insights that are not limited to a single physical manifestation of 'the environment'. In addition, the broader GCC agenda has important equity and human rights elements to it and one might expect to see work at the intersection of these two arenas. Finally, while accounting has tended to concentrate on organizational entities, the multiple scales on which carbon is counted provide opportunities for accounts to non-organizational entities such as cities (indeed, Milne and Grubnic, 2011, touch on national level reporting as being a possible base from which to contextualize entity accounts).

## Concluding comments

The aim of this chapter was to provide readers with an entry point into the rapidly emerging field of carbon accounting. In a relatively short time, a literature has developed within accounting that starts the process of reflecting on GCC and the sorts of accounting and reporting technologies that are being developed by organizations. The literature has identified that there are distinctive reporting frames at play, sometimes described as: counting carbon; carbon accounting; and accountability for carbon (Bowen and Wittneben, 2011). Likewise, internal management processes (and accounting information related to them) are starting to be documented. What emerges clearly from the literature is that what we have done to date is not up to the challenge posed by GCC (see Boston and Lempp, 2011) and, as a result, this field is one that will grow and develop over time. As well as the 'normal' proliferation of studies that seek to better understand the relevance of new and existing findings, a number of areas might usefully attract the attention of researchers going forward in time.

Given that national governments are adopting a variety of approaches to achieving emissions targets (with the United Kingdom and Scotland being the first countries – in 2008 and 2009 respectively – to pass legislation to achieve reduction trajectories) it is likely that particular countries will provide an early lead on carbon governance, accounting and reporting. For example, one 'interesting' aspect of the United Kingdom Climate Change Act is that it gives the Secretary of State the power to require reporting by entities (that exercise functions of a public nature) about what they are doing to adapt to GCC (this is called the adaptation reporting power). Organizations that are producing these reports (including both public and private sector organizations) are those that operate key parts of the infrastructure (such as roads, rails, ports, airports, networks, utility providers, regulators and some public bodies). While these reports have yet to be subject to academic accounting investigations they do fit within the ambit of the discipline (but see Cooper and Pearce, 2011 at p. 1106 where they note that more than one-third of their local government respondents gave priority to GCC adaptation which might relate to this regulation).

It is also likely that sector focused research will emerge going forward, as dynamics created by both production activities and institutional settings will affect GCC responsiveness (the insurance industry would be a good example of a sector that is being impacted in particular ways by GCC). At times one would also expect that this will cross-cut with country level analysis – the Australian mining industry being a case in point – already subject to investigation by accountants. Likewise, a formal consideration of the role of forests (and economic activities around them) is likely as the UN REDD (Reducing Emissions from Deforestation and Forest Degradation) programme moves forward (see Neeff and Ascui, 2009). Moreover, as there are now projects developed under the Clean Development Mechanism, an analysis of their impacts (which are amenable to social accounting analysis) might also be anticipated.[6]

The suggestions made here are not conclusive but we hope they might stimulate readers of this chapter into extending analysis beyond information disclosure of large public listed companies (which is the predominant focus of existing social and environmental accounting work). It seems to us that accounting for carbon provides a context where the accounting literature can move beyond legitimacy and stakeholder theory-informed work to more systematically consider the context within which reporting practice is emerging and the multiple institutional pressures that might lead to reporting activities. Indeed, the findings of Rankin *et al.* (2011, p. 1039) that reporting was influenced by the combined effect of ISO certification, GRI reporting activities and engagement with the CDP, alongside links to internal governance and information systems, points to a more sophisticated conceptualization of influences on disclosure. It is also the case that carbon regimes' failures to curb emissions at an appropriate level will continue to challenge businesses and, consequently, organizational responses to the GCC agenda will multiply. This is an area, therefore, where there will be no shortage of empirical sites around which investigations might emerge. Likewise, it is possible that this area might provide a bridge between social and environmental accountants and the mainstream of accounting theorizing as well as being a site upon which insights from a whole variety of related disciplines might be brought together. The practice, policy and intellectual ramifications of the GCC agenda and accounting for carbon, we would suggest, are only just starting to be realized.

## Notes

1   A number of accounting papers cover this background including: Bebbington and Larrinaga (2008); Ascui and Lovell (2011); Milne and Grubnic (2011) and Boston and Lempp (2011). Observations of how organizations have interacted with the international processes can be found (for example) in Kolk and Levy (2001); Begg *et al.* (2005); Pinkse and Kolk (2007); and Kolk *et al.* (2008).
2   The Kyoto Protocol does not seek to govern all greenhouse gases. Rather, it focuses on those that have the greatest link to human activity and subsequent changes in atmospheric concentrations. The main gases covered by Kyoto are carbon dioxide, methane, nitrous oxide and a number of other gases (hydrofluorocarbons, perfluorocarbons and sulphur hexafluoride). These gases are generated by a range of human activities (as well as natural processes) in which organizations of various types play a part.
3   We are using 'carbon' as shorthand to cover the constituent elements of the carbon cycle that are of concern to policymakers. This includes the Kyoto basket of six greenhouse gases as well as carbon tied up in terrestrial ecosystems (such as soils, oceans and forests).
4   Numerous journals focus on GCC, many of them based on natural science investigations. Social science journals that contribute to our understanding of GCC and which might be familiar to accountants include *Ecological Economics*; *Energy Policy*; the *Environment and Planning* series of journals; *Global Environmental Change: Human and Policy Dimensions*; and the *Journal of Environmental Management*. In addition, other journals carry relevant material from time to time, including: *Climate Change*; *Climate Change Journal*; *Climate Change Economics*; *Climate Policy*; *Ecology and Society*; *Geoforum*; *Society & Natural Resources: An International Journal*; and *Wiley Interdisciplinary Reviews*.
5   As might be expected, the conversion of a physical impact into a marketable commodity is not without critics (see, for example, McNicholas and Windsor, 2011) and reflects the same concerns that were raised in the mid-1990s around the development of an $SO_2$ market in the United States (Gibson, 1996; Lehman, 1996; and Wambsganss and Sanford, 1996).
6   While the social and environmental accounting literature has concentrated on carbon markets in a limited range of countries (Europe, Australia and New Zealand) the CDM mechanism should also attract our attention. For example, the CDM has delivered over 3,000 projects and catalysed over $140 billion in investment (by mid-2011), fundamentally enabled by the development, from scratch, of several hundred different methodologies for accounting project-level emission reductions which have yet to be subject to sustained empirical investigation. We are grateful for the input of Francisco Ascui on this point.

## References

Acquaye, A., Wiedmann, T., Feng, K., Crawford, R., Barrett, J., Kuylenstierna, J., Duffy, A. P., Koh, S. C. L. and McQueen-Mason, S. (2011), 'Identification of "carbon hot-spots" and quantification of GHG intensities in the biodiesel supply chain using hybrid LCA and structural path analysis', *Environmental Science & Technology*, 45(6): 2471–78.

Andrew, J. and Cortese, C. (2011), 'Accounting for climate change and the self-regulation of carbon disclosures', *Accounting Forum*, 35(3): 130–38.

Archel, P., Fernandez, M. and Larrinaga, C. (2008), 'The organizational and operational boundaries of triple bottom line reporting: A survey', *Environmental Management*, 41(1): 106–17.

Ascui, F. and Lovell, H. (2011), 'As frames collide: Making sense of carbon accounting', *Accounting, Auditing and Accountability Journal*, 24(8): 978–99.

Ascui, F. and Lovell, H. (2012), 'Carbon accounting and the construction of competence', *Journal of Cleaner Production*, 36: 48–59.

Ball, A., Mason, I., Grubnic, S. and Hughes, P. (2009), 'The carbon neutral public sector: Early developments and an urgent agenda for research', *Public Management Review*, 11(5): 575–600.

Bebbington, J. and Barter, N. (2011), *Strategic Responses to Global Climate Change: A UK Analysis*. London: Chartered Institute of Management Accountants (CIMA).

Bebbington, J. and Larrinaga, C. (2008), 'Carbon trading: Accounting and reporting issues', *European Accounting Review*, 17(4): 697–717.

Bebbington, J., Kirk, E. and Larrinaga, C. (2012), 'The production of normativity: A comparison of reporting regimes in Spain and the UK', *Accounting, Organizations and Society*, 37(2): 78–94.

Begg, K., Van der Woerd, F. and Levy, D. (eds) (2005), *The Business of Climate Change: Corporate Responses to Kyoto*. London: Greenleaf.

Boston, J. and Lempp, F. (2011), 'Climate change: Explaining and solving the mismatch between scientific urgency and political inertia', *Accounting, Auditing and Accountability Journal*, 24(8): 1000–21.

Bowen, F. and Wittneben, B. (2011), 'Carbon accounting: Negotiating accuracy, consistency and certainty across organisational fields', *Accounting, Auditing and Accountability Journal*, 24(8): 1022–36.

Braun, M. (2009), 'The evolution of emissions trading in the EU – the role of policy networks, knowledge and policy entrepreneurs', *Accounting, Organisations and Society*, 34(3/4): 469–87.

Burritt, R., Schaltegger, S. and Zvezdov, D. (2011), 'Carbon management accounting: Explaining practice in leading German companies', *Australian Accounting Review*, 21(1): 80–98.

Busch, T. and Hoffmann, V. (2007), 'Emerging carbon constraints for corporate risk management', *Ecological Economics*, 62: 518–28.

Callon, M. (2009), 'Civilizing markets: Carbon trading between in vitro and in vivo experiments', *Accounting, Organizations and Society*, 34(3–4): 535–48.

Cook, A. (2009), 'Emission rights: From costless activity to market operations', *Accounting, Organizations and Society*, 34(3–4): 456–68.

Cooper, S. and Pearce, G. (2011), 'Climate change performance measurement, control and accountability in English local authority areas', *Accounting, Auditing and Accountability Journal*, 24(8): 1097–118.

Engels, A. (2009), 'The European Emissions Trading Scheme: An exploratory study of how companies learn to account for carbon', *Accounting, Organizations and Society*, 34(3/4): 488–98.

Freedman, M. and Jaggi, B. (2005), 'Global warming, commitment to the Kyoto protocol, and accounting disclosures by the largest global public firms from polluting industries', *International Journal of Accounting*, 40: 215–32.

Gibson, K. (1996), 'The problem with reporting pollution allowances: Reporting is not the problem', *Critical Perspectives on Accounting*, 7(6): 655–65.

Green, W. and Li, Q. (2012), 'Evidence of an expectation gap for greenhouse gas emissions assurance', *Accounting, Auditing and Accountability Journal*, 25(1): 146–73.

Haigh, M. and Shapiro, M. (2012), 'Carbon reporting: Does it matter?', *Accounting, Auditing and Accountability Journal*, 25(1): 105–25.

Henderson, C. and Hughes, K. (2010), 'Valuation implications of regulatory climate for utilities facing future environmental costs', *Advances in Accounting, incorporating Advances in International Accounting* 26(1): 13–24.

Hrasky, S. (2012), 'Carbon footprints and legitimation strategies: Symbolism or action?' *Accounting, Auditing and Accountability Journal*, 25(1): 174–98.

Johnston, D., Sefcik, S. and Soderstrom, N. (2008), 'The value relevance of greenhouse gas emissions allowances', *European Accounting Review*, 17(4): 749–66.

Knox-Hayes, J. (2009), 'The developing carbon financial service industry: Expertise, adaption and complementarity in London and New York', *Journal of Economic Geography*, 9(6): 749–77.

Kolk, A. and Levy, D. (2001), 'Winds of change: Corporate strategy, climate change and oil multinationals', *European Management Journal*, 19(5): 501–9.

Kolk, A., Levy, D. and Pinkse, J. (2008), 'Corporate responses in an emerging climate regime: The institutionalization and commensuration of carbon disclosure', *European Accounting Review*, 17(4): 719–45.

Lee, K. (2010), 'Integrating carbon footprint into supply chain management: The case of Hyundai Motor Company (HMC) in the automobile industry', *Journal of Cleaner Production*, 19(11): 1216–23.

Lee, K. (2012), 'Carbon accounting for supply chain management in the automobile industry', *Journal of Cleaner Production*, 36: 89–93.

Lehman, G. (1996), 'Environmental accounting: Pollution permits or selling the environment', *Critical Perspectives on Accounting*, 7(6): 667–76.

Lodhia, S. (2011), 'The Australian National Greenhouse and Energy Reporting Act and its implications for accounting practice and research', *Journal of Accounting and Organizational Change*, 7(2): 190–8.

Lohmann, L. (2009), 'Toward a different debate in environmental accounting: The cases of carbon and cost-benefit', *Accounting Organizations and Society*, 34(3–4): 499–534.

Lovell, H. and MacKenzie, D. (2011), 'Accounting for carbon: The role of accounting professional organisations in governing climate change', *Antipode*, 43(3): 704–30.

Lovell, H., Aguiar, T., Bebbington, J. and Larrinaga, C. (2010), *Accounting for Carbon*. London: Association of Chartered Certified Accountants (ACCA).

Lovell, H., Bebbington, J., Larrinaga, C. and Sales de Aguiar, T. (2013), 'Putting carbon markets into practice: A case study of financial accounting in Europe', *Environment and Planning C*, 31(4): 741–57.

MacKenzie, D. (2009), 'Making things the same: Gases, emission rights and the politics of carbon markets', *Accounting, Organizations and Society*, 34(3–4): 440–55.

McNicholas, P. and Windsor, C. (2011), 'Can the financialised atmosphere be effectively regulated and accounted for?', *Accounting, Auditing and Accountability Journal*, 24(8): 1071–96.

Matthews, H., Hendrickson, C. and Weber, C. (2008), 'The importance of carbon footprint estimation boundaries', *Environmental Science & Technology*, 42(16): 5839–42.

Milne, M. and Grubnic, S. (2011), 'Climate change accounting research: Keeping it interesting and different', *Accounting, Auditing and Accountability Journal*, 24(8): 948–77.

Neeff, T. and Ascui, F. (2009), 'Lessons from carbon markets for designing an effective REDD architecture', *Climate Policy*, 9: 306–15.

Okereke, C. (2007), 'An exploration of motivations, drivers and barriers to carbon management: The UK FTSE 100', *European Management Journal*, 25(6): 475–86.

Olson, E. (2010), 'Challenges and opportunities from greenhouse gas emissions reporting and independent auditing', *Managerial Auditing Journal* 25(9): 934–42.

Pellegrino, C. and Lodhia, S. (2012), 'Climate change accounting and the Australian mining industry: Exploring the links between corporate disclosure and the generation of legitimacy', *Journal of Cleaner Production*, 36: 68–82.

Pfeifer, S. and Sullivan, R. (2008), 'Public policy, institutional investors and climate change: A UK case-study', *Climate Change*, 89(3–4): 245–62.

Pinkse, J. and Kolk, A. (2007), 'Multinational corporations and emissions trading: Strategic responses to new institutional constraints', *European Management Journal*, 25(6): 441–52.

Prado-Lorenzo, J., Rodriguez-Dominguez, L., Gallego-Álvarez, I. and Garcia-Sánchez, I. (2009), 'Factors influencing the disclosure of greenhouse gas emissions in companies world-wide', *Management Decision*, 47(7): 1133–57.

Rankin, M., Windsor, C. and Wahyuni, D. (2011), 'An investigation of voluntary corporate greenhouse gas emissions reporting in a market governance system: Australian evidence', *Accounting, Auditing and Accountability Journal*, 24(8): 1037–70.

Ratnatunga, J. (2008), 'Carbonomics: Strategic management accounting issues', *Journal of Applied Management Accounting Research*, 6(1): 1–10.

Ratnatunga, J. and Balachandran, K. (2009), 'Carbon business accounting: The impact of global warming on the cost and management accounting profession', *Journal of Accounting, Auditing & Finance*, 24(2): 333–55.

Schaltegger, S. and Csutora, M. (2012), 'Carbon accounting for sustainability and management. Status quo and challenges', *Journal of Cleaner Production*, 36: 1–16.

Scipioni, A., Manzardo, A., Mazzi, A. and Mastrobuono, M. (2012), 'Monitoring the carbon footprint of products: A methodological approach', *Journal of Cleaner Production*, 36: 94–101.

Simnett, R., Nugent, M. and Huggins, A. (2009), 'Developing an international assurance standard on carbon emissions disclosures', *Accounting Horizons*, 23(4): 347–63.

Solomon, J., Solomon, A., Norton, S. and Joseph, N. (2011), 'Private climate change reporting: An emerging discourse of risk and opportunity?', *Accounting, Auditing and Accountability Journal*, 24(8): 1119–48.

Stechemesser, K. and Guenther, E. (2012), 'Carbon accounting: A systematic literature review', *Journal of Cleaner Production*, 36: 17–38.

Stern, N. (2006), *The Economics of Climate Change: The Stern Review*. Cambridge: Cambridge University Press.

Sullivan, R. and Gouldson, A. (2012), 'Does voluntary carbon reporting meet investors' needs?', *Journal of Cleaner Production*, 36: 60–7.

Tsai, W., Shen, Y., Lee, P., Chen, H., Kuo, L. and Huang, C. (2012), 'Integrating information about the cost of carbon through activity-based costing', *Journal of Cleaner Production*, 36: 102–11.

Wambsganss, J. R. and Sanford, B. (1996), 'The problem with reporting pollution allowances', *Critical Perspectives on Accounting*, 7(6): 643–52.

Wiedmann, T., Minx, J., Barrett, J. and Wackernagel, M. (2006), 'Allocating ecological footprints to final consumption categories with input–output analysis', *Ecological Economics*, 56(1): 28–48.

World Business Council for Sustainable Development/World Resources Institute (WBCSD/WRI) (2004), *The Greenhouse Gas Protocol, A Corporate Accounting and Reporting Standard* (rev. edn). *Geneva*: World Business Council for Sustainable Development.

# 13 Accounting and accountability for fresh water

## Exploring initiatives and innovations

*Shona Russell[1] and Linda Lewis[2]*

## Introduction

The relationship between humans and the planet is changing. Planetary boundaries for climate change, biodiversity loss and the nitrogen cycle have been exceeded, while we are approaching other limits including global freshwater use (Rockström *et al.* 2009). In the twenty-first century, global change processes mean that we face challenges including 'the scarcity of critical resources, degradation of ecosystem services, [and] erosion of the planet's capability to absorb our wastes' (Steffen *et al.* 2011: 739). The scale, speed and complexity of challenges constitute these as 'wicked problems' (Rittel and Webber 1973). Transformative changes are required across multiple scales, crossing national and organizational boundaries. Knowledge from natural and social sciences, including accounting and management, will need to be integrated in order to support transitions to sustainability (Future Earth 2013).

As we approach the planetary boundary for fresh water, challenges (such as drought, flooding, food security and climate change) have significant, increasing and dangerous threats to ecosystems and human well-being. The availability, affordability and adequacy of fresh water to meet basic needs continue to be central to the international sustainable development agenda (UN-Water 2011), supplemented by recognition of the need to overcome challenges of unsustainable use and competition for water resources to meet current and future needs of people and of freshwater ecosystems. Inadequate water governance has been identified as a major constraint to sustainable water resource management leading to calls for the involvement of those 'outside the water box' (WWAP 2009). Initiatives and innovations, concerning both the provision of water services and the management of fresh water, attempt to take account of multi-stakeholder perspectives, including those from the private sector (Kaika 2003). These initiatives blur responsibilities, alter decision-making processes and draw on various expertises, including accounting, to inform how water is used, allocated and managed (Lewis and Russell 2011).

While social and environmental accounting research (hereafter SEAR) has a long history of engaging in such sustainability challenges, there has been limited research concerning fresh water. Recent exceptions concern those relating to sustainability in the water sector (Cashman and Lewis 2007; Kennedy 2011); water disclosures (ACCA 2010; Crowther *et al.* 2006; Egan and Frost 2010; Tredgida and Milne 2006); and the development of 'water accounting' (Chalmers *et al.* 2012; Godfrey and Chalmers 2012; Hazelton 2013). These studies follow earlier research concerning accounting in the water sector, in relation to privatization and organizational change (see for example Ogden 1995, 1997, 1999; Rahaman *et al.* 2007; Shaoul 1997). In this chapter, drawing on a review of academic literatures, primarily those associated with SEAR,[3] and publicly available documents[4] we examine initiatives and accounting innovations concerning water resource management, responding to calls for SEAR to engage with policy, practice, society and ecology (Parker 2011). The rest of the chapter is structured as follows: first, we frame the review in the context of sustainability accounting; second, we present an overview of freshwater challenges and responses; this is followed in the third and fourth sections by a deeper examination and discussion of the emergence of accounting research, initiatives and accounting innovations for fresh water. Finally, we outline two possible streams for SEAR concerning fresh water.

## Sustainability accounting and accountability

Accounting is recognized to represent, construct, problematize, and to measure the vision, conduct and practices of organizations (Dey *et al.* 2010). In particular, accounting renders entities visible through numerical representations (Hines 1991). Interest in sustainability accounting and accountability has blossomed in recent years (Unerman *et al.* 2007), with a growing emphasis on issues such as climate change (Bebbington and Larrinaga 2008; Milne and Grubnic 2011); biodiversity (Jones and Solomon 2013); and human rights (McPhail and McKernan 2011). Accounting technologies for sustainability can inform decision making, and communicate aspects of organizational performance to a range of stakeholders, and enable managers to discharge duties of accountability (Unerman *et al.* 2007: 3). Examples include the sustainability assessment model, full-cost accounting, indicators and reporting guidelines, and assurance practices that seek to operationalize and embed sustainability in practice (see discussions in Hopwood et al. 2010; Unerman *et al.* 2007). These technologies may be powerful tools in the management, planning, control and accountability with regard to social and environmental sustainability of organizations (Unerman *et al.* 2007), of supply chains (Spence and Rinaldi 2012) and of nations (Russell and Thomson 2009).

Despite the *potential* of sustainability accounting and accountability research and practice, accounting and accounts fall short of a full account for sustainability but provide a partial picture to evaluate impacts (Bebbington *et al.* 2007: 348). Furthermore, accounting technologies can problematize and inform decision making to support longer term transitions to sustainability (Russell and Thomson 2009). Thomson's (2007) review of SEAR highlights a divergence in the field whereby empirical studies, particularly content analysis of annual financial reports, are distinct from a growing area characterized as adopting normative, engaged and critical perspectives on the developments in accounting technologies for sustainability (Thomson 2007: 33). The latter area is orientated towards consideration of accounting and accountability in contested arenas (Georgakopoulos and Thomson 2008).

Sustainability accounting and accountability cuts across sub-disciplines of management and financial accounting; blurs the boundaries of accounting entities and responsibilities of impacts; requires engagement with other disciplines and expertise; and appreciates the nature of sustainability as a spatial concept concerned with equitable and distributive justice (Bebbington et al. 2007). Accounting technologies sit alongside many others, including deliberative and participative processes (e.g. citizen juries and scenarios) and voluntary governance programmes (e.g. certification schemes) that endeavour to engage with sustainability challenges – or 'wicked problems' – through messy processes involving various stakeholders generating clumsy solutions for sustainability (Frame 2008; Russell and Frame 2013). In this chapter, we examine initiatives and accounting innovations for fresh water contributing to the reorganization of human activities to meet needs of current and future generations, as well as those of the ecosystems (Gray 2006).

## Fresh water: challenges and responses

Fresh water is essential for ecosystems, for human well-being and for sustainability. While freshwater ecosystems provide a range of goods and services, they also enhance resilience against negative impacts of environmental change (UNEP 2012: 100). Yet global change processes are threatening the sustainability of fresh water with multiple impacts that may vary both spatially and temporally. Availability, affordability, adequacy of fresh water to meet basic needs continue to be central to the international sustainable development agenda (UN-Water 2011). Global withdrawals of water have tripled in the last 50 years to meet the demands of a growing population and are projected to rise, placing additional pressure on freshwater ecosystems, which need water of suitable quantity, quality and availability to sustain the provision of goods and services (WWAP 2012).

In both the Global North and South, inadequate water governance has been identified as a major constraint to sustainable water resource management (UNEP 2012: 122). Previous centralized, technocratic and top-down approaches are being modified to take account of multi-stakeholder perspectives through participatory and deliberative processes to address environmental issues through nested decision making (Benson *et al.* 2013; Kaika 2003; Lankford and Hepworth 2010; Neef 2009; Pahl-Wostl 2009). Significant reforms have addressed these challenges endeavouring to promote water use efficiency,[5] achieve water, energy and food security, and protect freshwater ecosystems through integrated and adaptive approaches. Alongside reforms that involve public-sector agencies and civil society, another stream seeks to engage the private sector, researchers,[6] non-governmental organizations[7] (NGOs) and the United Nations.

The 'soft path' to water management is one such approach (Gleick 2003). In contrast to prior supply-management (or hard path) approaches characterized by large infrastructure projects, the soft path implies an emphasis on demand management of water rather than that of supply. It focuses on changing practices of water use, with an emphasis on asking why water is used for certain tasks. It also implies adaptability in the ways water is managed in the short and long term to suit the particular contexts (e.g. homes, factories, farms, catchments, river basins) with an emphasis on ecological sustainability. The soft path implies engagement with various disciplines with an interest in water alongside policy makers, planners, and politicians. Moreover, it requires questioning of the values that inform how water is used and management (water resource management) and how water-related decisions are made (water governance).

The soft path is just one of many approaches, including integrated water resource management (IWRM), which is altering water management and governance to address freshwater challenges in the twenty-first century. In doing so, these approaches that incorporate stakeholder engagement and strategic decision making can lead to a redistribution of responsibilities among those involved in water resource management, such as the public sector. For example, in Canterbury, New Zealand, concerns about over-allocation of water resources led to the development of a regional water strategy, published in 2009 after seven years in development, that incorporated a number of participatory and deliberative initiatives involving stakeholders representing interests from the local government, iwi,[8] agricultural and recreational sectors (see Lennox *et al.* 2011; Russell *et al.* 2011). During 2013, the strategy was being implemented creating hybrid water governance comprising collaborative, decentralized and participatory initiatives organized around sub-catchments, one which continues to emerge and develop (Holley and Gunningham 2011).

Common to these approaches are the following characteristics: (i) (re)distribution and blurring of responsibilities among communities, organizations and governments; (ii) changes in the scales at which water resources management is undertaken; and (iii) developments of initiatives, tools and skills to support decision making. As a result, complex, dynamic and diverse arrangements are emerging. Water governance is no longer the sole responsibility of public agencies in accordance with national legislation. Instead, the decision-making processes and operational water management programmes comprise various actors (public, private and from civil society) and initiatives (voluntary and mandatory).

## Accounting and accountability for fresh water: innovations and initiatives

Empirical and theoretical enquiries within the accounting community diverge into two areas, namely that pertaining to the *water sector* (to denote the provision of water and wastewater services); and that associated with *water resource management* (a term used to describe the use, allocation and regulation of water resources themselves). A substantial volume of work examined accounting and accountability in the water sector, particularly in the context of privatization, in England and Wales in the late 1980s and in Africa (Rahaman *et al.* 2007). Often in connection with corporate social responsibility (CSR) and social and environmental accounting (SEA), literature considered the role of accounting in organizational change (Ogden 1995, 1997; Ogden and Anderson 1995); regulation of the sector (Shaoul 1997); and sustainability accounting and sustainability in the water sector (Cashman and Lewis 2007; Kennedy 2011; Larrinaga and Perez-Chamorro 2008; Letza and Smallman 2001; von Schwedler 2011). More recently, a growing body of work engages directly with aspects of *water resource management*. For example, development of accounting to address challenges associated with climate change in Australia (Chalmers *et al.* 2012; Godfrey and Chalmers 2012); water governance in the Barbados (Cashman 2011); the use of accounts in relation to pollution (Solomon and Thomson 2009); levels of corporate water disclosure (Egan and Frost 2010) and accounting information could support rights to water (Hazelton 2013).

Three themes emerge from these two areas of literature. First, water accounts include much more than those included in annual reports or CSR reports. Interest in water-related accounting research may initially focus on levels of disclosure by organizations that use large volumes of water; interest that is being located within a broader range of water-related accounts that are used in various contexts and produced in relation to various temporal and spatial scales. Second, accounting research is beginning to take account of a diverse range of entities across multiple scales spanning the sector and projects alongside, as noted by Hazelton (2013), organizations, catchments and products. For example, other accounts could include adverts or media releases produced in relation to a weather-related event (Larrinaga and Perez-Chamarro 2008); submissions to regulatory authorities concerning water abstraction or pollution in a particular catchment (Hazelton 2013); or periodic 'state of water resources' reports by national or international agencies (see for example WWAP 2009, 2012); and as part of efforts to transform water management in one particular river (Solomon and Thomson 2009). Third, research appears orientated towards water-related issues, whether those be transformation of the sector (as was the case with privatization), or threats to the availability and accessibility of the resource stemming from drought, floods or pollution. For example, water-related accounting is understood to problematize and seek change, as illustrated in Braithwaite's account of the River Wandle that documented the quality of water, river flow rate, water use, pollutants and source of pollution (Solomon and Thomson 2009), or contribute to the reform of water resource management in Australia (Chalmers *et al.* 2012).

Corporate engagement in water has grown substantially in the last decade marked by international initiatives; partnerships between corporations and non-governmental organizations; increasing corporate water disclosures; supporting the financial sector's engagement with water issues,[9] and a burgeoning market of water-related expertise estimated in 2011 to be worth US$30m per year,[10] having grown from virtually nothing in 2002 (Gasson 2011). In addition to large international initiatives, individual corporations have undertaken efforts to reduce water impacts on quantity and quality across activities of production and distribution, and sometimes even use by consumers (see Lambooy 2011). Corporations are also undertaking individual projects to address water concerns, sometimes in response to threats or protests, such as Coca-Cola in India (Burnett and Welford 2007; Hills and Welford 2005); or in partnerships with NGOs to reduce water-related impacts, such as SABMiller and the World Wildlife Fund (WWF)'s work on water footprints (SABMiller and WWF 2009). Despite such developments, the area remains of limited interest in SEAR and the wider research community has been slow (Hepworth 2012).

Here, we focus on the initiatives and accounting innovations rather than individual organizational efforts to engage in water resource management. A range of water-related initiatives have been developed that are characterized as voluntary and are linked to international agencies or involve partnerships with non-government agencies. Many initiatives appear tied to the activities of the United Nation's CEO Water Mandate, which is itself linked to the UN Global Compact.[11] Originally established in 2007, the mandate aims to assist companies in the development, implementation and disclosure of water sustainability policies and practices across six areas: direct operations, supply chain and watershed management, collective action, public policy, community engagement, and transparency (UN Global Compact 2011). The mandate has reiterated the need for collective action with regard to water issues by calling for governments to 'make water sustainability a priority', calling for commitments to long-term planning and international coordination, and collaborating actively with the private sector and civil society (UN CEO Water Mandate 2012).

A number of accounting innovations have emerged concerning fresh water and efforts to conserve water, understand relations between water, energy and climate change; manage water-related risks; invest in upgrading and expanding water-related assets; and develop opportunities ensuring long-term operational viability or maintaining/improving the social licence to operate (Egan 2009). In this section, we focus on three innovations concerning *water accounting*, *whole-life costing*, and *water disclosures*. The third acts as a bridge to examine other initiatives for fresh water, where accounting innovations are emerging in practice but subject to little attention from SEAR.

*Water accounting* (hereafter WA) is arguably emerging as a distinct accounting practice (Chalmers et al. 2012). In Australia, WA has developed as part of reforms under the National Water Initiative (NWI) that led to the development of general purpose water accounting (GPWA) system. The GPWA system is based on financial accounting models and comprises water accounting standards, a conceptual framework and the establishment of a Water Accounting Standards Board (WASB) (Chalmers *et al.* 2012; Godfrey and Chalmers 2012). Registers of water rights and periodic national water accounts have been developed in an effort to meet the information needs of different water systems in respect to monitoring, trading, environmental management and on-farm management in order to improve transparency and provide good information and assurance for decision making. Other forms of WA could include an organizational perspective that may focus on accounting and reporting on use and discharge of water with regard to volume, timing and location of impacts (Morrison et al. 2010). In addition, WA may refer to measurement and disclosure of information concerning for example: (i) physical volumes of water in the economy and environment, and economic aspects of water use and supply in the management of national and regional water resources (Vardon et al. 2007); or (ii) water used and embedded in products, also known as a water footprint (Hoekstra *et al.* 2011). One may also argue that the US Toxic Release Inventory that collates and reports on pollution by organizations constitutes another form of WA (see Hazelton 2013).

Corporate WA tools have been identified as informing water-related decisions (Morrison et al. 2010). Early tools appeared to focus primarily on internal water use, particularly at the level of facilities (e.g. the World Business Council for Sustainable Development (WBCSD)'s Global Water Tool and GEMI's Sustainability Planner). This was followed by 'corporate water accounting tools' such as life cycle assessments, water footprints and other assessment tools (Morrison *et al.* 2010), which address issues of efficiency, investments, water risk assessment and management of impacts, alongside the communication of risks and performance with stakeholders and engagement with water policy.

This early cluster of organizational-centred tools has been linked to others that seek to assess water risks in catchments (e.g. the Aqueduct Water Risk Atlas) in order to support decision making and disclosure. For example, the Water Risk Filter, launched in 2012 by WWF and Deutsche Investitions und Entwicklungsgesellschaft (DEG),[12] uses scarcity data from the Water Footprint Network to construct risk metrics; results will be reported to provide the user with the information required for the Carbon Disclosure Project (CDP)'s Water Disclosure Questionnaire. Thus, there seems to be a degree of integration of tools, perhaps creating stability and norms in this particular trajectory of water governance.

*Whole-life costing* (WLC) is an example of accounting innovation designed to facilitate the management of water infrastructure to provide services in the *water sector*. WLC is a means to determine the costs of building and maintaining the infrastructure necessary to provide water services. In contrast to conventional accounting that distinguishes between capital investment costs and operational, maintenance costs for the purposes of annual accounts, 'whole-life' is as it sounds. It attempts to calculate the total costs of building, maintaining, replacing and where necessary, disposing of parts of the infrastructure, taking a long-term view of the costs involved and the likely demands made on that infrastructure (Skipworth et al. 2002).

WLC is a technique often employed in public sector service provision or in the provision of utilities by the private sector where, regardless of provider, there are significant infrastructure assets to protect and maintain. The use of WLC may differ depending on the context. For many organizations, particularly in countries where water service provision has been privatized, the infrastructure may already exist, so it is the long-term replacement and maintenance costs that are significant. In addition, costs need to recognize the regulatory and information costs that are likely to be incurred to ensure availability of resources, affordability, transparency and account-ability. Developing countries particularly often lack the capital investment for appropriate water infrastructure to ensure adequate, affordable and clean water supplies to all inhabitants; this in conjunction with water scarcity compounds problems about how to provide water and sanitation services. By comparison, developed nations are beginning to find that maintaining their water infrastructure is expensive and that it is difficult to recover the costs in prices that are affordable to the consumers. One consequence of a lack of adequate maintenance of that infrastructure is leakage. This can lead to shortages that are further exacerbated by climate change that further leads to water supplies draining rivers and underwater aquifers.

The long-term view that is taken within WLC lends itself to issues of sustainability, not just of the infrastructure itself, but of the resource, in this case water, that is being provided.

From an SEA perspective it allows consideration of all types of cost to be incorporated into a WLC analysis. Environmental impacts can be assessed and costs incorporated for pollution caused by dirty water and breakdowns in sanitation, by way of the remedial or avoidance costs to ensure this does not happen; and for social costs such as designing schemes to provide subsidies and/or preferential pricing to ensure no-one is denied access to water (as a human right) not to mention conventional economic costs. The resulting WLC analysis, which calculates total costs and discounts these over the projected lifetime of the infrastructure, can then be used in deciding when is the best time to incur the costs to most effectively maintain the infrastructure.

A third area of *water disclosures* is emerging across research and practice. Water disclosures spans the collection of data, assessing and evaluating information; developing strategic responses and reporting information to stakeholders is integral to water management efforts. In an effort to address such absence of information, there have been many recommendations of what companies could or should disclose (see Table 13.1). Voluntary initiatives such as the Global Reporting Initiative (GRI), the Water Disclosure Programme, and most recently, the UN CEO Water Mandate, have sought to develop guidelines to support common – or standardized approaches – to water disclosures (UN CEO Water Mandate 2012). This short report frames detailed disclosure of current state, implications and response supported by information about the company's water profile and an explanation of how a company determines what topics to disclose (see Table 13.1).

A growing number of studies have examined disclosures concerning organizational use and impacts on water resources in sustainability or CSR accounts, or stand-alone reports for water-intensive industries (ACCA 2010; Adrio 2012; Egan 2009; Egan and Frost 2010) and water supply organizations in the United Kingdom (von Schwedler 2011) and in New Zealand (Tredgida and Milne 2006). Levels of reporting have been found lacking, despite evidence that companies in water-intensive industries report water information as standard practice (Egan and Frost 2010; Morikawa et al. 2007). Specifically, there is a lack of quantitative indicators or details of impacts that are specific to particular operations; instead many reports contain strategic and qualitative information about water-related impacts and use. Furthermore, the growth in initiatives has led to confusion over terminology; a growing emphasis on external as well as internal aspects of water impacts; lack of harmonization of approaches to measure and report risks and impacts; an absence of methods to characterize watershed conditions and assess risks; and an under-emphasis of water issues across supply chains. However, companies were found

*Table 13.1* Possible water-related disclosure

| INTERNAL issues concerning operations at sites or across organization | EXTERNAL issues concerning catchments, river basins or countries in which operations are based |
|---|---|
| Reports of past use and management of water resources | Availability and accessibility of water |
| Strategic water plans concerning quality and quantity | Rights to water |
| | Pricing |
| | Stakeholder engagement |
| | Ecological, social and economic impacts |
| | Water resource management in the supply chain |
| | Human health issues |

Source: Derived from Egan 2009; Irbaris 2009; Morrison *et al.* 2010.

to acknowledge water-related impacts associated with energy use and carbon emissions (CDP 2010: 7–8).

Indicators provide quantitative measures that sit alongside qualitative narratives. As illustrated in Table 13.2, various indicators have been suggested in relation to water disclosures. The examples listed suggest first, that there is a commonality of indictors across a variety of sources indicating efforts to perhaps standardize disclosure practice, including the use of indicators (CDP 2012). Second, there are numerous indicators related to quantity rather than quality concerns, suggesting a potential gap in the reporting of water impacts. Third, distinctions are being made between cumulative indicators concerning organizations (e.g. GRI) and those that relate directly to specific sites, catchments, and/or geographical regions. Further work is required to understand the extent to which there is awareness of site-specific, or rather catchment-specific, impacts associated with water and the extent to which this is reflected in the reporting practices of organizations. In addition, the apparent alignment of indicators and disclosure practices across various initiatives indicates the production of normativity within corporate engagement with water and water governance more broadly (Bebbington et al. 2012).

## Discussion

The emergence of voluntary initiatives for water governance adds further complexity to examining accounting and accountability for water. No longer is the focus solely on an individual organization's conduct or that of public sector authorities with water resource management responsibilities. Furthermore, the interests in water are not solely economic with regard to the use of water; instead consideration of social, ecological and cultural values of water are intertwined in decision-making processes. As we approach the boundaries of the planet's freshwater system, it is pertinent to examine the effectiveness and contributions of initiatives and accounting innovations to the organizational and societal use and management of water (Hepworth 2012).

The initiatives and accounting innovations described above involve multiple participants operating in specific contexts, prompting questions about 'ownership', 'responsibility' and 'accountability' with regard to the initiatives themselves, and the wider impacts on water. As responsibilities are (re)distributed among actors in changing water governance, the nature of decision making and the implications of those decisions (see Bakker 2007), and the interests, expertise and responsibilities of the stakeholders involved (Ioris 2008) remain pertinent concerns. Furthermore, it is important to attend to the appropriateness of applying initiatives that originated outwith water resource management and the social, political, environmental and cultural issues that may influence the application of these initiatives. These considerations are part of the 'Pandora's Box', where benefits of corporate engagement with water such as provision of an essential water supply may be countered by risks of policy and regulatory capture by corporations, and the perpetuation of inequities embedded within the initiatives and accounting innovations (Hepworth 2012).

There are a number of common characteristics between initiatives and innovations with accounting practice. Table 13.3 provides an overview of a number of these tools in order to demonstrate the variety and commonality of tools in existence and to identify a range of areas worthy of investigation by accounting scholars. For example, each initiative seeks to support decision making through the production of accounts and the use of technologies that integrate data from a number of sources. Furthermore, there is recognition of stakeholder engagement, particularly with regard to government that draws out questions about accountability regarding social and environmental impacts. Chalmers et al. (2012) suggest

*Table 13.2* A selection of indicators and metrics concerning water

| Issue | Indicator/metric | Source |
|---|---|---|
| Freshwater | EN8: total water withdrawal by source | GRI (2011) |
| | EN9: water resources that are significantly affected by withdrawal of water | G3 Guidance; CDP (2012) |
| | EN10: total volume of water recycled and reused | Guidance |
| Wastewater | EN21: total volume water discharge by quality and destination | |
| | EN25: Identity, size, protected status and biodiversity value of water bodies and related habitats significantly affected by the reporting organization's discharges of water and run-off | |
| | Volumes and costs of water disposed of, including the volumes of waste disposed of in sewerage (details of targets) | Egan and Frost (2010) |
| | Impact of water disposal on external water bodies | |
| Water reduction and efficiency | Water saving achievements, targets, related management control approaches and future plans for making further savings* | |
| | Capital costs of any infrastructure investments designed to save water | |
| Water management and governance (internal to organizations) | percentage of respondents with water policy, strategy or plan in place | CDP Water (2011 Guidance) |
| | percentage of respondents with board-level oversight of policy, strategy or plan | |
| | percentage of respondents with concrete targets or goals in place | |
| Water-related risks and opportunities affecting operations | List the water-stressed regions where you have operations and proposal of total operations in that area (%)* | |
| | Type of risk affecting operations (e.g. flooding, inadequate water infrastructure, regulatory uncertainty, poor water quality)* | |
| | A total proportion of operations that are located in regions at risk (100%) | |
| Water-related risks and opportunities affecting supply chain | Proportion of input or material that comes from a region at risk (%) expressed in units such as value of material purchased, volume or weight of material purchased | |
| Trade-offs between water and carbon | Linkages or trade-offs identified between water and carbon emissions in operations or supply chains * | |
| Connecting water and financial issues | Financial intensity to aggregate or compare water use across businesses that produce different products (Financial output (US$)/volume of water withdrawn, used or discharged [mega-litres]) | |
| | Water intensity to aggregate or compare businesses that have similar products (volume of water used in making product (water unit)/output or volume of product created (product unit) | |
| Water footprint | Total volume of fresh water that is used to produce the goods and services consumed by the individual, community or business. | (Hoekstra *et al.*, 2012) |

*indicates qualitative indicator

Table 13.3 A selection of tools associated with water initiatives

| Title (date launched if available) | Description | Lead organizations or initiative | Intended users | Entities to which tools relate |
|---|---|---|---|---|
| Aqua Gauge Framework (2011) | Aims to inform companies' water management strategies and allow investors to evaluate companies' activities against definitions of leading practice. Features four categories of water practices: 1. Measurement, 2. Management, 3. Stakeholder engagement, 4. Disclosure. | Ceres | Investors Organizations | Organizations |
| Aqueduct Water Risk Atlas (2012) | Publicly available online global database of local-level water risk indicators and global standard for measuring and reporting geographic water risk. Framework for risk assessment is comprised of 1. Access and growth constraints, 2. Cost risks, 3. Disruption potential, and looks across water supply issues, water quality, regulatory pressure, governance, etc. | World Resources Institute | Organizations Governments | Watersheds, organizations |
| GEMI Water Sustainability Planner Tool (2007) | Aims to help companies understand water-related needs and circumstances. Two tools: 1. Assesses companies' relationship to water, identifies associated risks, and describes business case for action. 2. Helps articulate operation or facilitates depending on water and state of local watershed | Global Environmental Water Management Initiative | Organizations | Facilities Organizations Watershed |
| Water footprint (2002) | Aims to allow entities to better understand relationship with watersheds, make informed management decisions and spread awareness of water challenges. Indicator of volume of freshwater consumed and/or polluted to produce goods and services consumed | Water Footprint Network | Individuals Organizations Governments | Products Organizations Watersheds Countries |
| Water Risk Filter (2012) | Online application to analyse impacts of activities on water supply, understand potential risk exposures and obtain ideas for risk mitigation. | WWF and DEG | Organizations Investors Organizations | Facilities Organizations Infrastructure |
| Whole life costing | Designed to facilitate the management of water infrastructure to provide water services. | | | |
| World Business Council's Global Water Tool (2007) | Free online platform that combines corporate water use, discharge and facility information input with watershed and country-level data to map water use and assess risks relative to global operations. | World Business Council for Sustainable Development | Organizations | Facility Organization Watershed Country |

that water accounting has now developed increased salience and is emerging as a discipline in itself, as well as having purchase with water-related policy and practice. These developments are worthy of further investigation particularly with regard to the pathways through which accounting-related concepts and practices are translated and altered in different contexts. By examining the adoption of water accounting practice, and its use in decision making, accounting communities (academic and professional) may identify further possibilities for other forms of natural resources accounting. Such investigations require consideration of the extent to which accounting practice alters the way we know, understand and manage water and relations with each other (Hines 1988, 1991); and more specifically, the implications (for example, theoretical, practical, material, discursive political and ethical) of adapting practices and institutional arrangements associated with financial accounting practice to the use and management of fresh water.

In reviewing initiatives and accounting innovations we can see that such technologies are aligned to catchment entities rather than that of an organization, in accordance with a central tenet of sustainability accounting (Milne and Gray 2007). The distinct nature of water and its connections to wider ecosystems requires us to reconsider ideas of an 'accounting entity' and the associated boundaries that frame accounting. Thus, investigations of water accounting may benefit from considering the implementation of particular technologies across different scales, rather than a singular focus on either the organization or the region. Furthermore, in contrast to a single zooming out of water accounting to align with particular catchments or ecosystems, Hazelton (2013) illustrates that there are multiple accounting technologies for water that sometimes overlap and are connected to particular legislative or regulatory regimes. This illustrates the complex and intertwined nature of decision making for water across various temporal and spatial scales.

In light of this sensitivity of multiple scales, we need to develop approaches to research that recognize and interact with the messiness and complexity of water governance by focusing on the technologies themselves that cross or blur organizational, political, catchment or ecosystem boundaries. In addition, it is important to attend to the specific context in which the technologies are being implemented, the aspects of water governance to which accounting innovations relate (such as those associated with the water sector or water resource management) and the responsibilities of those involved (including environmental protection agencies or local authorities). This frames a consideration of accountability, particularly by whom and how accountability may be discharged through accounts (Hazelton 2013).

The disclosure of water accounts is one mechanism by which water users, and managers of water resources, can discharge accountability with regard to adhering to terms of permits, agreements and associated legislation. Yet such water accounts may not be presented in corporate disclosures, such as annual reports or stand-alone sustainability reports, so that those wishing to investigate use and management of water and associated impacts by organizations may choose to look at alternative sources of information. Thus the particular methodologies for accounting for water, and associated reporting, may differ in accordance with the specific organizations' responsibilities. This has implications for those wishing to access water-related information with regard to the source of such information and its timeliness. Moving beyond the bounds of accounting for water by organizations, we may also want to explore and experiment with the theory and practice of alternative accounts of water. This may involve consideration of the knowledge required to understand water, which includes but may not be limited to that associated with expertise in hydrology, geomorphology, environmental management and engineering, for example. It may also require consideration and engagement with social science, anthropology and political science as part of the exploration of ways of knowing and valuing water; and how this shapes, and is shaped by, accounting practice. In broadening the parameters of what may constitute a water account, the characteristics of the account may differ with regard to the metrics, language(s) and format produced by those with scientific and/or experiential knowledge of water (Strang 2004).

In reviewing the initiatives, there appear to be efforts to standardize approaches and align each initiative within a programme of initiatives to support corporate engagement with water management. Standardization is emerging through collaboration among corporations operating in particular countries rather than being prescribed by national governments. Calls for, and developments in, standardized approaches to water accounting and to corporate engagement attempt to meet the needs required to potentially improve water resource management both within and between organizations. However, further investigation is required in the development of such approaches and how they are tested, refined and implemented in particular contexts with specific water users. Such research would support emergent policy and practice in the field of water resource management (e.g. the development of an International Water Stewardship Standard by the Alliance for Water Stewardship).[13]

Finally, it is pertinent to undertake comparative examinations of voluntary initiatives and certification schemes in the fields of water, carbon and biodiversity. For example, the Water Disclosure Project asks respondents the extent to which each are identified as strategic issues requiring board oversight and consideration of trade-offs between carbon and water in the CDP Guidance (CDP 2012). The GRI indicator EN25 requires organizations to disclose information regarding the identity, size, protected status and biodiversity value of water bodies and habitats affected by discharge and run-off, evidencing some consideration of water use and biodiversity. We find that many water-related initiatives emerge from voluntary programmes involving the CDP and Ceres and the UN Global Compact, which have a record of past engagement in areas of carbon and biodiversity. As examples of sustainability accounting that are emerging in practice, it is important to examine these initiatives for water, carbon and biodiversity, and consider implications for accounting and accountability, and how they may contribute, or hamper, transitions for sustainability.

## Concluding comments

Water is integral to ecosystems, societies, economies and cultures. Organizations, from the public, private and third sector, are dependent on water and influence how it is used, managed and governed. Water resource management can include legislation and policies, educational and awareness campaigns, pricing, technological developments to improve water efficiency and investments in infrastructure. In this chapter, we have sought to identify and describe recent developments in the area of voluntary initiatives and accounting innovations in the water sector and water resource management, focusing primarily on efforts concerning corporations using large volumes of water. In tracing some of the recent developments, we find there is a proliferation of accounting technologies to address challenges with regard to water both in organizations, and in relation to legislative and policy frameworks to support water resource management. Developments in the areas of water sector and water resource management offer many theoretical and empirical opportunities for SEAR, and engagement with practice and policy. There are also opportunities, if not imperatives, to draw on and engage with other disciplines, in both the natural and social sciences. While research is growing in this area, there are two possible streams of further research concerning accounting technologies and accountability.

First, each initiative incorporates accounting technologies to support the collection, interpretation and dissemination of information to support decision making for water resource management. Future research could examine these accounting technologies in organizations, communities or policy agencies using in-depth case studies, within particular water-intensive sectors or across sectors. This research may be the extent to which these technologies shape, mould and influence the use, allocation and management of water; and the short- and long-term environmental, social, economic and cultural impacts for societies and ecosystems. For example, how might an accounting system or accounting technology shape our understandings of water? Would such a system lead us to consider water as a resource similar to other financial assets? Or would the models need to be adjusted, altered or transformed to take account of the fact that it is the particular characteristics of water that make it an 'uncooperative commodity' (Bakker 2004).

Initiatives and accounting innovations are part of ongoing shifts in water governance, raising questions of who are decision makers and how decisions are made – what information is used in decision making, and how decision makers are held to account remains limited (Bakker 2007). As such, accountability in relation to water is another area for future research. For example, research may examine accountability in relation to incidents of water pollution or over-abstraction of water; or consideration of the emergence of different accountability systems in voluntary water governance initiatives; or participatory initiatives within government-led programmes for water resource management.

In conclusion, there are rich opportunities for future research concerning accounts, accounting technologies and accountability, spanning challenges with regard to the use, allocation and management of fresh water. Such research may be orientated towards particular issues and ecosystems, rather than organizational entities, and may require engagement with other researchers, practitioners and communities. As the field of research develops, theoretically, methodologically and empirically, we hope that SEAR continues to contribute to addressing particular freshwater challenges, and broader transitions to sustainability.

## Notes

1 sr65@st-andrews.ac.uk.
2 l.a.lewis@shef.ac.uk.
3 These include *Accounting, Auditing & Accountability Journal*; *Accounting, Organisations & Society*; *Critical Perspectives on Accounting*; and *Social and Environmental Accountability Journal*.
4 Reports and web-based resources concerned review water accounting practice (Adrio 2012; Barton and Morgan-Knott 2010; Morrison *et al.* 2010; UNEP 2011) and water disclosures (for example, CDP 2010, 2011); and proposals for new initiatives (Barton et al. 2011; Hoekstra *et al.* 2011; Irbaris 2009; Shiao *et al.* 2012).
5 For example, the Water Footprint, Neutrality and Efficiency (WaFNE) project aims to engage public and private sectors to collaborate with the United Nations Environment Programme (UNEP) in areas of water use efficiency. The project attends specifically to geographical locations and water intensive sectors such as agrifood, pulp and paper, apparel, chemicals and metals under the aim of ensuring those industries that are highly dependent on water, particularly in developing countries, promote sustainable water use through collaborative public–private partnerships and changes in operations. Further details on this project are available at www.unep.fr/scp/water/WAFNE.htm, accessed 5 November 2012.
6 For example, the UNESCO Institute for Water Education. Further details are available at http://www.unesco-ihe.org/, accessed 5 November 2012.
7 These reports were produced by those engaged in developing corporate responses to sustainability concerns or climate change, including Ceres (available at www.ceres.org, accessed 11 September 2013) and the Carbon Disclosure Project (available at www.cdpproject.net, accessed 11 September 2013).

8  The term 'iwi' may be translated as an extended kinship group or tribe and often refers to a large group of people with common ancestry. (Definition available at http://www.maoridictionary.co.nz/, accessed 11 September 2013).

9  The UNEP Finance Initiative (UNEP FI) aims to understand the impacts of environmental and social considerations on financial performance. Further information is available at www.unepfi.org, accessed 5 November 2012.

10  This figure was published by Global Water Intel which describes itself as a market leader in the provision of high-value information for the water industry. Available at http://www.globalwaterintel.com/home/, accessed 5 November 2012.

11  The United Nations Global Compact is an initiative encouraging businesses to adopt sustainable and socially responsible policies and to report on their implementation. Further information is available at www.unglobalcompact.org, accessed 11 September 2013.

12  Further information on the Water Risk Filter is available at http://waterriskfilter.panda.org/, accessed 11 September 2013. DEG (Deutsche Investitions und Entwicklungsgesellschaft) is a subsidiary of KfW Bank Group, available at https://www.deginvest.de/I, accessed 11 September 2013.

13  The Alliance for Water Stewardship is developing an International Water Stewardship Standard that defines principles, criteria and indicators for water stewardship at a site and catchment level. Further information is available at http://www.allianceforwaterstewardship.org/what-we-do.html#water-stewardship-standard, accessed 11 September 2013.

## Acknowledgement

Thank you to the editors for patience and support during the writing process. Errors remain ours alone.

## References

Adrio, B. 2012. *Clearing the Waters: A Review of Corporate Water Risk Disclosures in SEC Filings.* Boston, MA: Ceres.

Association of Chartered Certified Accountants (ACCA) 2010. Discussion Report. Water: The Next Carbon?, available at http://www2.accaglobal.com/documents/WaterFootprinting.pdf, accessed 30 October 2012.

Bakker, K. 2004. *An Uncooperative Commodity: Privatizing Water in England and Wales.* Oxford: Oxford University Press.

Bakker, K. (ed.) 2007. *Eau Canada—The Future of Canada's Water.* Vancouver, BC: UBC Press.

Barton, B. and Morgan-Knott, S. 2010. *Murky Waters? Corporate Reporting on Water Risk.* Boston, MA: Ceres.

Barton, B., Adrio, B., Hampton, D. and Lynn, W. 2011. *The Ceres Aqua Gauge: A Framework for 21st Century Water Risk Management.* Boston, MA: Ceres.

Bebbington, J. and Larrinaga, C. 2008. Carbon trading: Accounting and reporting issues. *European Accounting Review*, 17(4): 697–717.

Bebbington, J., O'Dwyer, B. and Unerman, J. 2007. Postscript and conclusions, in J. Unerman, J. Bebbington and B. O'Dwyer (eds) *Sustainability Accounting and Accountability.* London: Routledge, pp. 345–9.

Bebbington, J., Kirk, E. A. and Larrinaga, C. 2012. The production of normativity: A comparison of reporting regimes in Spain and the UK. *Accounting, Organizations and Society*, 37(2): 78–94.

Benson, D., Jordan, A., Cook, H. and Smith, L. 2013. Collaborative environmental governance: Are watershed partnerships swimming or are they sinking? *Land Use Policy*, 30(1): 748–57.

Burnett, M. and Welford, R. 2007. Case study: Coca-Cola and water in India: Episode 2. *Corporate Social Responsibility and Environmental Management*, 14(5): 298–304.

Carbon Disclosure Project (CDP) 2010. *CDP Water Disclosure 2010 Global Report.* London: CDP.

Carbon Disclosure Project (CDP) 2011. *CDP Water Disclosure Global Report 2011: Raising Corporate Awareness of Global Water Issues.* London: CDP.

Carbon Disclosure Project (CDP) 2012. *Collective Responses to Rising Water Challenges*. London: CDP.

Cashman, A. 2011. 'Our water supply is being managed like a rumshop': Water governance in Barbados. *Social and Environmental Accountability Journal*, 31(2): 155–66.

Cashman, A. and Lewis, L. 2007. Topping up or watering down? Sustainable development in the privatized UK water industry. *Business Strategy and the Environment*, 105(July 2006): 93–105.

Chalmers, K., Godfrey, J.M. and Lynch, B. 2012. Regulatory theory insights into the past, present and future of general purpose water accounting standard setting. *Accounting, Auditing & Accountability Journal*, 25(6): 1001–24.

Crowther, D., Carter, C. and Cooper, S. 2006. The poetics of corporate reporting: Evidence from the UK water industry. *Critical Perspectives on Accounting*, 17(2–3): 175–201.

Dey, C., Russell, S. and Thomson, I. 2010. Social accounting and the external problematisation of institutional contact: Exploring the potential of shadow accounts, in S. Osbourne and A. Ball (eds) *Social Accounting and Public Management: Accountability for the Public Good*. London: Routledge, pp. 64–75.

Egan, M. 2009. Sydney water sector change and industrial water management. *Journal of Accounting & Organizational Change*, 5(2): 277–93.

Egan, M. and Frost, G. 2010. *Corporate Water Reporting: A Study of the Australian Food, Beverage and Tobacco Sector*. Southbank, VIC: CPA Australia.

Frame, B. 2008. 'Wicked', 'messy', and 'clumsy': Long-term frameworks for sustainability. *Environment and Planning C: Government and Policy*, 26(6): 1113–28.

Future Earth 2013. *Future Earth Initial Design: Report of the Transition Team*. Paris: International Council for Science (ICSU).

Gasson, C. 2011. The case for corporate water. Need to know and analysis. Global Water Intel, September 2011, available at www.globalwaterintel.com/, accessed 31 October 2012.

Georgakopoulos, G. and Thomson, I. 2008. Social reporting, engagements, controversies and conflict in an arena context. *Accounting, Auditing & Accountability Journal*, 21(8): 1116–43.

Gleick, P. H. 2003. Global freshwater resources: The concept of water soft paths. *Science*, 302: 1524–8.

Global Reporting Initiative (GRI) 2011. *Sustainability Reporting Guidelines, version 3.1*. Amsterdam: GRI.

Godfrey, J. M. and Chalmers, K. (eds) 2012. *Water Accounting: International Approaches to Policy and Decision-making*. Cheltenham: Edward Elgar.

Gray, R. 2006. Social, environmental and sustainability reporting and organisational value creation?: Whose value? Whose creation? *Accounting, Auditing & Accountability Journal*, 19(6): 793–819.

Hazelton, J. 2013. Accounting as a human right: The case of water information. *Accounting, Auditing & Accountability Journal*, 26(2): 267–311.

Hepworth, N. 2012. Open for business or opening Pandora's box? A constructive critique of corporate engagement in water policy: An Introduction. *Water Alternatives*, 5(3): 543–62.

Hills, J. and Welford, R. 2005. Case study: Coca-Cola and water in India. *Corporate Social Responsibility and Environmental Management*, 12: 168–77.

Hines, R. 1991. On valuing nature. *Accounting, Auditing & Accountability Journal*, 4(3): 27–9.

Hines, R.D. 1988. Financial accounting: in communicating reality, we construct reality. *Accounting, Organizations and Society*, 13(3): 251–61.

Hoekstra, A.Y., Chapagain, A.K., Aldaya, M.M. and Mekonnen, M.M. 2011. *The Water Footprint Assessment Manual: Setting the Global Standard*, available at: www.waterfootprint.org/downloads/TheWaterFootprintAssessmentManual.pdf, accessed 13 May 2013.

Holley, C. and Gunningham, N. 2011. Natural resources, new governance and legal regulation: When does collaboration work? *New Zealand Universities Law Review*, 24: 309–27.

Hopwood, A., Unerman, J. and Fries, J. 2010 *Accounting for Sustainability: Practical Insights*. London: Earthscan.

Ioris, A. A. R. 2008. Water institutional reforms in Scotland: Contested objectives and hidden disputes. *Water Alternatives*, 1(2): 253–70.

Irbaris, 2009. *CDP Water Disclosure: The Case for Water Disclosure*, London: Irbaris.

Jones, M. and Solomon, J. 2013. Problematising accounting for biodiversity. *Accounting, Auditing & Accountability Journal*, 26(5): 668–87.

Kaika, M. 2003. The water framework directive: A new directive for a changing social, political and economic European framework. *European Planning Studies*, 11(3): 299–316.

Kennedy, S. 2011. Stakeholder management for sustainable development implementation: The case of a sustainable urban drainage system. *Social and Environmental Accountability Journal*, 31(2): 139–53.

Lambooy, T. 2011. Corporate social responsibility: Sustainable water use. *Journal of Cleaner Production*, 19(8): 852–66.

Lankford, B. and Hepworth, N. 2010. The cathedral and the bazaar: Monocentric and polycentric river basin management. *Water Alternatives*, 3(1): 82–101.

Larrinaga, C. and Perez-Chamorro, V. 2008. Sustainability accounting and accountability in public water companies. *Public Money and Management*, 28(6): 337–43.

Lennox, J., Proctor, W. and Russell, S. 2011. Structuring stakeholder participation in New Zealand's water resource governance. *Ecological Economics*, 70(7): 1381–94.

Letza, S. and Smallman, C. 2001. Est in aqua dulci non invidiosa voluptas [In pure water there is a pleasure begrudged by none]: On ownership, accountability and control in a privatized utility. *Critical Perspectives on Accounting*, 12(1): 65–85.

Lewis, L. and Russell, S. 2011. Permeating boundaries : Accountability at the nexus of water and climate change. *Social and Environmental Accountability Journal*, 31(2): 37–41.

McPhail, K. and McKernan, J. 2011. Accounting for human rights: An overview and introduction. *Critical Perspectives on Accounting*, 22(8): 733–37.

Milne, M.J. and Gray, R.H. 2007. Future prospects for corporate sustainability reporting, in J. Unerman, J. Bebbington and B. O'Dwyer (eds) *Sustainability Accounting and Accountability*. London: Routledge, pp. 184–208.

Milne, M. J. and Grubnic, S. 2011. Climate change accounting research: Keeping it interesting and different. *Accounting, Auditing & Accountability Journal*, 24(8): 948–77.

Morikawa, M., Morrison, J. and Gleick, P. 2007. *Corporate Reporting on Water*, available at www.pacinst.org/reports/water_reporting/corporate_reporting_on_water.pdf, accessed 13 May 2013.

Morrison, J., Schulte, P. and Schenck, R. 2010. *Corporate Water Accounting: An Analysis of Methods and Tools for Measuring Water Use and its Impacts*. Oakland CA and Vashon, WA: Pacific Institute and Institute for Environmental Research and Education (IERE).

Neef, A. 2009. Transforming rural water governance: Towards deliberative and polycentric models? *Water Alternatives*, 2(1): 53–60.

Ogden, S. 1995. Transforming frameworks of accountability: The case of water privatisation. *Accounting, Organizations and Society*, 20(2/3): 193–218.

Ogden, S. 1997. Accounting for organisational performance: The construction of the customer in the privatised water industry. *Accounting, Organizations and Society*, 22(6): 529–56.

Ogden, S, 1999. The role of accounting in organizational change: promoting performance improvements in the privatised U.K. water industry. *Critical Perspectives on Accounting*, 10, pp. 91–124.

Ogden, S. and Anderson, F. 1995. Representing customers' interests: The case of the privatised water industry in England and Wales. *Public Administration*, 73: 535–59.

Pahl-Wostl, C. 2009. A conceptual framework for analysing adaptive capacity and multi-level learning processes in resource governance regimes. *Global Environmental Change*, 19: 354–65.

Parker, L. D. 2011. Building bridges to the future: Mapping the territory for developing social and environmental accountability. *Social and Environmental Accountability Journal*, 31(1): 7–24.

Rahaman, A. S., Everett, J. and Neu, D. 2007. Accounting and the move to privatize water services in Africa. *Accounting, Auditing & Accountability Journal*, 20(5): 637–70.

Rittel, H. W. J. and Webber, M. M. 1973. Dilemmas in a general theory of planning. *Policy Sciences*, 4: 155–69.

Rockström, J., Steffen, W. and Noone, K. 2009. A safe operating space for humanity. *Nature*, 461: 472–65.

Russell, S., Frame, B. and Lennox, J. 2011. *Old Problems New Solutions: Navigating Water Governance*. Lincoln, NZ: Landcare Research.

Russell, S.L. and Thomson, I. 2009. Analysing the role of sustainable development indicators in accounting for and constructing a sustainable Scotland. *Accounting Forum*, 33(3): 225–44.

SABMiller and World Wildlife Fund (WWF) 2009. *Water Footprinting: Identifying and Addressing Water Risks in the Value Chain*, available at http://www.sabmiller.com/files/reports/water_footprinting_report.pdf, accessed 30 October 2012.

Shaoul, J. 1997. A critical financial analysis of the performance of privatised industries: The case of the water industry in England and Wales. *Critical Perspectives on Accounting*, (8): 479–505.

Shiao, T., Reig, P., Gassert, F. and Chatikavanij, V. 2012. *Aqueduct Water Risk Atlas – Basin Maps Summary Methodology Document*: Washington, DC: World Resources Institute.

Skipworth, P., Engelhardt, M., Cashman, A., Savic, D., Saul, A. and Walters, G. 2002. *Whole Life Costing for Water Distribution Network Management*. London: Thomas Telford.

Solomon, J. F. and Thomson, I. 2009. Satanic mills? *Accounting Forum*, 33(1): 74–87.

Spence, L. J. and Rinaldi, L. 2012. Governmentality in accounting and accountability: A case study of embedding sustainability in a supply chain. *Accounting, Organizations and Society*, ISSN 0361–3682, available at http://dx.doi.org/10.1016/j.aos.2012.03.003, accessed 19 April 2012.

Steffen, W., Persson, Å., Deutsch, L., Zalasiewicz, J., Williams, M., Richardson, K., Crumley, C. et al. 2011. The anthropocene: From global change to planetary stewardship. *Ambio*, 40(7): 739–61.

Strang, V. 2004. *The Meaning of Water*. New York: Berg.

Thomson, I. 2007. Mapping the terrain of sustainability accounting, in J. Unerman, J. Bebbington and B. O'Dwyer (eds) *Sustainability Accounting and Accountability*. London: Routledge, pp. 19–36.

Tregidga, H. and Milne, M. 2006. From sustainable management to sustainable development: A longitudinal analysis of a leading New Zealand environmental reporter. *Business Strategy and the Environment*, 241: 219–41.

UN CEO Water Mandate 2012. *Corporate Water Disclosure Guidelines: Towards a Common Approach to Reporting*. Oakland, CA: Pacific Institute.

UNEP 2011. *Water Footprint and Corporate Water Accounting for Resource Efficiency*, available at http://www.waterfootprint.org/Reports/UNEP-2011.pdf, accessed 30 March 2013.

UNEP 2012. *Global Environment Outlook 5: Environment for the Future we Want*, available at http://www.unep.org/geo/geo5.asp, accessed at 30 March 2013.

Unerman, J., Bebbington, J. and O'Dwyer, B. (eds) 2007. *Sustainability Accounting and Accountability*. London: Routledge.

United Nations Global Compact (UNGC) 2011. *The CEO Water Mandate: An Initiative by Business Leaders in Partnership with the International Community*. New York: United Nations, available at http://ceowatermandate.org/, accessed 30 March 2013.

UN-Water 2011. *Water in a Green Economy: A Statement by UN-Water for the UN Conference on Sustainable Development*, available at http://www.unwater.org/downloads/UNW_RIOSTATEMENT.pdf, accessed 30 March 2013.

Vardon, M., Lenzen, M., Peevor, S. and Creeser, M. 2007. Water accounting in Australia. *Ecological Economics*, 61(4): 650–9.

Von Schwedler, M. 2011. CSR in the UK water industry: 'Doing the Right Thing'? A case study. *Social and Environmental Accountability Journal*, 31(2): 125–38.

Water Accounting Standards Board (WASB) 2011. *International Water Accounting: Current Practice and Potential Development*. Commonwealth of Australia: Bureau of Meteorology.

World Water Assessment Programme (WWAP) 2009. *The United Nations World Water Development Report 3: Water in a Changing World*. Paris and London: UNESCO and Earthscan.

World Water Assessment Programme (WWAP) 2012. *The United Nations World Water Development Report 4: Managing Water under Uncertainty and Risk*. Paris: UNESCO.

**Part V**

# Conceptual interpretations of accounting for sustainable development

# 14 Legitimating the social accounting project

## An ethic of accountability

*Jesse Dillard*

## Introduction

Philosophically, the social accounting[1] project[2] is, at least on the surface, pragmatic (Gray, 2002), and quite proud of its proclivity for "getting its hands dirty." "If social accounting is anything, it is the opening of new spaces, of new accountings, not simply reacting to old ones. The project seeks engagement and the changing of practice. Imagining, engagement, and change practice are not easy activities to undertake" (Gray, 2002: 698). Though there is much debate,[3] generally those pursuing the project recognize the need to change current accounting techniques and practices to include new descriptions, an expanded set of events, and a more inclusive user group. Environmental accounting provides an example. The new descriptions should include the effects of organizational action on the natural system. This would require expanding the relevant set of events recognized by the accounting system to include descriptions of such events as greenhouse gas emissions. The primary user set expands beyond the shareholders to include a broader set of affected constituencies, including future generations.

The practitioners of social accounting seem more oriented toward action than theorizing, and given the current rate of deterioration in both the natural and social systems, such a position seems imminently logical. However, there appears to be a growing affinity with social theory,[4] especially that typically characterized as alternative/critical.[5] The social accounting project is enhancing, and reaffirming, a growing awareness that the objectives of a sustainable natural and social world are probably not attainable within the current context of global market capitalism. The unfettered demand of capital markets for growth and wealth accumulation subordinates all other objectives. The social accounting project has experienced frustrations with creating and implementing more complete accountings for organizations that recognize and report on their rights and responsibilities to various constituencies. Alternative/critical accounting studies provide support for this position. However, there is an obvious and irre-solvable tension between the practicalities of a new accounting and the ideological purity of the philosophical basis upon which one might be constructed.[6]

With this in mind, I wish to consider a philosophical frame within which the social accounting project might be situated. This includes considering the pragmatic philosophical perspective as well as elaborating on its critical energy. The next major section, A Philosophical Framework for the Social Accounting Project, identifies acting in the public interest as the fundamental legitimating criterion for the social accounting project and proposes an ethic of accountability as a legitimating basis upon which the project might move forward. A discussion of the rights and responsibilities of the accounting profession and the accounting academy related to the social accounting project comprise the closing remarks.

## A philosophical framework for the social accounting project

Gray (2002) states that the social accounting project is a response to Medawar (1976), empowered by Bronner (1994). From an implementation perspective, Medawar, taking a pointedly pragmatic and practical perspective, argues that precise measurement and objectivity in reporting should not be allowed to impede the implementation of social accounting, while independence is critical. Critical theory provides the theoretical and philosophical base for the social accounting project. As discussed in Bronner, critical theory holds that through critique people can come to understand and live in more enlightened ways. The process and possibilities associated with this critique and the necessary engagement provide the energizing dimensions of the social accounting project.[7] Thus, from a philosophical perspective, it seems appropriate to consider the pragmatic groundings of the project and then to explore sustainability, accounting, and accountability through a critical theory lens. The following discussion attempts to provide a more complete articulation.

### A pragmatic perspective

Pragmatism[8] is "a philosophy that stresses the relation of theory to praxis and takes the continuity of experience and nature as revealed through the outcome of directed action as the starting point for reflection" (Audi, 1995: 638). Subject and object are constituted and reconstituted within, and because of, the flow of lived experience. Truth can only be determined by the outcome of inquiry and cannot be derived apart from the contextually defined goals and values. Knowledge is an instrumental tool that constitutes the basis for discerning truth. Thus, truth claims are validated through experience, and, as such, truth is subject to revision.

Generally following Burrell and Morgan's (1979)[9] philosophy of science typology, ontology[10] can be positioned along a continuum from subjective to objective. Epistemology[11] is specified along a continuum from positivist to anti-positivist. Human nature is viewed as ranging from determinist to voluntarist, and applicable methodologies range from ideographic to nomothesistic. As a point of reference, functionalism is the predominant category of traditional accounting research[12] suggesting that, to varying degrees, it is philosophically objectivist, positivist, deterministic, and nomothesist. This presumes that there is an external world separate and distinct from the observer and that world can be known through empirical exploration and measurement. Although a majority of the empirical based social accounting studies, especially the work evaluating the information content and economic effects of social and environmental reporting, fall into this category, the social accounting literature has spanned the spectrum of alternative approaches and theories.[13] There is a growing recognition that reality may be, at least at some level, socially constructed, and interpretivist type methodologies such as case studies and in depth interviews are being more extensively employed.[14] This expanding horizon naturally follows with the centrality of critique to the project's energy and direction.

Consistent with its pragmatic nature, the current body of social accounting research appears to be somewhat inconsistent with respect to the philosophy of science underpinnings. Take, for example, the environment. There is little doubt that it exists separately from the human beings who are destroying it at an unprecedented rate. How could such a world be socially constructed? However, human beings understand this world through their shared perceptions and as such construct and reconstruct it in their own image – an objective world, subjectively reconstructed.[15]

Critical theory provides the theoretical context for the social accounting project and is predicated on metaphysical, and therefore contestable, values such as justice, equity, and trust. These values are realized through a process of enlightenment, empowerment, and emancipation. The philosophical dimensions of critical theory are a mirror image of the functionalist perspective. A comparison of the alternative perspectives provides insights and a synthesis whereby the social accounting project can continue to move in a direction of enhancing the human condition through harmonizing the relationships between human beings and the natural systems and among those who inhabit the social systems they create.

### The social accounting project as a critical undertaking

Following Gray (2002), critical theory provides the empowering theoretic of the social accounting project. In a previous essay (Dillard, 1991), I concluded that, given the capture of conventional accounting by financial capital, it seemed impossible to consider accounting to be an instrumental means for emancipatory action. That is, can accounting as currently practiced assist members of society in gaining enlightenment, empowerment, and emancipation?[16] However, if conventional accounting represents a subset of what is here termed social accounting, and if the social accounting project can accurately be described as being on the "frontiers of environmental and social justice" (Gray, 2002: 689) with its principal justification being "in its emancipatory and radical possibilities," then such a conclusion may warrant review.

Critical theory sees understanding as a means for facilitating a society so configured as to foster the realization of its human potential, whereas the traditional functionalist perspective sees understanding as an end in itself. Critical theory ontology is a subjective one where the social world is created and recreated by the social actors. The epistemology is anti-positivist. It makes the voluntaristic assumption that individuals possess agency, and thus can act otherwise if they so choose. Following the ontological and epistemological positions, the preferred methodological approach focuses on subjective and historical accounts of actions and events by the individuals carrying out the actions and living through the events.

Applying critical theory as an empowering philosophy provides insights into social accounting's idealized objectives, a basis for designing research and application programs as well as a set of criteria by which progress can be measured. Human agency is central, and self-understanding provides the motivating factor as well as the guiding force for change. Human beings are presumed to be estranged from their natural and intended state of existence. Under the capitalist mode of production, human beings, just as with all other resources, are means to the ends of economic growth and wealth accumulation. An individual's worth is only that which is reflected in the market value of the person's commodified labor. Thus, the individual is estranged from him or herself, from their fellow human beings, and the natural system within which they live. The natural and intended state is that human beings live in harmony with themselves, with the other members of society, and with the natural system. This is accomplished through self-reflection motivated by the insights gained from a more realistic understanding of one's current physical and social existence as well as an appreciation of future possibilities. Individuals gain emancipation through empowerment that is motivated by enlightenment. Each step results in a change within the actor as well as within their social context. While traditionally critical theory has been concerned with the revolutionary praxis at a societal level, Laughlin (1987, 1988) has applied these ideas to the study of accounting and accountability systems.[17] Following Habermas (1984, 1987), recognized as the current leading critical theorist (e.g., see Held, 1980; White, 1988), Laughlin's analysis focuses on the emancipatory potential of language.

Following Fay (1987), critical theory can be described using four related components that concern the interrelationships between individual self perceptions and social practices and institutions. These form the context and means by which change is brought about. The four primary categories are characterized as: false consciousness, crisis, education, and transformative action. If social accounting is to be empowered by these ideas, the ideas must be understood and addressed in research and applications projects.

## False consciousness

Critical theory is based on the assumption of self-estrangement. Self-estrangement presumes that human existence is comprised of two spheres. One is that manifested in one's conscious understanding of the everyday activities and the other is embedded within ideologically prescribed social structures and hidden from view within the unconscious. Self-estrangement concerns the way self-understandings are artificial and, at times, incoherent. As a result, the lived experience is needlessly frustrating and opaque, leading to unsatisfying and in some situations detrimental, modes of existence. Through critique (enlightenment), these illusions must be recognized in order to overcome the false consciousness that is impeding growth and fulfillment. Critical theory presumes that the ideological critique will reveal alternatives superior to the prevailing social context. As the enlightened understanding of the social context expands, the individual recognizes that preferable alternatives are possible and conceives of means for attaining them. As a result, one's existence becomes more satisfying, increasing the likelihood of realizing one's full potential. For example, the prevailing neoliberal ideology, at least implicitly, purports that the good of society can best be achieved through the success of economic organizations (i.e., corporations); therefore, what is good for the corporation is good for the individual.

## Crisis

Crises that spur change are presumed to be inherent within the extant social system. These perturbations provide a stimulus for self-reflection and inquiry that reveal the nature and causes inherent within the prevailing social systems. An understanding of the genesis of crisis includes a historical appreciation of how the interaction between social structures and false consciousness results in crisis. Under the current social order, alienation and social instability cannot be overcome because of individual false consciousness coupled with the basic organization of society. The current environmental crisis is an example. Over the years, the dominant neoliberal ideology claims that the allocation of scarce resources is best carried out through market regimes. As such, there has been a general abdication of moral responsibility, allowing markets, and those who operate within them, to make the requisite and responsible trade-offs between current and future benefits and costs incurred from the exploitation of natural resources. The growing evidence of climate change and the uneven impact on various groups has forced some to reevaluate the neoliberal assumptions upon which the "business case" (market) solution is predicated.

## Education

Education makes people aware of the possibility for change. This awareness arises out of the self-awareness and the recognition of crises, revealing shared beliefs and possible means for changing the beliefs. Initial conditions as well as the mechanisms for emancipatory enlightenment are specified. Within the context and limitations of rational reflection, necessary and sufficient conditions for emancipatory change are specified, and the likelihood of realizing these conditions through critical analysis increases. Here, social and environmental accounting

(SEA) can play an important role in making transparent the effects of corporate action on the environment. From this expanded understanding, new alternative organizational structures and action sets may emerge or be evaluated.

## Transformative action

The preceding categories are primarily concerned with informing and motivating transformative action by revealing the alienating aspects of life and what must be changed if reconciliation is to be achieved. Transformative action requires a program indicating how, and by whom, emancipatory change can be brought about. In order to appropriately resolve crises, the conditions for the requisite changes in self perception and in social organizations must be specified followed by a plan of action including a program for its implementation. The resulting social transformations bring about emancipatory change at both the individual and corporate levels. This would precipitate and characterize the social accounting project whereby new accounting and accountability regimes are developed and implemented. The basis for the transformational programs moves beyond the neoliberal market focus to include the critical elements associated with the long-term viability of social and ecological systems. These programs might emerge from within the democratic structures that facilitate contested polylogical dialogue and debate (e.g., Brown, 2009; Brown and Dillard, 2013a; Dillard and Brown, 2012).

## Limitations

As we contemplate the application of critical theory in facilitating the social accounting project, we must be cognizant of, and attentive to, the theory's limitations. The efficacy of human reason in initiating change is central to critical theory; ideas represent the sole determinant of behavior, and clarity of vision leads to emancipatory action. If these assumptions do not hold, the means for overcoming oppression and alienation are not operative. These assumptions have their limitations, which are relevant to the theory's constructive application to social accounting. There appear to be limits on the extent to which human beings are, or can be, activists within given institutional contexts, thus limiting the effect of enlightenment. Due to the inherent indeterminacy of human existence and the historicity and physicality of human situatedness, human beings cannot achieve the level of self clarity necessary for the rational analysis presumed as the basis for enlightened understanding leading to emancipatory action. Humans are always already active participants and perpetuators of the emerging existence and as such cannot overcome this situatedness by stepping outside of their circumstances as required for rational analysis. Internally, somatically acquired traits and dispositions are not necessarily accessible or modifiable through mental processes. Externally applied force can also be a significant impediment to individual emancipation, with death being the ultimate impediment to a satisfying and fulfilled existence. Further, there are severe limitations in the, at least implicit, assumption that freedom equates with happiness or that freedom necessarily leads to consensus of opinion or action following from collective autonomy.

In summary, the energetic and pragmatic approach taken by the social accounting project is compatible with, and a consequence of, its acquaintance with critical theory. While there are significant limitations, they do not negate the value of critical theory as a useful theoretic. What it does suggest is the need to incorporate a theoretical formulation that explicitly considers the interaction of the agent with the social structures that enable and constrain the realization of enlightenment, empowerment, and emancipation as well as the conflicts and antagonisms inherent within the extant social systems. The dispersion and diversity of the current offerings seem to suggest a need at this point to become more attentive to the project's moral groundings and how they might be useful in legitimating and organizing social accounting, providing a framework for developing, focusing, and evaluating this ongoing research program. Thus, one might conclude that critical theory as an empowering philosophical basis, while reflecting the passion and critique of "critical theory and its theorists," could do with just a bit more development. I propose the collective public interest responsibilities as one dimension along which this development might proceed in that it is a common evaluation criterion for both individual action and societal structures.

## The legitimating criteria of social accounting

Acting in the public interest is acting so as to enhance the well being of society within the context of sustainable natural, social, and economic systems. The moral legitimacy of the social accounting project both individually and societally rests on acting in the public interest. Not only does acting in the public interest provide the moral context wherein an action or activity is contemplated and legitimized, it also represents a central tenet of social integration.[18] Acting in the public interest represents a central component of an individual or a profession's social and professional responsibility and legitimizes the distinguishing characteristics of the social relationships by articulating rights, privileges, and status.

The object of the social accounting project has been primarily business or work organizations, generally corporations.[19] Within this context, the purpose of social accounting is to assist these organizations in fulfilling their public interest responsibility. Business organizations represent one of the primary institutions within western societies and play a central role in ensuring the long-term viability of a democratically governed society grounded in justice, equality, and trust and supported by sustainable natural, social, and economic systems. Organizational management is specifically granted fiduciary responsibility over society's economic resources.[20] By exercising these rights, an *ethic of accountability* is established whereby the actor agrees to being held accountable by those who grant these rights, and those who grant the rights accept the responsibility for holding the recipients accountable for the related outcomes. Providing relevant and understandable information is a necessary condition for being held accountable. In addition, accountability requires that actual outcomes be evaluated relative to a set of relevant criteria. The grantors of the rights are also responsible for establishing the evaluation criteria used in holding the organizations accountable. Care must be taken so that the evaluation criteria reflect the norms and values of the society, not those of special interests or those in power.

### An ethic of accountability[21]

An ethic of accountability situates the actor as a member of an ongoing community and consists of four primary elements: solidarity, interpreted actions, the contemplated action, and accountability. Solidarity refers to the ongoing, situated, purposeful interrelatedness of human agents as they act as members of social and natural systems. Social solidarity recognizes that action takes place within the context of an ongoing community. Natural solidarity recognizes that action of human agents[22] also takes place within, and has an effect on, natural systems. Interpreted action refers to the recognition that moral behavior requires the actor to be aware of the historic and physical interrelatedness of events as evidenced by observed outcomes from previous acts with respect to their effect on both social and natural systems. Contemplated action refers to actor's deliberations with respect to the act to be carried out.

As a member of an ongoing community, the actor is obliged to consider the anticipated act and its propriety in light of the projected effect as judged by the effect of past actions and the anticipated implications for members of the community. An ethic of accountability requires a moral act to be preceded by a serious and conscious consideration of the physical and historical context within which an act is to be carried out. The actor acts within, and as a responsible member of, an ongoing community, accepting the right of the community to require an account of both process and outcome. In turn, the community accepts its responsibility to hold the actor accountable. A part of this process includes establishing and implementing, through enlightened democratic processes, evaluation criteria, as well as effective monitoring mechanisms and reporting requirements.[23]

Conceptually, an ethic of accountability is not a one time, isolated event, but an ongoing conversation between that actor and all affected parties, carried out within a sustaining, and sustainable, community. An ethic of accountability does not seek "the good" in a utilitarian sense or "the right" in a deontological sense, though both are consistent with the ideal. The good and the right are delineated as part of the process of determining the appropriate action within the ongoing community. An ongoing community presumes sustainable natural and social systems.

Fitting action as well as the act of holding accountable depends upon open and trustworthy discourse between the actor and the community members as well as among the community members themselves. A preliminary condition in implementing an ethic of accountability requires the stipulation of what constitutes legitimate communal dialogue whereby the rights and responsibilities of all community members are recognized. The level of trustworthiness among the actors is developed as a result of ongoing interactions and is central to establishing a sense of loyalty and responsibility. If the communal discourse is controlled by powerful, self-interested agents who exploit the social and physical resources to achieve self serving objectives, an ethic of accountability becomes impossible, and its pretense becomes a means for manipulation and exploitation with any possibility of solidarity destroyed.

Following Habermas (1984: 92–104), legitimate communication provides the basis for ethical action. Communication is legitimate if it satisfies the follow three validity claims:

1. propositional validity – (physical) concerns the correspondence between the claim and the external or objective evidence and requires the speaker to provide the grounds upon which the claim is being made;
2. normative validity – (social) concerns the degree to which the claim is consistent with the extant social norms and requires the speaker to provide justification;
3. subjective authenticity – (personal) concerns the correspondence between perceived and actual intent of the speaker and relates to the extent that a claim is genuine, as opposed to strategic/manipulative. The speaker is required to prove her or his trustworthiness.

These claims define the conditions under which an ethic of accountability can be successfully pursued.

Clearly, these conditions are restrictive and difficult to obtain.[24] Nonetheless, they represent criteria for initiating and sustaining meaningful and ongoing dialogue among members of an ongoing community seeking to identify and carry out moral courses of action. Inability to satisfy these validity claims calls into question the veracity of the communal discourse, thus imposing limiting conditions on the operationalization of an ethic of accountability. Alternatively, actors (e.g., work organizations) committed to acting sustainably can use these criteria as guidelines for facilitating open discussion and community dialogue. For example, emerging issues arise from, and relate to, unique contextual circumstances. Legitimate communal dialogue provides the means for selecting and prioritizing interests and outcomes, with alternatives chosen based on the strength of the better argument.

Seriously implementing an ethic of accountability results in an expanded scope of behavior alternatives, a framework for setting priorities, more widely understood and accepted sets of evaluation criteria, and a higher likelihood of successful applications. The process does not prescribe a set of generally applicable rules but emphasizes the importance of context and accountability in issues associated with sustainability and thus related to the social accounting project.

### The action space

A social accounting project based on an ethic of accountability as discussed above presumes that to act in the public interest requires the explicit consideration of natural, social, and economic systems. Natural systems provide the context and the sustenance for social systems and social systems provide the context and objectives for economic systems. All three systems must be respected, nurtured, and sustained, and an ethic of accountability requires that accountability systems address all three. The social accounting project sees the accounting profession's responsibility as facilitating and monitoring organizational management in carrying out their fiduciary responsibility with respect to the natural, social, and economic systems. As such, accountants are concerned with the integrity and accountability of reporting and administrative systems and those who design, implement, and use them.

The social accounting project presumes that the academic accounting community has a responsibility to facilitate, and engage in, dialogue among members of the community regarding accounting's (the profession, the professionals, the systems) and organizational management's public interest responsibilities. Accountants, the business community, members of academy, and representatives of the civil community have a responsibility to engage in and sustain this discourse. Applying the tenets of critical theory, the action space of the accounting academic related to the social accounting project includes scholarly activities leading to enlightenment, educational innovation leading to empowerment, and community action/interaction facilitating emancipation.

### Enlightenment

In developing and implementing an ethic of accountability, the expertise of faculty, students, and the business and civil communities can be brought together to identify and consider the critical public interest issues associated with sustainability and accountability. At a general level, the quest for enlightenment deems it important to identify critical sustainability issues and responsibilities facing accounting and organizational management. Such an undertaking requires an appreciation of the historical and current role of organization management, accounting, the accounting profession, and accounting systems. This entails studying these within the current and historical economic, political, social, ecological, and organizational contexts, utilizing a broad range of methodologies, addressing a wide variety of research topics.

Much of the extant research contributes to a more complete understanding with respect to the availability, use, and implications of social and environmental information.[25] For example, a significant portion of the empirical work addresses publicly reported information and the associated market and stakeholder reactions (for a review see Thomson, 2007, also Deegan, 2002). Internally, the related research considers the social and environmental implications of the interplay between autonomy and control within work organizations and the related technological (scientific as well as administrative) applications such as material conversion processes as well as budget and management control systems (see Thomson, 2007, Deegan, 2002, and Mathews, 1997 for a review of the work in these areas).

The research agenda must continue to enlighten our understanding of issues surrounding the social accounting project. Sustainability issues should become an integral part of corporate governance, especially as these issues relate to legislation and regulation; and the scope of disclosure should include any affected constituency, past, present, and future.[26] Management information systems, of which social and environmental accounting systems are a part, must provide information relevant for effectively managing a sustainable organization. Also, in designing these systems, issues such as the social consequences of information access, implications for creating human capabilities, as well as the moral implications of technological applications must be considered.

*Empowerment*

Empowerment follows from enlightenment as the deeper understanding is conveyed to members of the ongoing community. The social accounting project is concerned with applying appropriate tools for constructing the sustainability related issues facing accounting and organizational management.[27] Community members gain an appreciation of current and historical context within which their life situation is enacted as well as the associated rights and responsibilities. The educational process also provides the means for identifying and developing new opportunities for responsible and responsive development especially as they relate to sustainability and accountability. This requires innovative thinking in terms of pedagogy, course, program, and curriculum development, as well as the accompanying teaching materials, case studies, and related research.[28]

The key to empowerment is critique. A realization of possibilities comes from critique of the current state of affairs. Critique must be embedded within educational undertakings that facilitate an appreciation of the complexities associated with the interface between organizations and social and natural systems. Relative to the social accounting project, this implies a much broader range of knowledge, transcending the understanding of rules and traditional practices. A social accounting approach integrates social and ecological literacy and technical competence with a deep understanding of the complex responsibilities of accounting to organizations, society, and the environment. For example, empowerment integrates an appreciation of the source and situatedness of professional roles, implicit and explicit multiple associated constituencies and responsibilities, and their interrelatedness with natural and social systems.

*Emancipation*

Emancipation is brought about through action carried out by enlightened members of the ongoing community that follows from their expanded appreciation of the possibilities and necessities arising from the new understandings. Within the context of this discussion, action facilitating sustainability through accountability follows from, and facilitates, enlightened and sustained discourse within the ongoing community.[29] Action is directed toward creating, identifying, and acting on opportunities for advancing the cause of sustainability, both environmental and social. All members of the community share these responsibilities. Emancipation is the result of an enabling and ongoing dialogue among all relevant constituents and becomes evident in actions to bring the anticipated world order to fruition through active engagement.

## Closing remarks

Social accounting includes all other accountings, both manifest and imagined. The legitimacy of the social accounting project is grounded in a responsibility to act in the public interest. Acting in the public interest recognizes the critical interrelationship among the natural, social, and economic systems. An ethic of accountability provides the legitimating justification for the social accounting project, and pragmatism provides the operational framework whereby the social accounting project is to be realized. Upon these tenets accountants' and accountings' moral obligations for a sustainable society are based, and a general plan for action can be formulated. The following are means consistent with these tenets whereby the social accounting project may be facilitated.

In light of the heightening awareness of the accelerating degradation of both social and natural systems, a larger segment of society appears to recognize the criticality of social and environmental sustainability. As one of the primary societal institutions, organizations are situated within, and dependent upon, both natural and social systems. If those responsible for managing these organizations are not keenly aware and held accountable for both, they cannot adequately address the risks, opportunities, and responsibilities associated with their actions. Given the constraints of global market capitalism and business' historical stance and traditional intransigence, we must seriously question organizational management's ability, motivation, and commitment to act in the public interest working toward a more sustainable society. While laws and regulations have begun to codify society's expectations, they cannot substitute for a genuine ethic of accountability accepted by all parties and supported by a comprehensive system of accountability.

Those associated with external auditing and related activities have a direct and unambiguous responsibility for rendering the actions of organizations transparent by facilitating the provision of relevant, reliable, and understandable information by the reporting entity to external and internal constituencies. Those associated with accounting in its organizationally related applications serve the ethic of accountability by providing the information necessary for others to understand the entities' actions and to hold those responsible for the outcomes. For example, the accounting function prepares communications used by creditors, owners, sponsors, contributors, employees, unions, managers, politicians, regulators, and society. All have the right to expect objective, understandable, and honest reporting by the entity and the responsible business professional.

The controllership function is a primary administrative component charged with ensuring that the organization fulfills its fiduciary responsibilities to society, responsibilities that extend substantially beyond the legal requirements stated in a corporate charter or codified in laws and regulations. To adequately fulfill the societal responsibilities, processes and associated reporting and administrative systems must be designed and implemented that safeguard social and environmental systems as well as economic ones. The social accounting project envisions that the controllership function will take a leading role in developing and implementing these information systems.

Relatedly, internal auditing and management accounting activities involve recognizing risks associated with legal, financial, social, and environmental implications of an organization's activities. Those associated with the collection and conveyance of organizational information enjoy a unique opportunity, and responsibility, to identify and communicate activities and behaviors that jeopardize or enhance the organization's ability to carry out its responsibilities. Social and environmental accounting issues should be at the forefront of these efforts.

Members of the accounting academy must recognize and embrace the scope and interdisciplinarity of the social accounting project, ensuring that it is represented in the accounting curriculum and in their research programs. As scholars, we must accept our responsibility as the thought leaders of society, recognizing that it is critique that energizes the social accounting project; and where appropriate help to more fully and clearly articulate the rights and responsibilities implicated in an ethic of accountability, building strategic alliances with other interested groups. If these responsibilities are embraced by those who teach and practice accounting, there is a modicum of hope that a social accounting can transcend the current constraints of its neoclassical economic proclivities and respond with an enabling and sustaining accounting grounded in an ethic of accountability.

## Notes

1   In the following discussion, this term is used as a collective to include sustainability, accounting, and accountability; also see Gray and Bebbington (2002).
2   The social accounting project refers to the work undertaken by a loosely connected, international network of social and environmental accounting academics and practitioners. See Dillard and Brown (2012); Gray and Bebbington (2002).
3   See Adams and Larrinaga-González (2007); Bebbington et al. (2007a, 2007b); Brown (2009, 2010); Burritt and Schaltegger (2010); Cooper et al. (2005); Dillard and Brown (2012); Dillard and Roslender (2011); Everett (2004, 2007); Everett and Neu (2000); Gray (2002, 2007, 2010); Gray et al. (2009); Lehman (2001, 2010); Neu et al. (2001); Owen (2008); Parker (2005, 2011); Shenkin and Coulson (2007); Spence (2009); Spence et al. (2010); Tinker and Gray (2003); Tinker et al. (1991).
4   For example, see Archel et al. (2011); Bebbington et al. (2007b); Brown (2009, 2010); Brown and Dillard (2013a); Dillard and Brown (2012); Everett (2004); Gray et al. (2010); Lehman (2010); Shenkin and Coulson (2007); Spence (2007, 2009).
5   Roslender and Dillard (2003) suggest that the alternative/critical project is far from a coherent project and care should be given in appropriating the label. Here, I reserve the term critical theory in referring to a particular branch of neomarxist social theory originally associated with the Frankfurt School (see Bronner, 1994; Held, 1980; White, 1988). Critical accounting studies include those studies that are motivated by the recognized need for radical politically motivated change. Alternative accounting studies are those providing a critique of the status quo without a specific political program.
6   For example, see Lehman (1995, 1996, 1999, 2001); Puxty (1991); Tinker and Gray (2003); Tinker et al. (1991); Spence (2007, 2009).
7   However, Bronner (1994) notes a general reluctance on the part of its advocates to participate in actual engagements.
8   This discussion follows from Audi (1995: 638–9).
9   See Chua (1986), Hopper and Powell (1985), Laughlin and Lowe (1989), Roberts and Scapens (1985) for a discussion of associated limitations.
10  Ontology refers to what there is to know. For example, is there an objective world to be discovered or is there only a subjectively created artifact?
11  Epistemology refers to how one comes to know what there is to know. Can one come to know the world through precise measurement and observation, or does one come to know the world through abstract mental reasoning?
12  A casual review of what some consider the traditional research journals (e.g., *The Accounting Review, Accounting Horizons*, etc.) in accounting will confirm this observation.
13  See Adams and Larrinaga (2007); Deegan (2002); Gray (2002, 2010); Gray and Laughlin (2012); Parker (2011); Mathews (1997).
14  See Archel et al. (2009); Bebbington (1997); Bebbington et al. (1999); Bebbington et al. (2007a, 2007b); Dey (2007); Everett (2004); Everett and Neu (2000); Georgakopoulos and Thomson (2007); Gray (1992, 2002); Gray and Milne (2004); Gray et al. (1997); Lehman (1995, 1996, 1999, 2001); O'Dwyer (2003, 2005, 2011); Power (1991, 1997); Tinker et al. (1991).
15  See Searle (1995) for a philosophical discussion of these permutations and combinations.

16  These attributes are relevant for enhancing the human condition with respect to both social and natural systems.
17  Also see Broadbent and Laughlin (1997, 1998); Broadbent et al. (1991); Laughlin (2007); Power and Laughlin (1996).
18  Social integration means facilitating individuals coming together and working together to accomplish common goals.
19  See Adams and Larrinaga (2007); Burritt and Schaltegger (2010); Deegan (2002); Gray (2010); Mathews (1997); Parker (2005, 2011).
20  These include natural, human, financial, and technological resources.
21  These ideas follow from Niebuhr's (1963) Responsibility Ethic as developed in Dillard and Yuthas (2001).
22  The focus is on the human agent as the only purposeful actor.
23  These ideas are not inconsistent with various forms of stakeholder theory such as normative stakeholder theory (Donaldson and Preston, 1995) and provide a moral grounding for them.
24  See Brown and Dillard (2013b) for a discussion of these debates as they relate to social and environmental accounting.
25  A complete review of the areas considered in the extant literature as well as the important areas in need of consideration is beyond the scope of this discussion. See, for example, Burritt (2012); Burritt and Schaltegger (2010); Deegan (2002); Gray (2002, 2004, 2010); Gray and Bebbington (2002); Gray and Laughlin (2012); Mathews (1997); Parker (2005, 2011); Thomson (2007).
26  For example, see the work by Owen et al. (2000, 2001) concerning stakeholder involvement.
27  For example, see Bebbington and Gray (2001) and Gray et al. (1997).
28  For work directly applying the ideas included in critical theory to education and educational processes see particularly Bebbington (1997); Thomson and Bebbington (2004, 2005).
29  Gray and Bebbington (2002) provide an illustration of the current social and environmental accounting practices as well as the substantial opportunities with respect to implementing the social accounting project.

## References

Adams, C.A. and Larrinaga-González, C. 2007. Engaging with organisations in pursuit of improved sustainability accounting and performance. *Accounting, Auditing and Accountability Journal.* 20(3): 333–55.

Archel, P., Husillos, J., Larrinaga, C. and Spence, C. 2009. Social disclosure, legitimacy theory and the role of the state. *Accounting, Auditing and Accountability Journal.* 22(8): 1284–307.

Archel, P., Husillos, J. and Spence, C. 2011. The institutionalisation of unaccountability: Loading the dice of Corporate Social Responsibility discourse. *Accounting, Organizations and Society.* 36(6): 327–43.

Audi, R. (ed.) 1995. *The Cambridge Dictionary of Philosophy.* Cambridge: Cambridge University Press.

Bebbington, J. 1997. Engagement, education and sustainability: A review essay on environment accounting. *Accounting, Auditing and Accountability Journal.* 10: 365–81.

Bebbington, J. and Gray, R. 2001. An account of sustainability: Failure, success and a reconceptualization. *Critical Perspectives on Accounting.* 12(5): 557–87.

Bebbington, K.J., Gray, R.H. and Owen, D.L. 1999. Seeing the wood for the trees: Taking the pulse of social and environmental accounting. *Accounting, Auditing and Accountability Journal.* 12(1): 47–51.

Bebbington, J., Brown, J. and Frame, B. 2007a. Accounting technologies and sustainability assessment models. *Ecological Economics.* 61(2/3): 224–36.

Bebbington, J., Brown, J., Frame, B. and Thomson, I. 2007b. Theorizing engagement: The potential of a critical dialogic approach. *Accounting, Auditing and Accountability Journal.* 20(3): 356–81.

Broadbent, J. and Laughlin, R. 1997. Developing empirical research: An example informed by a Habermasian approach. *Accounting, Auditing and Accountability Journal.* 10(5): 622–48.

Broadbent, J. and Laughlin, R. 1998. Resisting the "new public management": Absorption and absorbing groups in schools and GP practices in the UK. *Accounting, Auditing and Accountability Journal.* 11(4): 403–35.

Broadbent, J., Laughlin, R. and Read, S. 1991. Recent financial and administrative changes in the NHS: A critical theory analysis. *Critical Perspectives on Accounting.* 2(1): 1–29.

Bronner, S. 1994. *Of Critical Theory and its Theorists.* Oxford: Blackwell.

Brown, J. 2009. Democracy, sustainability and dialogic accounting technologies: Taking pluralism seriously. *Critical Perspectives on Accounting.* 20(3): 313–42.

Brown, J. 2010. Accounting and visual cultural studies: Potentialities, challenges and prospects. *Accounting, Auditing and Accountability Journal.* 23(4): 482–505.

Brown, J. and Dillard, J. 2013a. Agonizing over engagement: SEA and the "Death of Environmentalism" debates. *Critical Perspectives on Accounting.* 24(1): 1–18.

Brown, J. and Dillard, J. 2013b. Critical accounting and communicative action: On the limits of consensual deliberation. *Critical Perspectives on Accounting.* 24(3): 176–90.

Burrell, G. and Morgan, G. 1979. *Social Paradigms and Organizational Analysis.* London: Heinemann.

Burritt, R. and Schaltegger, S. 2010. Sustainability accounting and reporting: Fad or trend? *Accounting, Auditing and Accountability Journal.* 23(7): 829–46.

Chua, W. 1986. Radical developments in accounting thought. *The Accounting Review.* 61(4): 601–32.

Cooper, C., Taylor, P., Smith, N. and Catchpowle, L. 2005. A discussion of the political potential of social accounting. *Critical Perspectives on Accounting.* 16(7): 951–74.

Deegan, C. 2002. The legitimizing effect of social and environmental disclosures – a theoretical foundation. *Accounting, Auditing and Accountability Journal.* 15(3): 282–311.

Dey, C. 2007. Social accounting at Traidcraft plc: A struggle for the meaning of fair trade. *Accounting, Auditing and Accountability Journal.* 20(3): 423–45.

Dillard, J. 1991. Accounting as a critical social science. *Accounting, Auditing, and Accountability Journal.* 4(1): 8–28.

Dillard, J. and Brown, J. 2012. Agonistic pluralism and imagining CSEAR into the future. *Social and Environmental Accounting Journal.* 32(1): 3–16.

Dillard, J. and Roslender, R. 2011. Taking pluralism seriously: Embedded moralities in management accounting and control systems. *Critical Perspectives on Accounting.* 22(3): 135–47.

Dillard, J. and Yuthas, K. 2001. A responsibility ethic of audit expert systems. *Journal of Business Ethics.* 30: 337–59.

Donaldson, T. and Preston, L. 1995. The stakeholder theory of the corporation: Concepts, evidence and implications. *Academy of Management Journal.* 20: 65–91.

Everett, J. 2004. Exploring (false) dualisms for environmental accounting praxis. *Critical Perspectives on Accounting.* 15: 1061–84.

Everett, J. 2007. Fear, desire, and lack in Deegan and Soltys's social accounting research: An Australasian perspective. *Accounting Forum.* 31(1): 91–7.

Everett, J. and Neu, D. 2000. Ecological modernization and the limits of environmental accounting. *Accounting Forum.* 24(1): 5–30.

Fay, B. 1987. *Critical Social Science.* Ithaca, NY: Cornell University Press.

Georgakopoulos, G. and Thomson, I. 2008. Social reporting, engagements, controversies and conflict in an arena context. *Accounting, Auditing and Accountability Journal.* 28(8): 1116–43.

Gray, R. 1992. Accounting and environmentalism: An exploration of the challenge of gently accounting for accountability, transparency, and sustainability. *Accounting Organizations and Society.* 17(5): 399–425.

Gray, R. 2002. The social accounting project and *Accounting, Organizations and Society*: Privileging engagement, imaginings, new accountings and pragmatism over critique? *Accounting, Organizations and Society.* 27: 687–709.

Gray, R. 2004. Why is social accounting so difficult? Part 1. *Social and Environmental Accounting Journal.* 24(1): 12–17.

Gray, R. 2007. Taking a long view on what we now know about social and environmental accountability and reporting. *Issues in Social and Environmental Accounting.* 1(2): 169–98.

Gray, R. 2010. Is accounting for sustainability actually accounting for sustainability … and how would we know? An exploration of narratives of organisations and the planet. *Accounting, Organizations and Society*. 35: 47–62.

Gray, R. and Bebbington, J. 2002. *Accounting for the Environment* (2nd edn). London: Sage Publications.

Gray, R. and Laughlin, R. 2012. It was 20 years ago today. *Accounting, Auditing and Accountability Journal*. 25(2): 228–55.

Gray, R. and Milne, M.J. 2004. Towards reporting on the triple bottom line: Mirages, methods and myths, in A. Henriques and J. Richardson (eds) *The Triple Bottom Line: Does it All Add Up?* London: Earthscan, pp. 70–80.

Gray, R., Dey, C., Owen, D., Evans, R. and Zadek, S. 1997. Struggling with the praxis of social accounting: Stakeholders, accountability, audits and procedures. *Accounting, Auditing and Accountability Journal*. 10(3): 325–64.

Gray, R., Dillard, J. and Spence, C. 2009. Social accounting as if the world matters. *Public Management Review*. 11(5): 545–73.

Gray, R., Owen, D. and Adams, C. 2010. Some theories for social accounting?: A review essay and a tentative pedagogic categorisation of theorisations around social accounting, in B. Jaggi and M. Freedman (eds) *Sustainability, Environmental Performance and Disclosures (Advances in Environmental Accounting and Management*, vol. 4). Bingley, Yorks: Emerald Group, pp. 1–54.

Habermas, J. 1984. *The Theory of Communicative Action*, vol. I. Trans. T. McCarthy. Boston, MA: Beacon Press.

Habermas, J. 1987. *The Theory of Communicative Action*, vol. II. Trans. T. McCarthy. Boston, MA: Beacon Press.

Held, D. 1980. *Introduction to Critical Theory: Horkheimer to Habermas*. Berkeley, CA: University of California Press.

Hopper, T. and Powell, A. 1985. Making sense of research into the organizational and social aspects of management accounting: A review of its underlying assumptions. *Journal of Management Studies*. 22(5): 429–65.

Laughlin, R. 1987. Accounting systems in organizational contexts: A case for critical theory. *Accounting, Organizations and Society*. 12(5): 479–502.

Laughlin, R. 1988. Accounting in its social context: Analysis of the accounting systems of the church of England. *Accounting, Auditing, and Accountability Journal*. 1(2): 19–42.

Laughlin, R. 2007. Critical reflections on research approaches, accounting regulation and the regulation of accounting. *British Accounting Review*. 39(4): 271–89.

Laughlin, R. and Lowe, A. 1989. A critical analysis of accounting thought: Prognosis and prospects for understanding and changing accounting systems, in D. Cooper and T. Hopper (eds) *Critical Accounting*. New York: Macmillan, pp. 15–43.

Lehman, G. 1995. A legitimate concern for environmental accounting. *Critical Perspectives on Accounting*. 6(6): 393–412.

Lehman, G. 1996. Environmental accounting: Pollution permits or selling the environment. *Critical Perspectives on Accounting*. 7(6): 667–76.

Lehman, G. 1999. Disclosing new worlds: A role for social and environmental accounting and auditing. *Accounting, Organizations and Society*. 24(3): 217–42.

Lehman, G. 2001. Reclaiming the public sphere: Problems and prospects for corporate social and environmental accounting. *Critical Perspectives on Accounting*. 12(6): 713–33.

Lehman, G. 2010. Perspectives on accounting, commonalities and the public sphere. *Critical Perspectives on Accounting*. 21(8): 724–38.

Mathews, R. 1997. Twenty-five years of social and environmental accounting research. *Accounting, Auditing, and Accountability Journal*. 10(4): 481–531.

Medawar, C. 1976. The social audit: A political view. *Accounting, Organizations and Society*. 1(4): 389–94.

Neu, D., Cooper, D.J. and Everett, J. 2001. Critical accounting interventions. *Critical Perspectives on Accounting*. 12(6): 735–62.

Niebuhr, R. 1963. *The Responsible Self.* San Francisco, CA: Harper Press.

O'Dwyer, B. 2003. Conceptions of corporate social responsibility: The nature of managerial capture. *Accounting, Auditing and Accountability Journal.* 16(4): 523–57.

O'Dwyer, B. 2005. The construction of a social account: A case study in an overseas aid agency. *Accounting, Organizations and Society.* 30(3): 279–96.

O'Dwyer, B. 2011. The case of sustainability assurance: Constructing a new assurance service. *Contemporary Accounting Research.* 28(4): 1230–66.

Owen, D. 2008. Chronicles of wasted time? A personal reflection on the current state of, and future prospects for, social and environmental accounting research. *Accounting, Auditing and Accountability Journal.* 21(2): 240–67.

Owen, D., Swift, T., Humphrey, C. and Bowerman, M. 2000. The new social audits: Accountability, managerial capture or the agenda of social champions? *European Accounting Review.* 9(1): 81–98.

Owen, D., Swift, T. and Hunt, K. 2001. Questioning the role of stakeholder engagement in social and ethical accounting. *Accounting Forum.* 25(3): 264–82.

Parker, L.D. 2005. Social and environmental accountability research: A view from the commentary box. *Accounting, Auditing and Accountability Journal.* 18(6): 842–60.

Parker, L.D. 2011. Twenty-one years of social and environmental accountability research: A coming of age. *Accounting Forum.* 35(1): 1–10.

Power, M. 1991. Auditing and environmental expertise: Between protest and professionalization. *Accounting, Auditing & Accountability Journal.* 4(3): 30–42.

Power, M. 1997. Expertise and the construction of relevance: Accountants and the environmental audit. *Accounting, Organizations and Society.* 22(2): 123–46.

Power, M. and Laughlin, R. 1996. Habermas, law and accounting. *Accounting, Organizations and Society.* 21(5): 441–65.

Puxty, A.G. 1991. Social accountability and universal pragmatics. *Advances in Public Interest Accounting.* 4: 35–45.

Roberts, J. and Scapens, R. 1985. Accounting systems and systems of accountability – understanding accounting practices in their organizational context. *Accounting, Organizations and Society.* 10(4): 443–56.

Roslender, R. and Dillard, J. 2003. Reflections on the interdisciplinary perspectives on accounting project. *Critical Perspectives on Accounting.* 14(3): 325–52.

Searle, J. (1995). *The Construction of Social Reality.* New York: The Free Press.

Shenkin, M. and Coulson, A. 2007. Accountability through activism: Learning from Bourdieu. *Accounting, Auditing and Accountability Journal.* 20(2): 297–317.

Spence, C. 2007. Social and environmental reporting and hegemonic discourse. *Accounting, Auditing and Accountability Journal.* 20(6): 855–82.

Spence, C. 2009. Social accounting's emancipatory potential: A Gramscian critique. *Critical Perspectives on Accounting.* 20(2): 205–27.

Spence, C., Husillos, J. and Correa-Ruiz, C. 2010. Cargo cult science and the death of politics: A critical review of social and environmental accounting research. *Critical Perspectives on Accounting.* 21(1): 76–89.

Thomson, I. 2007. Mapping the terrain of sustainability accounting, in J. Unerman, J. Bebbington and B. O'Dwyer (eds) *Sustainability Accounting and Accountability.* London: Routledge, Ch. 1, pp. 19–36.

Thomson, I. and Bebbington, J. 2004. It doesn't matter what you teach? *Critical Perspectives on Accounting.* 15(4/5): 609–28.

Thomson, I. and Bebbington, J. 2005. Social and environmental reporting in the UK: A pedagogic evaluation. *Critical Perspectives on Accounting.* 16(5): 507–33.

Tinker, T. and Gray, R. 2003. Beyond critique of pure reason: From policy to policies to praxis in environmental and social accounting. *Accounting, Auditing, and Accountability Journal.* 16(5): 727–61.

Tinker, T., Lehman, C. and Neimark, M. 1991. Falling down the hole in the middle of the road: Political quietism in corporate social accounting. *Accounting, Auditing, and Accountability Journal.* 4(2): 28–54.

White, S. 1988. *The Recent Works of Jurgen Habermas.* New York: Cambridge University Press.

# 15 An overview of legitimacy theory as applied within the social and environmental accounting literature

*Craig Deegan* ( 2014)

## Introduction

This chapter provides an overview of legitimacy theory as applied within the social and environmental accounting literature. In doing so it first defines *organizational legitimacy* and describes how organizational legitimacy can be considered to be a *resource* that is necessary to the survival of an organization. We then proceed to describe legitimacy theory as a *positive theory* that embraces a *systems-oriented perspective* and which is often considered as being derived from *political economy theory*.

Often linked to legitimacy theory is the theoretical construct known as the *social contract*. We will explore the meaning of the *social contract* and discuss how compliance with it is often considered as essential for establishing and maintaining *organizational legitimacy*. We will consider the implications that will flow should an organization breach its 'social contract' and we will describe the strategies that managers of organizations might adopt should the social contract be perceived as violated.

We will briefly review a number of studies that have utilized legitimacy theory to explain corporate motivations for disclosing social and environmental information. We will also question whether organizations that appear to be behaving in accordance with legitimacy theory are actually acting in the broader interests of society. We will conclude the chapter by considering some of the limitations of legitimacy theory and some future research directions.[1]

## Organizational legitimacy – what is it?

From an organization's perspective, *legitimacy* has been defined by Lindblom (1993, p. 2) as:

> a condition or status which exists when an entity's value system is congruent with the value system of the larger social system of which the entity is a part. When a disparity, actual or potential, exists between the two value systems, there is a threat to the entity's legitimacy.

Legitimacy is a relative concept – it is relative to the social system in which the entity operates and is *time* and *place* specific. As Suchman (1995, p. 574, emphasis in the original) states:

> 'Legitimacy is a generalised perception or assumption that the actions of an entity are desirable, proper, or appropriate *within* some socially constructed system of norms, values, beliefs, and definitions.'

Legitimacy can be considered as a *resource* upon which an organization is dependent for survival (Dowling and Pfeffer, 1975; O'Donovan, 2002). It is something that is conferred upon the organization by society, and it is something that is desired or sought by the organization. However, unlike many other 'resources', it is a resource that the organization is considered able to impact or manipulate through various disclosure-related strategies. Proponents of legitimacy theory would suggest that whenever managers consider that the supply of the particular resource – *legitimacy* – is vital to organizational survival, then they will pursue strategies to ensure the continued supply of that resource. Strategies aimed at gaining, maintaining, or repairing legitimacy (often referred to as legitimation strategies) typically rely upon targeted disclosures.

For an organization seeking to be legitimate (and therefore in compliance with community expectations) it is not the *actual* conduct of the organization that is important, it is what society collectively knows or *perceives* about the organization's conduct that shapes legitimacy. As Suchman (1995, p. 574) states:

> An organisation may diverge dramatically from societal norms yet retain legitimacy because the divergence goes unnoticed. Legitimacy is socially constructed in that it reflects a congruence between the behaviours of the legitimated entity and the shared (or assumed shared) beliefs of some social group; thus legitimacy is dependent on a collective audience, yet independent of particular observers.

Consistent with the view that legitimacy is based on *perceptions*, Nasi *et al.* (1997, p. 300) state:

> A corporation is legitimate when it is judged to be 'just and worthy of support' (Dowling and Pfeffer, 1975). Legitimacy therefore is not an abstract measure of the 'rightness' of the corporation but rather a measure of societal perceptions of the adequacy of corporate behaviour (Suchman, 1995). It is a measure of the attitude of society toward a corporation and its activities, and it is a matter of degree ranging from highly legitimate to highly illegitimate. It is also important to point out that legitimacy is a social construct based on cultural norms for corporate behaviour. Therefore, the demands placed on corporations change over time, and different communities often have different ideas about what constitutes legitimate corporate behaviour.

## What 'type' of theory is legitimacy theory?

Legitimacy theory has been utilized by researchers, particularly social and environmental accounting researchers, when seeking to explain *why* corporate management undertake certain actions – such as disclosing particular items of social and environmental information. It is not a theory that is used to provide prescription about what management *ought* or *should* do. Hence, it is generally accepted that legitimacy theory is a *positive theory* (it seeks to explain or predict particular managerial activities).

Legitimacy theory has also been described as a systems-based theory. According to Gray *et al.* (1996, p. 45): 'a systems-oriented view of the organisation and society…. permits us to focus on the role of information and disclosure in the relationship(s) between organisations, the State, individuals and groups'.

Within a systems-oriented perspective (also sometimes referred to as an open-systems perspective), the entity is assumed to be influenced by, and in turn, to have influence upon, the society in which it operates. Within a broader systems-oriented perspective, the perceptions of the organization, as held by other parties within that social system, are of importance to the survival of the organization. Commenting on the use of open-systems theorizing Suchman (1995, p. 571) states:

> Open-system theories have reconceptualised organisational boundaries as porous and problematic, and institutional theories (Powell and DiMaggio, 1991) have stressed that many dynamics in the organisational environment stem not from technological or material imperatives, but rather, from cultural norms, symbols, beliefs and rituals. Corporate disclosure policies are considered to represent one important means by which management can influence external perceptions about their organisation. At the core of this intellectual transformation lies the concept of organisational legitimacy.

Suchman (1995) also identifies that studies of legitimacy seem to fall within two distinct groups, these being the *strategic* and the *institutional* groups. In explaining the difference, Suchman (1995, p. 572) states:

> Work in the strategic tradition ... adopts a managerial perspective and emphasizes the ways in which organisations instrumentally manipulate and deploy evocative symbols in order to garner societal support. In contrast, work in the institutional tradition ... adopts a more detached stance and emphasises the ways in which sector-wide structuration dynamics generate cultural pressures that transcend any single organisation's purposive control.

The vast majority of research that has utilized legitimacy theory, and which has focused on social and environmental or sustainability reporting, has been informed by the strategic (or managerial) perspective of legitimacy theory in which actions are taken to legitimate a particular organization within a particular (given) social system – and this will be the focus of this chapter.[2] Nevertheless, it needs to be appreciated that a relatively limited number of researchers have used the tenets of legitimacy theory to show how actions (such as government or corporate disclosures) can be used more broadly to legitimize certain practices, processes, or 'institutions' within society (for example, see Archel *et al.*, 2009).

Legitimacy theory (which we have so far described as a positive, systems-based theory which can have either a managerial or an institutional focus) originates from another theory – political economy theory. According to Deegan (2014, p. 341, emphasis in the original):

> The 'political economy' itself has been defined by Gray *et al.* (1996, p. 47) as 'the social, political and economic framework within which human life takes place'. Political economy theory explicitly recognises the power conflicts that exist within society and the various struggles that occur between various groups within society. The perspective embraced in political economy theory, and also in legitimacy theory, is that *society*, *politics* and *economics* are inseparable and economic issues cannot meaningfully be investigated in the absence of considerations about the political, social and institutional framework in which the economic activity takes place. It is argued that by considering the *political economy* a researcher is better able to consider broader (societal) issues which impact how an organisation operates, and what information it elects to disclose.

Following on from the above point, Guthrie and Parker explain the relevance of accounting within a political economy perspective. They state (1990, p. 166): 'The political economy perspective perceives accounting reports as social, political, and economic documents. They serve as a tool for constructing, sustaining, and legitimising economic and political arrangements, institutions, and ideological themes which contribute to the corporation's private interests.'

Consistent with the view that organizations are part of a broader social system, the perspectives provided by legitimacy theory (which, as stated, are fundamentally built upon foundations provided by political economy theory) indicate that organizations are not considered to have any inherent right to resources. Organizations exist to the extent that the particular society considers that they are *legitimate*, and if this is the case, the society 'confers' upon the organization the 'state' of *legitimacy*. If 'society' considers that organizations are not legitimate then this will have potential implications for the ongoing support and survival of the organization.

While legitimacy theory is considered to derive from political economy theory, political economy theory itself has two broad branches. Legitimacy theory is derived from one of these branches. As Deegan (2014, p. 342) states:

> Political Economy Theory has been divided (perhaps somewhat simplistically, but nevertheless usefully) into two broad streams which Gray *et al.* (2010, p. 20) have labelled 'classical' and 'bourgeois' political economy. Classical political economy is related to the works of philosophers such as Karl Marx, and explicitly places 'sectional (class) interests, structural conflict, inequity, and the role of the State at the heart of the analysis' (Gray *et al.*, 2010, p. 20). This can be contrasted with 'bourgeois' political economy theory which, according to Gray *et al.* (1995, p. 53), largely ignores these elements and, as a result, is content to perceive the world as essentially pluralistic.

Classical political economy would tend to explain corporate disclosures as being a tool that powerful individuals (perhaps those in control of capital) use to maintain their own positions to the detriment of those individuals without power (for example, workers). Classical political economy focuses on the structural conflicts within society.[3]

By contrast, legitimacy theory – which is often seen as being embedded in the 'bourgeois' branch of political economy theory – does not consider or question structural or class-based conflicts within society. It assumes that the views of a reasonably unified and pluralistic society shape the activities of organizations.[4] It is the failure to consider class struggles that has fuelled criticisms of legitimacy theory from many researchers working from within the critical perspective of accounting.

Hence, to this point we can summarize the above discussion by noting that:

- Within legitimacy theory, the resource of importance is *organizational legitimacy*.
- Legitimacy theory is a *positive* theory.
- Legitimacy theory is a *systems-oriented* (or open-system) theory.
- Legitimacy theory has a *managerial branch* and an *institutional branch*, with most of the related research in the social and environmental accounting literature being informed by the managerial branch.
- Legitimacy theory, as applied by many social and environmental accounting researchers, derives from the *bourgeois branch* of political economy theory, and as a result typically assumes a *pluralistic society*.

It should also be stressed that legitimacy theory has many similarities with another theory frequently used within the social and environmental accounting literature – this being stakeholder theory – which in itself is considered to have a managerial and ethical branch.

Stakeholder theory (from the managerial branch) provides a view that organizations will react to the demands of those stakeholder groups that control resources necessary to the organization's operations (deemed to be 'powerful stakeholders') and will tend to disregard the concerns of those groups without power.[5] As Ullmann (1985, p. 2) states: 'Our position is that organisations survive to the extent that they are effective. Their effectiveness derives from the management of demands, particularly the demands of interest groups upon which the organisation depends.'

According to stakeholder theory, the disclosure of particular types of information can be used to gain or maintain the support of particular groups. That is, corporate disclosure is a strategy for managing, or perhaps *manipulating*, the demands of particular groups (Gray *et al.*, 1996).

Because of the many similarities between stakeholder theory and legitimacy theory, any attempt to treat them as sharply discrete theories would be wrong. As Deegan and Blomquist (2006) state:

> Both theories [legitimacy theory and stakeholder theory] conceptualize the organisation as part of a broader social system wherein the organisation impacts, and is impacted by, other groups within society. Whilst legitimacy theory discusses the expectations of society in general (as encapsulated within the 'social contract'), stakeholder theory provides a more refined resolution by referring to particular groups within society (stakeholder groups). Essentially, stakeholder theory accepts that because different stakeholder groups will have different views about how an organisation should conduct its operation, there will be various social contracts 'negotiated' with different stakeholder groups, rather than one contract with society in general. Whilst implied within legitimacy theory, stakeholder theory explicitly refers to issues of stakeholder power, and how a stakeholder's relative power impacts their ability to 'coerce' the organisation into complying with the stakeholder's expectations.

Legitimacy theory also has many similarities with institutional theory. Indeed, Deegan (2014) argues that institutional theory provides a useful complement to both legitimacy theory and stakeholder theory. Specifically, Deegan (2014, p. 386) states:

> A key reason why institutional theory is relevant to researchers who investigate voluntary corporate reporting practices is that it provides a complementary perspective, to both stakeholder theory and legitimacy theory, in understanding how organisations understand and respond to changing social and institutional pressures and expectations. Among other factors, it links organisational practices (such as accounting and corporate reporting) to the values of the society in which an organisation operates, and to a need to maintain organisational legitimacy. There is a view that organisational form and practices might tend towards some form of homogeneity – that is, the structure of the organisation (including the structure of its reporting systems) and the practices adopted by different organisations tend to become similar to conform with what society, or particular powerful groups, consider to be 'normal' … Organisations that deviate from being of a form that has become 'normal' or expected will potentially have problems in gaining or retaining legitimacy.

While we will not pursue further discussion of stakeholder theory or institutional theory, those individuals interested in applying legitimacy theory should make the effort to consider the many similarities legitimacy theory has with both stakeholder theory and institutional theory. It should also be noted that if we consider the 'richness' of institutional theory, and all that it can offer, then we might find, as some authors suggest, that institutional theory provides all of the insights that legitimacy theory provides, plus even more (Ji, 2013).[6] Nevertheless, legitimacy theory provides a more focused or narrow perspective of the strategic management role of corporate activities and it has appeared to provide a high level of explanatory power in terms of explaining corporate social and environmental disclosure.

Returning to legitimacy theory, one theoretical construct that is very important to the utilization of legitimacy theory is the 'social contract', which we will now discuss.

## The social contract and its relevance to legitimacy theory

A central premise of legitimacy theory is that organizations can maintain their operations only to the extent that they have the support of the community. Such support is earned as a result of the organization being *perceived* by society as complying with the expectations of the society with which they interact. While researchers outside of the social and environmental accounting literature do not tend to link legitimacy with compliance to the 'social contract', the two have tended to be linked within the social and environmental accounting literature. That is, within the social and environmental accounting literature expectations that society has with regards to how an entity shall act are often considered to constitute the *social contract* negotiated between the organization and society. Specifically, it is considered that an organization's survival will be threatened if society perceives that the organization has breached its social contract. As Deegan (2014, p. 346, emphasis in the original) states:

> Where society is not satisfied that the organisation is operating in an acceptable, or *legitimate* manner, then society will effectively revoke the organisation's 'contract' to continue its operations. This might be evidenced through, for example, consumers reducing or eliminating the demand for the products of the business, factor suppliers eliminating the supply of labour and financial capital to the business, or constituents lobbying government for increased taxes, fines or laws to prohibit those actions which do not conform with the expectations of the community.

It is emphasized that the social contract is a theoretical construct, and hence an individual cannot simply go out and find a copy of the contract. Different managers will have different perceptions about how society expects the organization to behave across the various attributes of its activities – and this in itself can explain, at least in part, why some managers will elect to do things differently from other managers. If a manager undertakes certain actions that are subsequently found to be unacceptable to the community (for example, sourcing clothing from Asian 'sweatshops' – an issue that recently outraged many people within the community) then legitimacy theory would explain this in terms of the manager misinterpreting the terms of the social contract. Consider the implications for Nike, GAP and other clothing and footwear manufacturers when the media ran campaigns about their association with various abusive 'sweatshops'.

The social contract is considered to be made up of numerous terms (or clauses) – some explicit and some implicit. As Deegan (2014, p. 346) states:

> Gray *et al.* (1996) suggest that legal requirements provide the explicit terms of the contract, while other non-legislated societal expectations embody the implicit terms of

the contract. That is, there is an imperfect correlation between the law and societal norms (as reflected in the social contract) and according to Dowling and Pfeffer (1975), there are three broad reasons for the difference. First, even though laws are reflective of societal norms and values, legal systems are slow to adapt to changes in the norms and values in society. Second, legal systems often strive for consistency whereas societal norms and expectations can be contradictory. Third, it is suggested that while society may not be accepting of certain behaviours, it may not be willing or structured enough to have those behavioural restrictions codified within law. It is in relation to the composition of the implicit terms of the 'contract' that we can expect managers' perceptions to vary greatly.[7]

## Implications of corporate non-compliance with the social contract

According to Deegan (2014), the term 'legitimacy gap' has been utilized to describe the situation where there appears to be a lack of correspondence between how society believes an organization *should* act and how it is *perceived* that the organization has acted. In relation to how legitimacy gaps arise, Sethi (1977) describes two major sources of the gaps. First, societal expectations might change, and this will lead to a gap arising even though the organization is operating in the same manner as it always has. As an example of this source of a legitimacy gap, Nasi *et al.* (1997, p. 301) state:

> For American tobacco companies in the 1970s, for example, the increasing awareness of the health consequences of smoking resulted in a significant and widening legitimacy gap (Miles and Cameron,1982). The tobacco companies had not changed their activities, and their image was much the same as it had been, yet they suddenly faced a significantly different evaluation of their role in society; they faced a significant and widening legitimacy gap.

As we have already emphasized, community expectations are not considered static, but rather, change across time thereby necessitating the organization to be responsive to current and future changes to the environment in which they operate. While organizations might modify their behaviour to conform with community expectations, if the momentum of their change is slower than the changing expectations of society, then legitimacy gaps will arise.

Legitimacy itself can be threatened even when an organization's performance is not deviating from society's expectations of appropriate performance. This might be because the organization has failed to make disclosures that show it is complying with society's expectations, which in themselves might be changing across time. That is, legitimacy is assumed to be influenced by disclosures of information, and not simply by (undisclosed) changes in corporate actions. If society's expectations about performance change, then arguably an organization will need to show that what it is doing is also changing (or perhaps it will need to explicitly communicate and justify why its operations have *not* changed). In relation to the dynamics associated with changing expectations, Lindblom (1993, p. 3) states:

> Legitimacy is dynamic in that the relevant publics continuously evaluate corporate output, methods, and goals against an ever evolving expectation. The legitimacy gap will fluctuate without any changes in action on the part of the corporation. Indeed, as expectations of the relevant publics change the corporation must make changes or the

*Shadow reports ?.*

legitimacy gap will grow as the level of conflict increases and the levels of positive and passive support decreases.

The second major source of a legitimacy gap, according to Sethi (1977), occurs when previously unknown information becomes known about the organization – perhaps through disclosure being made within the news media. In relation to this possibility, Nasi *et al.* (1997, p. 301) make an interesting reference to 'organizational shadows'. They state:

> The potential body of information about the corporation that is unavailable to the public – the corporate shadow (Bowles, 1991) – stands as a constant potential threat to a corporation's legitimacy. When part of the organisational shadow is revealed, either accidentally or through the activities of an activist group or a journalist, a legitimacy gap may be created.

In relation to the above source of a legitimacy gap, we can consider how society reacted to media revelations made about certain sportswear companies alleged to be sourcing products from sweatshops in Asia (for example, Nike); revelations about the pollution being caused by mining companies' tailings dams in remote environments (for example, BHP Billiton's operations in Papua New Guinea); or revelations about how the products of particular companies impact consumer health (for example, the reaction to the McDonalds investigation as told in the movie *Supersize Me*). All these revelations arguably had significant cost implications for the respective companies involved – and to solve the legitimacy problems the organizations typically relied upon various disclosure strategies. However, the legitimacy-threatening activities were potentially going on for years before the news media ran stories on the adverse social and environmental activities – it was the news media coverage that ultimately created the threats to the corporations, not necessarily the actions themselves.

## How will an organization respond when a legitimacy gap is perceived to exist?

Much of the work that has been undertaken within the social and environmental accounting area, and which has embraced legitimacy theory, has typically addressed actions undertaken by organizations to *regain* their legitimacy after some form of legitimacy threatening event occurs. Indeed, legitimacy theory was refined and used by social and environmental accounting researchers who had a fascination with understanding and explaining why companies were voluntarily making social and environmental disclosures within such media as annual reports. Because corporations internationally appeared to significantly increase their social and environmental disclosures from around the late 1980s this was also the time when research aimed at understanding the disclosure started to boom.

As authors such as Suchman (1995) and O'Donovan (2002) indicate, legitimation strategies might be used to either *gain, maintain,* or *repair* legitimacy. According to O'Donovan (2002, p. 349): 'Legitimation techniques/tactics chosen will differ depending upon whether the organisation is trying to gain or extend legitimacy, to maintain its current level of legitimacy, or to repair or to defend its lost or threatened legitimacy.'

While researchers have proposed that legitimation tactics might differ depending upon whether the entity is trying to *gain, maintain,* or *repair* legitimacy, the theoretical development in this area remains weak. Although the literature provides some general commentary, there is a lack of guidance about the relative effectiveness of legitimation strategies with regards to either gaining, maintaining or regaining legitimacy. In terms of the general commentary provided within the literature, gaining legitimacy occurs when an organization moves into a new area of operations in which it has no past reputation. In such a situation the organization suffers from the 'liability of newness' (Ashforth and Gibbs, 1990) and it needs to proactively engage in activities to win acceptance.

The task of *maintaining* legitimacy is typically considered easier than *gaining* or *repairing* legitimacy (Ashforth and Gibbs, 1990; O'Donovan, 2002). One of the 'tricks' in maintaining legitimacy is to be able to anticipate changing community perceptions. According to Suchman (1995, p. 594), strategies for maintaining legitimacy fall into two groups – forecasting future changes, and protecting past accomplishments. In relation to monitoring or forecasting changing community perceptions, Suchman (1995, p. 595) states:

> Managers must guard against becoming so enamored with their own legitimating myths that they lose sight of external developments that might bring those myths into question. With advanced warning, managers can engage in pre-emptive conformity, selection, or manipulation, keeping the organisation and its environment in close alignment; without such warning, managers will find themselves constantly struggling to regain lost ground. In general, perceptual strategies involve monitoring the cultural environment and assimilating elements of that environment into organizational decision processes, usually by employing boundary-spanning personnel as bridges across which the organization can learn audience values, beliefs, and reaction.

In relation to protecting past (legitimacy enhancing) accomplishments, Suchman (1995, p. 595) states:

> In addition to guarding against unforeseen challenges, organizations may seek to buttress the legitimacy they have already acquired. In particular, organizations can enhance their security by converting legitimacy from episodic to continual forms. To a large extent this boils down to (a) policing internal operations to prevent miscues, (b) curtailing highly visible legitimation efforts in favour of more subtle techniques, and (c) developing a defensive stockpile of supportive beliefs, attitudes and accounts.

In relation to *maintaining* legitimacy, the greater the extent to which the organization trades on its level of legitimacy, the more crucial it will be for that organization to ensure that it does not deviate from the high standards that it has established. Conversely, the less 'legitimacy' an existing organization has to begin with, the less it needs to maintain. As Deegan states:

> For example, compare an armaments manufacturer with, say, The Body Shop (a shop that had developed a reputation for sound social and environmental practices). The products of armaments manufacturers are designed to kill – such an organisation arguably has less to worry about in terms of its legitimacy than The Body Shop. The Body Shop [had, for many years, traded on a] reputation for caring about the environment, society and the welfare of animals. If, perhaps, an organisation within the supply chain of The Body Shop—and without the knowledge of the Body Shop—undertook activities that were somehow related to animal testing or with particular environmental damage, and such facts were found out by the media, for example, then this could be extremely costly to the organisation. It has a lot of *investment in legitimacy* to lose.
>
> (2014, p. 350, emphasis in the original)

In considering *repairing* legitimacy, Suchman (1995, p. 597) suggests that related legitimation techniques tend to be reactive responses to often unforeseen crises. In many respects, *repairing* and *gaining* legitimacy are similar. As O'Donovan (2002, p. 350) states:

> Repairing legitimacy has been related to different levels of crisis management (Davidson, 1991; Elsbach and Sutton, 1992). The task of repairing legitimacy is, in some ways, similar to gaining legitimacy. If a crisis is evolving proactive strategies may need to be adopted, as has been the case for the tobacco industry during the past two decades (Pava and Krausz, 1997). Generally, however, the main difference is that strategies for repairing legitimacy are reactive, usually to an unforeseen and immediate crisis, whereas techniques to gain legitimacy are usually *ex ante*, proactive and not normally related to crisis.

In the discussion that follows we will consider the strategies that can be used by corporate management in an effort to *gain*, *maintain*, or *regain* legitimacy. As we have already indicated, our theoretical development has not developed sufficiently to link specific legitimation techniques with efforts to either gain, maintain, or regain legitimacy. Most of the proposed legitimation techniques appear to relate to regaining legitimacy in the light of particular crises – something that has tended to be the focus of many researchers working within the social and environmental accounting area (and who embrace legitimacy theory). Nevertheless, all legitimation strategies rely upon disclosure.

In considering organizational strategies for maintaining or creating congruence between the social values implied by an organization's operations, and the values embraced by society, we can usefully apply the insights provided by Dowling and Pfeffer (1975). Dowling and Pfeffer outline the means by which an organization, when faced with legitimacy threats, may legitimate its activities (1975, p. 127). Tactics might include the following:

- The organization can adapt its output, goals and methods of operation to conform to prevailing definitions of legitimacy.
- The organization can attempt, through communication, to alter the definition of social legitimacy so that it conforms to the organization's present practices, output, and values.
- The organization can attempt through communication to become identified with symbols, values, or institutions that have a strong base of legitimacy.

Consistent with Dowling and Pfeffer's (1975) strategy of 'communication', Lindblom (1993) proposes that an organization can adopt a number of strategies where it perceives that its legitimacy is in question because its actions (or operations) are perceived to be at variance with society's expectations and values. Lindblom (1993) identifies four courses of action (there is some overlap with Dowling and Pfeffer) that an organization can take to obtain, or maintain, legitimacy in these circumstances. The organization can:

1. seek to educate and inform its 'relevant publics' about (actual) changes in the organization's performance and activities which bring the activities and performance more into line with society's values and expectations;
2. seek to change the perceptions that 'relevant publics' have of the organization's performance and activities – but not change the organization's actual behaviour (while using disclosures in corporate reports to falsely indicate that the performance and activities have changed);

3.   seek to manipulate perception by deflecting attention from the issue of concern onto other related issues through an appeal to, for example, emotive symbols, thus seeking to demonstrate how the organization has fulfilled social expectations in other areas of its activities;
4.   seek to change external expectations of its performance, possibly by demonstrating that specific societal expectations are unreasonable.

In all cases, the disclosure of information to 'relevant publics' is essential for influencing legitimacy. A corporation may use a variety of legitimating techniques to execute its chosen strategy. Consistent with the above discussion, Ashforth and Gibbs (1990) provide two general categories of legitimating techniques that a corporation may adopt – substantive and symbolic management techniques. The use of *substantive* management techniques 'involves real, material change in organisational goals, structures, and processes or socially institutionalised practices' (Ashforth and Gibbs, 1990, p. 178). Alternatively, the corporation may change its relevant publics, or the degree to which it is dependent on those publics' resources. At the other end of the spectrum the corporation may adopt techniques to actively align the values of society to those of the corporation (Ashforth and Gibbs, 1990). Regardless of the approach adopted, substantive management techniques involve a *real* change in the behaviour of the corporation.

In contrast, *symbolic* management techniques of legitimation involve the *portrayal* of corporate behaviour in a manner to 'appear consistent with social values and expectations' (Ashforth and Gibbs, 1990, p. 180). Companies may publish policies on various issues including the environment, but may not enforce or set in place mechanisms for the full adoption of such policies. According to Ashforth and Gibbs (1990), it is not necessary to use either substantive or symbolic management techniques exclusively. Corporations may adopt a mix of substantive and/or symbolic legitimating techniques and may apply these with varying levels of intensity.[8]

Whichever one of the above legitimizing strategies is adopted will rely upon disclosure if it is to be successful, as we again emphasize. In providing an illustration of the first strategy proposed by Dowling and Pfeffer we can refer to the leading sportswear company, Nike. As Deegan (2012, p. 1141) explains, Nike had been heavily criticized because people manufacturing its products were paid extremely low (and perceived unfair) wages, and were sometimes subject to various types of abuse. This impacted the sales of Nike's products. In reaction to the community concern Nike ultimately undertook reviews (or social audits) of the various factories supplying its goods. The background to the reviews, the results of the reviews, and the organizational changes brought about as a result of the reviews were publicized by Nike in its publicly available social report, as well as being provided in detailed commentary on its website. Legitimacy theory would suggest that Nike took the action it did because the revelations about sweatshop abuses (heavily publicized in the media) had created a significant *legitimacy gap* which in turn was undermining the entity's performance. The gap needed to be reduced and the disclosure of information about various activities would be expected to help reduce the gap.

In relation to the second approach to legitimation described by Dowling and Pfeffer (1975) we might consider tobacco companies. In recent years tobacco companies have been heavily criticized because of their impacts on addicted consumers. A number of the major producers have responded by releasing social reports, which among other things emphasize that consumers make the choice to smoke cigarettes and that the companies are simply satisfying a legal demand. The reports also tend to emphasize the work of tobacco companies within the community – for example, supporting sporting events and putting in place mechanisms to discourage young smokers.

As an example of the third legitimating tactic identified by Dowling and Pfeffer (1975) we could consider the example of where industry bodies develop social and environmental codes of conduct. Deegan and Blomquist (2006) provide an Australian example wherein the Australian Mineral Council developed a Code of Environmental Management to be followed by its members. The code was considered to be a symbol of legitimacy. Hence, legitimizing strategies can also occur at an industry level. Having a code of environmental management could arguably be seen as a symbolic commitment to improved environmental performance by the industry body that developed the code, and by those companies who commit to it.

## Does there come a time when the legitimacy gap becomes so wide that actions to repair lost legitimacy are deemed to be forlorn?

As Deegan (2014, p. 364) states:

> whilst much of the research efforts have considered efforts to defend legitimacy, there might come a time – which we refer to as the 'loss phase'– when an organisation decides there is no point trying to defend legitimacy and therefore it might decide to discontinue its legitimation activities.

In this regard we can consider Tilling and Tilt (2010) and their study of the annual report disclosures made by the tobacco company, Rothmans Ltd (which ultimately became part of British American Tobacco Australia), for the period from 1955 to 1999. According to the authors, issues to do with the health aspects of smoking started gaining momentum in the mid-1960s. At this point in time the company was publicly questioning the veracity of the evidence about the health effects of tobacco products, and as such, this could be construed as a legitimation tactic. As Tilling and Tilt state (2010, p. 71):

> This would appear to be an attempt at knowledge dissociation. From 1966 to 1971 the disclosures remain fairly consistent, focusing on the various specific company activities associated with sports, fine arts and education. Then in 1972 (the year compulsory health warnings were introduced) there is no mention of social activities. From 1973 onwards the focus shifts to the three Rothmans' foundations (Rothmans National Sport Foundation, Rothmans University Endowment Fund and Peter Stuyvesant Trust for the Development of the Arts). One significant difference is the 1980 annual report, which was presented more as a history of Rothmans' 25 years in Australia. It contained a substantial section on community service (pp. 14–15). In 1995 the last social disclosure is made, referring to the work undertaken by the Rothmans Foundation in Australia, and states that the decision to close the foundation 'was made in light of the adverse impact of anti-tobacco legislation which had severely hindered the Foundation in its work'. No more disclosures of a social kind were made in the annual reports of Rothmans.

In reflecting upon their results, they go on to state:

> The tobacco industry in general, and Rothmans specifically, had one major threat to its legitimacy: the smoking and health issue. Other than in 1964 it chose not to engage with

this issue, instead focusing on community service and charitable works. This could appear to be an attempt to engage in Lindblom's (1993) third strategy, trying to get the community to accept the company's legitimacy, not in terms of the health issue, but instead highlighting the organisation's engagement in good works, therefore trying to bolster its position as a legitimate organisation without having to engage in change. Ultimately this would appear to have failed, at least to the extent that the industry is now highly regulated, scrutinised and taxed, although it continues to survive. When there no longer seemed to be value in even trying to defend legitimacy, the analysis suggests the company ultimately gave up its charitable community involvement and reporting on it.

As Deegan (2014, p. 365) notes, the tobacco industry is an interesting industry in the sense that, unlike many other industries, it can survive, albeit probably at a reduced level of operations, even when the legitimacy of the industry has been eroded. In large part this is due to the addictive qualities of the product. However, the lower level of legitimacy in the broader (non-addicted) community may lead to higher taxes being imposed on the products of the industry, higher salaries required to be paid to attract quality staff, and higher returns required to be paid to capital providers.

Hence, while most social and environmental accounting researchers consider legitimacy in three phases (gain, maintain, and repair legitimacy), works of authors such as Tilling and Tilt (2010) emphasize that legitimacy threatening events will not always be expected to evoke a disclosure reaction from corporations – things might become so bad that managers resign themselves to the view that lost or damaged legitimacy can no longer be repaired. This might be referred to as an 'abandonment phase'.

## Use of legitimacy theory in studies of social and environmental reporting

There have been numerous studies in the social and environmental accounting literature that have embraced legitimacy theory. While the following discussion is far from comprehensive, it does provide reference to some relevant research papers in the area. As noted earlier, much of the research occurred from the late 1980s (although there were some notable earlier papers, such as Hogner, 1982, as discussed in the following paragraph).

One of the early studies to embrace legitimacy theory was that of Hogner (1982). Hogner examined corporate social reporting in the annual reports of US Steel Corporation over a period of 80 years, commencing in 1901, the data being analysed for year to year variation. Hogner showed that the extent of social disclosures varied from year to year and he speculated that the variation could represent a response to society's changing expectations of corporate behaviour.

Another influential paper was that of Guthrie and Parker (1989). Guthrie and Parker sought to match the disclosure practices of BHP Ltd (BHP Ltd is a large Australian company and has subsequently become BHP Billiton) across the period from 1885 to 1985 with a historical account of major events relating to BHP Ltd. The argument was that if corporate disclosure policies are reactive to major social and environmental events, then there should be correspondence between peaks of disclosure and events that are significant in BHP Ltd's history. While this paper did not provide evidence supportive of legitimacy theory (perhaps due to data limitations, as Deegan *et al.*, 2002, explain) a large number of subsequent research studies have used and refined their arguments.

Another important paper was that of Patten (1992), which focused on the change in the extent of environmental disclosures made by North American oil companies, other than just

Exxon Oil Company, both before and after the *Exxon Valdez* incident in Alaska in 1989. Patten argued that if the Alaskan oil spill resulted in a threat to the legitimacy of the petroleum industry, and not just to Exxon, then legitimacy theory would suggest that companies operating within that industry would respond by increasing the amount of environmental disclosures in their annual reports. Patten's results indicate that there were increased environmental disclosures by the petroleum companies for the post-1989 period, consistent with a legitimation perspective. This disclosure reaction took place across the industry, even though the incident itself was directly related to one oil company.

Gray *et al.* (1995) performed a longitudinal review of UK corporate social and environmental disclosures for the period 1979 to 1991. After considering the extent and types of corporate disclosures, they stated (1995, p. 65): 'Increasingly, companies are being required to demonstrate a satisfactory performance within the environmental domain. Corporate social reporting would appear to be one of the mechanisms by which the organisations satisfy (and manipulate) that requirement.'

In relation to trends found in regard to health and safety disclosures Gray *et al.* (1995, p. 65) stated:

> We are persuaded that companies were increasingly under pressure from various 'relevant publics' to improve their performance in the area of health and safety and employed corporate social reporting to manage this 'legitimacy gap'. That is, while the disclosure did not, as such, demonstrate improved health and safety records (lack of previous information makes such assessment impossible), it did paint a picture of increasing concern being given by companies to the matter of protecting and training their workforce. This disclosure then helped add to the image of a competent and concerned organisation which took its responsibilities in this field seriously.

Deegan and Rankin (1996) utilized legitimacy theory to try to explain systematic changes in corporate annual report environmental disclosure policies around the time of proven environmental prosecutions. Deegan and Rankin found that prosecuted firms disclosed significantly more environmental information (of a favourable nature) in the year of prosecution than in any other year in the sample period. Consistent with the view that companies increase disclosure to offset any effects of environmental prosecutions, the prosecuted firms also disclosed more positive environmental information, relative to non-prosecuted firms.

Brown and Deegan (1998) extended the legitimacy theory literature by incorporating media agenda-setting theory. Media agenda-setting theory – a theory that has been utilized by various researchers for a number of decades, including those within journalism schools – is explained by Ader (1995, p. 300):

> The agenda-setting hypothesis ... posits a relationship between the relative emphasis given by the media to various topics and the degree of salience these topics have for the general public. Individuals note the amount of and distribution of media coverage among issues, and this determines the salience of each issue for the individuals. According to the agenda-setting hypothesis, the media do not mirror public priorities as much as they influence them.[9]

Brown and Deegan used the extent of media coverage given to a particular environmental issue as a measure (or proxy) of community concern. In terms of causality, increased media attention is believed to lead to increased community concern for a particular issue and a consequent increased need for legitimizing strategies, corporate disclosure being one such reaction. The results in Brown and Deegan (1998) indicate that for the majority of the industries studied, higher levels of media attention given to specific social and environmental issues (as determined by a review of a number of print media newspapers and journals) are significantly associated with higher levels of annual report environmental disclosures in relation to such issues. In concluding their study, Brown and Deegan (1998, p. 34) stated:

> This study has contributed to the literature because it has shown, unlike any other known study, that the environmental disclosure strategies of management within some industries is [sic] associated with the extent of media attention. More specifically, variations in media attention appear to be associated with variations in corporate disclosures. It has further contributed to the literature by showing that not all industries react in the same manner to variation in the level of media attention. Taken together, the results provide a further resource for those individuals/organisations attempting to explain or understand what drives particular entities to voluntarily disclose environmental information in their annual report.

Within the context of companies that source their products from developing countries, Islam and Deegan (2010) undertook a review of the social and environmental disclosure practices of two leading multinational sportswear and clothing companies, Nike and Hennes & Mauritz. Islam and Deegan found a direct relationship between the extent of global news media coverage of a critical nature being given to particular social issues relating to the industry, and the extent of social disclosure. In particular, they found that, once the news media started running a campaign that exposed poor working conditions and the use of child labour in developing countries, it appeared that the multinational companies then responded by making various disclosures identifying initiatives that were being undertaken to ensure that the companies did not source their products from factories that had abusive or unsafe working conditions or used child labour.

Islam and Deegan (2010) found the evidence to be consistent with the view that the news media influenced the expectations of western consumers (consistent with Media Agenda-Setting Theory), thereby causing a legitimacy problem for the companies. The companies then responded to the legitimacy crisis by providing disclosures within their annual report that particularly focused on the highlighted issue. Islam and Deegan showed that, prior to the time at which the news media started running stories about the labour conditions in developing countries (media attention to these issues appeared to gain greater momentum in the early 1990s), there was a general absence of disclosures being made by the companies. This was despite the fact that evidence suggests that poor working conditions and the use of child labour existed in developing countries for many years prior to the newspapers beginning coverage of the issues. Islam and Deegan (2010) speculate that had the western news media not run stories exposing the working conditions in developing countries – which created a legitimacy gap for the multinational companies – the multinational companies would not have embraced initiatives to improve working conditions, nor provided disclosures about the initiatives being undertaken in relation to working conditions. Work by Deegan and Islam (2009) has also shown that non-government organizations (NGOs) including labour rights and environmental organizations often use the media as a means of disseminating information about poor labour practices in developing countries (Deegan and Islam, 2009). Without the use of the media, consumers would generally not have knowledge of poor workplace practices. As they state (p. 1):

> Our results show that social and environmental NGOs strategically use the news media to effect changes in the operating and disclosure policies pertaining to corporate labour practices. More particularly, both the NGOs and the news media representatives stated that NGOs would be relatively powerless to create changes in corporate accountability without media coverage.

While the above papers have generally provided support for legitimacy theory it also needs to be acknowledged that some studies have not. For example, Wilmshurst and Frost (2000) conducted a questionnaire survey among a sample of chief financial officers (CFOs) which asked the executives to rank the importance of various factors in environmental disclosure decisions. Wilmshurst and Frost then analysed environmental disclosures within the annual reports of the companies for whom their sample of CFOs worked, and found (2000, p. 22) 'the influences of the competitor response to environmental issues and customer concerns to have predictive power'. This provided 'limited support for the applicability of Legitimacy Theory'.

O'Dwyer (2002) interviewed 29 senior executives from 27 large Irish companies and found that managerial motives for engaging in corporate social and environmental reporting were only sometimes consistent with a legitimacy theory explanation. This was despite many managers perceiving clear threats to their organizations' legitimacy in the eyes of a range of powerful stakeholders. O'Dwyer states (2002, p. 416) that detailed and close questioning revealed:

> an overwhelming perception of CSD [corporate social disclosure] as an unsuccessful legitimation mechanism. Therefore, while CSD is sometimes perceived as being employed as part of a legitimacy process, its employment in this manner is ultimately viewed as failing to aid in securing a state of legitimacy for organisations. Furthermore, despite the predominant view [among senior managers] that CSD is incapable of facilitating the achievement of a state of legitimacy, research into the CSD practices [of the companies interviewed] subsequent to the interviews … reveals that many of the interviewees' companies continue to engage in some form of CSD. In conjunction with the interviewees' perspectives, this questions the pervasive explanatory power of Legitimacy Theory with respect to the motives for CSD when considered in the Irish context.

Therefore, while there has been a vast body of work, particularly undertaken by social and environmental accounting researchers that has supported legitimacy theory, there are also a number of papers that have not provided results supporting the explanatory power of legitimacy theory. However, as Deegan (2014) emphasizes, we should not expect theories of human behaviour (and legitimacy theory is one such theory as it seeks to explain how particular people – for example, managers – will act or react when confronted with particular situations, for example legitimacy threatening events) to provide perfect predictions in all cases. Sometimes a theory that explains behaviour in the majority of cases is argued to be useful, particularly until such time that a 'better' theory comes along.

## Are legitimating strategies in the interests of society?

In this chapter we have provided evidence to suggest that, consistent with legitimacy theory, corporate social and environmental disclosures appear to react to community expectations – but we can briefly reflect upon whether this is actually a 'good thing'. Further, are such corporate disclosures really reflective of an acceptance that an organization has an accountability issue for its social and environmental performance, *or are they merely a mechanism to support the existence of the organization?* As Deegan et al. (2002) state:

> Legitimising disclosures mean that the organisation is responding to particular concerns that have arisen in relation to their operations. The implication is that unless concerns are aroused (and importantly, the managers *perceive* the existence of such concerns) then unregulated disclosures could be quite minimal. Disclosure decisions driven by the desire to be legitimate are not the same as disclosure policies driven by a management view that the community has a *right-to-know* about certain aspects of an organisation's operations. One motivation relates to survival, whereas the other motivation relates to responsibility. Arguably, companies that simply react to community concerns are not truly embracing a notion of accountability. Studies providing results consistent with Legitimacy Theory (and there are many of them) leave us with a view that unless specific concerns are raised then no *accountability* appears to be due. Unless community concern happens to be raised (perhaps as a result of a major social or environmental incident which attracts media attention), there will be little or no corporate disclosure.

Further, and utilizing the work of Cooper and Sherer (1984), Deegan *et al.* (2002) argue that legitimizing disclosures simply act to sustain corporate operations that are of concern to some individuals within society. To the extent that the corporate social and environmental disclosures reflect or portray management concern as well as corporate moves towards actual change, the corporate disclosures may be merely forestalling any *real* changes in corporate activities. Taking this position even further, Puxty (1991, p. 39) states: 'I do not accept that I see legitimation as innocuous. It seems to me that the legitimation can be very harmful indeed, insofar as it acts as a barrier to enlightenment and hence progress.'

From the above discussion we can argue that organizations that are shown to be embracing legitimizing strategies – and evidence indicates that there are many of them – are not really likely to be embracing a broader sustainability ethos. 'True' sustainability would require management to accept that they have a responsibility and accountability to the environment and to current and future generations which would not simply be reactive to community concerns. The evidence provided in numerous social and environmental accounting research studies suggests that higher levels of social and environmental disclosure will only occur when community concerns are aroused. Globally, there is a general lack of regulatory requirements for corporations to make sustainability-related disclosures, meaning that corporate management is typically in charge of determining the extent of disclosure. In this regard, Deegan *et al.* (2002) emphasize that if corporate legitimizing activities are successful, then public pressure for government to introduce disclosure legislation will be low and managers will retain control of their social and environmental reporting practices. Accountability will be 'captured' and progress towards sustainability will be hindered.

## Limitations of legitimacy theory and future 'ways forward'

While legitimacy theory is widely used in social and environmental accounting research, it nevertheless is not without its critics. Some of the criticisms include:

- There is a lack of research that demonstrates that legitimizing disclosures *actually* work in reducing *legitimacy gaps.*

- Tied to the above point, there is a lack of research that explores which specific types of disclosures are relatively more effective in changing community expectations.
- There are problems of resolution – legitimacy theory tends to focus on society at large and does not explore whether particular groups within society might be relatively more influenced by corporate disclosures (and what types of disclosure).
- Research utilizing legitimacy theory fails to provide insights about the attributes of managers that influence how they respond to legitimacy threats – or indeed, how they perceive the existence of *legitimacy threats*.
- Proponents of legitimacy theory often talk about 'society', and compliance with the expectations of society (as embodied within the *social contract*); however, this provides poor resolution given that *society* is clearly made up of various groups having unequal power or ability to influence the activities of other groups.
- While researchers have proposed that legitimation tactics might differ depending upon whether the entity is trying to *gain*, *maintain*, or *repair* legitimacy, the theoretical development in this area remains weak.
- While there are many studies that identify particular adverse social and environmental events as reducing the legitimacy of an organization such studies typically do not try to provide any form of measurement of the supposed changes in legitimacy.
- The use of legitimacy theory in social and environmental accounting typically assumes that all action is driven by self-interest motivations, with corporate survival at the heart of corporate action.
- Much of legitimacy theory as applied in the social and environmental accounting literature ignores the legitimation of particular social structures – rather it tends to simply focus upon efforts by organizations to legitimate their own existence.

In concluding this paper we have chosen a number of the above limitations for further discussion.

### *Failure to measure changes in legitimacy*

As we have seen, a number of studies have investigated corporate reporting behaviour around the time of major adverse social and environmental events. The argument typically used is that the events cause erosion in the 'legitimacy' of the organization thereby necessitating disclosures aimed at restoring lost legitimacy. That is, the adverse social or environmental event causes the perceived legitimacy of the organization to fall following the event. But can we actually place a measure on this reduction in legitimacy? Can we actually measure it before and after the adverse social or environmental event?

   As Deegan (2014, p. 365) emphasizes, most researchers do not attempt to measure any perceived reduction in legitimacy. They typically assume, or infer, that the particular adverse event caused a reduction in legitimacy (and the claim might be bolstered by counting the number of newspaper articles that addressed the event) and the organization will thereafter respond strategically with legitimacy enhancing disclosures. While many studies (perhaps too many?) have been published showing a relationship between certain adverse social and environmental events – which are simply inferred as impacting an entity's legitimacy or not, in an apparent binary *0/1* or *yes legitimacy has been eroded/no legitimacy has not been eroded* type of classification – and corporate disclosures, it is questionable whether such studies can continue to be published in the absence of further refinement. One refinement would be to move away from a binary classification of legitimacy threatening events to an approach that attempts to place some form of measurement on movements in legitimacy. But as Deegan (2014, p. 366) notes:

> Obviously, placing a measurement on 'legitimacy' would be a very subjective exercise, influenced by a number of factors not the least of which would be the researchers' own values and perspectives. Therefore, rather than trying to gauge an organisation's legitimacy directly, we can perhaps infer its existence through the actions of various parties within society. One way to do this is to consider the flow of resources going to an organisation – something that perhaps can be more objectively determined (Tilling and Tilt, 2010; Hybels, 1995).

As Hybels (1995, p. 243) states:

> Legitimacy itself has no material form. It exists only as a symbolic representation of the collective evaluation of an institution, as evidenced to both observers and participants perhaps most convincingly by the flow of resources. Resources must have symbolic import to function as value in social exchange. But legitimacy is a higher-order representation of that symbolism. Terreberry (1968, p. 608) well explained the relationship between resources and organisational legitimacy nearly thirty years ago when he said 'the willingness of firm A to contribute to X, and of agency B to refer personnel to X, and C to buy X's product testifies to the legitimacy of X'.

The view being promoted in the above quote is that if people continue to provide resources to the entity then, in a sense, they must believe that organization is worthy of support. Hence, the level of resource transfer can be used, perhaps somewhat imperfectly, as a measure of the legitimacy of an organization. As Hybels (1995, p. 245) states:

> Legitimation derives from increases in the flow of resources, while delegitimation occurs as the flow of resources declines. I do not mean to imply, however, that resources and legitimacy are synonymous, only that resource flows are among the best evidence of legitimacy.

As Hybels (1995, p. 244) explains, we can consider the resource flows from different stakeholder groups. Such resource flows need to be considered with some imagination and not simply restricted to direct transactions with associated cash flows. For an example of some resource flows, the media provide resources (positive or negative) in terms of media exposure; consumers provide resources in terms of sales; and government provides inflows and outflows of resources in terms of regulation, tariff protection, and so forth. As Hybels (1995, p. 243) states:

> To build a well-grounded theory of legitimation of organizations, it is necessary above all to identify the critical actors, both internal and external, whose approval is necessary to the fulfilment of an organization's functions. Each influences the flow of resources crucial to the organization's establishment, growth, and survival, either through direct control or by the communication of goodwill.

From the above brief discussion we can see how a difficult construct, such as legitimacy, might be measured (albeit, imperfectly) by measuring resource flows. Again, it has probably come time for researchers to be a bit more sophisticated in their research and provide some form of measurement of changes in legitimacy rather than simply inferring that particular events have changed corporate legitimacy, and then searching for a related disclosure reaction.

### *Assumptions that disclosure strategies are driven by self-interest*

As Deegan (2014) stresses, in many theories – particularly those emanating from the economics literature – there is an explicit simplifying assumption that all actions by all people are driven by self-interest. This is often criticized by social and environmental accounting researchers in large part because of its overt simplicity and because such an assumption, if accepted, destroys hope for sustainable development. But similar criticisms could be made of legitimacy theory in that it assumes that actions – such as corporate reporting – are strategically undertaken for advancement and/or survival purposes. Obviously this is a rather simplistic assumption. As Oliver (1991) points out, socially responsible organizations may choose to undertake actions beyond self-interest:

> For example, corporate social responsibility and the maintenance of sound organizational ethics may not be invariably reducible to strategic behaviours induced by the anticipation of organizational gain. Organisations may act ethically or responsibly not because of any direct link to a positive organizational outcome (e.g., greater prestige or more resources) but merely because it would be unthinkable to do otherwise. In this way, organizational behaviour may be driven not by processes of interest mobilization (DiMaggio 1988), but by preconscious acceptance of institutionalized values or practices. (pp. 148–9)

Further, certain actions may become 'institutionalised'. As Deegan (2014, p. 368) states:

> That is, managers and organisations themselves will be influenced by their social environments and will naturally embrace certain social norms and values, rather than consciously and instrumentally choosing actions – such as making disclosures – for strategic surviving or advancement purpose (for legitimacy). Oliver (1991, p. 148) argues when external social norms and practices 'obtain the status of a social fact, organisations may engage in activities that are not so much calculative or self-interested'. That is, 'the exercise of strategic choice may be pre-empted' (Oliver, 1991, p. 148) when managers and organisations unconsciously conform to taken-for-granted social norms and practices. Therefore we must act with caution before simply assuming that all corporate action is driven by survival considerations – an assumption made by many proponents of legitimacy theory.

Therefore, legitimacy theorists must be careful and acknowledge simplifying assumptions they are making when trying to explain corporate conduct.

### *Researchers who apply legitimacy theory typically do not consider actions that are aimed at legitimizing the broader social system*

While the research we have briefly discussed in this chapter has looked mainly at how organizations attempt to legitimize their own existence within a particular society (with the associated assumption, often implicit, of a pluralist society), Deegan (2014, p. 368) also highlights that disclosures might be taken to legitimize particular aspects of the broader social system in place at a particular point in time. Archel *et al.* (2009) suggest that, while individual organizations might be making disclosures to create 'organizational-level legitimacy' on a strategic basis, the same organizations as well as governments (the state, which might work in conjunction with the organization to legitimize particular elements of society) might also be making related disclosures to legitimize particular systems that they hope will become institutionalized within the broader society.

As we noted in the section entitled Organizational Legitimacy, legitimacy theory is typically considered to be derived from political economy theory. We also learned that political economy theory has been divided into two broad streams, which have been labelled 'classical' and 'bourgeois' political economy. Classical political economy theory explicitly places sectional (class) interests, structural conflict, inequity, and the role of the state at the heart of the analysis. By contrast, 'bourgeois' political economy theory largely ignores these elements and perceives the world as essentially pluralistic. Most researchers who apply legitimacy theory embrace a view consistent with the 'bourgeois' branch of political economy theory.

According to Archel *et al.* (2009, p. 1288), once we start considering the role of government (the state) in supporting particular processes, including an analysis of government disclosures, then:

> This conceptualisation of the State moves us into a more critical branch of Legitimacy Theory that has more in common with classical political economy theory (Gray *et al.*, 1995, 1996). Whereas the bourgeois branch of Legitimacy Theory exhibits a more immediate concern with how the firm becomes legitimate in the eyes of its stakeholders, the critical branch of Legitimacy Theory 'raises questions about the legitimacy of the system (e.g. capitalism) as a whole' (Gray *et al.*, 1995, p. 47). Studying social and environmental disclosures through the lens of this second variant of Legitimacy Theory links the legitimising strategies identified at an organisational level with an economic, political and social setting that is at odds with the essentially pluralist one assumed by the bourgeois approach (see for example, Tinker and Neimark, 1987; Tinker *et al.*, 1991; Neimark, 1992) ... Through the lens of this variant of Legitimacy Theory grounded in the Classical branch of Political Economy Theory, not only can social and environmental disclosures serve to legitimise firms' outputs, methods and goals but it can also serve to legitimise the economic, social and political system as a whole (Gray *et al.*, 1995, 1996). Therefore, when authors support the Legitimacy Theory argument by analysing the firm's behaviour, that is, when they show how firms are trying to inform, educate or manipulate society using social information, they could be identifying strategies with a broader impact. This has not been explicitly considered in previous Legitimacy Theory studies, including those that investigate how companies try to circumvent public policy processes and regulation.

Archel et al. (2009) applied this more 'critical perspective' to consider the disclosures made by the car producer VW in Navarra, Spain between the years 1986 and 2005. During this period the car manufacturer moved from a standardized and common method of car manufacture to a new production process (known as lean production). This new process was deemed to have led to a severe deterioration in working conditions for employees, but was good for profits and share value and was also favoured by government because of the increased efficiency and economic benefits it would create in the region. Applying legitimacy theory, Archel *et al.* (2009) argued that the corporate and government disclosures had two purposes. They were not only undertaken to legitimize the existence of the company within society (which is the view traditionally embraced by advocates of legitimacy theory), but they were also taken to try to legitimize the particular production process within the broader society (which is an aspect most legitimacy theory-related research does not consider).

Effectively, the disclosures made by the company and the government reinforced each other – something that would not be considered if a researcher only investigates the corporation's disclosures in isolation from the disclosures being made by other entities that were also addressing the same issue. Because the government was publicly supporting the company's processes, the need for the company to undertake certain legitimation strategies was reduced.

In concluding their paper, Archel *et al.* (2009) suggest that researchers think more broadly about the legitimation strategies undertaken by organizations. While disclosure strategies might be undertaken to inform, educate, or even manipulate society in a manner intended to provide legitimacy to the organization, researchers should also consider whether the disclosures might have a broader impact in terms of efforts to legitimize particular economic, social, and political systems that potentially undermine the interests of particular stakeholders (such as employees). Researchers should also consider complementary disclosures that might also be made by government, as the disclosures made by government could influence the necessity for legitimizing disclosures by a corporation.

We could list more potential criticisms of, or gaps in, legitimacy theory other than those provided above. But what is being emphasized here is that there is much scope for developing and improving legitimacy theory. The generation of insightful developments in the theory now seems overdue. Undertaking such theory 'extension' such as that suggested above would provide a valuable contribution to the social and environmental accounting literature and would provide a means for an up-and-coming researcher to be associated with a highly cited research paper. We must remember that no 'theory' will ever be perfect, but further advancement in legitimacy theory is required if the theory is expected to retain its place as a dominant theory in the social and environmental accounting literature. Perhaps because of the lack of refinement, and other perceived limitations, Gray *et al.* (2010) have gone so far as to suggest that institutional theory may in due course become the 'mainstream theory', replacing legitimacy theory as the dominant theory used in the social and environmental accounting (SEA) literature. Time will tell.

## Notes

1  The material in this chapter is largely based on material that appears in Deegan (2014).

2  In such research, the researcher typically does not consider or critique any structural or procedural inequities in the various social systems. This has been a source of criticism of such research because of the associated assumption of a pluralist society wherein no particular groups act to undermine the interests of other groups.

3  Authors such as Puxty (1991) have indicated that legitimizing disclosures made by corporations tends to allow businesses to continue in a 'business-as-usual' way, even when the corporations are creating harm to other less powerful sectors of society.

4  A pluralistic perspective assumes (typically implicitly) that many classes of stakeholders have the power to influence various decisions by corporations, government, and other entities. Within this perspective, accounting is not considered to be put in place to favour specific interests (sometimes referred to as 'elites'), but can be used to provide advantage to specific groups within a pluralistic society. By using 'society' as the topic of focus rather than *subgroups* within society, theories such as Legitimacy Theory – as usually applied – ignores 'struggles and inequities within society' (Puxty, 1991).

5  It should be appreciated however that 'stakeholder theory' is a broad 'umbrella' term for a number of theoretical perspectives; hence, the use of the label 'stakeholder theory' can create some confusion. As discussed in Deegan (2014) there is a normative branch of stakeholder theory which prescribes

how organizations *should* interact with their stakeholders (for example, see Freeman and Reed, 1983; Hasnas, 1998). There is also a managerial branch of stakeholder theory that explains how organizations do interact with their stakeholders (for example, Ullman, 1985; Roberts, 1992; Nasi *et al.*, 1997).

6  Ji (2013) also suggests that it is predominantly in the social and environmental accounting literature that 'legitimacy theory' is referred to. Other disciplines simply refer to the construct of 'legitimacy', but with the underlying theory being institutional theory. Ji's concern is that in taking a core component of institutional theory – the component being 'legitimacy' – and then restricting the insights to those available from 'legitimacy theory' (as progressively developed, in large part, by social and environmental accounting researchers) we are ignoring a rich body of literature that provides insights into both the strategic management perspective of legitimacy (on which social and environmental accounting researchers typically focus), and the institutional perspective of legitimacy. We will not pursue this issue further in this chapter, but will continue with the assumption that legitimacy theory is a theory in its own right and not simply a sub-part of institutional theory. Nevertheless, we would encourage interested readers to consider the extent to which institutional theory provides many of the insights also available from legitimacy theory.

7  As Deegan (2014) indicates, the theoretical construct of the social contract is not new, having been discussed by philosophers such as Thomas Hobbes (1588–1679), John Locke (1632–1704), and Jean-Jacques Rousseau (1712–78).

8  This idea that corporations will make disclosures that are symbolic and detached from their actual activities or processes is consistent with the idea of decoupling as provided within institutional theory (DiMaggio and Powell, 1983).

9  For an explanation of Media Agenda Setting Theory, see McCombs and Shaw (1972); Zucker (1978); Blood (1981); Eyal *et al.* (1981); McCombs (1981); Ader (1995).

## References

Ader, C. (1995), 'A longitudinal study of agenda setting for the issue of environmental pollution', *Journalism & Mass Communication Quarterly*, 72(3): 300–11.

Archel, P., Husillos, J., Larringa, C. and Spence, C. (2009), 'Social disclosure, legitimacy theory and the role of the state', *Accounting, Auditing and Accountability Journal*, 22(8): 1284–307.

Ashforth, B. and Gibbs, B. (1990) 'The double edge of legitimization', *Organization Science*, 1: 177–94.

Blood, R. W. (1981), 'Unobtrusive issues and the agenda-setting role of the press', unpublished Doctoral dissertation, Syracuse University, New York.

Brown, N. and Deegan, C. (1998), 'The public disclosure of environmental performance information – A dual test of media agenda setting theory and legitimacy theory', *Accounting and Business Research*, 29(1): 21–41.

Cooper, D. J. and Sherer, M. J. (1984), 'The value of corporate accounting reports – Arguments for a political economy of accounting', *Accounting, Organizations and Society*, 9(3/4): 207–32.

Deegan, C. (2012), *Australian Financial Accounting*, 7th edn. Sydney, NSW: McGraw Hill.

Deegan, C. (2014), *Financial Accounting Theory*, 4th edn. Sydney, NSW: McGraw Hill.

Deegan, C. and Blomquist, C. (2006) 'Stakeholder influence on corporate reporting: An exploration of the interaction between WWF-Australia and the Australian Minerals Industry', *Accounting, Organizations and Society*, 31(4): 343–72.

Deegan, C. and Islam, M. A. (2009), *NGOs' use of the Media to Create Changes in Corporate Activities and Accountabilities: Evidence from a Developing Country*, paper presented to the Accounting and Finance Association of Australia and New Zealand Annual Conference, Adelaide, July.

Deegan, C. and Rankin, M. (1996), 'Do Australian companies report environmental news objectively? An analysis of environmental disclosures by firms prosecuted successfully by the environmental protection authority', *Accounting, Auditing and Accountability Journal*, 9(2): 52–69.

Deegan, C., Rankin, M. and Tobin, J. (2002), 'An examination of the corporate social and environmental disclosures of BHP from 1983–1997', *Accounting, Auditing and Accountability Journal*, 15(3): 312–43.

DiMaggio, P. J. and Powell, W. W. (1983), 'The iron cage revisited: institutional isomorphism and collective rationality in organizational fields', *American Sociological Review*, 48: 146–60.

Dowling, J. and Pfeffer, J. (1975), 'Organisational legitimacy: Social values and organisational behavior', *Pacific Sociological Review*, 18(1): 122–36.

Eyal, C. H., Winter, J. P. and DeGeorge, W. F. (1981), 'The concept of time frame in agenda setting', in G. C. Wilhoit (ed.) *Mass Communication Yearbook*, Beverly Hills, CA: Sage Publications, pp. 212–18.

Freeman, R. and Reed, D. (1983), 'Stockholders and stakeholders: A new perspective on corporate governance', *Californian Management Review*, 25(2): 88–106.

Gray, R., Kouhy, R. and Lavers, S. (1995), 'Corporate social and environmental reporting: A review of the literature and a longitudinal study of UK disclosure', *Accounting, Auditing and Accountability Journal*, 8(2): 47–77.

Gray, R., Owen, D. and Adams, C. (1996), *Accounting and Accountability: Changes and Challenges in Corporate Social and Environmental Reporting*. London: Prentice-Hall.

Gray, R., Owen, D. and Adams, C. (2010), 'Some theories for social accounting?: A review essay and a tentative pedagogic categorisation of theorisations around social accounting', *Advances in Environmental Accounting & Management*, 4: 1–54.

Guthrie, J. and Parker, L. (1989), 'Corporate social reporting: A rebuttal of legitimacy theory', *Accounting and Business Research*, 19(76): 343–52.

Guthrie, J. and Parker, L. (1990), 'Corporate social disclosure practice: A comparative international analysis', *Advances in Public Interest Accounting*, 3: 159–75.

Hasnas, J. (1998), 'The normative theories of business ethics: A guide for the perplexed', *Business Ethics Quarterly*, 8(1): 19–42.

Hogner, R. H. (1982), 'Corporate social reporting: Eight decades of development at US steel', *Research in Corporate Performance and Policy*, 4: 243–50.

Hybels, R. (1995), 'On legitimacy, legitimation, and organizations: A critical review and integrative theoretical model, *Academy of Management Journal*, Special Issue (best papers procedures): 241–45.

Islam, M. A. and Deegan, C. (2010), 'Media pressures and corporate disclosure of social responsibility performance information: A study of two global clothing and sports retail companies', *Accounting and Business Research*, 40(2): 131–48.

Ji, S. (2013), 'The disclosure of environmental remediation obligations on contaminated sites in annual reports: An Australian exploratory study', PhD thesis, RMIT University, Melbourne, VIC.

Lindblom, C. K. (1993), *The Implications of Organisational Legitimacy for Corporate Social Performance and Disclosure*, paper presented to the *Critical Perspectives on Accounting Conference*, New York, April.

McCombs, M. (1981), 'The agenda-setting approach', in D. Nimmo and K. Sanders (eds) *Handbook of Political Communication*, Beverly Hills, CA: Sage, pp. 121–40.

McCombs, M. and Shaw, D. (1972), 'The agenda setting function of mass media', *Public Opinion Quarterly*, 36(2): 176–87.

Nasi, J., Nasi, S., Phillips, N. and Zyglidopoulos, S. (1997), 'The evolution of corporate social responsiveness – An exploratory study of Finnish and Canadian forestry companies', *Business & Society*, 38(3): 296–321.

O'Donovan, G. (2002), 'Environmental disclosures in the annual report: Extending the applicability and predictive power of legitimacy theory', *Accounting, Auditing and Accountability Journal*, 15(3): 344–71.

O'Dwyer, B. (2002), 'Managerial perceptions of corporate social disclosure: An Irish story', *Accounting, Auditing and Accountability Journal*, 15(3): 406–36.

Oliver, C. (1991) 'Strategic responses to institutional processes', *Academy of Management Review*, 16(1): 145–79.

Patten, D. M. (1992), 'Intra-industry environmental disclosures in response to the Alaskan oil spill: A note on legitimacy theory', *Accounting, Organizations and Society*, 15(5): 471–5.

Powell, W. W. and DiMaggio, P. J. (eds) (1991), *The New Institutionalism in Organizational Analysis*. Chicago, IL: University of Chicago Press.

Puxty, A. (1991), 'Social accountability and universal pragmatics', *Advances in Public Interest Accounting*, 4: 35–46.

Roberts, R. (1992), 'Determinants of corporate social responsibility disclosure: An application of stakeholder theory', *Accounting, Organizations and Society*, 17(6): 595–612.

Sethi, S. P. (1977) 'Dimensions of corporate social performance: An analytical framework', in A. B. Carroll (ed.) *Managing Corporate Social Responsibility*. Boston, MA: Little Brown.

Suchman, M. C. (1995), 'Managing legitimacy: Strategic and institutional approaches', *Academy of Management Review*, 20(3): 571–610.

Tilling, M. and Tilt, C. (2010), 'The edge of legitimacy: Voluntary social and environmental reporting in Rothmans' 1956–1999 annual reports', *Accounting, Auditing and Accountability Journal*, 23(1): 51–81.

Ullman, A. (1985), 'Data in search of a theory: A critical examination of the relationships among social performance, social disclosure, and economic performance of US firms', *Academy of Management Review*, 10(3): 540–57.

Zucker, H. G. (1978), 'The variable nature of news media influence', in B. D. Rubin (ed.) *Communication Yearbook No. 2*, New Brunswick, NJ: Transaction, pp. 225–45.

Zucker, L. G. (1987), 'Institutional theories of organizations', *Annual Review of Sociology*, 13: 443–64.

# 16 Sustainability reporting

## Insights from institutional theory

*Colin Higgins and Carlos Larrinaga*

## Introduction

Over the past few years, more and more business organizations have started reporting details of their social and environmental performance in comprehensive, stand-alone sustainability reports (KPMG, 2011). Some commentators suggest that this type of reporting is becoming mainstream, and a common and expected part of regular business practice (Borkowski *et al.*, 2010). Close inspection of reporting trends, however, raises some important questions about how sustainability reporting is spreading and why it is spreading in the way it is.

In this chapter, we offer institutional theory as way of understanding the uptake and spread of sustainability reporting. Institutional theory emphasizes the conditioning role of the social context. Most theoretical explanations of sustainability reporting, including stakeholder theory and legitimacy theory, suggest reporting is something carefully and deliberately planned by managers to meet (or shape) the expectations of powerful stakeholders or those of the general community (Deegan, 2002; Roberts, 1992). Theorists who emphasize account-ability, or a moral obligation to disclose social/environmental information, similarly emphasize deliberate action on the part of sustainability-conscious managers (Gray *et al.*, 1996). An institutional theory of sustainability reporting, in contrast, downplays rational and calculative managerial behaviour, suggesting instead that, in the absence of a clear rationale, firms undertake this activity because their peers do so, and because it has come to be 'taken for granted' in the contexts where they operate. Institutional theory provides insights into why this is so, and how such effects come about.

Institutional analysis has been applied to various organizational initiatives, including understanding responsible and sustainable business behaviour and, increasingly, sustainability reporting and sustainability management accounting (Chen and Roberts, 2010). Our aim in this chapter is to provide an overview of institutional theory – particularly neo-institutional theory and how it can explain (some aspects of) sustainability reporting. We draw on a growing body of empirical studies to illustrate the presence and effects of organizational fields, and the types of institutions that are influencing reporting activity. We also discuss the prospects for sustainability reporting becoming institutionalized.

### Institutions and organizational fields

Institutional theory is concerned with 'how social choices are shaped, mediated, and channeled by the institutional environment' (Hoffman, 1999, p. 351). Core to institutional theory are 'institutions' and 'organizational fields'. Institutions are rules and regulations as well as ideas, understandings and cultural frameworks (e.g. neoliberal economics) which have achieved a degree of social permanency (Zucker, 1987) in a particular context. They are experienced as 'possessing a reality of their own, a reality that confronts the individual as an external and coercive fact' (Berger and Luckmann, 1966, p. 58) and thus shape how organizations act and why they do so. Ideas and practices that have reached such a state of influence are said to be 'institutionalized' – and bring about a homogenization of organizations (a process DiMaggio and Powell (1983) call isomorphism). This process arises as organizations respond to institutional expectations, which help to guarantee their survival and increase their success possibilities in a particular environment. In a similar vein, Scott (1995) develops the notion of legitimacy as 'not a commodity to be possessed or exchanged but a condition reflecting cultural alignment, normative support, or consonance with relevant rules or laws' (p. 45).

Organizational fields demarcate the specific context in which institutions influence organizations. An organizational field is formed by those organizations that collectively constitute a recognized area of institutional life (DiMaggio and Powell, 1983), 'that partake of a common meaning system and whose participants interact more frequently and fatefully with one another than with actors outside the field' (Scott, 1995, p. 56). Sometimes considered analogous to industry, the institutional analysis literature has also identified fields around common technologies or common regulation, such as the electricity industry or the public hospitals in a given geographical area. Those fields would include 'key suppliers, resource and product consumers, regulatory agencies, and other organizations that produce similar services or products' (DiMaggio and Powell, 1983, p. 145).

The social accounting literature has long noted that sustainability reporting (SR) has been more common among firms in 'dirty and naughty' industries (Brown and Deegan, 1999), theorized from legitimacy (Deegan, 2002) and stakeholder perspectives (Roberts, 1992). However, from an institutional perspective, specific reporting patterns may be explained rather by stronger institutional influences taking place inside this particular organizational field (e.g. the industry). Among multinational firms, Kolk (2010b) described such reporting patterns:

- Industrial, more 'polluting' sectors have been the most active reporters, while banking, insurance, finance, trade and retail, services and communications and media have been much less so.
- Banks and insurance firms are under-represented among consistent reporters, whereas electronics and computers, chemicals and pharmaceuticals, and automotive are over-represented among this group.
- Reporting has become 'normal' in the utilities, chemicals, pharmaceuticals, electronics and computer sectors.

The question that arises is whether in addition to industries, common technologies or regulation, organizational fields can be identified around other dimensions. In this respect, Hoffman (1999) found the development of fields around issues – he investigated the US chemical industry between 1962 and 1993 – and concluded that fields can form around issues that become important to the interests and objectives of the organizations in the field. Similarly, Levy and Kolk's (2002) study of how European and US oil multinationals converged in their response to climate change also demonstrates the development of an issues-based field. Organizational fields may also form around common organizational strategies. In the case of a small number of New Zealand firms, Bebbington *et al.*'s (2009) analysis of reporting patterns hints at the institutionalization of SR among firms wanting to be seen as responsive to or differentiated by sustainability (see also Higgins *et al.* (2011) for speculation about similar processes among Australian firms).

If organizational fields can be recognized around issues, strategies and industries, an important question is whether there exists a unique global organizational field for SR, or whether there are different local organizational fields (Blasco and Zølner, 2010; Perez-Batres *et al.*, 2010). Most studies find that SR is shaped predominantly by institutional pressures at the local, rather than global level. Kolk (2010b), in her study of multinational corporations, found that:

- US multinationals are consistent non-reporters, when compared to other geographical regions.
- French and Japanese firms have been laggards and late adopters of SR, respectively, but the recent uptake of reporting by firms in these countries has been swift.
- UK multinationals were early adopters of SR, and have been consistent reporters – much more so than firms in continental Europe, Japan and the USA.
- Japanese firms report much more detail on the internal accounting of their environmental management systems and policies – including environmental indicators and environmental costs and benefits. US and European firms, in contrast, exhibit more of an external orientation – focusing on the international sustainability discussion.
- US and European firms have been gradually moving towards 'sustainability reports', while Japanese firms have continued to issue 'environmental reports'.
- European firms are more likely to have their reports externally verified than are US and Japanese firms.

However, this portrait seems to be changing, with some recent trends in SR suggesting a gradual process of convergence among the world's largest companies. The triennial surveys of corporate responsibility reporting by KPMG, for example, illustrate that reporting among this group has grown from 50 per cent of the G250 in 2005 to 79 per cent in 2008 and to 95 per cent in 2011 (KPMG, 2011). A global, issues-based field for SR is starting to replace the influence of local geographical or industry-based fields (Kolk, 2011). Banks, insurance and finance firms are, for example, starting to resemble the reporting patterns of the early heavier impact industries (Kolk, 2010b; see also KPMG, 2011). This process of global convergence is being shaped by the development and institutionalization of global corporate social responsibility (CSR) and reporting standards – particularly the global reporting initiative (GRI) (Kolk, 2011); but also, to a lesser extent, the UN Global Compact (Chen and Bouvain, 2009) and the Carbon Disclosure Project (Kolk *et al.*, 2008).

These insights suggest that convergence in reporting practice is mostly occurring among global multinationals, and within countries or regions. This begs the question about processes of institutional change – particularly about the way in which fields come about and how institutions within them change over time to induce different reporting patterns. We discuss these issues after we describe the different types of institutions and their effects on organizational practice in the next section, Mechanisms of Institutionalization.

## Mechanisms of institutionalization

As fields demarcate the context in which systems of shared beliefs, symbols and regulations (Scott and Meyer, 1991) develop to influence organizational activity, it is necessary to distinguish the different types of institutional influences, and the sorts of pressures they exert. The basic premise of institutional theory is that a variety of institutional mechanisms exert pressures on individual organizations within fields, which results in isomorphism – or homogenization – of organizational structures and practices. Isomorphism is driven by three different types of institutional mechanisms: coercive, normative and mimetic (DiMaggio and Powell, 1983) – or, as Scott (1995) describes, three pillars (regulative, normative and cognitive). A basic correspondence between Scott's pillars and DiMaggio and Powell's mechanisms is explained in Table 16.1 and the next paragraphs. The existence of different mechanisms does not mean that they exclude each other, but that rather they are likely to operate at different levels. Further, different approaches to the study of institutions stress the importance of each one of these levels, with institutional economics (Williamson, 1985) focusing on the regulative/coercive elements and neo-institutional sociology favouring the normative and, especially, the cognitive elements. Which view is utilized varies in the different approaches to institutional theory.

In the context of SR, institutional theorists would suggest that reporting is not necessarily the outcome of a rational process of decision making by organizations acting independently. Rather, reporting could be institutionalized within fields, determining whether firms will publish a sustainability report or not, and how they will do so. As an institution, SR would consist of regulative, normative and cognitive structures and activities which would describe what type of reporting is produced, for whom, by whom and with what assumed purpose. Each element is further delineated below.

### Regulatory institutional mechanisms

The regulative pillar (coercive isomorphic mechanism) of institutions is based on rule setting, monitoring, recompense and punishment. In this case, the field acts over individual organizations through the imposition of structures (DiMaggio and Powell, 1983; Scott, 1987). Examples of coercive mechanisms are the enforcement of regulation, the discipline of markets or the exercise of power. Regulation may be considered broadly to include requirements set down by professional bodies (e.g. those necessary to maintain professional registration as accountants) or industry bodies (e.g. conditions of membership such as real estate industry associations in some countries). Coercive mechanisms lead the organization, and/or its members, to comply and align its structures with the dominant rules in order to gain legitimacy and survive (see Table 16.1). For example, manufacturers adopt health and safety procedures in order to comply with regulation, for otherwise public agencies could decide to close or fine them. The underlying logic is based on the interests of the organization (or those of the leading actors in the organization), in terms of acquiring or maintaining organizational resources.

Different regulatory regimes influence how SR is developing and converging. In the USA, for example, a long history of corporate reporting on various environmental matters to the Securities and Exchange Commission, as well as 'adversarial legalism' that characterizes business activity generally, emphasizes formal legal governance (Kagan and Axelrad, 2000). At the same time, these regulatory institutions inhibit the development of extended, voluntary reporting (Kolk, 2005), not only as regards SR but also external verification (Kolk, 2010a); corporate governance (Kolk, 2008); and climate change (Kolk et al., 2008).

Regulatory pressures may also influence some aspects of reporting in EU countries, such as the spread of environmental management and reporting as a consequence of the voluntary adoption of the European Eco-Management and Audit Scheme (EMAS) sponsored by the EU. Similarly, disclosure of environmental issues in corporate financial statements in European countries can be partly explained by a 2001 EU Recommendation to member countries to legislate in the matter (Criado et al., 2008).

*Table 16.1* Elements of institutionalization

| DiMaggio and Powell (1991) | Scott (1995) | Examples |
|---|---|---|
| Coercive mechanisms, such as the law or professional requirements, lead organizations to comply and to align with the requirements in such a way that behaviour becomes very similar in all of them. | Regulative structures, such as the law or the market, involve the capacity to establish rules, inspect conformity and manage sanctions in order to influence future behaviour. | Environmental regulation makes companies adopt new technologies. |
| Normative mechanisms, propelled through professionalization, formal education and professional networks, lead individuals to act according to values and norms. | Normative structures are based on social values and norms, leading individuals to act according to societal expectations. | Philanthropy among business in the USA; perceived 'appropriateness' of the UN Global Compact |
| Mimetic mechanisms. Organizations imitate those peer organizations that seem to be more successful and legitimate. | Cognitive structures are taken for granted symbols, meanings and roles that support the legitimacy of organizations. | It is argued that waves in the use of some concepts and techniques by organizations are associated with vogues (imitation) rather than with rationality. |

In Japan, the voluntary, but detailed, environmental reporting guidelines issued by the Japanese government have exerted quasi-regulatory pressure on Japanese firms to specify the internal accounting processes of their environmental responsiveness (Kolk, 2005). Malaysian firms face regulatory-type pressure in order to secure lucrative government contracts (Amran and Haniffa, 2011).

### Normative institutional mechanisms

The normative pillar of institutional theory (see Table 16.1) focuses on values and norms that could be applicable to all members of the collectivity or to specific actors. To understand the difference between the regulative and the normative pillars, the logic of each should be distinguished. While instrumentalism is the basic logic of why firms respond to the regulatory pillars, it is the 'appropriateness' of normative pillars that shape organizational responses (March and Olsen, 2006). Thus, while self-interest is compatible with a regulative conception of institutions, a normative conception leads individuals to follow perceived expectations about the 'right thing to do'. For example, there is a lot of controversy over whether CSR makes good economic sense (from the organizational viewpoint). But it could be simply argued that organizations engage in socially responsible practices, regardless of their revenue, because they have emerged as shared social values that organizations, and actors within these organizations, have to apply to be legitimate. One illustration of normative pressures is philanthropy in the USA, where there is a generally and widely held social expectation that business organizations will make philanthropic donations to various causes, e.g. business schools. A further example could be companies signing the principles of the Global Compact. Such examples could be described as voluntary initiatives, but such description would ignore the importance of normative pressures. Companies might engage partly (or wholly) because a set of given values and norms have spread through professionalization, formal education and professional networks (DiMaggio and Powell, 1983) to acquire a normative authority (Scott, 1987), because they conform to patterns of expected behaviour in the organizational field or in society at large (Bebbington *et al.*, 2012).

A combination of regulative and normative pressures may fully or partially explain patterns of SR in the UK. As an example of normative pressures, the ACCA established in 1991 the UK Environmental Reporting Awards, which in 2001 transformed into the Awards for Sustainability Reporting. The awards scheme provided a forum for the establishment of norms about expected behaviour in corporate SR (Bebbington *et al.*, 2012). For example, one of the key qualities of environmental reporting that emerged through the years was external verification: it has become a norm that a proper sustainability report should be externally verified, beyond the calculus of the consequences for the organization. Normative pressures were complemented by political pressure by the UK government (Kolk, 2005). In April 1998, for example, at an ACCA awards ceremony, Michael Meacher MP, UK Minister of the Environment, named and shamed some non-reporters and stated that if reporting did not develop voluntarily then legislation would be enacted (Bebbington *et al.*, 2012). The symbolic potential of winning reporting awards, demonstrating compliance with social expectations, is also influencing SR among Malaysian firms (Amran and Haniffa, 2011).

Normative pressures may also explain some differences in SR among European countries, with a particular case being how in some countries, particularly Germany, different industry groups created a structure to implement EMAS in such a way that it became the norm to publish an environmental report (Wenk, 2004). Additionally, social expectations about business behaviour can differ between countries, and emphasize different concerns. In the UK, for example, there is considerable community interest in ethical sourcing and supply chain practices. These concerns create expectations that firms will disclose information about their purchasing practices (Chen and Bouvain, 2009).

### Cognitive institutional mechanisms

Institutions can also be founded on a cognitive dimension. Sociology has long acknowledged the importance of symbols and meanings in social action, but (according to Scott, 1995) the change introduced in new institutionalism is the treatment of symbolic systems and cultural rules as objective and external to individuals. That is, symbols, meanings and rules are considered to be social constructions that are created, sustained and changed by social interaction (Berger and Luckmann, 1966). Once those constructions are established they exert on individuals and organizations a strong pull towards stability and compliance because they make a given behaviour appear as either taken for granted or inconceivable (Scott, 1995). Thus, cognitive structures 'form a culturally supported and conceptually correct support of legitimacy that becomes unquestioned' (Hoffman, 1999). For example,

> [i]nstitutional rules in the West have accorded greater individual autonomy and independence to social actors – both persons and firms – than have related rules in Eastern societies ... Relations among persons or firms that the West views as collusion, the East sees as normal, inevitable and beneficial.
>
> (Scott, 1995, pp. 43–4)

The isomorphic mechanism in organizations that, according to DiMaggio and Powell (1991), better captures the cognitive dimension is imitation (mimetic processes). Organizations imitate those peer organizations that seem to be more successful and legitimate (Tolbert and

Zucker, 1983), the underlying logic being that of 'orthodoxy': we prefer to act in conventional ways, to act according to routines (DiMaggio and Powell, 1991).

The existence of cognitive structures is very difficult to prove empirically. However, their existence can be inferred indirectly from the observation that for some it is taken for granted that a company will publish a sustainability report. This is almost certainly the case with the convergence of reporting activity among the world's largest multinational firms (see Kolk, 2011; KPMG, 2011). It would be almost unthinkable for many firms of this size and profile to now not report sustainability information. Similarly, for firms that are pursuing a sustainability or values-based positioning strategy, SR has often become 'normal' and 'taken-for-granted' – it is, in Oliver's (1992) words 'obvious and proper' that they do so. In Bebbington *et al.*'s (2009) study of a small number of NZ reporters, for example, reporting was largely a 'second order' effect for these firms that sought a *symbol* of their responsiveness to sustainability and their values-based competitive positioning. In a similar way, reporting has been influenced by the broader institutionalization of the GRI (Kolk, 2011). Firms might adopt the GRI because it has come to be seen as the legitimate standard for SR, to such a point that failing to adopt this standard would threaten the legitimacy of their reporting efforts. There is, thus, some evidence of a mimetic process in SR that is connected with the convergence hypothesis: organizations follow the route of orthodoxy once a given reporting practice in the organizational field has attained a tipping point (Bebbington *et al.*, 2012).

The previous analysis of mechanisms of institutionalizations shows that SR can be regarded as resting on a range of intersecting regulatory, normative and cognitive institutional pressures (Bebbington *et al.*, 2009; Gonzalez, 2010), which develop and evolve through multiple organizational fields (Kolk, 2011).

## Institutionalization and change

For the most part, institutional theory has been concerned with stability and inertia or the processes by which organizations converge around common structures and practices. It has been charged for its failure to address change (Greenwood and Hinings, 1996; Hoffman, 1999) and for ignoring the role of social actors (including managers) in the institutionalization process (Oliver, 1991). Among the studies that have considered change, Hoffman (1999) illustrated how organizations and fields evolve in light of environmental issues. He demonstrated that individual coercive, normative and cognitive pressures have different importances over time and that organizational fields can and do change as a result. Thus, while coercive, normative and cognitive structures (DiMaggio and Powell, 1983; Scott, 1995) are thought to lead to inertia and stability, organizational evolution takes place unexpectedly and produces discontinuities.

As regards change and the institutionalization of SR, four themes deserve closer inspection: (a) the initiating event that may alter institutional arrangements; (b) whether or not (and if so, how) fields evolve; (c) which coercive, normative and cognitive structures might lead to change and how; and (d) what is the relationship between competitive forces and institutional structures in the process of institutionalization.

### *Initiating events of institutional change*

The initiating event of institutional change can take different forms. Utilizing Lounsbury's (1997) institutional toolkit, Ball and Craig (2010) illustrate that changes to enable SR require shifts in habits and routines (activities) and also values and interests (ideas, priorities, norms) at the organizational and the broader societal level. Events and factors leading to such change can include: milestones, catastrophes and legal/administrative happenings (Hoffman, 1999) that reshape organizational activity and/or the rationale for that activity. Considering the institutional evolution of SR, it is not difficult to think of events that have shaped changes – and considering the diversity of SR fields, the initiating events are dependent on context. Hoffman (1999) found that the Bhopal accident, the Exxon Valdez oil spill, Superfund regulation and the Montreal Protocol all contributed to environmental reporting being adopted by a number of US firms (in addition to other organizational and strategic innovations). Conversely, in the European context it seems that catastrophes played a less significant role, and European organizations have been more attentive to governmental (EU's Environmental Action Programmes and EMAS) and private initiatives (GRI) encouraging SR (Kolk, 2005).

Sometimes organizations respond on the basis of the uncertainty created when fields start to change – experimenting and going beyond established practice. At other times, change is forced on organizations, where acquiescence to new institutional pressures will be necessary for legitimacy and survival. Initiating events can also arise from pressure exerted by social movements that reshape normative expectations of business activity (Ball and Craig, 2010; Qian and Burritt, 2008). Institutional theory directs researchers to reconsider the level of analysis for understanding the drivers and motivations of SR. While the literature to date has tended to emphasize the rational and strategic motivations of legitimacy and the business case, analysis of institutions and fields draws attention to more subtle social processes as initiating events for SR.

### Evolution of institutional fields

According to Hoffman (1999) institutional fields evolve, changing the composition and the balance of power of participants. Changes bring about a redefinition of institutions that reflects the interests of the newly formed field. The early development of SR was driven in part by interactions between a relatively tight-knit coalition of global companies, trans-governmental agencies (e.g. the UN), international bodies (e.g. the World Business Council for Sustainable Development [WBCSD]) and global NGOs. Livesey and Kearins (2002) reveal, for example, how in the early days of SR, this coalition cross-referenced each other in their literatures, and also worked together in various organizations that made up the emerging network. Such field-level interactions shaped the development of material practices (e.g. standards and guidelines) as well as the rhetoric and the rationality that accompanied them. The field members shared 'the common language of transparency and caring ... and the cross-referencing among groups working on corporate social responsibility and socially responsible companies, was mutually reinforcing and mutually legitimating' (Livesey and Kearins, 2002, p. 247).

Further, companies increasingly submit their reports to reporting awards schemes; attend meetings and conferences on SR; and participate in the EMAS or GRI schemes all organized and sponsored by the same coalition of field-level participants. Progressively, new guidelines are issued and there are new prized reports to benchmark. Analyses of how Integrated Reporting (see Chapter 4) is developing show a similar level of interaction among the same types of organizations. Institutional change rests on new field-level participants, and their interactions; it also rests on a process of *deinstitutionalization* where existing institutionalized routines and practices gradually lose legitimacy (Oliver, 1992) and a void is created for the new ones. Social movement organizations, as new or renewed field-level participants, can be critical for shaping new normative institutions, and ultimately regulatory changes (Ball and Craig, 2010). Efforts to facilitate interdisciplinary interactions (e.g. between environmental specialists and accountants) will also be required for institutional change (Qian and Burritt, 2008).

### *The role of different structures on institutional change*

Scott (1995) contends that coercive, normative and cognitive structures are a matter of emphasis and underlying assumptions, i.e. one has to choose between perspectives because they are not logically consistent, as one should be either a social constructionist (preferring cognitive structures) or a social realist (endorsing coercive structures), but not both at the same time. However, Hoffman (1999) proposes that those structures are not analytically and operationally distinct, and that regulative, normative and cognitive pillars are connected. In particular, in his study Hoffman found four periods of response from the US chemical industry from 1962 to 1993 that followed a sequence that began with a questioning of prior institutional beliefs and evolved through regulative and normative institutions, to finish as a cognitive institution.

In terms of SR, the process of institutionalization of the GRI also shows a mix of normative, cognitive and, to varying degrees, regulatory institutional mechanisms. Initially born out of a process of normative concern over the business and society relationship (Livesey, 2001), the founders of the GRI moved quickly to create a new normative reporting standard, which simultaneously became a cognitive institutional influence. That the GRI occurred during a time of renewed interest in harmonizing international accounting standards (Kolk, 2011) and included some involvement of the international accounting bodies lent it the promise of regulatory power.

### *Competitive forces and institutional structures*

A further aspect of institutional evolution is ambiguity regarding the drivers of early adopters. Institutional theorists (DiMaggio and Powell, 1991) have tended to suggest that early adoption tends to be related to competitive isomorphism (economic or technical explanations) and is supplanted later by institutional explanations (coercive, normative and cognitive structures). In terms of organizational sustainability strategy, Bansal (2005) hypothesized that in early years some firms will benefit by 'generating rents from resources and capabilities because of imperfectly competitive strategic factor markets … created by the ambiguity of the meaning and impact of sustainable development' (p. 203). Following this hypothesis, the firms that do not act early will imitate other firms, facilitating the institutionalization of sustainability in later years. This appears to be the case with the adoption and spread of the GRI among multinational companies. An early need to reduce the inter-institutional incompatibilities about sustainability arising from participating in multiple (geographically based) fields, and a need to create a new order of global business responsibility that would safeguard the global legitimacy of the business system, facilitated the early adoption of the new GRI reporting standard (Nikolaeva and Bicho, 2011). Its later adoption and spread is attributable to information-based imitative behaviour (Lieberman and Asaba, 2006) in which later adopters were influenced by media pressure and observation of successful early adopters.

The more organizations that adopted the GRI, the more reputable it became. In terms of the broader adoption of sustainability strategies, Bansal (2005) found, in contrast, that institutional pressures (rather than economic or technical explanations) can play a part in early adoption. Media attention (a surrogate she used for normative structures) and mimicry (related with cognitive structures) were positively associated in Bansal's study with sustainability strategy adoption. She found that for later adopters of sustainability strategies, the importance of media attention diminishes while mimicry remains equally important. As these findings contradict Bansal's propositions, she explains that in this particular case, institutional pressures could be important because of the ambiguity associated with the meaning, measurement and impact of sustainable development (Bansal, 2005). Regardless, institutional theory provides new insights into the spread and uptake of reporting.

Considering the multiple field levels that shape SR, the process of institutional change is likely to be context specific, dependent on the specific mix of initiating events, the interactions between particular field-level participants, and the perceived availability and desirability of economic, technical and institutional benefits.

## Institutionalism and legitimacy theory

In this section, we briefly explore the overlap between institutional theory and legitimacy theory. There is an apparent overlap between institutional arguments about SR and the overwhelming amount of legitimacy theory literature in social and environmental accounting. Legitimacy is an element of institutions: Scott (1995) contends that legitimacy explains organizational stability, by giving a normative dignity to its practical imperatives (Berger and Luckmann, 1966). However, the usual approach to legitimacy in social and environmental accounting is not always consistent with its use in institutional theory. A more resource based view of legitimacy is common: it is conceived in accounting literature as a resource or it enables organizations to attract resources that are employed in pursuit of organizational goals (Tilling, 2004).

While there is overlap between institutional theory and legitimacy theory (Deegan, 2002), it could be said that the former is more ambitious than the latter. The legitimacy in social and environmental accounting literature assumes a manipulative logic, based on self-interest, which could correspond with coercive structures. Deegan (2002), for example, explains that 'legitimacy is considered to be a resource on which an organization is dependent for survival ... that the organization also can impact or manipulate' (p. 293). Likewise, Patten (1992) argues that 'social disclosures represent one of the methods that firms can use to influence the public policy process ... The desired effect ... is to reduce ... the "exposure" of the company to the social and political environment' (p. 472).

Institutional theory, however, also permits different motives to be explored, primarily based on the logics of appropriateness and on the social construction of reality. In particular, the theory does not privilege any of the three explanations (coercive, normative or cognitive), but argues that they operate at different levels and moments through the institutionalization process. Additionally, this theoretical framework allows for organizations to be examined in their context; the notion of organizational fields is examined and helps to explain the behaviour inside firms. Finally, institutional theory is above all a theory of institutionalization: its main interest is the longitudinal study of institutional change and how organizations became institutionalized. Thus, it could be argued that while legitimacy theory could be more useful in determining in the short term why a given organization is making particular sustainability disclosures, institutional theory could be more helpful in the explanation of why given practices of SR become common practice in a particular context.

## Concluding comments

This chapter commenced questioning why we can observe some patterns of convergence in SR practice and proposed that institutional theory could provide some explanations, together with other chapters in this book. Along these lines, the chapter has presented the main elements of institutional theory and has discussed their relevance for SR.

We observed that a growing body of empirical studies in SR is pointing towards the existence of organizational fields around this issue. Further, although those organizational fields tended to be local, determining a diversity of SR in different parts of the world, some recent trends suggest the emergence of one (or more) global SR field(s), which is eliciting a worldwide convergence of SR (especially among multinational companies). We moved on to explain the coercive, normative and mimetic mechanisms of institutionalization, and illustrated how they can explain different processes of institutionalization in SR. Coercion can account for SR as a response to regulation, investors or consumer pressure. Normative mechanisms can explain SR as a response to voluntary initiatives on the grounds of social responsibility. Finally, mimicry could enlighten how SR could transform into something that is taken for granted for a given kind of firm and how those companies engage in SR simply to follow the orthodoxy in its organizational field. It is likely that SR is the result of a mixture of those three mechanisms, taking different weights in different contexts and in different stages of the institutionalization of SR.

The discussion over the relationship between institutionalization and change also revealed some patterns that could be observed in the case of SR. In this respect, we illustrated how different events served to initiate SR in different contexts and how the evolving composition of organizational fields allowed the redefinition of the institution, emerging in the last few years as SR. One direction in which this may evolve from here is Integrated Reporting. However, other propositions made in the strategic management literature do not appear to be supported and reveal the use of disputed notions of sustainability.

As regards the commonalities and differences between institutionalism and the often used legitimacy theory, it seems that the latter is a particular case of the former, related to the regulative pillar. The precision of legitimacy theory makes it testable, but at the same time opens it to question, as legitimacy, being a concept drawn from neo-institutional theory, has a wider meaning than is often recognized in the social and environmental accounting and accountability literature.

## References

Amran, A. and Haniffa, R. 2011. Evidence in development of sustainability reporting: A case of a developing country. *Business Strategy and the Environment*, 20(3): 141–56.

Ball, A. and Craig, R. 2010. Using neo-institutionalism to advance social and environmental accounting. *Critical Perspectives on Accounting*, 21(3): 283–93.

Bansal, P. 2005. Evolving sustainability: A longitudinal study of corporate sustainable development. *Strategic Management Journal*, 26: 197–218.

Bebbington, J., Higgins, C. and Frame, B. 2009. Initiating sustainable development reporting: Evidence from New Zealand. *Accounting, Auditing and Accountability Journal*, 22(4): 588–625.

Bebbington, J., Kirk, E. A. and Larrinaga, C. 2012. The production of normativity: A comparison of reporting regimes in Spain and the UK. *Accounting, Organizations and Society*, 37(2): 78–94.

Berger, P. and Luckmann, T. 1966. *The social construction of reality: A treatise in the sociology of knowledge*. New York: Doubleday.

Blasco, M. and Zølner, M. 2010. Corporate social responsibility in Mexico and France: Exploring the role of normative institutions. *Business and Society*, 49(2): 216–51.

Borkowski, S. C., Welsh, M. J. and Wentzel, K. 2010. Johnson & Johnson: A model for sustainability reporting. *Strategic Finance*, 92(3): 29–37.

Brown, N. and Deegan, C. 1999. The public disclosure of environmental performance information: A dual test of media agenda setting theory and legitimacy theory. *Accounting and Business Research*, 37(1): 21–41.

Chen, J. and Roberts, R. W. 2010. Toward a more coherent understanding of the organization–society relationship: A theoretical consideration for social and environmental accounting research. *Journal of Business Ethics*, 97(3): 651–65.

Chen, S. and Bouvain, P. 2009. Is corporate responsibility converging? A comparison of corporate responsibility reporting in the USA, UK, Australia, and Germany. *Journal of Business Ethics*, 87: 299–317.

Criado, I., Fernandez, M., Husillos, F. J. and Larrinaga, C. 2008. Compliance with mandatory environmental reporting in financial statements: The case of Spain (2001–2003). *Journal of Business Ethics*, 79(3): 245–62.

Deegan, C. 2002. The legitimising effect of social and environmental disclosures: A theoretical foundation. *Accounting, Auditing and Accountability Journal*, 15(3): 282–311.

DiMaggio, P. and Powell, W. 1983. The iron cage revisited: Institutional isomorphism and collective rationality in organizational fields. *American Sociological Review*, 48: 147–60.

DiMaggio, W. and Powell, P. 1991. Introduction, in P. Powell and W. DiMaggio (eds) *The new institutionalism in organizational analysis*. Chicago, IL and London: University of Chicago Press, pp. 1–38.

Gonzalez, J. 2010. Determinants of socially responsible corporate behaviours in the Spanish electricity sector. *Social Responsibility Journal*, 6(3): 386–403.

Gray, R., Owen, D. and Adams, C. 1996. *Accounting and accountability: Changes and challenges in corporate social and environmental reporting*. London: Prentice Hall.

Greenwood, R. and Hinings, C. 1996. Understanding radical organizational change: Bringing together the old and the new institutionalism. *Academy of Managment Review*, 21: 1022–54.

Higgins, C., Milne, M. and van Gramberg, B. 2011. *Towards a more nuanced understanding of sustainable development reporting in Australia*, paper presented to The 10th Australasian Conference on Social and Environmental Accounting Research (CSEAR), Launceston, TAS, December.

Hoffman, A. J. 1999. Institutional evolution and change: Environmentalism and the US chemical industry. *Academy of Management Journal*, 42(4): 351–71.

Kagan, R. and Axelrad, L. 2000. *Regulatory encounters: Multinational corporations and American adversarial legalism*. Berkeley, CA: University of California Press.

Kolk, A. 2005. Environmental reporting by multinationals from the triad: Convergence or divergence? *Management International Review*, 45(1): 145–66.

Kolk, A. 2008. Sustainability, accountability and corporate governance: Exploring multinationals' reporting practices. *Business, Strategy & the Environment*, 17(1): 1–15.

Kolk, A. 2010a. Determinants of the adoption of sustainability assurance statements: An international investigation. *Business, Strategy & the Environment*, 19(3): 182–98.

Kolk, A. 2010b. Trajectories of sustainability reporting by MNCs. *Journal of World Business*, 45(4): 367–74.

Kolk, A. 2011. Harmonization in CSR reporting MNEs and global CSR standards. *Management International Review*, 51(5): 665–96.

Kolk, A., Levy, D. and Pinkse, J. 2008. Corporate responses in an emerging climate regime: The institutionalisation and commensuration of carbon disclosure. *European Accounting Review*, 17(4): 719–45.

KPMG 2011. *The KPMG survey of corporate social responsibility reporting*. London: KPMG.

Levy, D. and Kolk, A. 2002. Strategic responses to global climate change: Conflicting pressures on multinationals in the oil industry. *Business and Politics*, 4(3): 275–300.

Lieberman, M. and Asaba, S. 2006. Why do firms imitate each other? *Academy of Management Review*, 31(2): 366–85.

Livesey, S. 2001. Eco-identity as discursive struggle: Royal Dutch/Shell, Brent Spar, and Nigeria. *Journal of Business Communication*, 38(1): 58–91.

Livesey, S. and Kearins, K. 2002. Transparent and caring corporations? – A study of sustainability reports by the Body Shop and Royal Dutch/Shell. *Organization & Environment*, 15(3): 233–58.

Lounsbury, M. 1997. Exploring the institutional toolkit: The rise of recycling in the US solid waste field. *American Behavioral Scientist*, 40(4): 465–78.

March, J. G. and Olsen, J. P. 2006. Elaborating the 'New Institutionalism', in R. A. W. Rhodes, S. A. Binder and B. A. Rockman (eds) *The Oxford handbook of political institutions.* Oxford: Oxford University Press, pp. 3–20.

Nikolaeva, R. and Bicho, M. 2011. The role of institutional and reputational factors in the voluntary adoption of corporate social responsibility reporting standards. *Journal of the Academy of Marketing Science*, 39(6): 136–57.

Oliver, C. 1991. Responses to institutional pressure. *Academy of Management Review*, 16(1): 145–79.

Oliver, C. 1992. The antecedents of deinstitutionalization. *Organization Studies*, 13(4): 563–88.

Patten, D. 1992. Intra-industry environmental disclosures in response to the Alaskan oil spill: A note on legitimacy theory. *Accounting, Organizations and Society*, 17: 471–5.

Perez-Batres, L., Miller, V. and Pisani, M. 2010. CSR, sustainability and the meaning of global reporting for Latin American corporations. *Journal of Business Ethics*, 91(2): 193–209.

Qian, W. and Burritt, R. 2008. The development of environmental management accounting: An institutional view, in S. Schaltegger, M. Bennett, R. Burritt and C. Jasch (eds) *Environmental management accounting for cleaner production.* Amsterdam: Springer, pp. 233–48.

Roberts, R. W. 1992. Determinants of corporate social responsibility disclosure. *Accounting, Organizations and Society*, 17(6): 595–612.

Scott, R. 1987. The adolescence of institutional theory. *Administrative Science Quarterly*, 32(3): 493–511.

Scott, R. and Meyer, J. 1991. The organization of societal sectors: propositions and early evidence, in W. W. Powell and P. J. DiMaggio (eds) *The new institutionalism in organizational analysis.* Chicago, IL: The University of Chicago Press, pp. 108–40.

Scott, W. R. 1995. *Institutions and organizations.* Thousand Oaks, CA: Sage.

Tilling, M. V. 2004. Some thoughts on legitimacy theory in social and environmental accounting. *Social and Environmental Accounting Journal*, 24(2): 3–7.

Tolbert, P. and Zucker, L. 1983. Institutional sources of change in the formal structure of organizations: The diffusion of civil service reform 1880–1935. *Administrative Science Quarterly*, 28(3): 22–39.

Wenk, M. 2004. EU's Eco-Management and Audit Scheme (EMAS). *Environmental and Quality Management*, 14(1): 59–70.

Williamson, O. E. 1985. *The economic institutions of capitalism: Firms, markets, relational contracting.* New York: Free Press.

Zucker, L. 1987. Institutional theories of organizations. *Annual Review of Sociology*, 13: 443–64.

# 17 Drawing to a close and future horizons

*Jan Bebbington, Jeffrey Unerman and Brendan O'Dwyer*

We should first congratulate you on making it to the closing book chapter. We trust that you have found much of interest in what you have read and are starting to see the outline of how the discipline of accounting has sought to engage with sustainable development debates and contribute to sustainable development. The connections between accounting and sustainable development are many but are also complex. It is not possible to summarize in a few short pages of this chapter all the themes that could be drawn from the various chapters of this book. Nor is such a task appropriate, because the chapters largely stand by themselves. What we wish to draw out, however, in this final chapter is a sense of the most important implications that face accounting practitioners and researchers who seek to develop a form of accounting that is sufficiently responsive to the demands of sustainable development.

## Future accounting contributions to sustainability transitions

Thomson's Chapter 2 in this book provides evidence that the academic accounting field is enlarging its domains of focus in response to sustainable development concerns. As we noted in Chapter 1, in this edition of the book we have included new material on both water accounting and carbon accounting because of the attention that is now being paid to these issues. We also noted in the Introduction to Chapter 1 that issues of accounting for biodiversity and human rights are starting to be examined, although are not yet at the stage of development in academic terms for the book to carry chapters devoted to these areas.

Given the interest in sustainable development issues within society more broadly, and the accounting academy in particular, we would expect that interest in many aspects of sustainability accounting and accountability among academics, practitioners, policymakers and society will continue to grow. As part of this growth we would expect to see more funding calls for academic research projects in this area and a growth in the amount and range of observed practices along with evolving networks of researchers with common interests. This should result in a continued increase in the number of topics addressed as well as the volume of papers produced. This means that reading accounting (and other) journals that publish sustainable development related material is likely to yield ever greater insights into the developing field – this book can only ever be a snapshot of a point in time.[1]

In addition, a literature is emerging that focuses more closely on how accounting might be seen to be a technology of control (and accountability) that operates with regimes of organizational governance that is itself aimed at sustainable development outcomes. This literature tends to focus on methods used within organizations to make assessments about current operations (and perhaps to inform choices about future courses of actions). Recent papers on this theme have tended to focus on the *sustainable assessment model* (see Bebbington, 2007) and its application in a variety of different contexts (Bebbington et al., 2007; Frame and Cavanagh, 2009; Xing *et al.*, 2009; Fraser, 2012). This *sustainable assessment model* tool built on previous work on full cost accounting (see Bebbington *et al.*, 2001; Herbohn, 2005; and for a broader summary Antheaume, 2007) but has extended its focus to encompass some of the complexities introduced by a sustainable development framing. Of more general interest in this literature is the conceptualization where monetization of elements of sustainable development might be useful (and where it might not – see Frame and Brown, 2008; and Frame and O'Connor, 2011, for additional insights on this matter). Given the tendency in accounting towards monetization (as well as concerns expressed in some sustainability accounting and accountability research about inappropriate monetization) it is likely that this small but growing stream of work might be influential in shaping future thinking about accounting as a calculative technology (which is itself a topic of accounting scholarship).

This literature is also informed by (and self-consciously draws from) what is often described as sustainability science. Sustainability science is a relatively new area of study (dating from about 2000) which seeks to describe what knowledge is needed for sustainable development to advance. In so doing it provides a chance for disciplines to explore their contribution to this goal. To help us answer the question of how accounting might develop in the future, Table 17.1 provides a summary of various aspects that sustainability science sees as being relevant for the understanding and pursuit of sustainable development.

We would suggest that accounting has the potential to provide insights into two of the elements in Table 17.1, namely:

- What systems of incentive structures – including markets, rules, norms and scientific information – can most effectively improve social capacity to guide interactions between nature and society towards more sustainable trajectories?
- How can today's operational systems for monitoring and reporting on environmental and social conditions be integrated or extended to provide more useful guidance for efforts to navigate a transition towards sustainability?

*Table 17.1* Questions to be addressed by sustainability science

---

- How can the dynamic interactions between nature and society – including lags and inertia – be better incorporated into emerging models and conceptualizations that integrate the earth system, human development and sustainability?
- How are long-term trends in environment and development, including consumption and population, reshaping nature–society interactions in ways relevant to sustainability?
- What determines the vulnerability or resilience of the nature–society system in particular kinds of places and for particular types of ecosystems and human livelihoods?
- Can scientifically meaningful 'limits' or 'boundaries' be defined that would provide effective warning of conditions beyond which the nature–society systems incur a significantly increased risk of serious degradation?
- What systems of incentive structures – including markets, rules, norms and scientific information – can most effectively improve social capacity to guide interactions between nature and society towards more sustainable trajectories?
- How can today's operational systems for monitoring and reporting on environmental and social conditions be integrated or extended to provide more useful guidance for efforts to navigate a transition towards sustainability?
- How can today's relatively independent activities of research planning, monitoring, assessment and decision support be better integrated into systems for adaptive management and societal learning?

---

Source: From Kates *et al.* (2001).

The provision of information to guide organizations' actions and to shape how they provide information with governance and accountability regimes is within the domain of the discipline of accounting. Indeed, many of this book's chapters consider routines of this sort.

What is less clear from the existing accounting literature is how our discipline might communicate its contribution to the two questions above to the rest of the sustainable development field. At the same time, sustainability science is likely to offer insights into the field of accounting and it is this synergistic interaction that is likely to shape the future of accounting for sustainable development.

## Closing points

As has been argued within this book, the sustainable development agenda poses crucial questions for the future of humanity. By focusing on the economic and largely ignoring the social and environmental impacts of entities, much accounting as it is currently structured operates in a manner which at best hides, and at worst reinforces and furthers, unsustainable development.

Addressing the questions posed by sustainable development is very far from easy. Accounting can play a number of potentially important roles in helping to address sustainable development and thus could help to make the world (or the manner in which humans through organizational operations impact on the world) less unsustainable. But to be effective, this would require a fundamental shift in a number of accounting practices and in the assumptions upon which a number of these practices are based.

We sincerely hope that this book reaches out not just to accounting students, but also to anyone else interested in developing a broader role for accounting in society in this manner. If the book is successful in helping to change perceptions regarding the impact of current accounting practices, and/or regarding the potential of accounting to help move us towards a more sustainable (or less unsustainable) future, it will have been a very worthwhile endeavour. We live in hope that societal commitments to sustainable development will develop sufficiently quickly and deeply to avoid environmental and social catastrophe, and hope that the material presented and discussed in this book will contribute towards much more socially and environmentally just and sustainable business, public sector and third sector (non-governmental organizations) practices.

## Note

1  These include the journals examined by Thomson (Chapter 2 of this book), as well as the likes of *Ecological Economics, Environment and Planning C* and *Futures*, which often publish relevant work in this area. In addition, as we were finalizing the text for this book there were four special issues that were imminent in the area of accounting for sustainable development. These are due to be published in: *Accounting, Organizations and Society; Accounting, Auditing and Accountability Journal* (in the context of higher education institutions); *Accounting Education: An International Journal*; and *Management Accounting Research*. It is likely that by the time this book emerges, material from these special issues will also be in the public domain and will build upon and strengthen the insights from this book.

## References

Antheaume, N. (2007). Full cost accounting: Adam Smith meets Rachel Carson?, in J. Unerman, J. Bebbington and B. O'Dwyer (eds) *Sustainability Accounting and Accountability*. London: Routledge, pp. 211–25.

Bebbington, J. (2007). *Accounting for Sustainable Development Performance*. London: Elsevier.

Bebbington, J., Gray, R., Hibbitt, C. and Kirk, E. (2001). *Full Cost Accounting: An Agenda for Action*. London: Association of Chartered Certified Accountants (ACCA).

Bebbington, J., Brown, J. and Frame, B. (2007). Accounting technologies and sustainability assessment models. *Ecological Economics*, 61(2–3): 224–36.

Frame, B. and Brown, J. (2008). Developing post-normal technologies for sustainability. *Ecological Economics*, 65(2): 225–41.

Frame, B. and Cavanagh, J. (2009). Experiences of sustainability assessment: An awkward adolescence. *Accounting Forum*, 33(3): 195–208.

Frame, B. and O'Connor, M. (2011). Integrating valuation and deliberation: The purposes of sustainability assessment. *Environmental Science & Policy*, 14(1): 1–10.

Fraser, M. (2012). Fleshing out an engagement with a social accounting technology. *Accounting, Auditing and Accountability Journal*, 25(3): 508–34.

Herbohn, K. (2005). A full cost environmental accounting experiment. *Accounting Organizations and Society*, 30(6): 519–36.

Kates, R. W., Clark, W. C., Corell, R., Hall, J. M., Jaeger, C. C., Lowe, I. et al. (2001). Sustainability science. *Science*, 292(5517): 641–2. doi: 10.1126/science.1059386.

Xing, Y., Horner, M., El-Haram, M. and Bebbington, J. (2009). A framework model for assessing sustainability impacts of urban development. *Accounting Forum*, 33(3): 209–24.

# Index

Page numbers in **bold** refer to figures, page numbers in *italic* refer to tables.